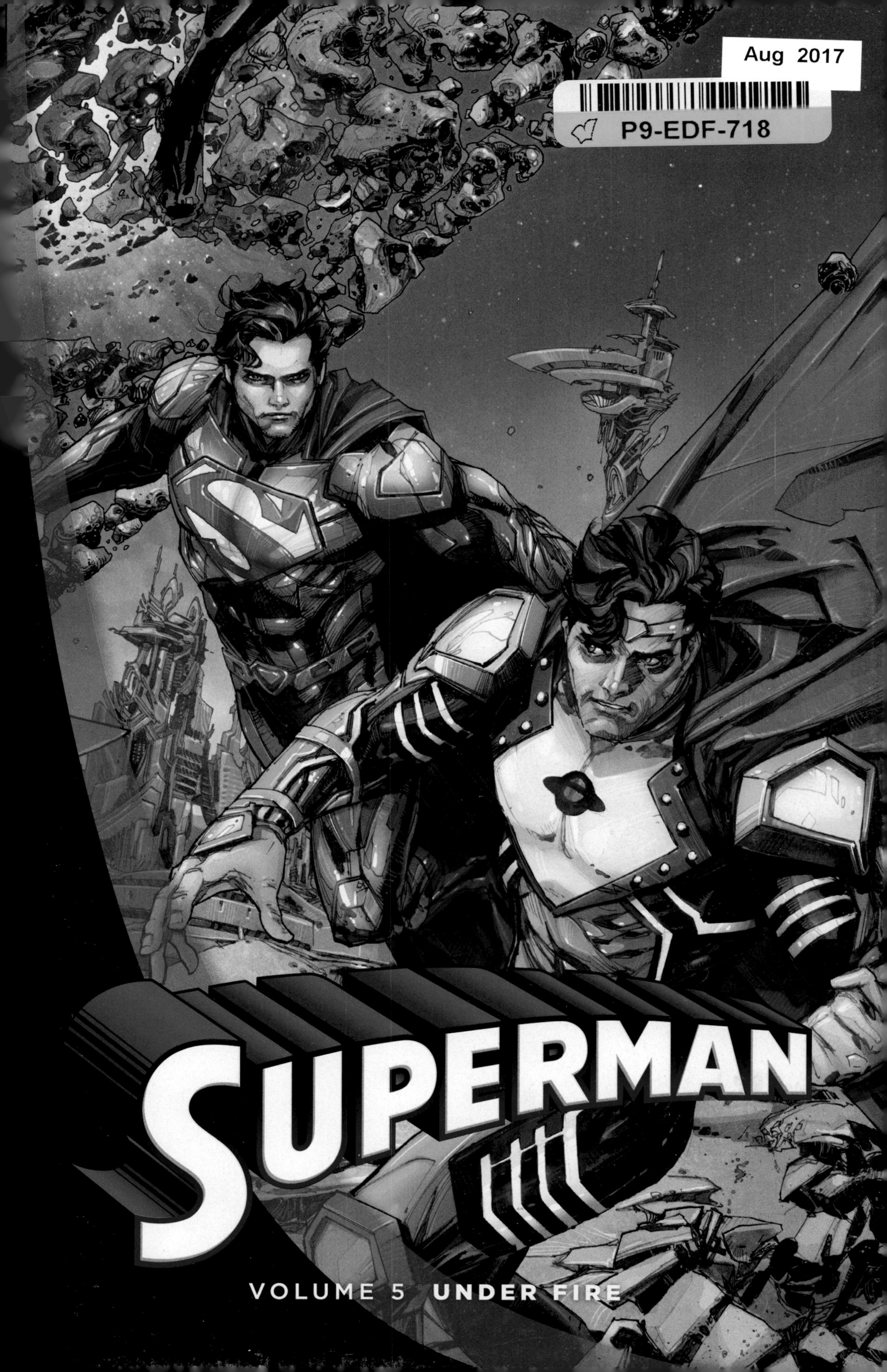
SUPERMAN
VOLUME 5 UNDER FIRE

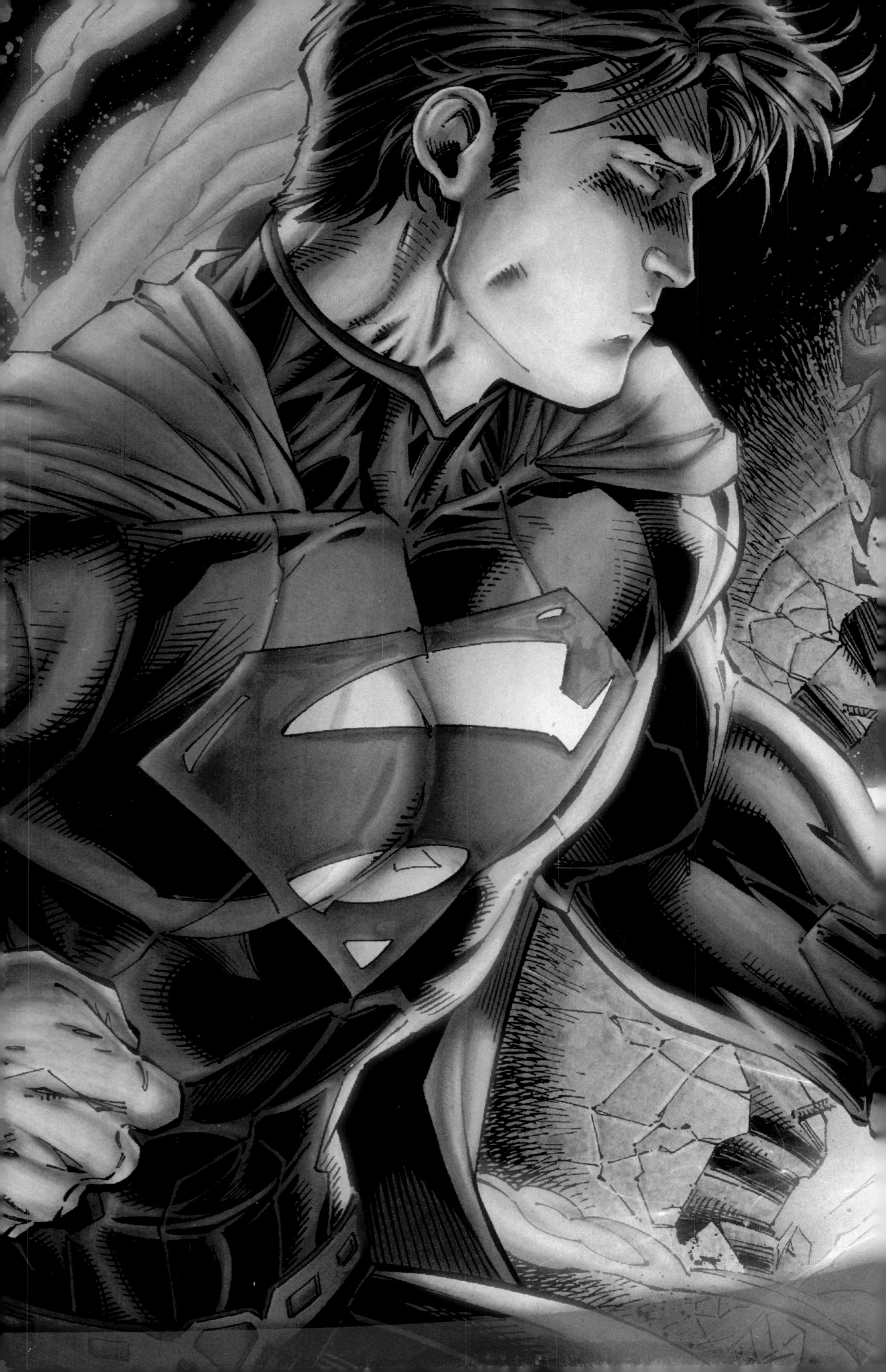

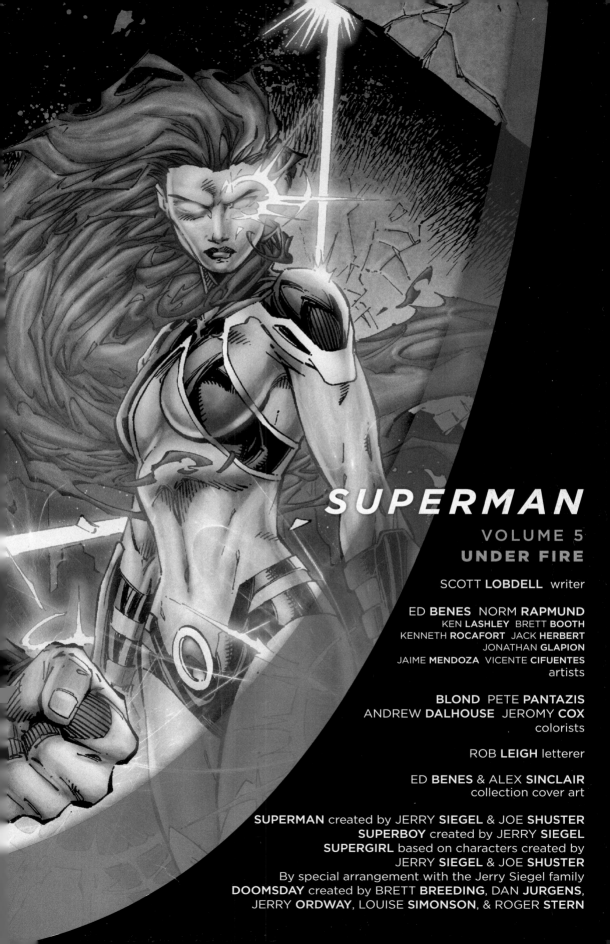

SUPERMAN

VOLUME 5
UNDER FIRE

SCOTT **LOBDELL** writer

ED **BENES** NORM **RAPMUND**
KEN **LASHLEY** BRETT **BOOTH**
KENNETH **ROCAFORT** JACK **HERBERT**
JONATHAN **GLAPION**
JAIME **MENDOZA** VICENTE **CIFUENTES**
artists

BLOND PETE **PANTAZIS**
ANDREW **DALHOUSE** JEROMY **COX**
colorists

ROB **LEIGH** letterer

ED **BENES** & ALEX **SINCLAIR**
collection cover art

SUPERMAN created by JERRY **SIEGEL** & JOE **SHUSTER**
SUPERBOY created by JERRY **SIEGEL**
SUPERGIRL based on characters created by
JERRY **SIEGEL** & JOE **SHUSTER**
By special arrangement with the Jerry Siegel family
DOOMSDAY created by BRETT **BREEDING**, DAN **JURGENS**,
JERRY **ORDWAY**, LOUISE **SIMONSON**, & ROGER **STERN**

EDDIE BERGANZA Editor – Original Series ANTHONY MARQUES Assistant Editor – Original Series
RACHEL PINNELAS Editor ROBBIN BROSTERMAN Design Director – Books ROBBIE BIEDERMAN Publication Design

BOB HARRAS Senior VP – Editor-in-Chief, DC Comics

DIANE NELSON President DAN DIDIO and JIM LEE Co-Publishers GEOFF JOHNS Chief Creative Officer
AMIT DESAI Senior VP – Marketing and Franchise Management AMY GENKINS Senior VP – Business and Legal Affairs
NAIRI GARDINER Senior VP – Finance JEFF BOISON VP – Publishing Planning
MARK CHIARELLO VP – Art Direction and Design JOHN CUNNINGHAM VP – Marketing
TERRI CUNNINGHAM VP – Editorial Administration LARRY GANEM VP – Talent Relations and Services
ALISON GILL Senior VP – Manufacturing and Operations HANK KANALZ Senior VP – Vertigo and Integrated Publishing
JAY KOGAN VP – Business and Legal Affairs, Publishing JACK MAHAN VP – Business Affairs, Talent
NICK NAPOLITANO VP – Manufacturing Administration SUE POHJA VP – Book Sales FRED RUIZ VP – Manufacturing Operations
COURTNEY SIMMONS Senior VP – Publicity BOB WAYNE Senior VP – Sales

SUPERMAN VOLUME 5: UNDER FIRE

DC Comics, 4000 Warner Blvd., Burbank, CA 91522
A Warner Bros. Entertainment Company.
Printed by RR Donnelley, Owensville, MO, USA. 7/3/15. First Printing.

ISBN: 978-1-4012-5542-8

Library of Congress Cataloging-in-Publication Data

Lobdell, Scott, author.
Superman. Volume 5, Under Fire / Scott Lobdell ; [illustrated by] Brett Booth, Ken Lashley.
pages cm. — (The New 52!)
ISBN 978-1-4012-5542-8
1. Graphic novels. I. Booth, Brett, illustrator. II. Lashley, Ken, illustrator. III. Title. IV. Title: Under fire.

PN6728.S9L5863 2015
741.5'973—dc23

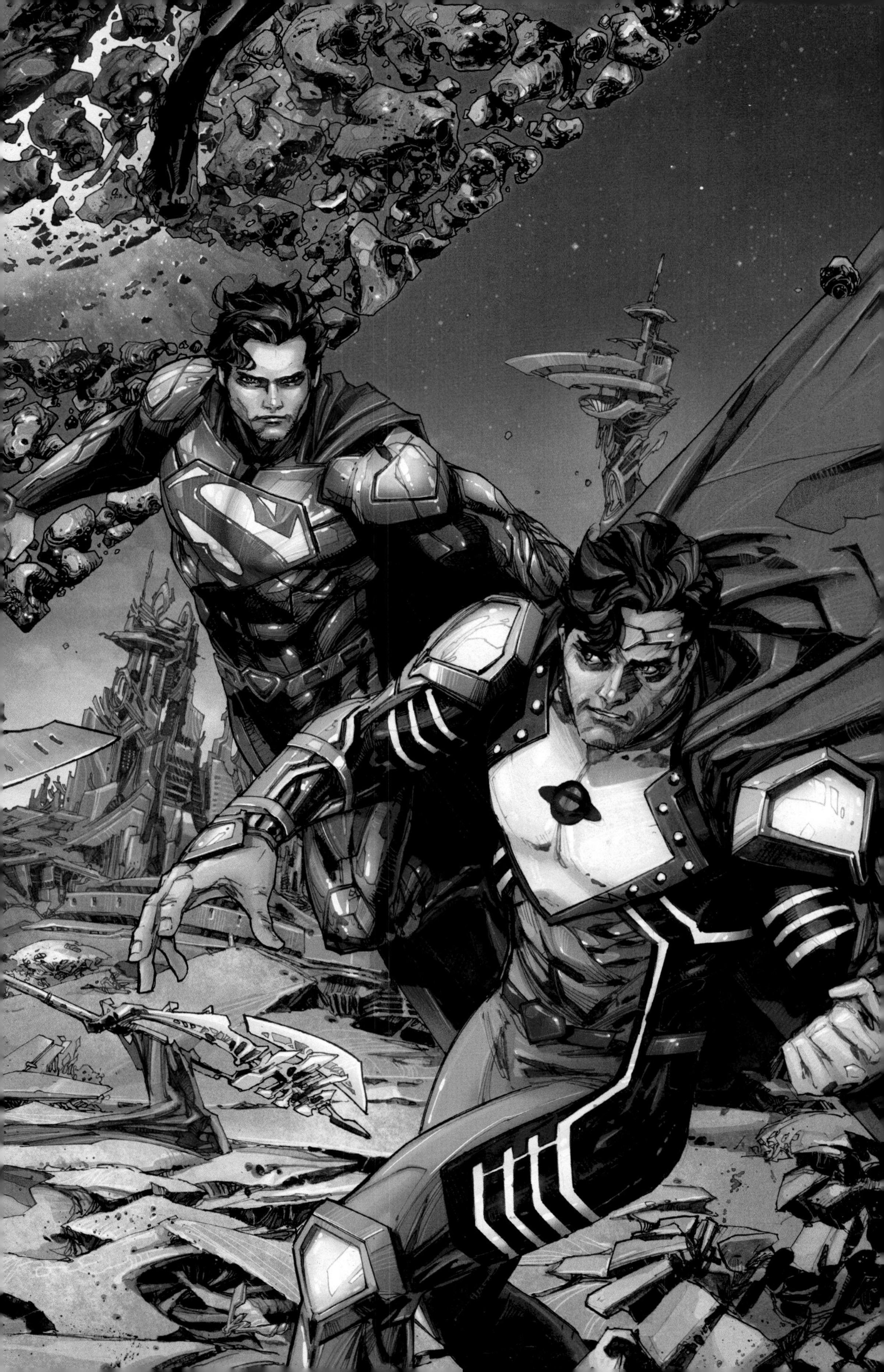

KRYPTON RETURNS

SCOTT LOBDELL writer **KENNETH ROCAFORT** penciller **BLOND** colorist cover art by **KENNETH ROCAFORT**

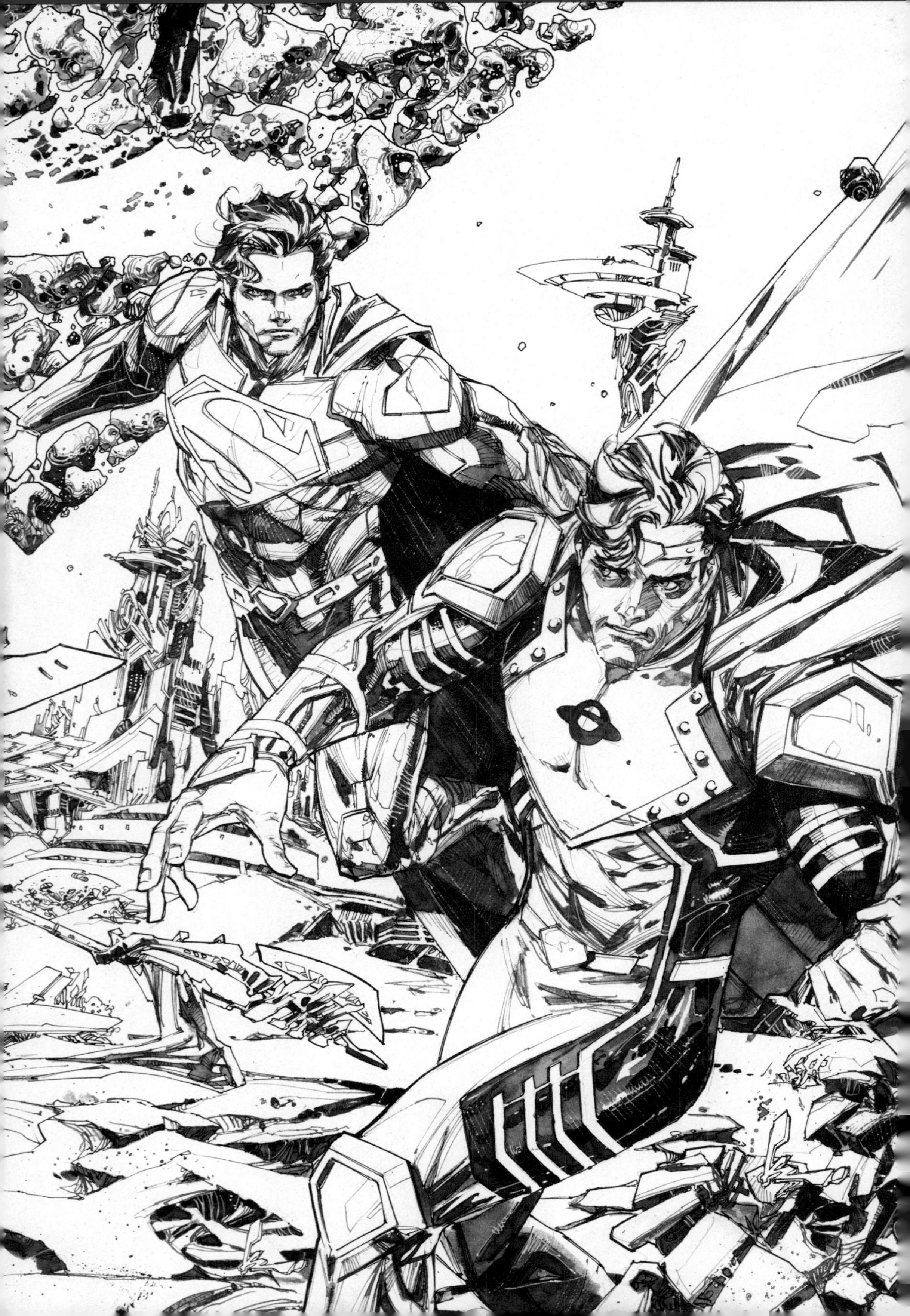

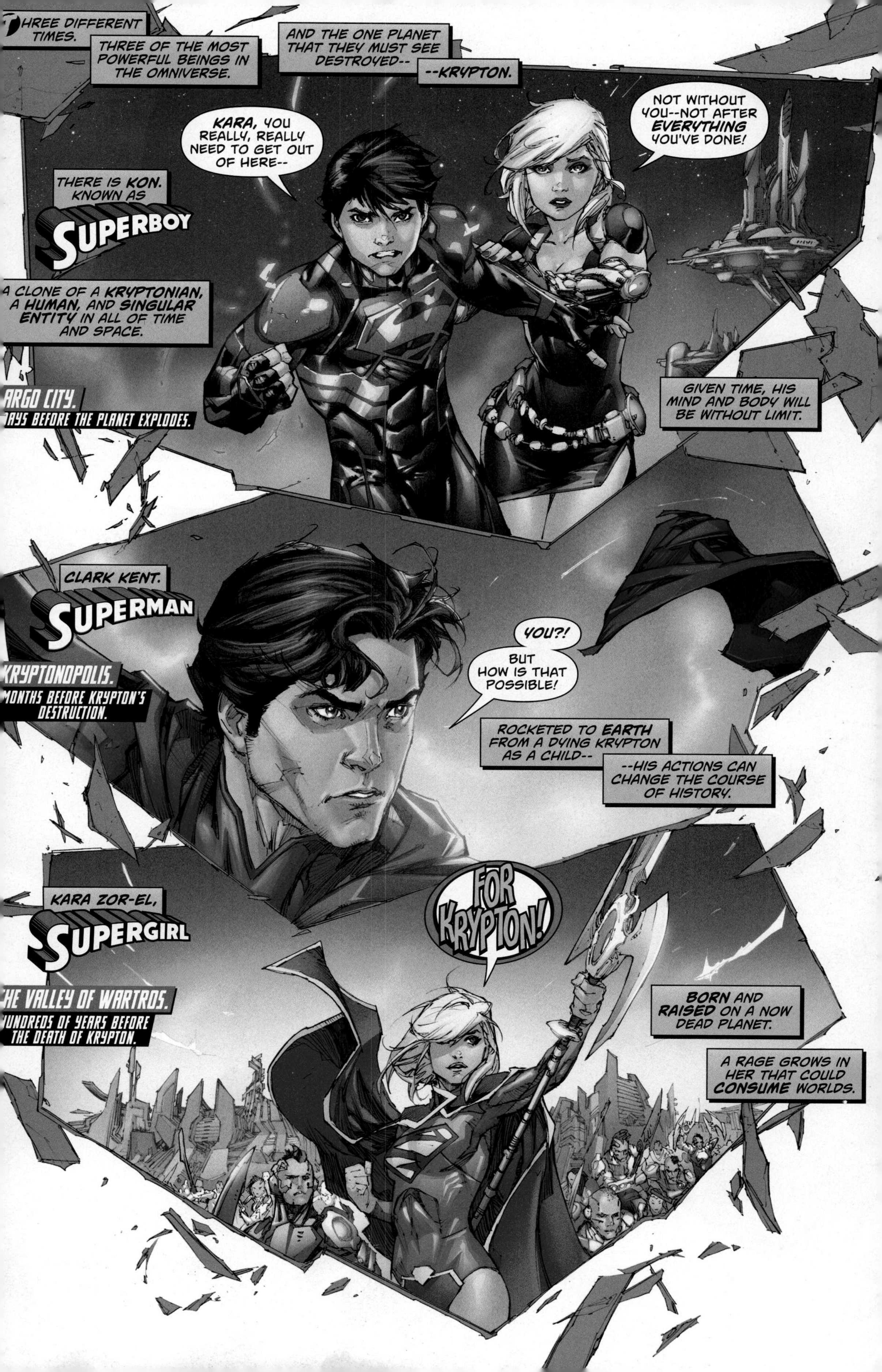
THREE DIFFERENT TIMES.
THREE OF THE MOST POWERFUL BEINGS IN THE OMNIVERSE.
AND THE ONE PLANET THAT THEY MUST SEE DESTROYED--
--KRYPTON.
KARA, YOU REALLY, REALLY NEED TO GET OUT OF HERE--
NOT WITHOUT YOU--NOT AFTER EVERYTHING YOU'VE DONE!
THERE IS KON. KNOWN AS
SUPERBOY
A CLONE OF A KRYPTONIAN, A HUMAN, AND SINGULAR ENTITY IN ALL OF TIME AND SPACE.
ARGO CITY.
DAYS BEFORE THE PLANET EXPLODES.
GIVEN TIME, HIS MIND AND BODY WILL BE WITHOUT LIMIT.
CLARK KENT.
SUPERMAN
KRYPTONOPOLIS.
MONTHS BEFORE KRYPTON'S DESTRUCTION.
YOU?!
BUT HOW IS THAT POSSIBLE!
ROCKETED TO EARTH FROM A DYING KRYPTON AS A CHILD--
--HIS ACTIONS CAN CHANGE THE COURSE OF HISTORY.
KARA ZOR-EL,
SUPERGIRL
FOR KRYPTON!
THE VALLEY OF WARTROS.
HUNDREDS OF YEARS BEFORE THE DEATH OF KRYPTON.
BORN AND RAISED ON A NOW DEAD PLANET.
A RAGE GROWS IN HER THAT COULD CONSUME WORLDS.

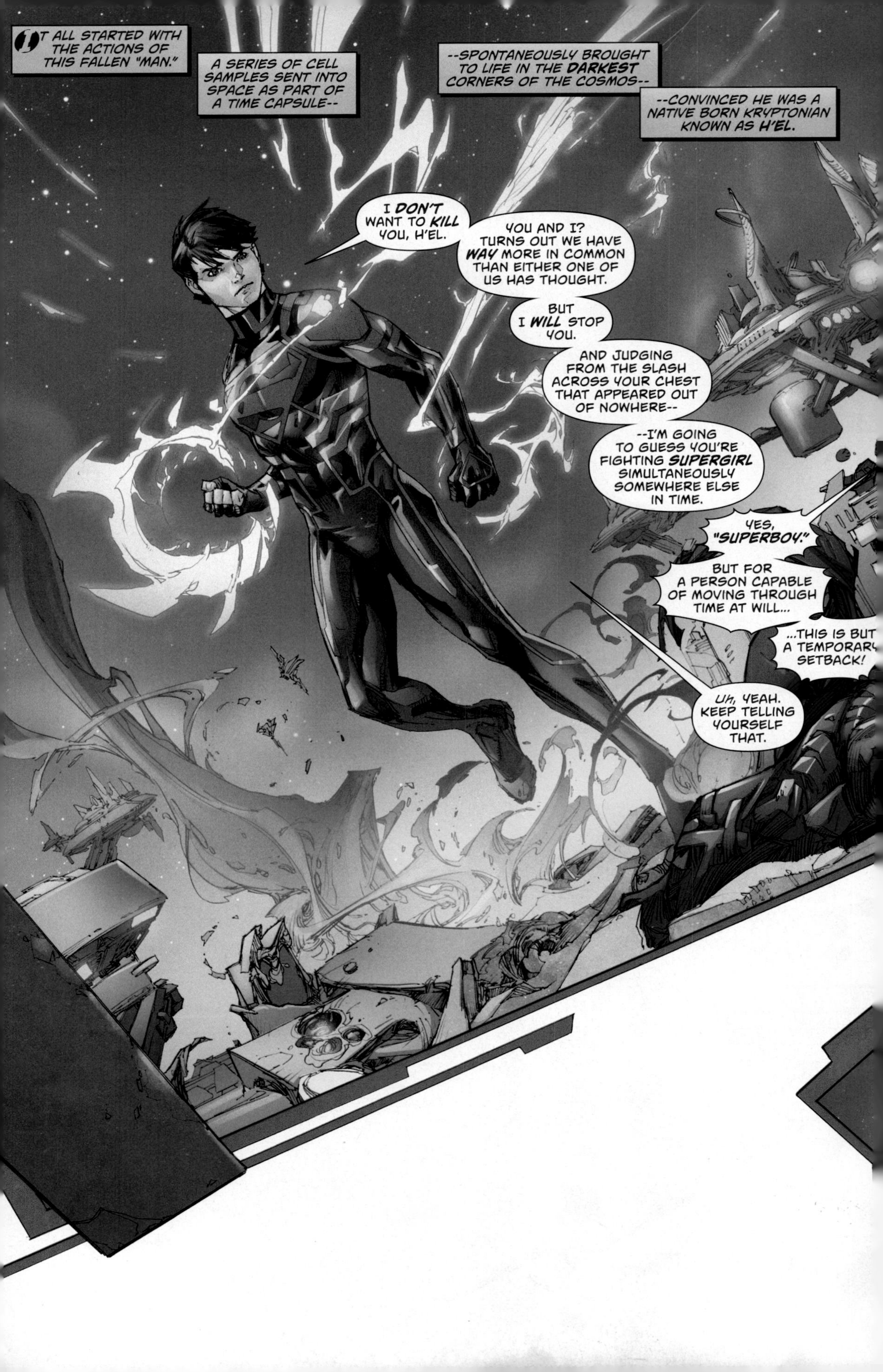
IT ALL STARTED WITH THE ACTIONS OF THIS FALLEN "MAN."
A SERIES OF CELL SAMPLES SENT INTO SPACE AS PART OF A TIME CAPSULE--
--SPONTANEOUSLY BROUGHT TO LIFE IN THE DARKEST CORNERS OF THE COSMOS--
--CONVINCED HE WAS A NATIVE BORN KRYPTONIAN KNOWN AS H'EL.
I DON'T WANT TO KILL YOU, H'EL.
YOU AND I? TURNS OUT WE HAVE WAY MORE IN COMMON THAN EITHER ONE OF US HAS THOUGHT.
BUT I WILL STOP YOU.
AND JUDGING FROM THE SLASH ACROSS YOUR CHEST THAT APPEARED OUT OF NOWHERE--
--I'M GOING TO GUESS YOU'RE FIGHTING SUPERGIRL SIMULTANEOUSLY SOMEWHERE ELSE IN TIME.
YES, "SUPERBOY."
BUT FOR A PERSON CAPABLE OF MOVING THROUGH TIME AT WILL...
...THIS IS BUT A TEMPORARY SETBACK!
UH, YEAH. KEEP TELLING YOURSELF THAT.

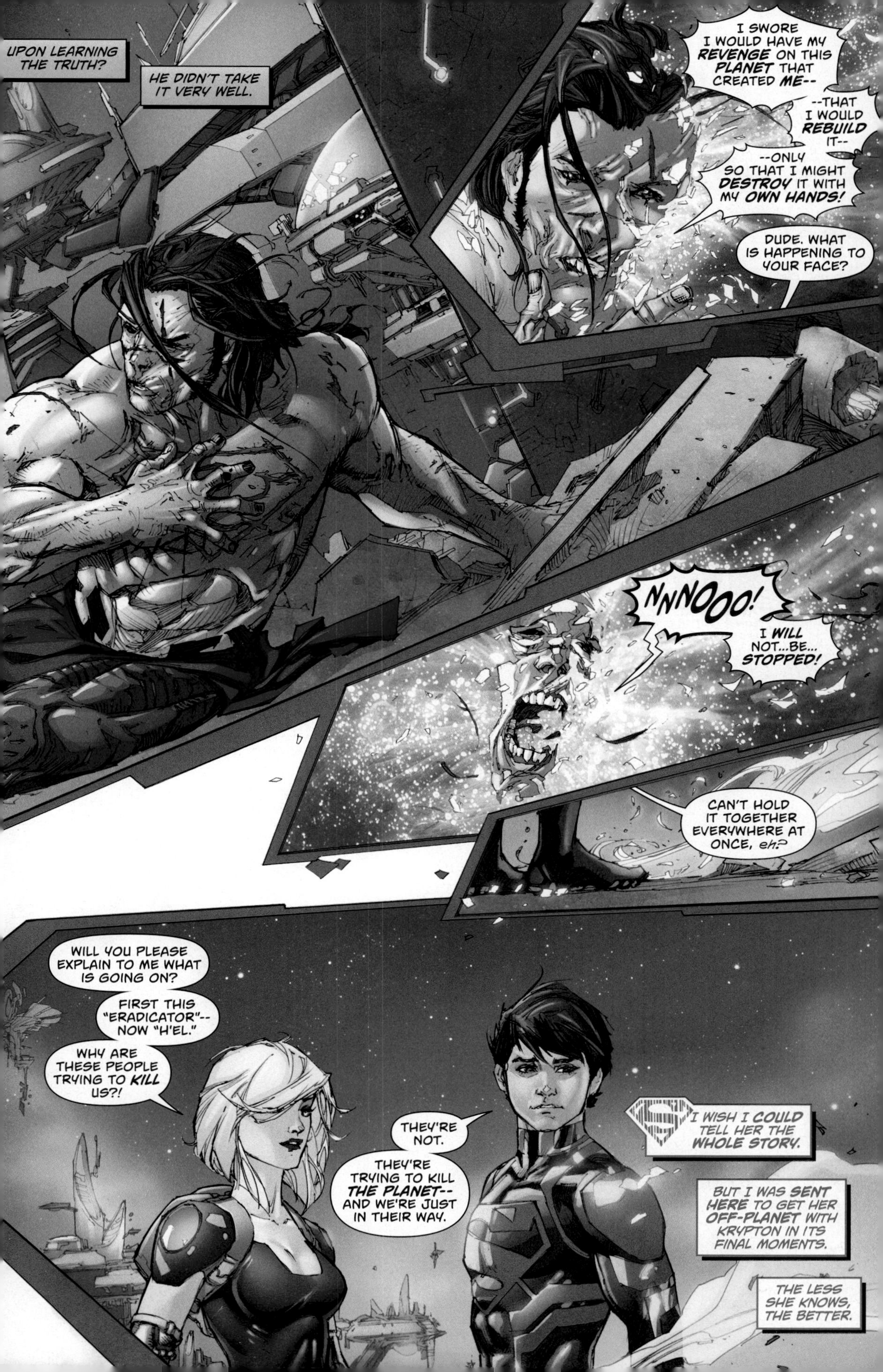
UPON LEARNING THE TRUTH?
HE DIDN'T TAKE IT VERY WELL.
I SWORE I WOULD HAVE MY REVENGE ON THIS PLANET THAT CREATED ME--
--THAT I WOULD REBUILD IT--
--ONLY SO THAT I MIGHT DESTROY IT WITH MY OWN HANDS!
DUDE. WHAT IS HAPPENING TO YOUR FACE?
NNNOOO!
I WILL NOT...BE... STOPPED!
CAN'T HOLD IT TOGETHER EVERYWHERE AT ONCE, eh?
WILL YOU PLEASE EXPLAIN TO ME WHAT IS GOING ON?
FIRST THIS "ERADICATOR"-- NOW "H'EL."
WHY ARE THESE PEOPLE TRYING TO KILL US?!
THEY'RE NOT.
THEY'RE TRYING TO KILL THE PLANET-- AND WE'RE JUST IN THEIR WAY.
I WISH I COULD TELL HER THE WHOLE STORY.
BUT I WAS SENT HERE TO GET HER OFF-PLANET WITH KRYPTON IN ITS FINAL MOMENTS.
THE LESS SHE KNOWS, THE BETTER.

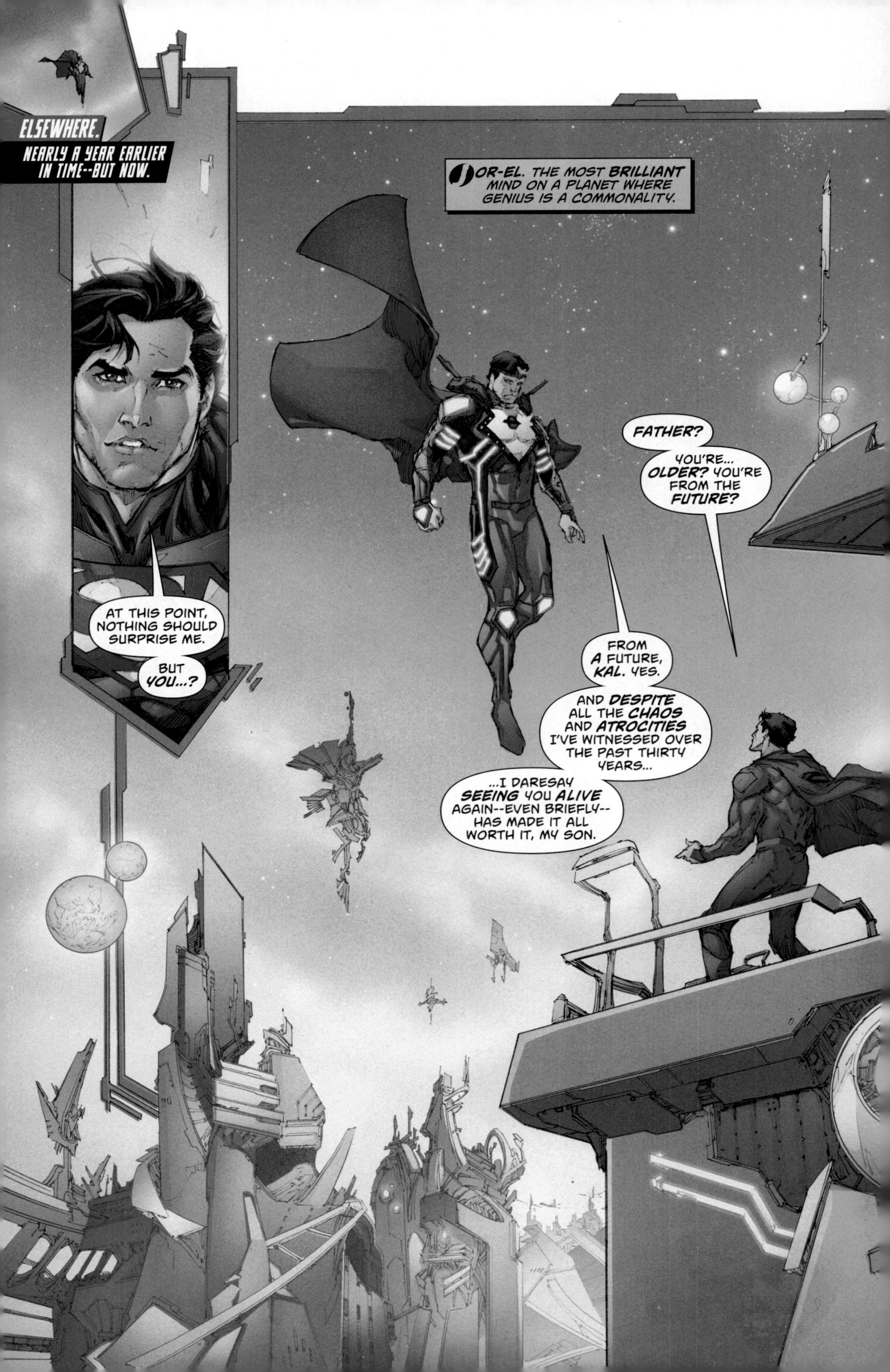
ELSEWHERE.
NEARLY A YEAR EARLIER IN TIME--BUT NOW.
JOR-EL. THE MOST BRILLIANT MIND ON A PLANET WHERE GENIUS IS A COMMONALITY.
AT THIS POINT, NOTHING SHOULD SURPRISE ME.
BUT YOU...?
FATHER?
YOU'RE... OLDER? YOU'RE FROM THE FUTURE?
FROM A FUTURE, KAL. YES.
AND DESPITE ALL THE CHAOS AND ATROCITIES I'VE WITNESSED OVER THE PAST THIRTY YEARS...
...I DARESAY SEEING YOU ALIVE AGAIN--EVEN BRIEFLY--HAS MADE IT ALL WORTH IT, MY SON.

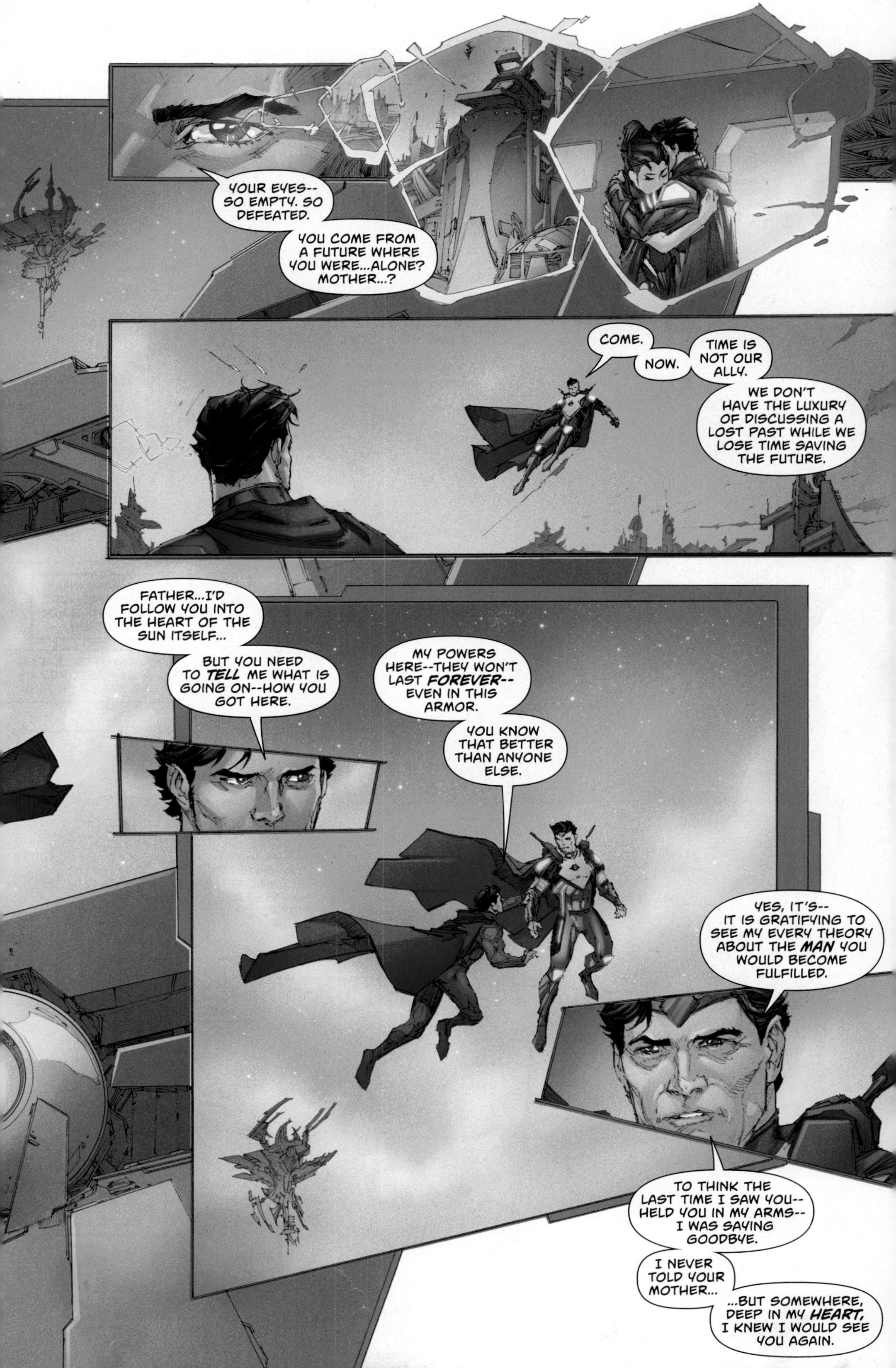
YOUR EYES-- SO EMPTY. SO DEFEATED.
YOU COME FROM A FUTURE WHERE YOU WERE...ALONE? MOTHER...?
COME.
NOW.
TIME IS NOT OUR ALLY.
WE DON'T HAVE THE LUXURY OF DISCUSSING A LOST PAST WHILE WE LOSE TIME SAVING THE FUTURE.
FATHER...I'D FOLLOW YOU INTO THE HEART OF THE SUN ITSELF...
BUT YOU NEED TO TELL ME WHAT IS GOING ON--HOW YOU GOT HERE.
MY POWERS HERE--THEY WON'T LAST FOREVER-- EVEN IN THIS ARMOR.
YOU KNOW THAT BETTER THAN ANYONE ELSE.
YES, IT'S-- IT IS GRATIFYING TO SEE MY EVERY THEORY ABOUT THE MAN YOU WOULD BECOME FULFILLED.
TO THINK THE LAST TIME I SAW YOU-- HELD YOU IN MY ARMS-- I WAS SAYING GOODBYE.
I NEVER TOLD YOUR MOTHER...
...BUT SOMEWHERE, DEEP IN MY HEART, I KNEW I WOULD SEE YOU AGAIN.

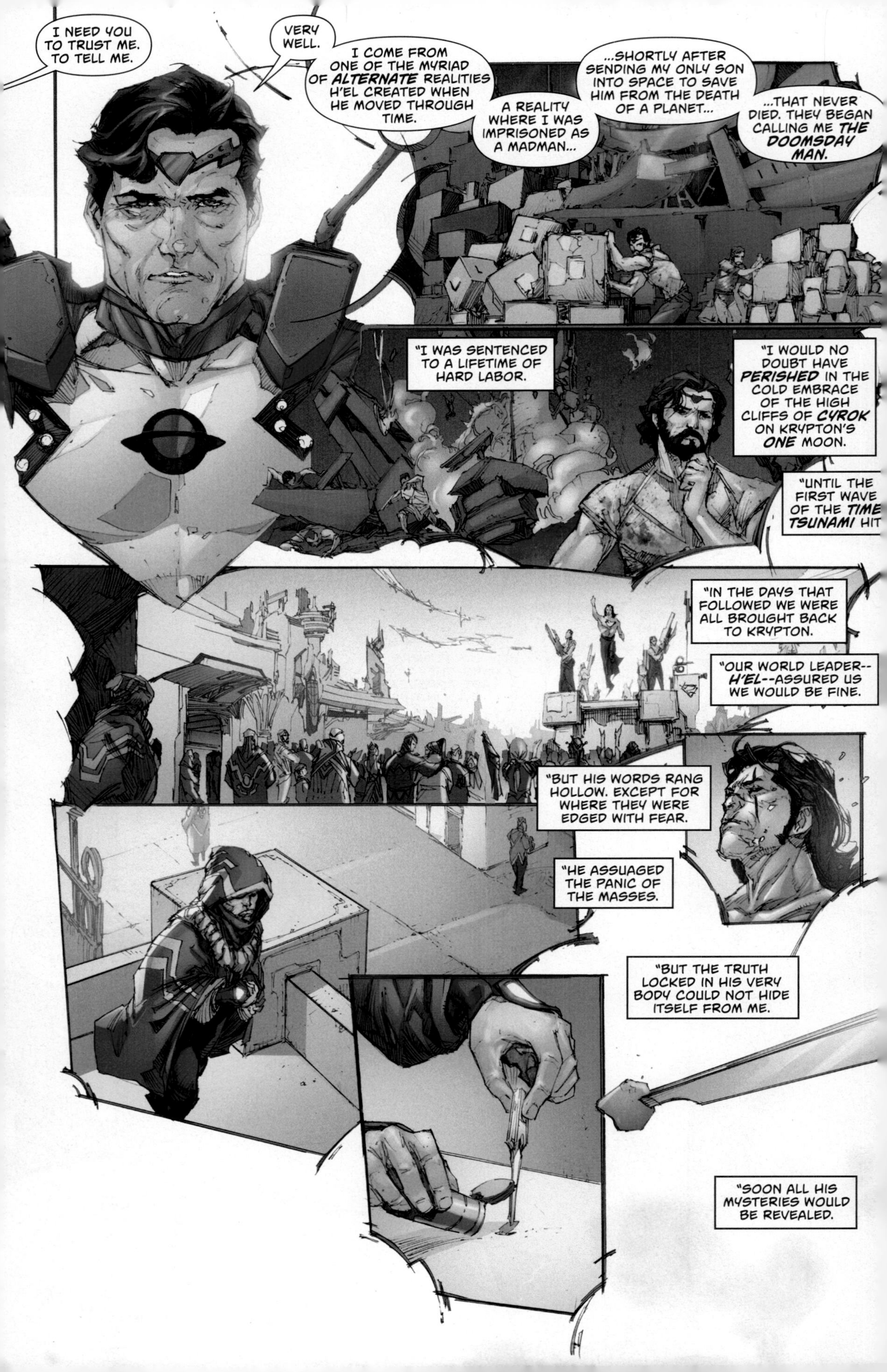
I NEED YOU TO TRUST ME. TO TELL ME.
VERY WELL.
I COME FROM ONE OF THE MYRIAD OF ALTERNATE REALITIES H'EL CREATED WHEN HE MOVED THROUGH TIME.
A REALITY WHERE I WAS IMPRISONED AS A MADMAN...
...SHORTLY AFTER SENDING MY ONLY SON INTO SPACE TO SAVE HIM FROM THE DEATH OF A PLANET...
...THAT NEVER DIED. THEY BEGAN CALLING ME THE DOOMSDAY MAN.
"I WAS SENTENCED TO A LIFETIME OF HARD LABOR.
"I WOULD NO DOUBT HAVE PERISHED IN THE COLD EMBRACE OF THE HIGH CLIFFS OF CYROK ON KRYPTON'S ONE MOON.
"UNTIL THE FIRST WAVE OF THE TIME TSUNAMI HIT.
"IN THE DAYS THAT FOLLOWED WE WERE ALL BROUGHT BACK TO KRYPTON.
"OUR WORLD LEADER--H'EL--ASSURED US WE WOULD BE FINE.
"BUT HIS WORDS RANG HOLLOW. EXCEPT FOR WHERE THEY WERE EDGED WITH FEAR.
"HE ASSUAGED THE PANIC OF THE MASSES.
"BUT THE TRUTH LOCKED IN HIS VERY BODY COULD NOT HIDE ITSELF FROM ME.
"SOON ALL HIS MYSTERIES WOULD BE REVEALED.

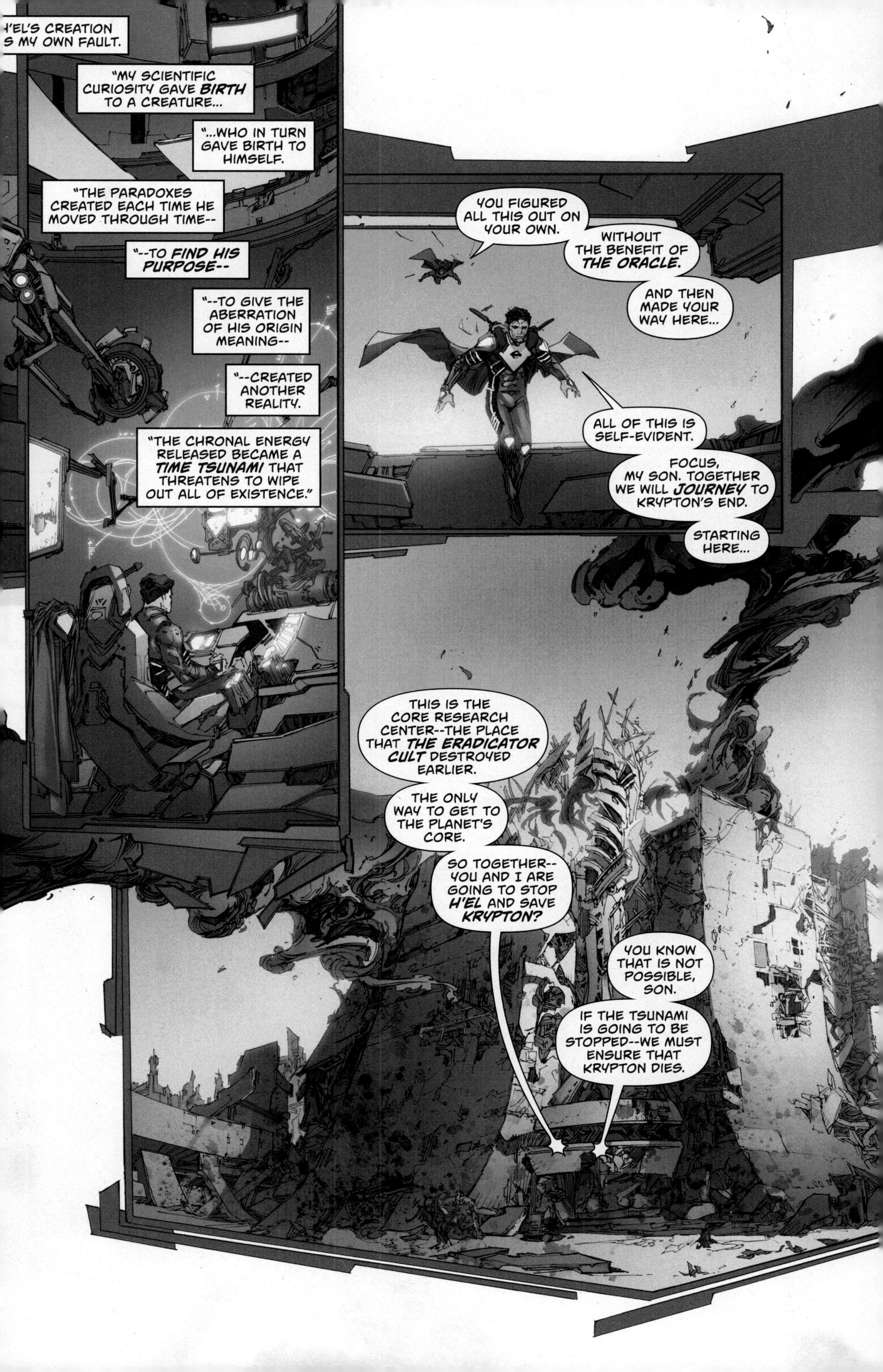

H'EL'S CREATION
S MY OWN FAULT.
"MY SCIENTIFIC CURIOSITY GAVE **BIRTH** TO A CREATURE...
"...WHO IN TURN GAVE BIRTH TO HIMSELF.
"THE PARADOXES CREATED EACH TIME HE MOVED THROUGH TIME--
"--TO **FIND HIS PURPOSE**--
"--TO GIVE THE ABERRATION OF HIS ORIGIN MEANING--
"--CREATED ANOTHER REALITY.
"THE CHRONAL ENERGY RELEASED BECAME A **TIME TSUNAMI** THAT THREATENS TO WIPE OUT ALL OF EXISTENCE."
YOU FIGURED ALL THIS OUT ON YOUR OWN.
WITHOUT THE BENEFIT OF **THE ORACLE**.
AND THEN MADE YOUR WAY HERE...
ALL OF THIS IS SELF-EVIDENT.
FOCUS, MY SON. TOGETHER WE WILL **JOURNEY** TO KRYPTON'S END.
STARTING HERE...
THIS IS THE CORE RESEARCH CENTER--THE PLACE THAT **THE ERADICATOR CULT** DESTROYED EARLIER.
THE ONLY WAY TO GET TO THE PLANET'S CORE.
SO TOGETHER-- YOU AND I ARE GOING TO STOP **H'EL** AND SAVE **KRYPTON?**
YOU KNOW THAT IS NOT POSSIBLE, SON.
IF THE TSUNAMI IS GOING TO BE STOPPED--WE MUST ENSURE THAT KRYPTON DIES.

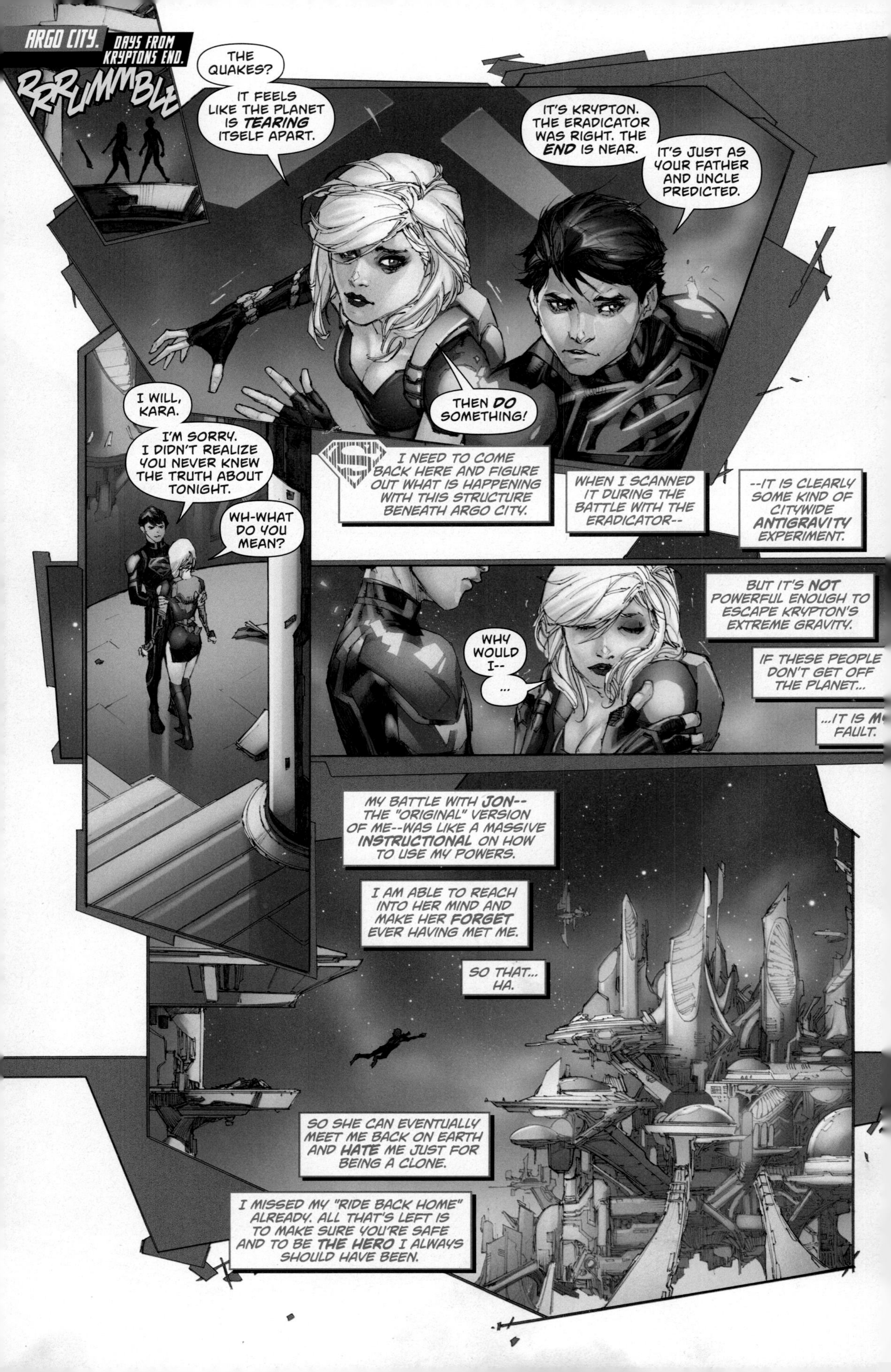
ARGO CITY.
DAYS FROM KRYPTONS END.
RRRUMMBLE
THE QUAKES?
IT FEELS LIKE THE PLANET IS TEARING ITSELF APART.
IT'S KRYPTON. THE ERADICATOR WAS RIGHT. THE END IS NEAR.
IT'S JUST AS YOUR FATHER AND UNCLE PREDICTED.
THEN DO SOMETHING!
I WILL, KARA.
I'M SORRY. I DIDN'T REALIZE YOU NEVER KNEW THE TRUTH ABOUT TONIGHT.
WH-WHAT DO YOU MEAN?
I NEED TO COME BACK HERE AND FIGURE OUT WHAT IS HAPPENING WITH THIS STRUCTURE BENEATH ARGO CITY.
WHEN I SCANNED IT DURING THE BATTLE WITH THE ERADICATOR--
--IT IS CLEARLY SOME KIND OF CITYWIDE ANTIGRAVITY EXPERIMENT.
WHY WOULD I-- ...
BUT IT'S NOT POWERFUL ENOUGH TO ESCAPE KRYPTON'S EXTREME GRAVITY.
IF THESE PEOPLE DON'T GET OFF THE PLANET...
...IT IS M FAULT.
MY BATTLE WITH JON-- THE "ORIGINAL" VERSION OF ME--WAS LIKE A MASSIVE INSTRUCTIONAL ON HOW TO USE MY POWERS.
I AM ABLE TO REACH INTO HER MIND AND MAKE HER FORGET EVER HAVING MET ME.
SO THAT... HA.
SO SHE CAN EVENTUALLY MEET ME BACK ON EARTH AND HATE ME JUST FOR BEING A CLONE.
I MISSED MY "RIDE BACK HOME" ALREADY. ALL THAT'S LEFT IS TO MAKE SURE YOU'RE SAFE AND TO BE THE HERO I ALWAYS SHOULD HAVE BEEN.

FAR INTO KRYPTON'S PAST...
HISTORICALLY, IT WAS CALLED **THE KON UPRISING**--AFTER ITS RUTHLESS LEADER.
THE LAST STAND OF THE **CLONES** WHO SOUGHT TO DESTROY THEIR CREATORS.
BUT IT TURNS OUT THE HISTORY BOOKS GOT IT WRONG.
ON THIS DAY THE **CLONES** RALLIED BEHIND A MYSTERIOUS YOUNG WOMAN--ME--WHO CONVINCED THEM TO BATTLE A THREAT **GREATER** THAN ANY KRYPTON HAD EVER KNOWN.
WITH JUST A TWIST OF MY LANCE-- I'LL HAVE WON.
BUT...CAN I DO IT?
WHAT ARE YOU WAITING FOR, KARA?
MY "**BELOVED.**"
IT WAS A SIMPLE MATTER TO BETRAY ME ONCE BEFORE.
DON'T PRETEND YOU CARE AT ALL WHAT HAPPENS TO ME.
BY **RAO!** YOU'RE AN IDIOT.
I **LOVED** YOU.
EVEN AFTER ALL YOUR LIES...YOUR MANIPULATION.
I UNDERSTOOD **WHAT** YOU **WANTED.**
IT WAS WHAT I WANTED WITH **ALL** MY HEART AND SOUL.
BUT **YOU** FORCED MY **HAND,** H'EL.
AND **DAMMIT** IF YOU'RE NOT GOING TO DO IT AGAIN!

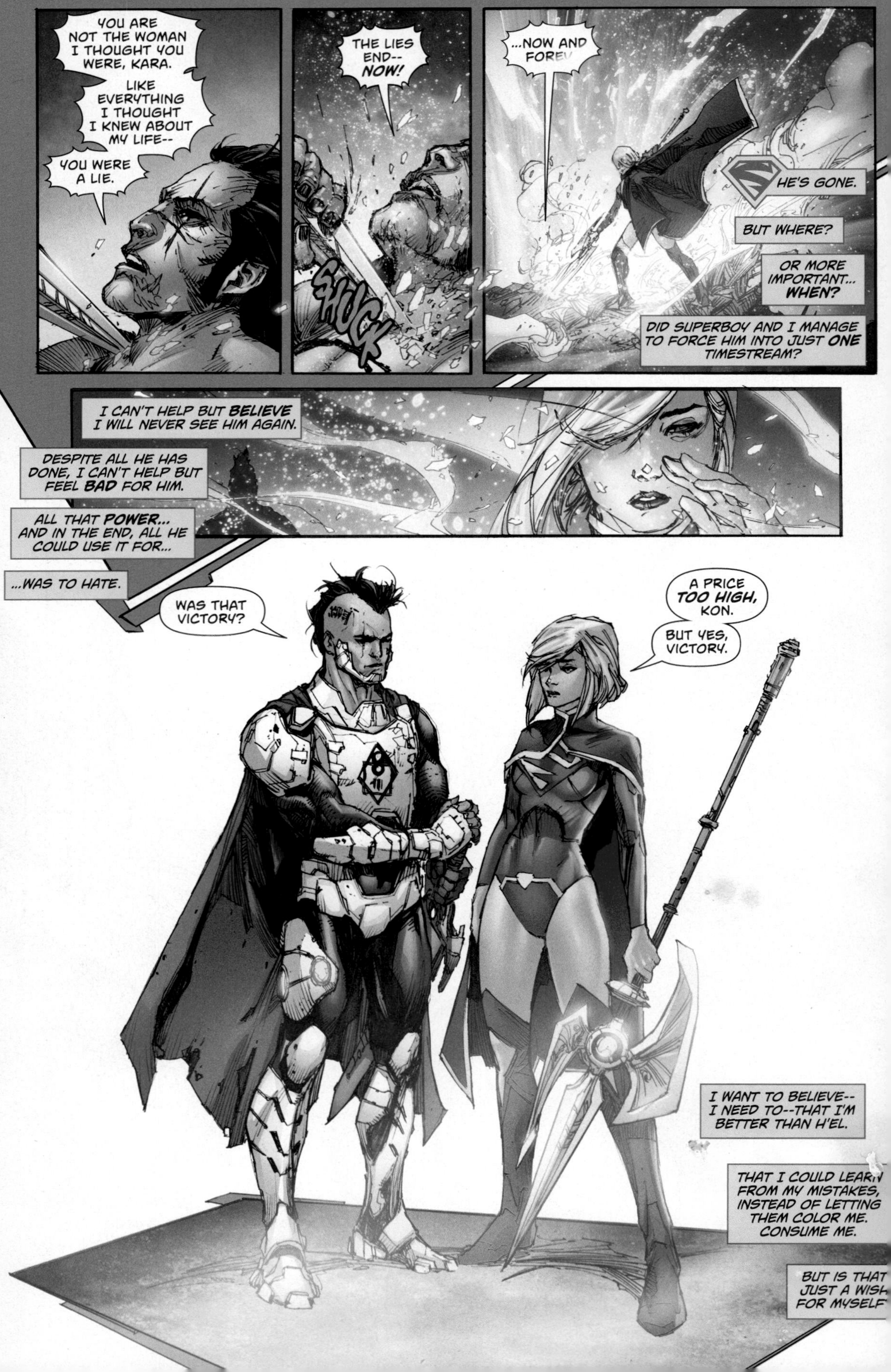

YOU ARE NOT THE WOMAN I THOUGHT YOU WERE, KARA.
LIKE EVERYTHING I THOUGHT I KNEW ABOUT MY LIFE--
YOU WERE A LIE.
THE LIES END-- NOW!
SHUCK
...NOW AND FOREV
HE'S GONE.
BUT WHERE?
OR MORE IMPORTANT... WHEN?
DID SUPERBOY AND I MANAGE TO FORCE HIM INTO JUST ONE TIMESTREAM?
I CAN'T HELP BUT BELIEVE I WILL NEVER SEE HIM AGAIN.
DESPITE ALL HE HAS DONE, I CAN'T HELP BUT FEEL BAD FOR HIM.
ALL THAT POWER... AND IN THE END, ALL HE COULD USE IT FOR...
...WAS TO HATE.
WAS THAT VICTORY?
A PRICE TOO HIGH, KON.
BUT YES, VICTORY.
I WANT TO BELIEVE-- I NEED TO--THAT I'M BETTER THAN H'EL.
THAT I COULD LEARN FROM MY MISTAKES, INSTEAD OF LETTING THEM COLOR ME. CONSUME ME.
BUT IS THAT JUST A WISH FOR MYSELF

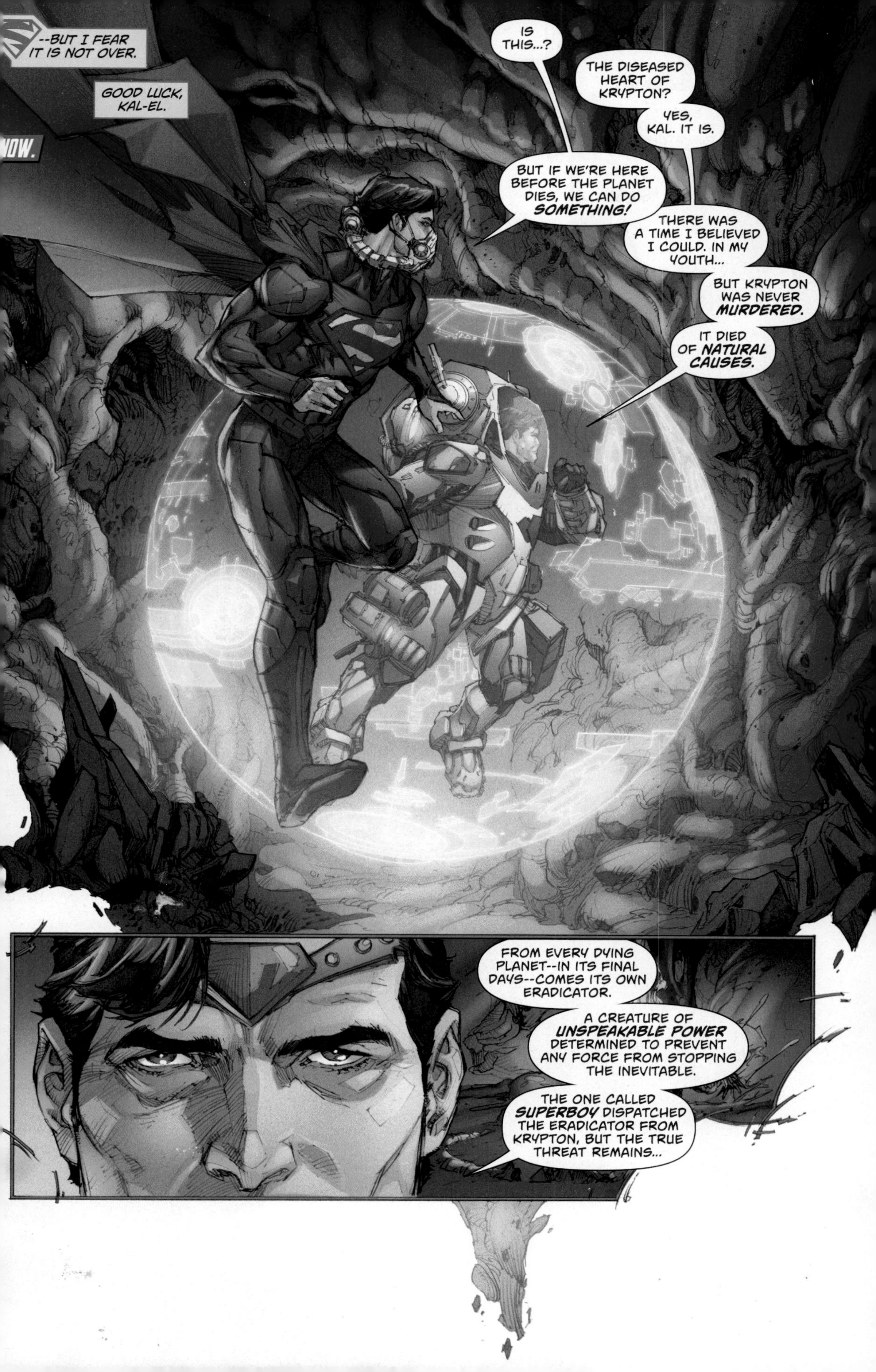
--BUT I FEAR IT IS NOT OVER.
GOOD LUCK, KAL-EL.
NOW.
IS THIS...?
THE DISEASED HEART OF KRYPTON?
YES, KAL. IT IS.
BUT IF WE'RE HERE BEFORE THE PLANET DIES, WE CAN DO SOMETHING!
THERE WAS A TIME I BELIEVED I COULD. IN MY YOUTH...
BUT KRYPTON WAS NEVER MURDERED.
IT DIED OF NATURAL CAUSES.
FROM EVERY DYING PLANET--IN ITS FINAL DAYS--COMES ITS OWN ERADICATOR.
A CREATURE OF UNSPEAKABLE POWER DETERMINED TO PREVENT ANY FORCE FROM STOPPING THE INEVITABLE.
THE ONE CALLED SUPERBOY DISPATCHED THE ERADICATOR FROM KRYPTON, BUT THE TRUE THREAT REMAINS...

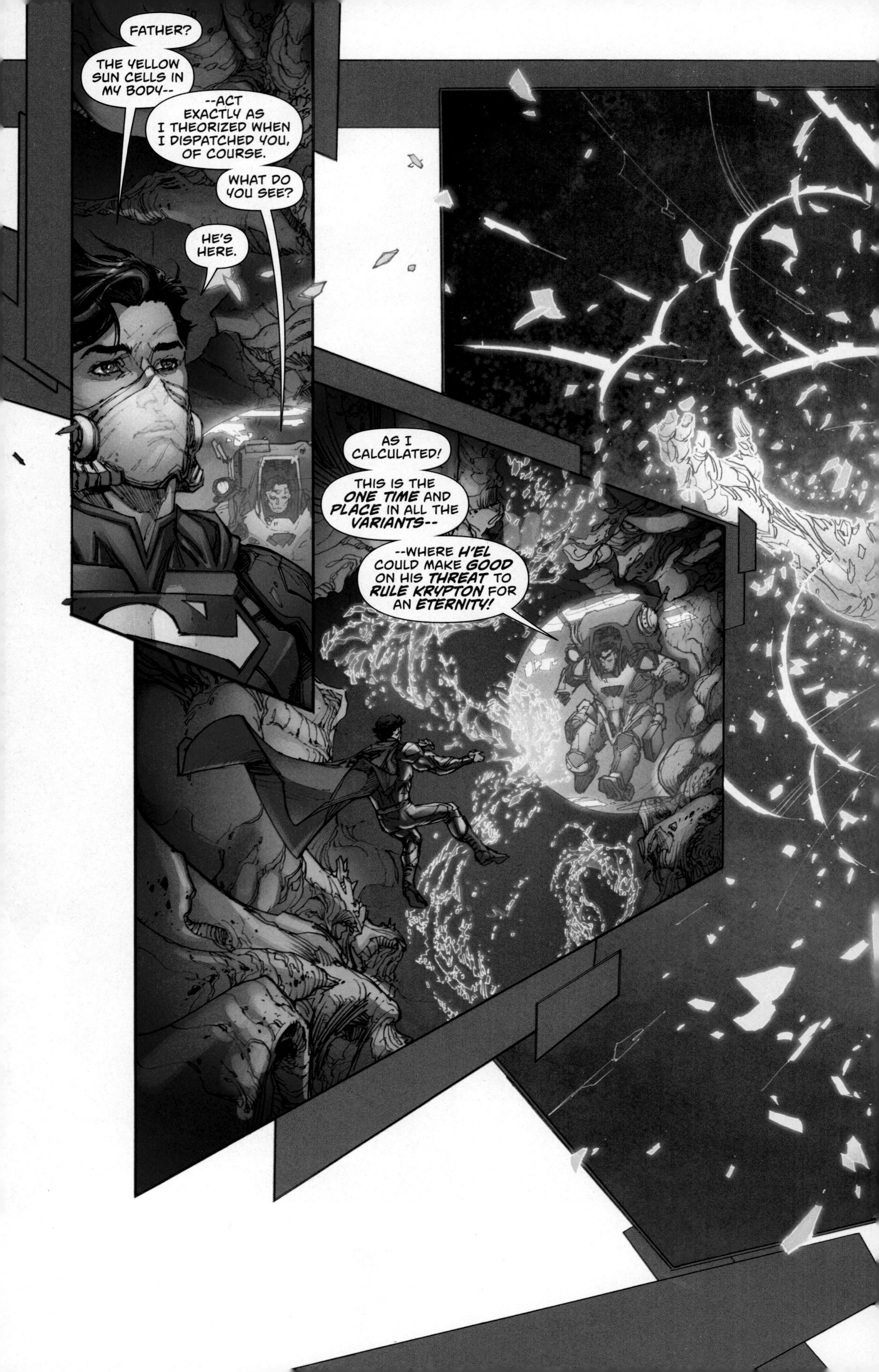
FATHER?
THE YELLOW SUN CELLS IN MY BODY--
--ACT EXACTLY AS I THEORIZED WHEN I DISPATCHED YOU, OF COURSE.
WHAT DO YOU SEE?
HE'S HERE.
AS I CALCULATED!
THIS IS THE ONE TIME AND PLACE IN ALL THE VARIANTS--
--WHERE H'EL COULD MAKE GOOD ON HIS THREAT TO RULE KRYPTON FOR AN ETERNITY!

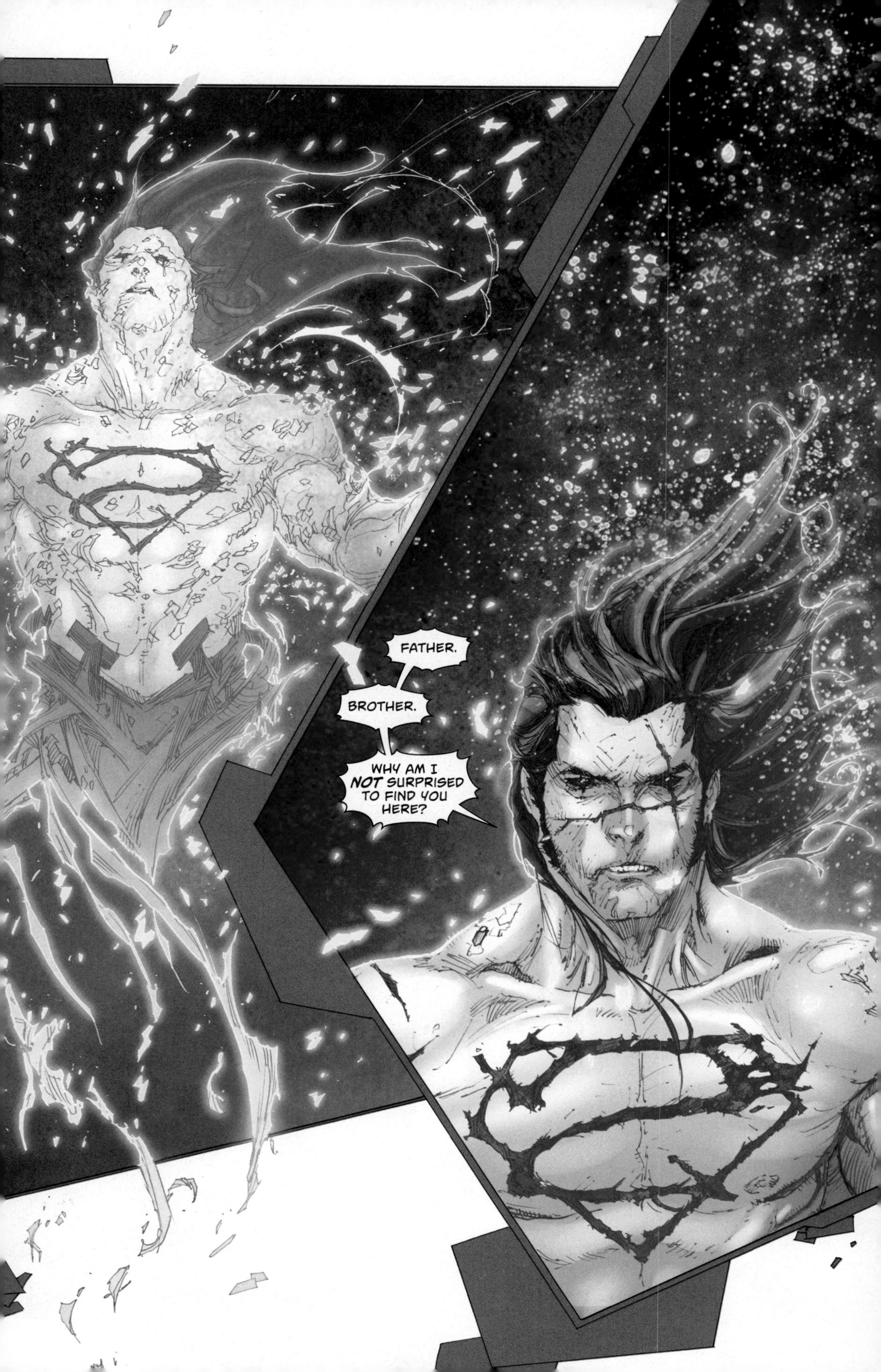
FATHER.
BROTHER.
WHY AM I *NOT* SURPRISED TO FIND YOU HERE?

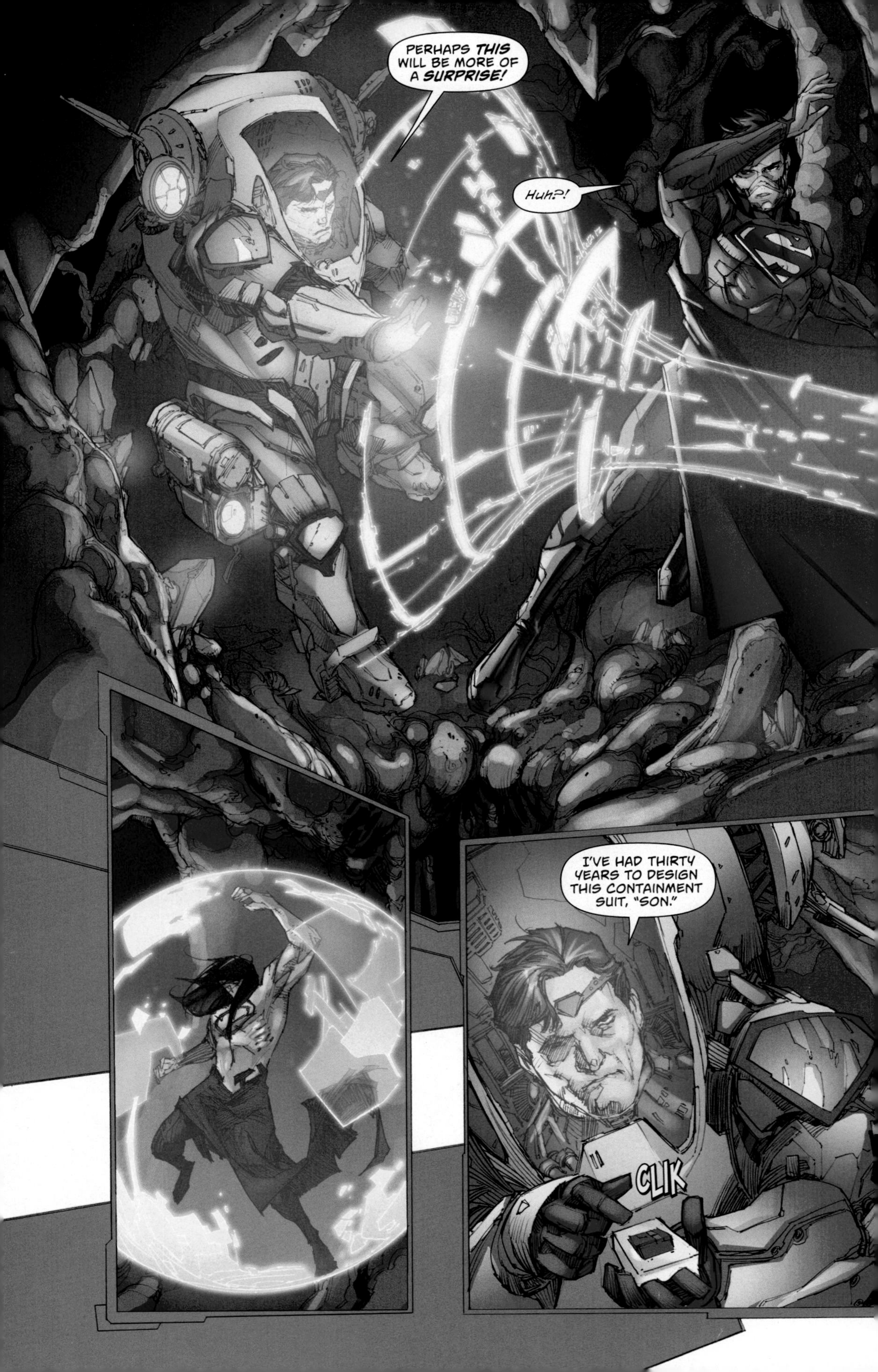
PERHAPS THIS WILL BE MORE OF A SURPRISE!
Huh?!
I'VE HAD THIRTY YEARS TO DESIGN THIS CONTAINMENT SUIT, "SON."
CLIK

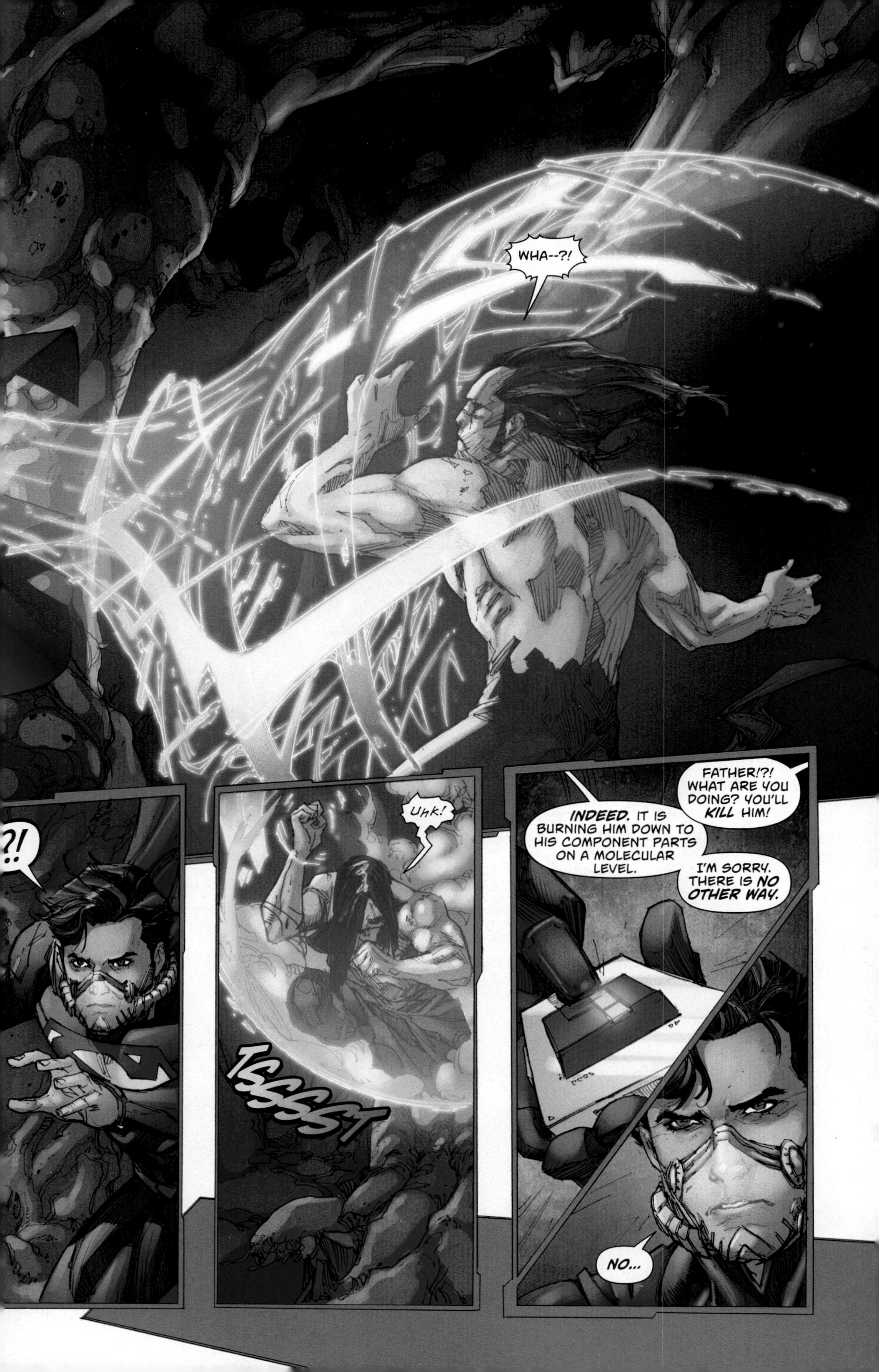
WHA--?!
?!
Uhk!
TSSSST
FATHER!?! WHAT ARE YOU DOING? YOU'LL KILL HIM!
INDEED. IT IS BURNING HIM DOWN TO HIS COMPONENT PARTS ON A MOLECULAR LEVEL.
I'M SORRY. THERE IS NO OTHER WAY.
NO...

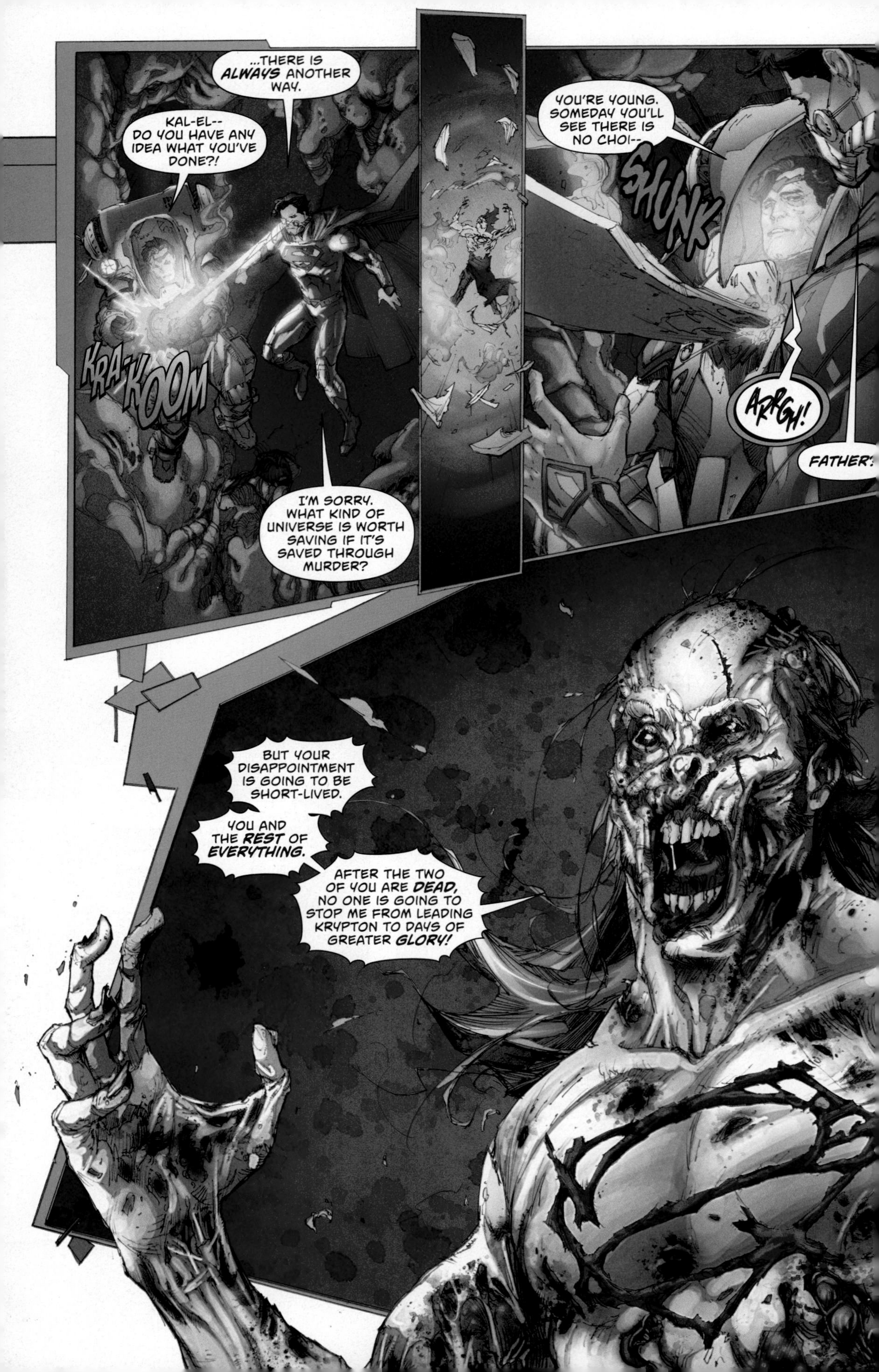
...THERE IS ALWAYS ANOTHER WAY.
KAL-EL-- DO YOU HAVE ANY IDEA WHAT YOU'VE DONE?!
KRA-KOOM
I'M SORRY. WHAT KIND OF UNIVERSE IS WORTH SAVING IF IT'S SAVED THROUGH MURDER?
YOU'RE YOUNG. SOMEDAY YOU'LL SEE THERE IS NO CHOI--
SHUNK
ARRGH!
FATHER!
BUT YOUR DISAPPOINTMENT IS GOING TO BE SHORT-LIVED.
YOU AND THE REST OF EVERYTHING.
AFTER THE TWO OF YOU ARE DEAD, NO ONE IS GOING TO STOP ME FROM LEADING KRYPTON TO DAYS OF GREATER GLORY!

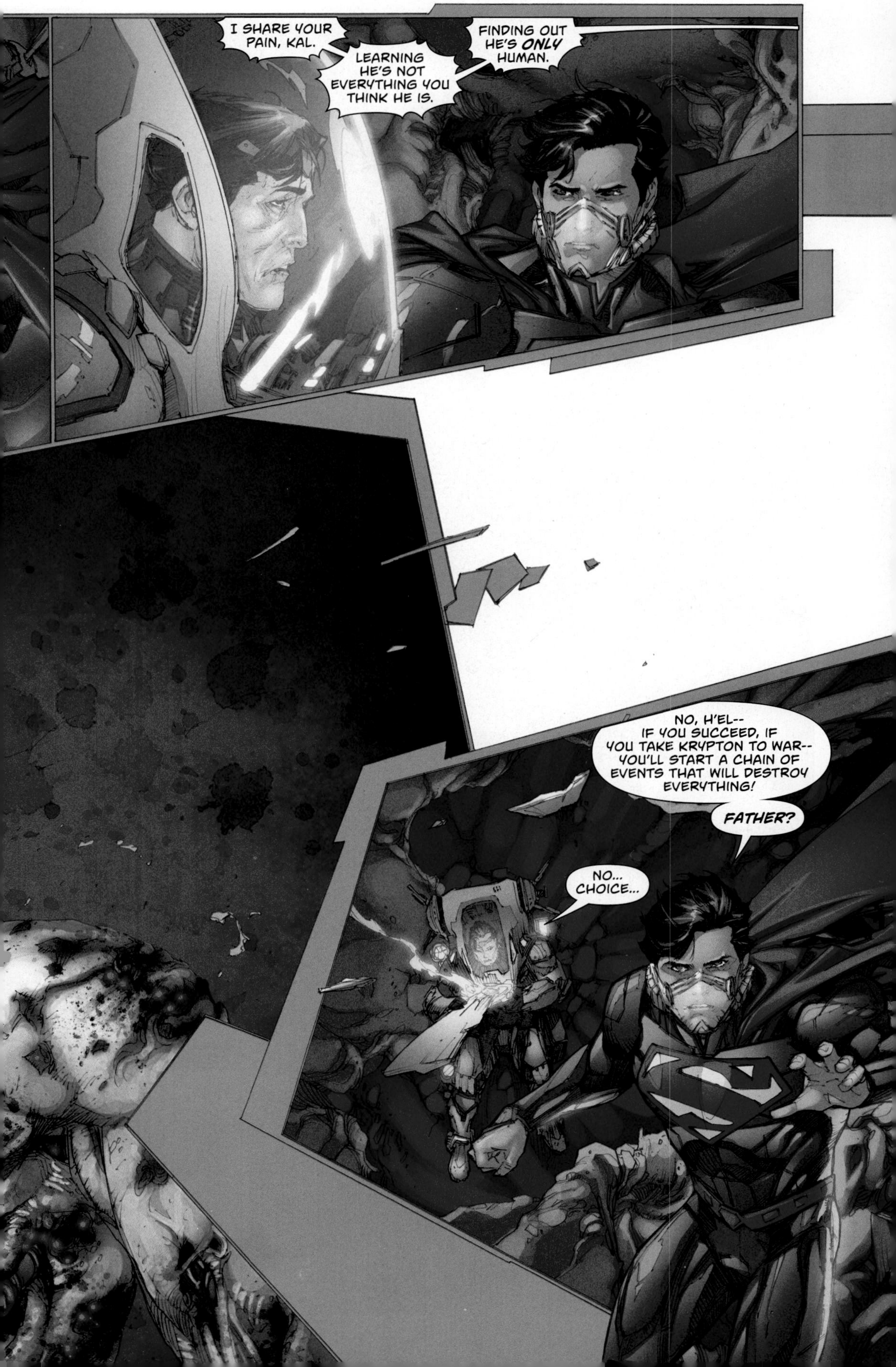
I SHARE YOUR PAIN, KAL.
LEARNING HE'S NOT EVERYTHING YOU THINK HE IS.
FINDING OUT HE'S *ONLY* HUMAN.
NO, H'EL-- IF YOU SUCCEED, IF YOU TAKE KRYPTON TO WAR-- YOU'LL START A CHAIN OF EVENTS THAT WILL DESTROY EVERYTHING!
FATHER?
NO... CHOICE...

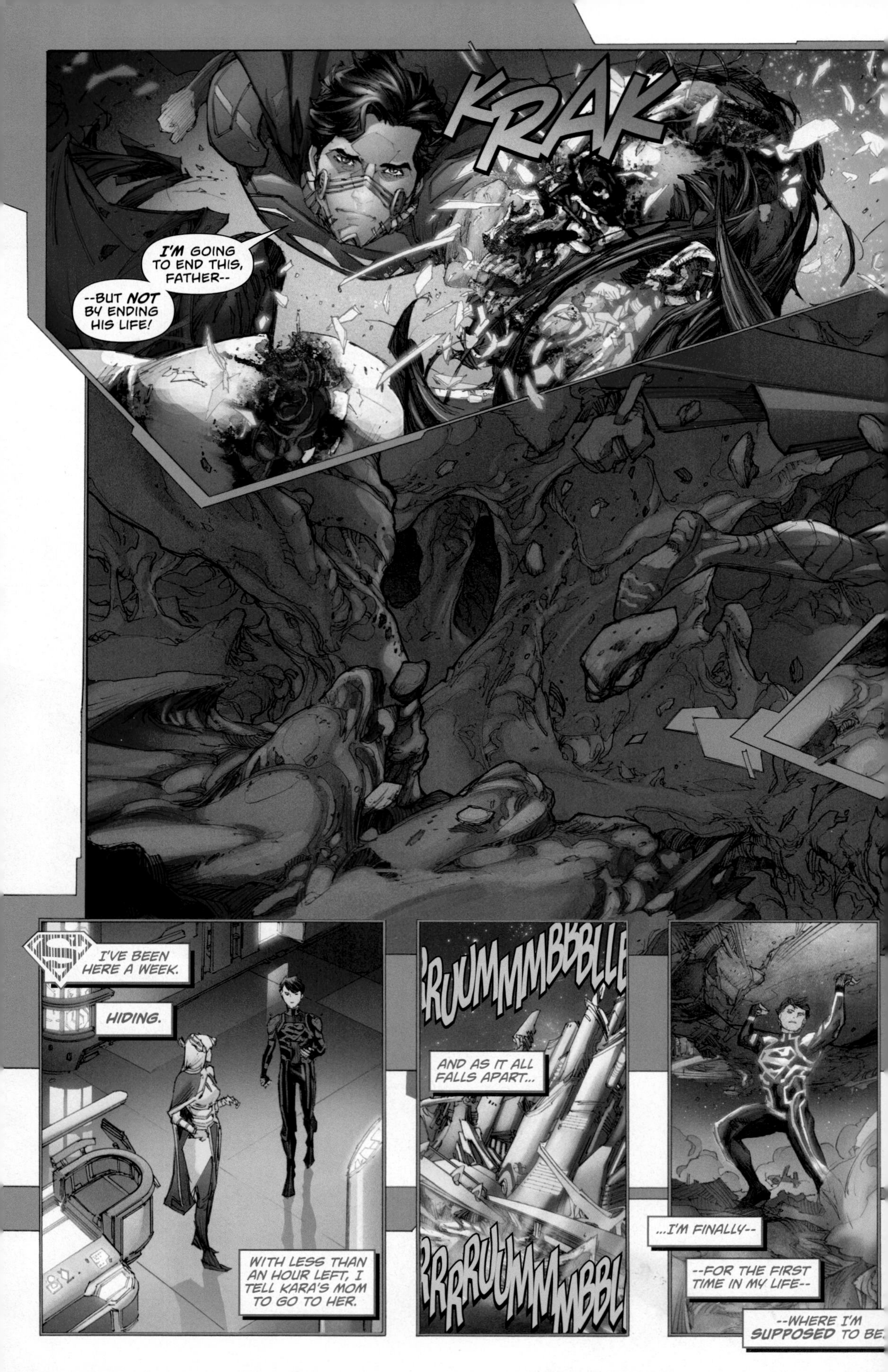
KRAK
I'M GOING TO END THIS, FATHER--
--BUT NOT BY ENDING HIS LIFE!
I'VE BEEN HERE A WEEK.
HIDING.
WITH LESS THAN AN HOUR LEFT, I TELL KARA'S MOM TO GO TO HER.
RRUUMMMBBBLLE
AND AS IT ALL FALLS APART...
RRRRUMMMBBL
...I'M FINALLY--
--FOR THE FIRST TIME IN MY LIFE--
--WHERE I'M SUPPOSED TO BE.

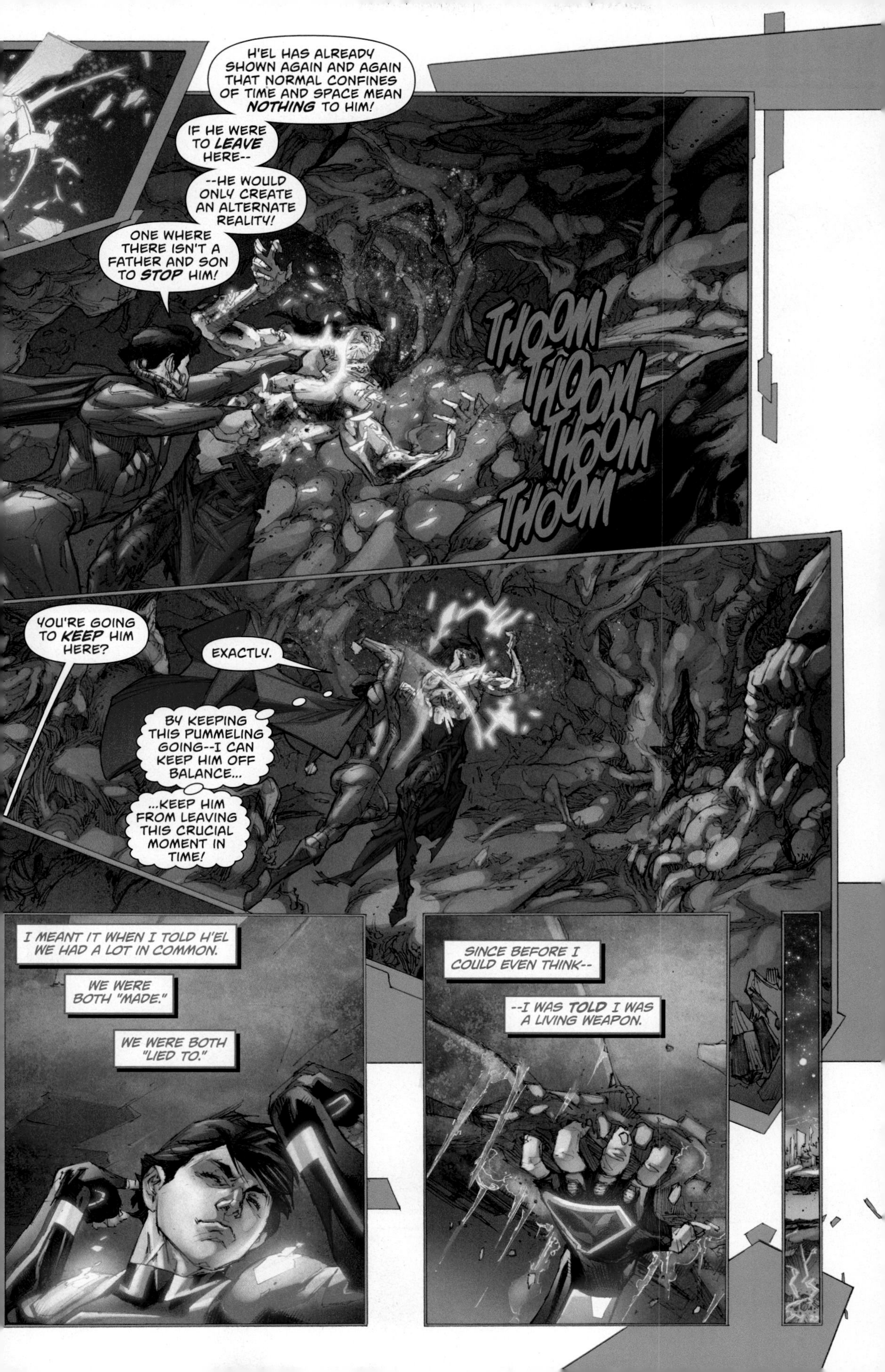
H'EL HAS ALREADY SHOWN AGAIN AND AGAIN THAT NORMAL CONFINES OF TIME AND SPACE MEAN NOTHING TO HIM!
IF HE WERE TO LEAVE HERE--
--HE WOULD ONLY CREATE AN ALTERNATE REALITY!
ONE WHERE THERE ISN'T A FATHER AND SON TO STOP HIM!
THOOM THOOM THOOM THOOM
YOU'RE GOING TO KEEP HIM HERE?
EXACTLY.
BY KEEPING THIS PUMMELING GOING--I CAN KEEP HIM OFF BALANCE...
...KEEP HIM FROM LEAVING THIS CRUCIAL MOMENT IN TIME!
I MEANT IT WHEN I TOLD H'EL WE HAD A LOT IN COMMON.
WE WERE BOTH "MADE."
WE WERE BOTH "LIED TO."
SINCE BEFORE I COULD EVEN THINK--
--I WAS TOLD I WAS A LIVING WEAPON.

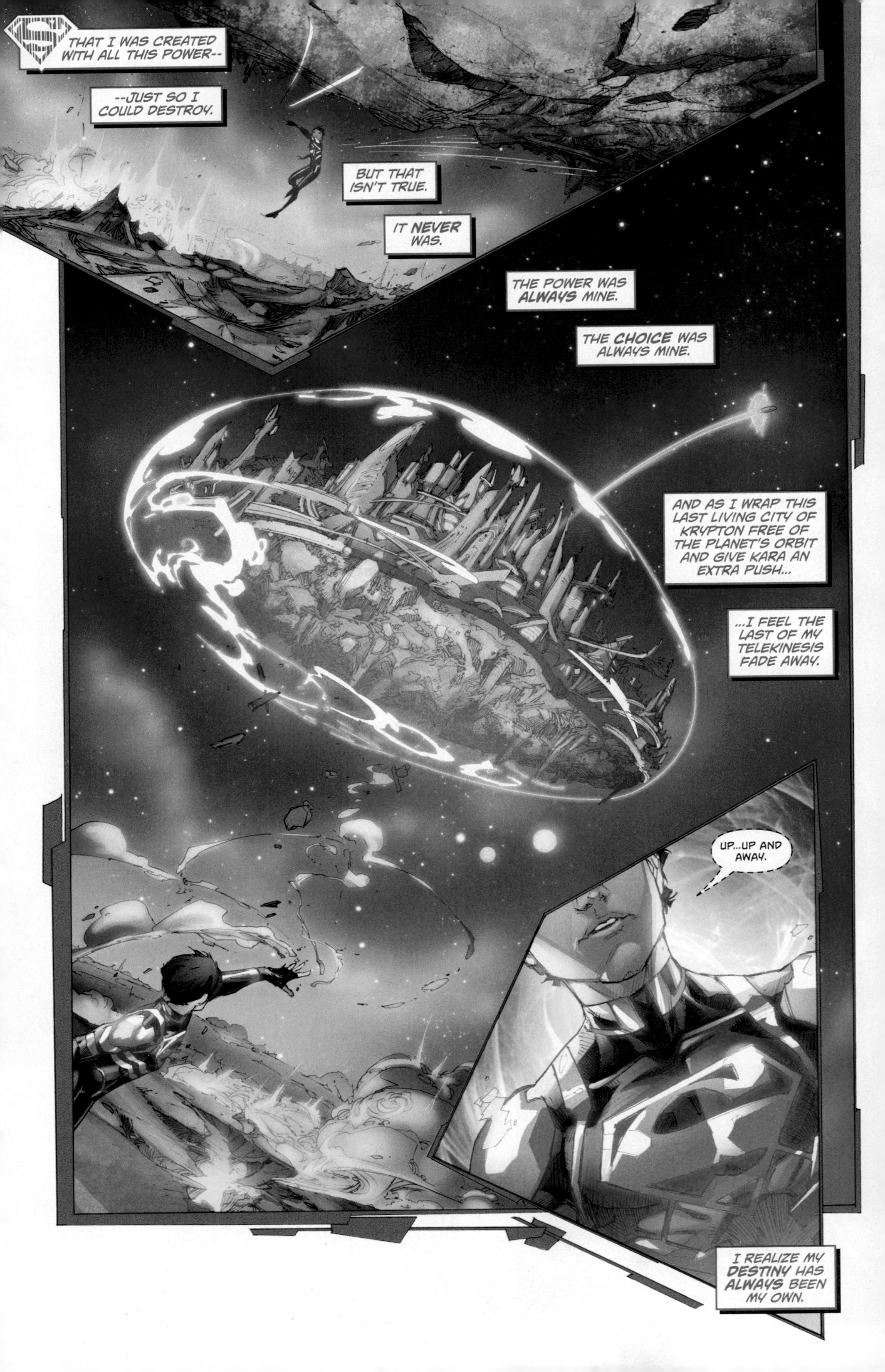

THAT I WAS CREATED WITH ALL THIS POWER--
--JUST SO I COULD DESTROY.
BUT THAT ISN'T TRUE.
IT NEVER WAS.
THE POWER WAS ALWAYS MINE.
THE CHOICE WAS ALWAYS MINE.
AND AS I WRAP THIS LAST LIVING CITY OF KRYPTON FREE OF THE PLANET'S ORBIT AND GIVE KARA AN EXTRA PUSH...
...I FEEL THE LAST OF MY TELEKINESIS FADE AWAY.
UP...UP AND AWAY.
I REALIZE MY DESTINY HAS ALWAYS BEEN MY OWN.

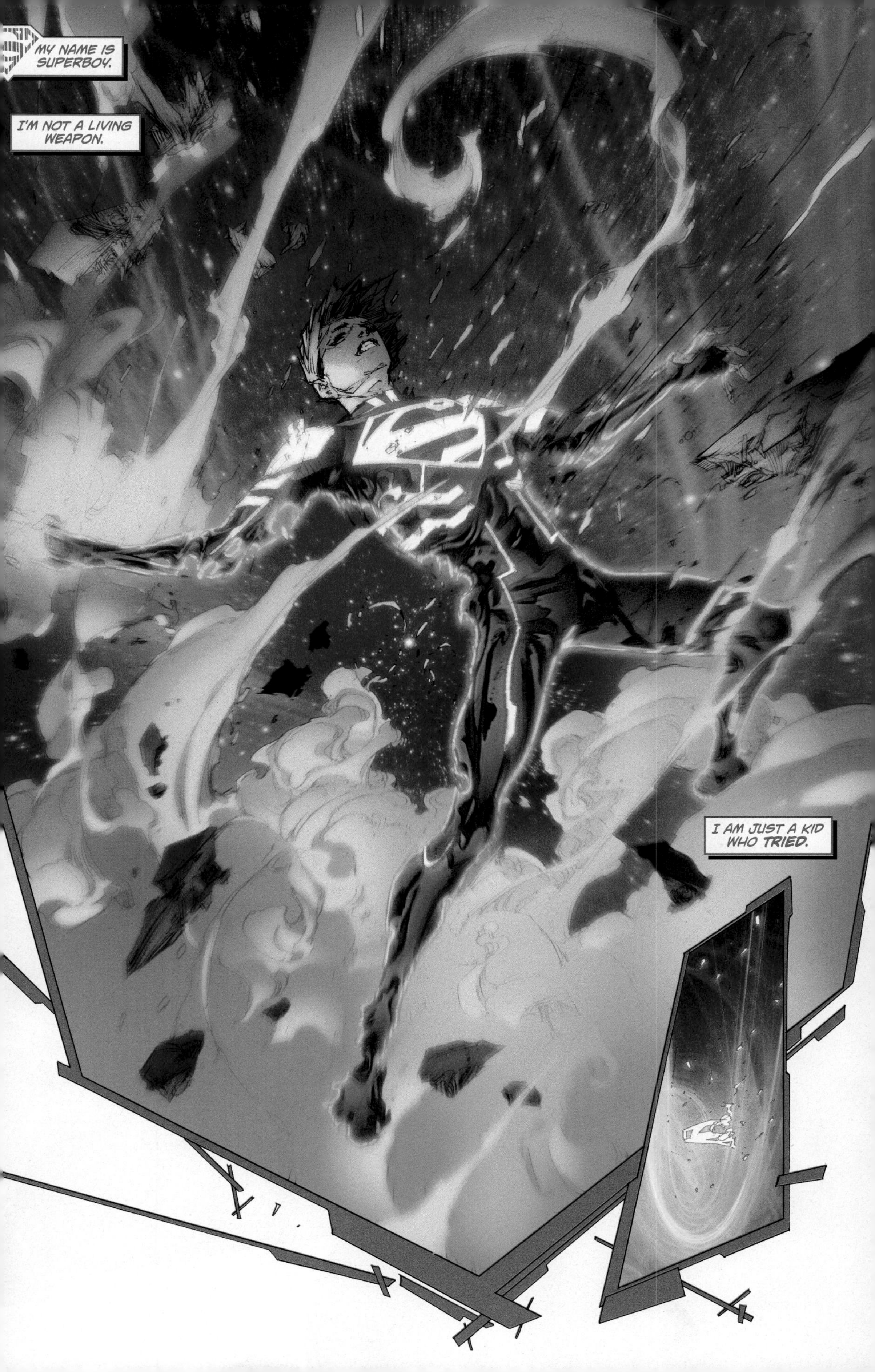

MY NAME IS SUPERBOY.
I'M NOT A LIVING WEAPON.
I AM JUST A KID WHO **TRIED.**

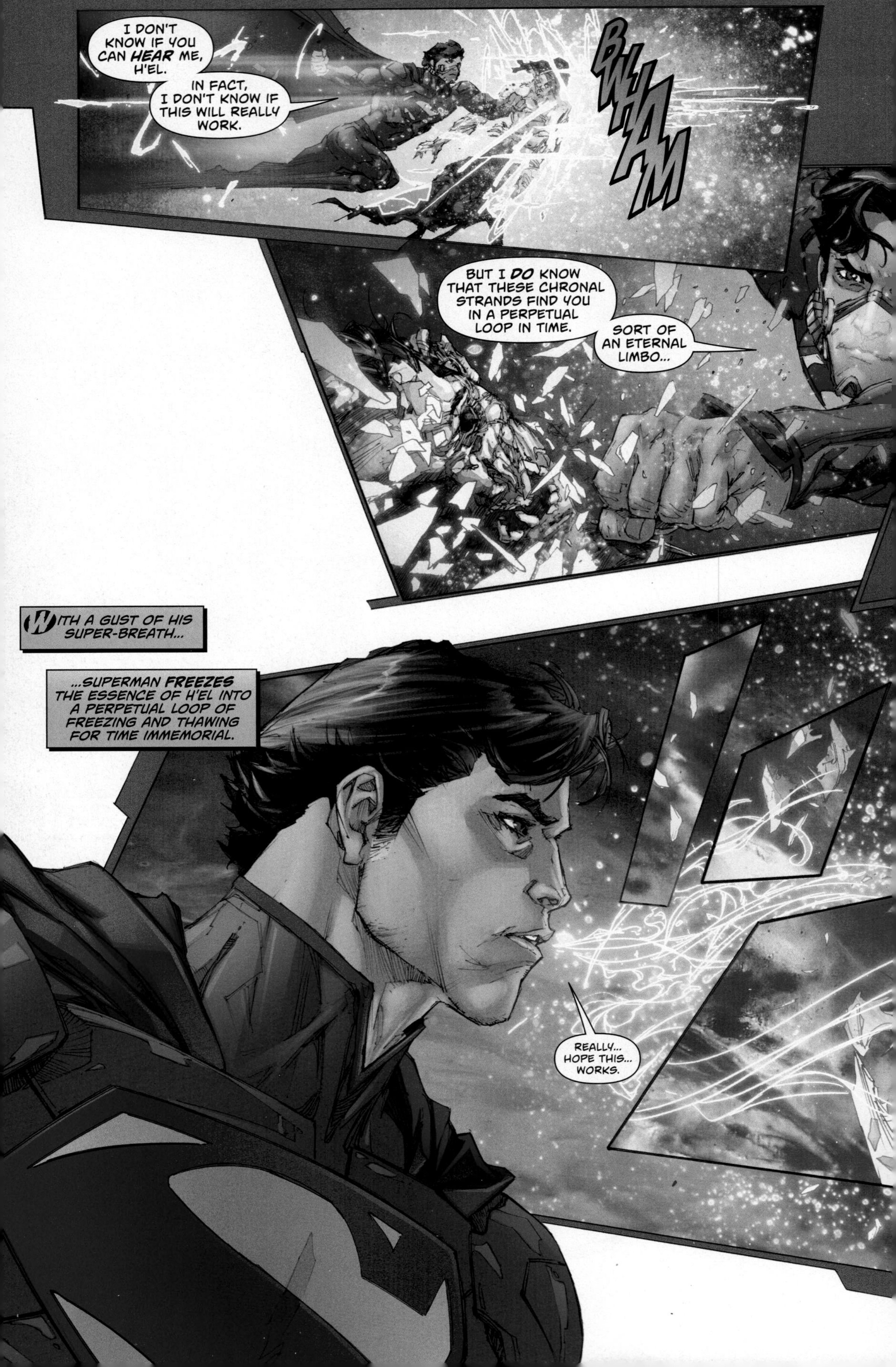
I DON'T KNOW IF YOU CAN HEAR ME, H'EL.
IN FACT, I DON'T KNOW IF THIS WILL REALLY WORK.
BWHAM
BUT I DO KNOW THAT THESE CHRONAL STRANDS FIND YOU IN A PERPETUAL LOOP IN TIME.
SORT OF AN ETERNAL LIMBO...
WITH A GUST OF HIS SUPER-BREATH...
...SUPERMAN FREEZES THE ESSENCE OF H'EL INTO A PERPETUAL LOOP OF FREEZING AND THAWING FOR TIME IMMEMORIAL.
REALLY... HOPE THIS... WORKS.

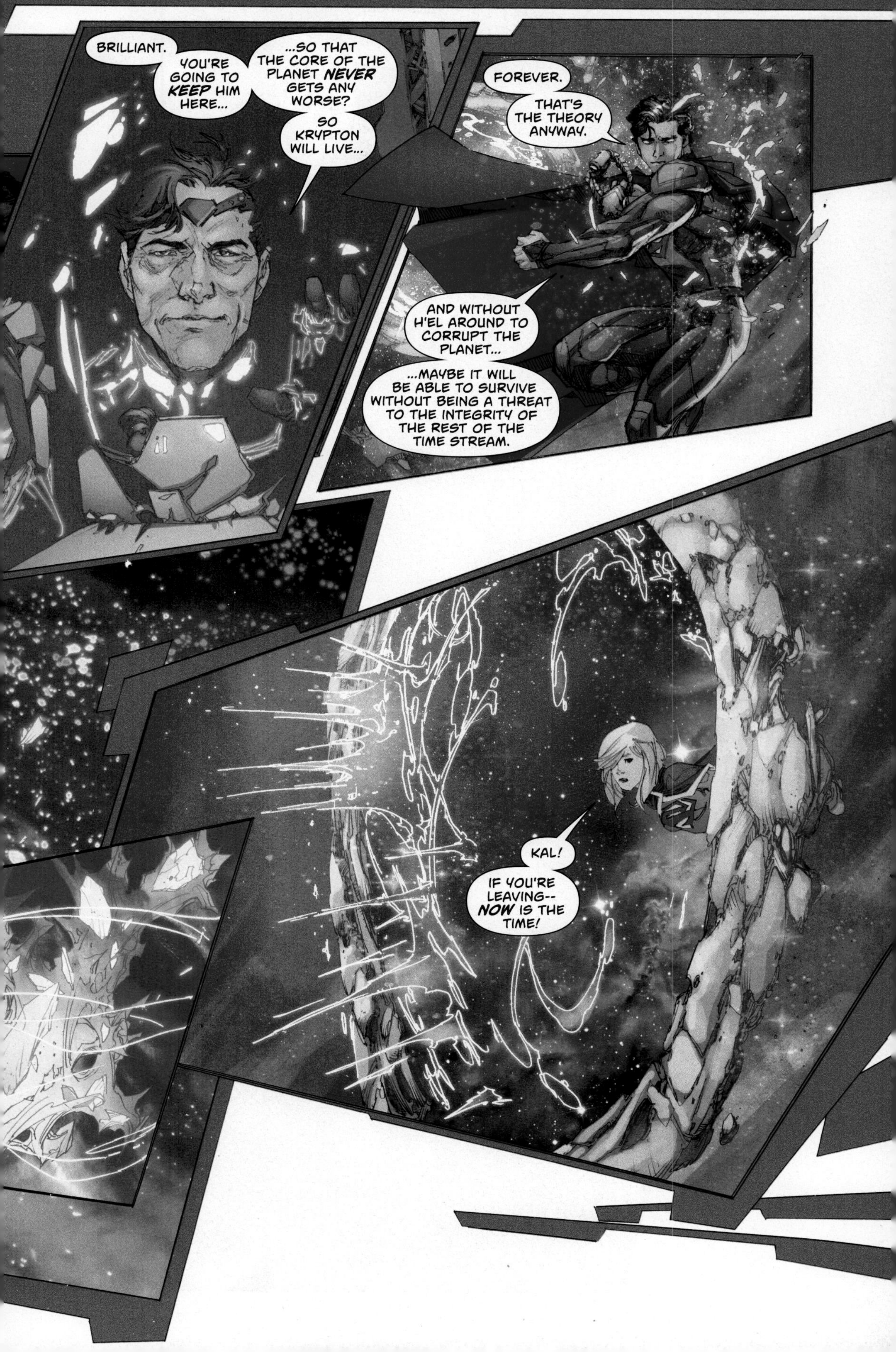
BRILLIANT.
YOU'RE GOING TO KEEP HIM HERE...
...SO THAT THE CORE OF THE PLANET NEVER GETS ANY WORSE?
SO KRYPTON WILL LIVE...
FOREVER.
THAT'S THE THEORY ANYWAY.
AND WITHOUT H'EL AROUND TO CORRUPT THE PLANET...
...MAYBE IT WILL BE ABLE TO SURVIVE WITHOUT BEING A THREAT TO THE INTEGRITY OF THE REST OF THE TIME STREAM.
KAL!
IF YOU'RE LEAVING-- NOW IS THE TIME!

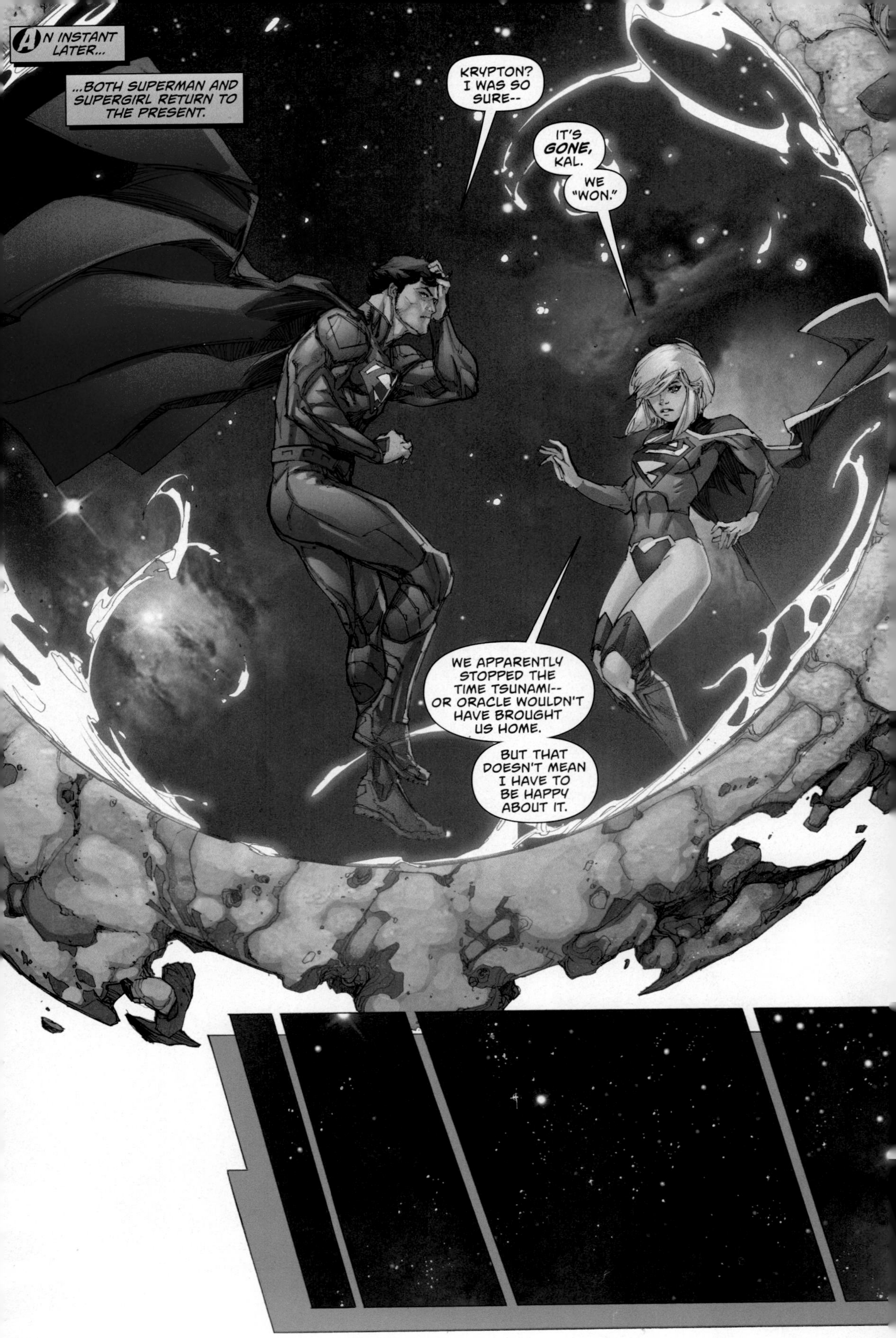
AN INSTANT LATER...
...BOTH SUPERMAN AND SUPERGIRL RETURN TO THE PRESENT.
KRYPTON? I WAS SO SURE--
IT'S GONE, KAL.
WE "WON."
WE APPARENTLY STOPPED THE TIME TSUNAMI-- OR ORACLE WOULDN'T HAVE BROUGHT US HOME.
BUT THAT DOESN'T MEAN I HAVE TO BE HAPPY ABOUT IT.

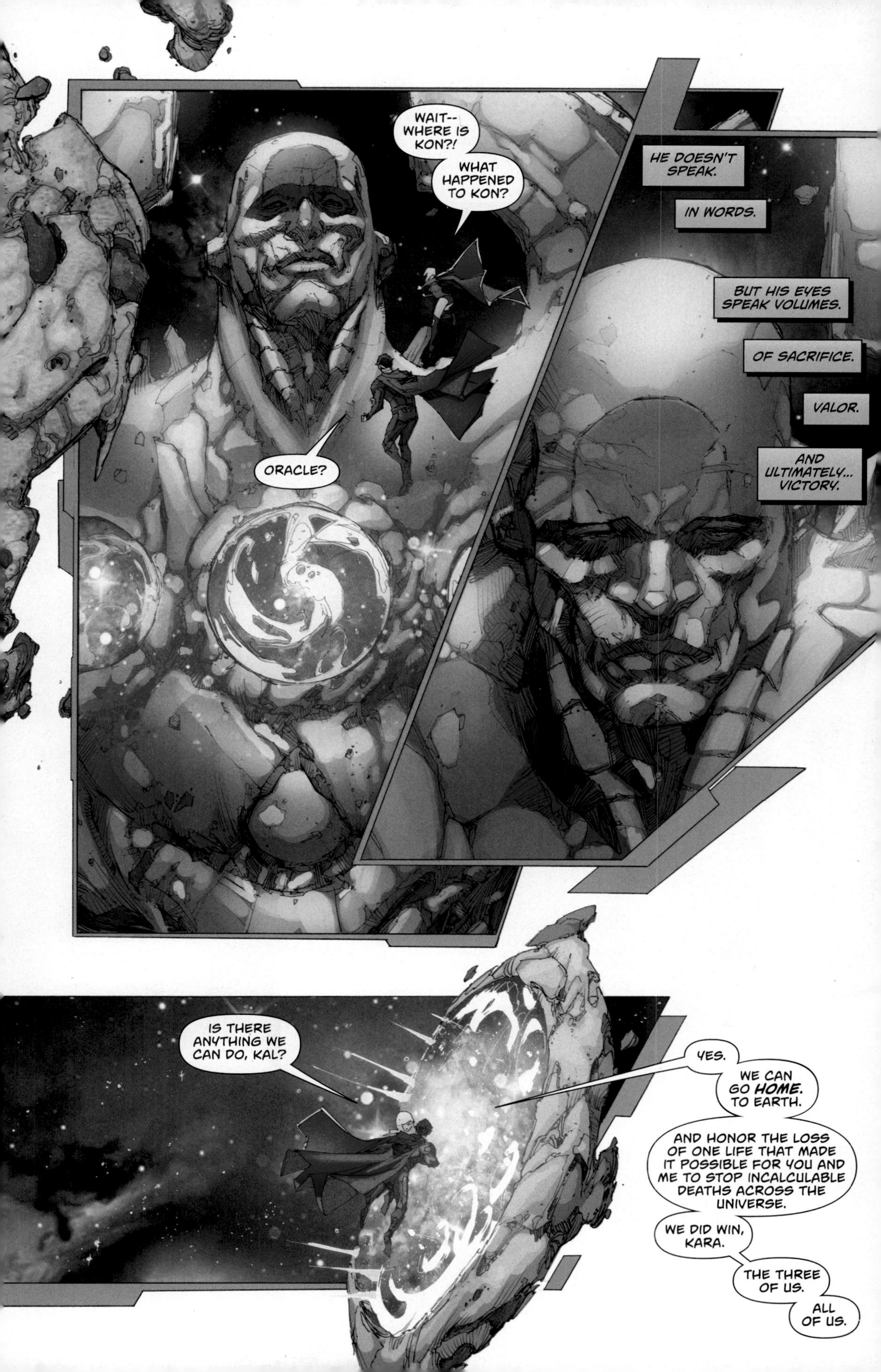
WAIT-- WHERE IS KON?!
WHAT HAPPENED TO KON?
ORACLE?
HE DOESN'T SPEAK.
IN WORDS.
BUT HIS EYES SPEAK VOLUMES.
OF SACRIFICE.
VALOR.
AND ULTIMATELY... VICTORY.
IS THERE ANYTHING WE CAN DO, KAL?
YES.
WE CAN GO HOME. TO EARTH.
AND HONOR THE LOSS OF ONE LIFE THAT MADE IT POSSIBLE FOR YOU AND ME TO STOP INCALCULABLE DEATHS ACROSS THE UNIVERSE.
WE DID WIN, KARA.
THE THREE OF US.
ALL OF US.

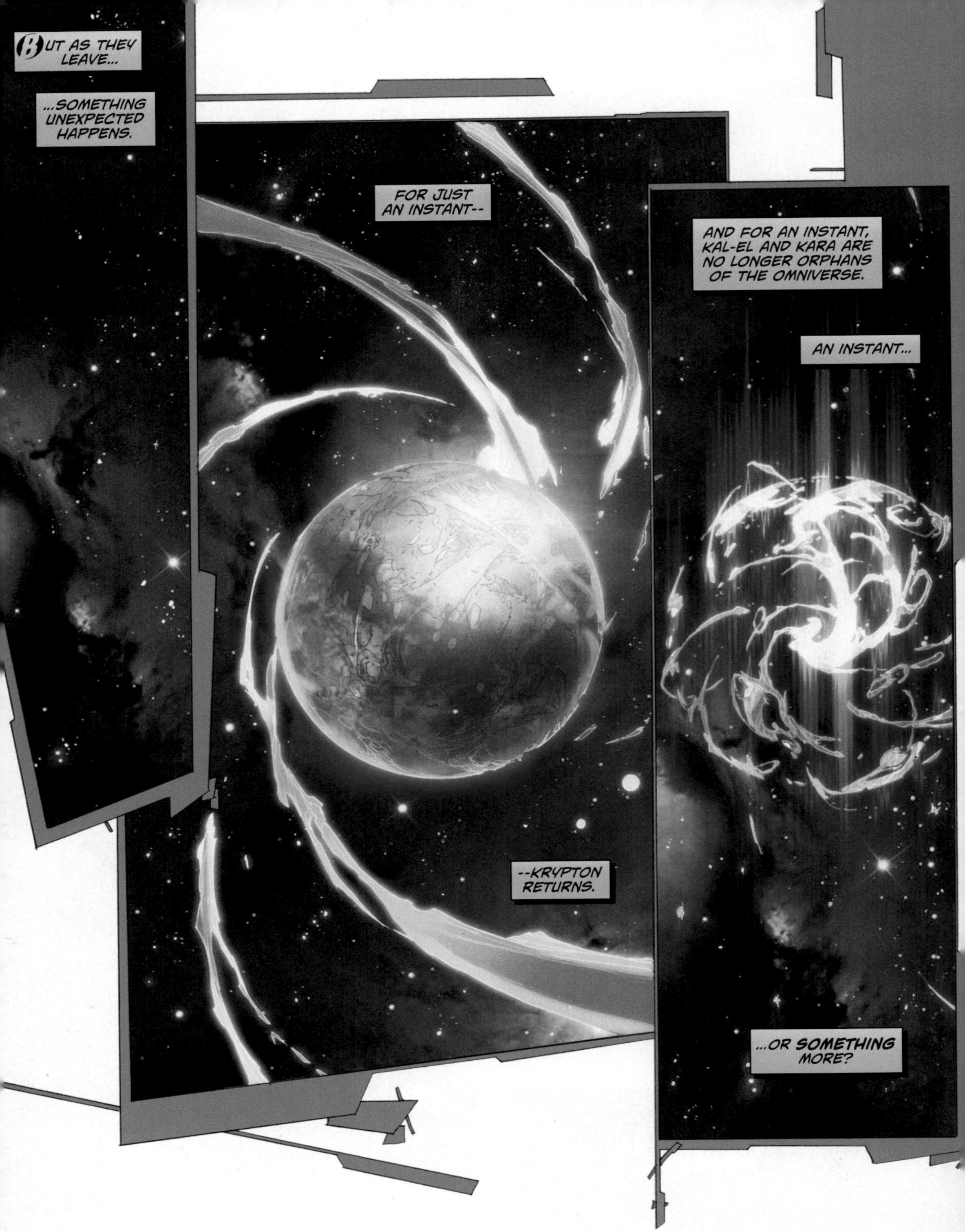
BUT AS THEY LEAVE...
...SOMETHING UNEXPECTED HAPPENS.
FOR JUST AN INSTANT--
--KRYPTON RETURNS.
AND FOR AN INSTANT, KAL-EL AND KARA ARE NO LONGER ORPHANS OF THE OMNIVERSE.
AN INSTANT...
...OR SOMETHING MORE?

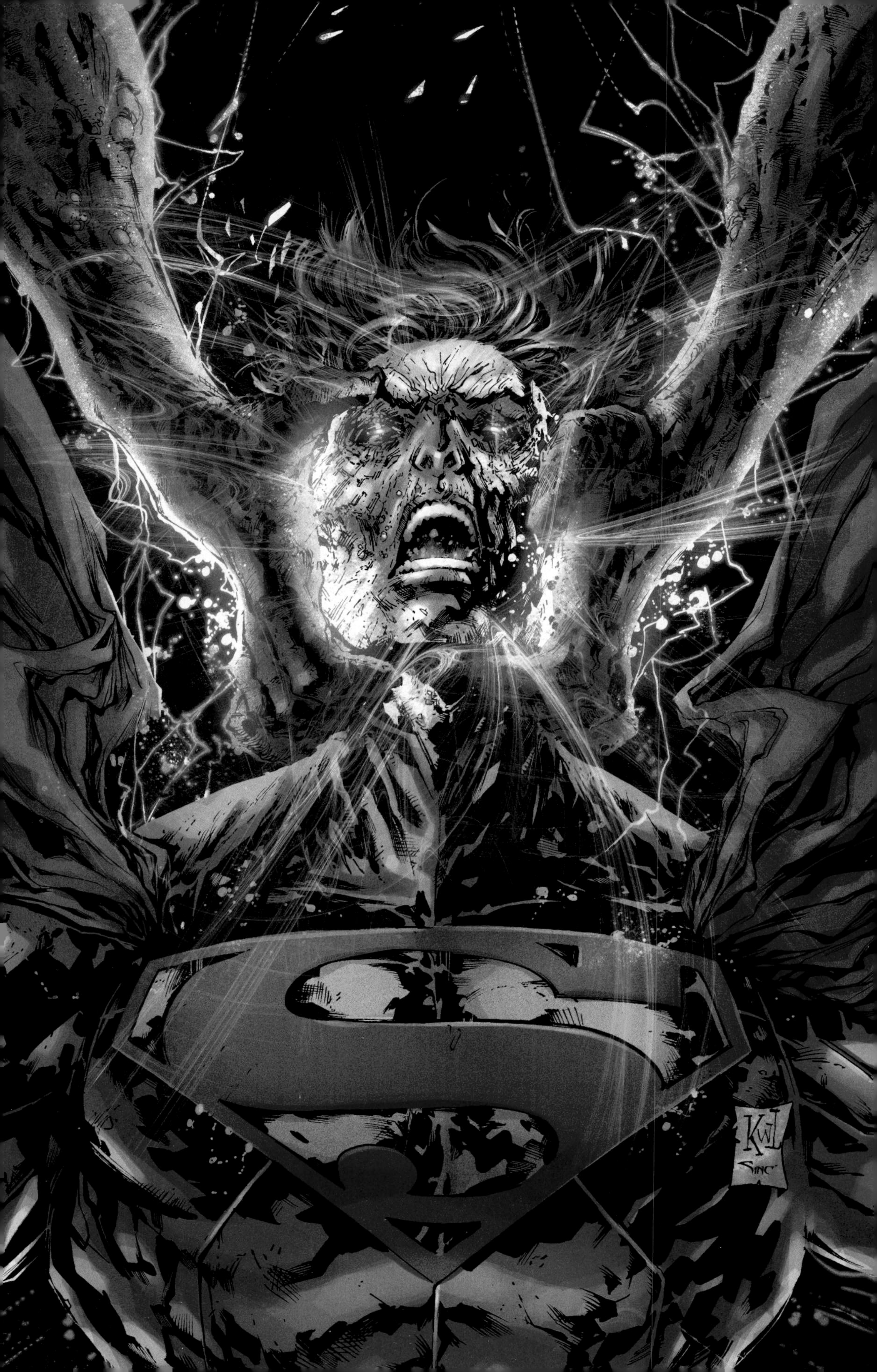

BRAIN DRAIN

SCOTT LOBDELL writer KEN LASHLEY artist PETE PANTAZIS colorist cover art by KEN LASHLEY and ALEX SINCLAIR

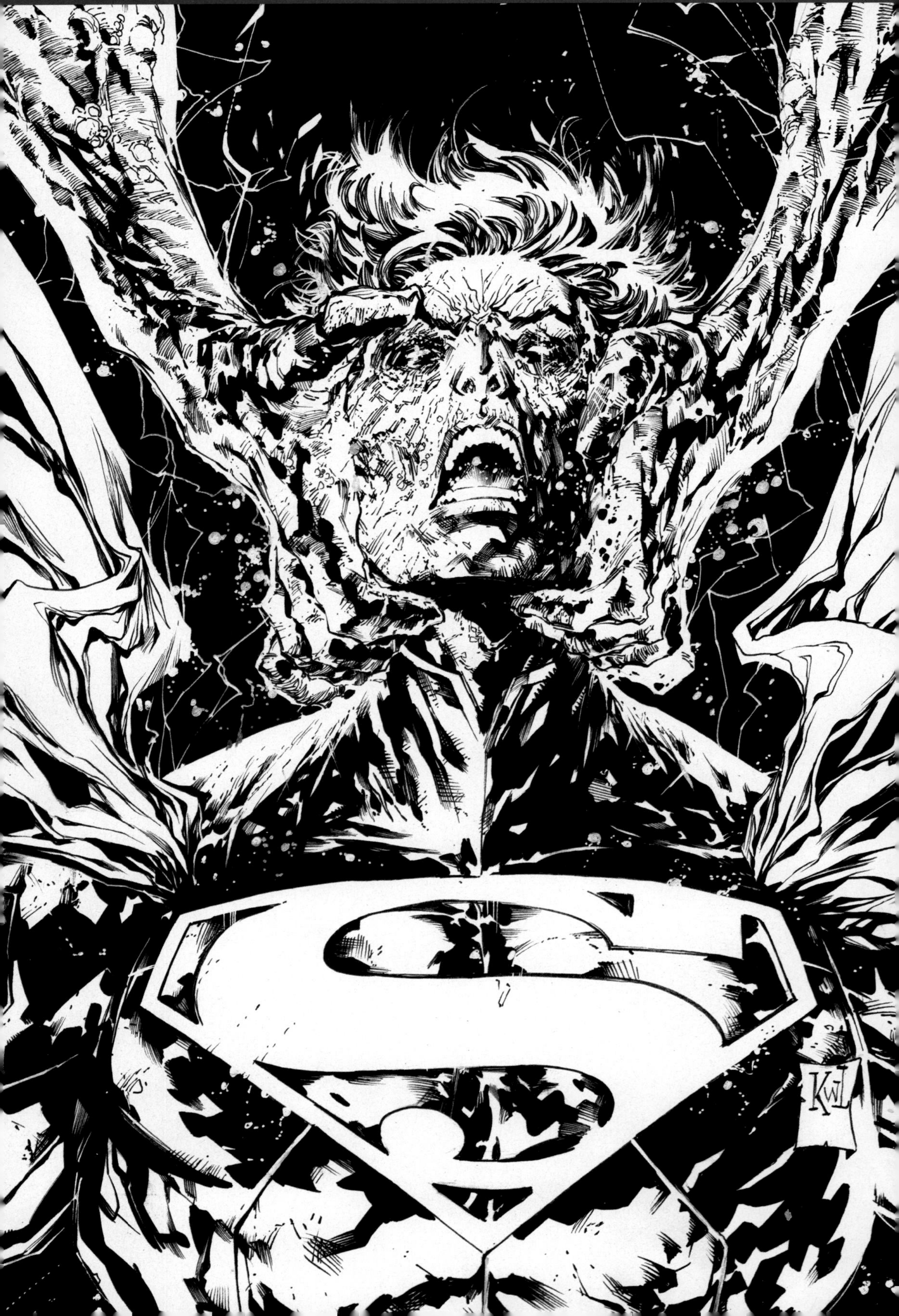

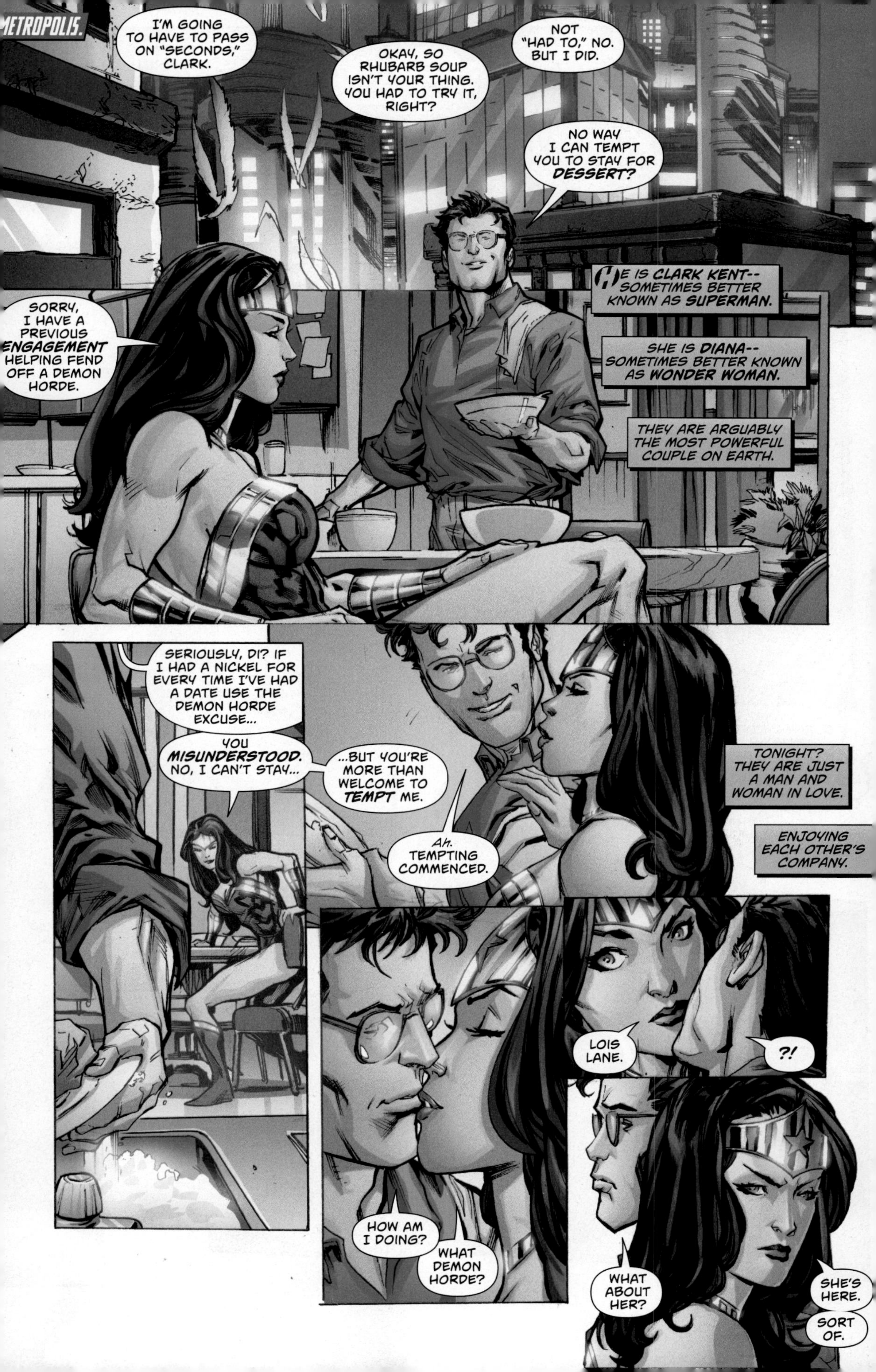
METROPOLIS.
I'M GOING TO HAVE TO PASS ON "SECONDS," CLARK.
OKAY, SO RHUBARB SOUP ISN'T YOUR THING. YOU HAD TO TRY IT, RIGHT?
NOT "HAD TO," NO. BUT I DID.
NO WAY I CAN TEMPT YOU TO STAY FOR DESSERT?
HE IS CLARK KENT-- SOMETIMES BETTER KNOWN AS SUPERMAN.
SHE IS DIANA-- SOMETIMES BETTER KNOWN AS WONDER WOMAN.
THEY ARE ARGUABLY THE MOST POWERFUL COUPLE ON EARTH.
SORRY, I HAVE A PREVIOUS ENGAGEMENT HELPING FEND OFF A DEMON HORDE.
SERIOUSLY, DI? IF I HAD A NICKEL FOR EVERY TIME I'VE HAD A DATE USE THE DEMON HORDE EXCUSE...
YOU MISUNDERSTOOD. NO, I CAN'T STAY...
...BUT YOU'RE MORE THAN WELCOME TO TEMPT ME.
Ah. TEMPTING COMMENCED.
TONIGHT? THEY ARE JUST A MAN AND WOMAN IN LOVE.
ENJOYING EACH OTHER'S COMPANY.
HOW AM I DOING?
WHAT DEMON HORDE?
LOIS LANE.
?!
WHAT ABOUT HER?
SHE'S HERE.
SORT OF.

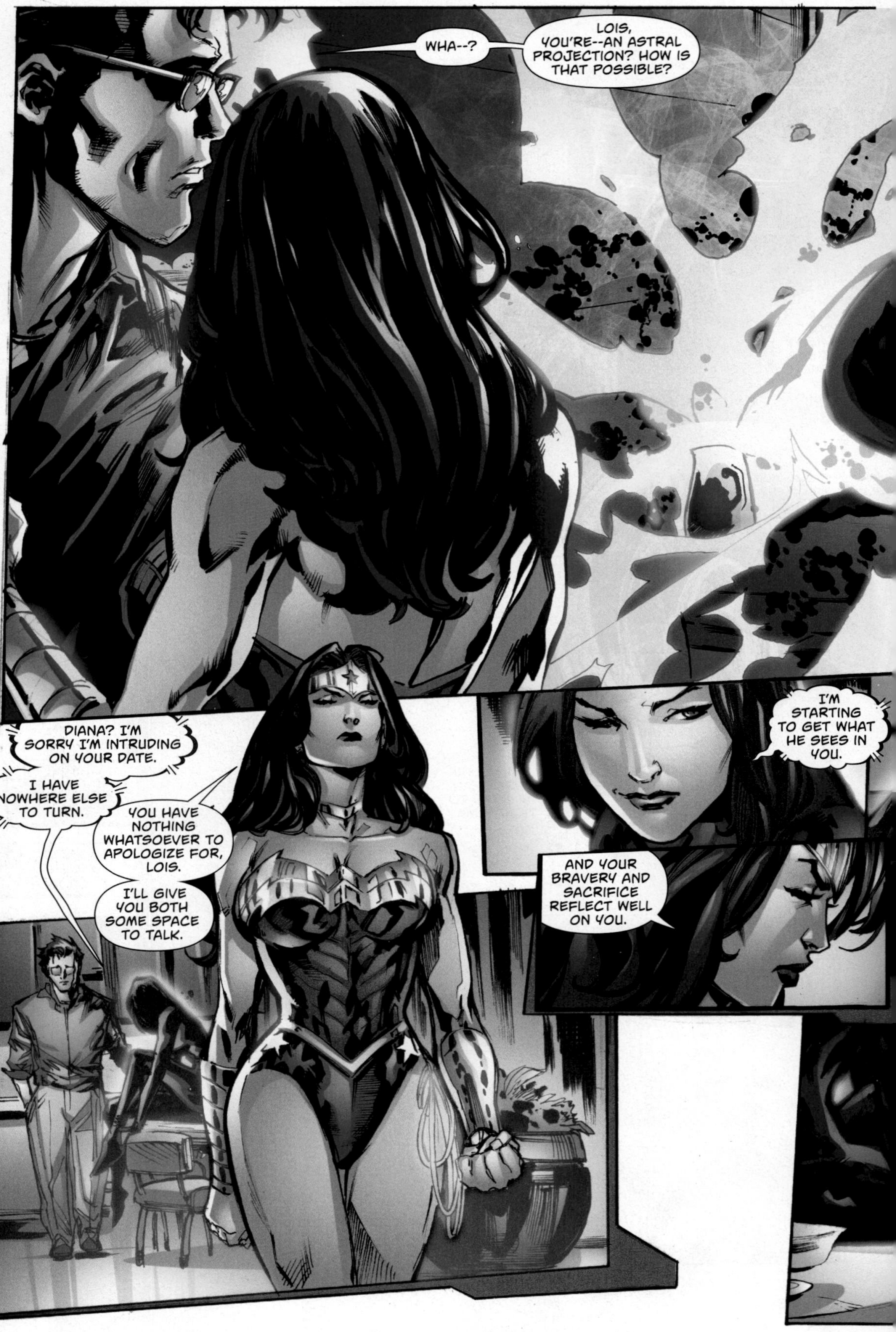
WHA--?
LOIS, YOU'RE--AN ASTRAL PROJECTION? HOW IS THAT POSSIBLE?
DIANA? I'M SORRY I'M INTRUDING ON YOUR DATE.
I HAVE NOWHERE ELSE TO TURN.
YOU HAVE NOTHING WHATSOEVER TO APOLOGIZE FOR, LOIS.
I'LL GIVE YOU BOTH SOME SPACE TO TALK.
I'M STARTING TO GET WHAT HE SEES IN YOU.
AND YOUR BRAVERY AND SACRIFICE REFLECT WELL ON YOU.

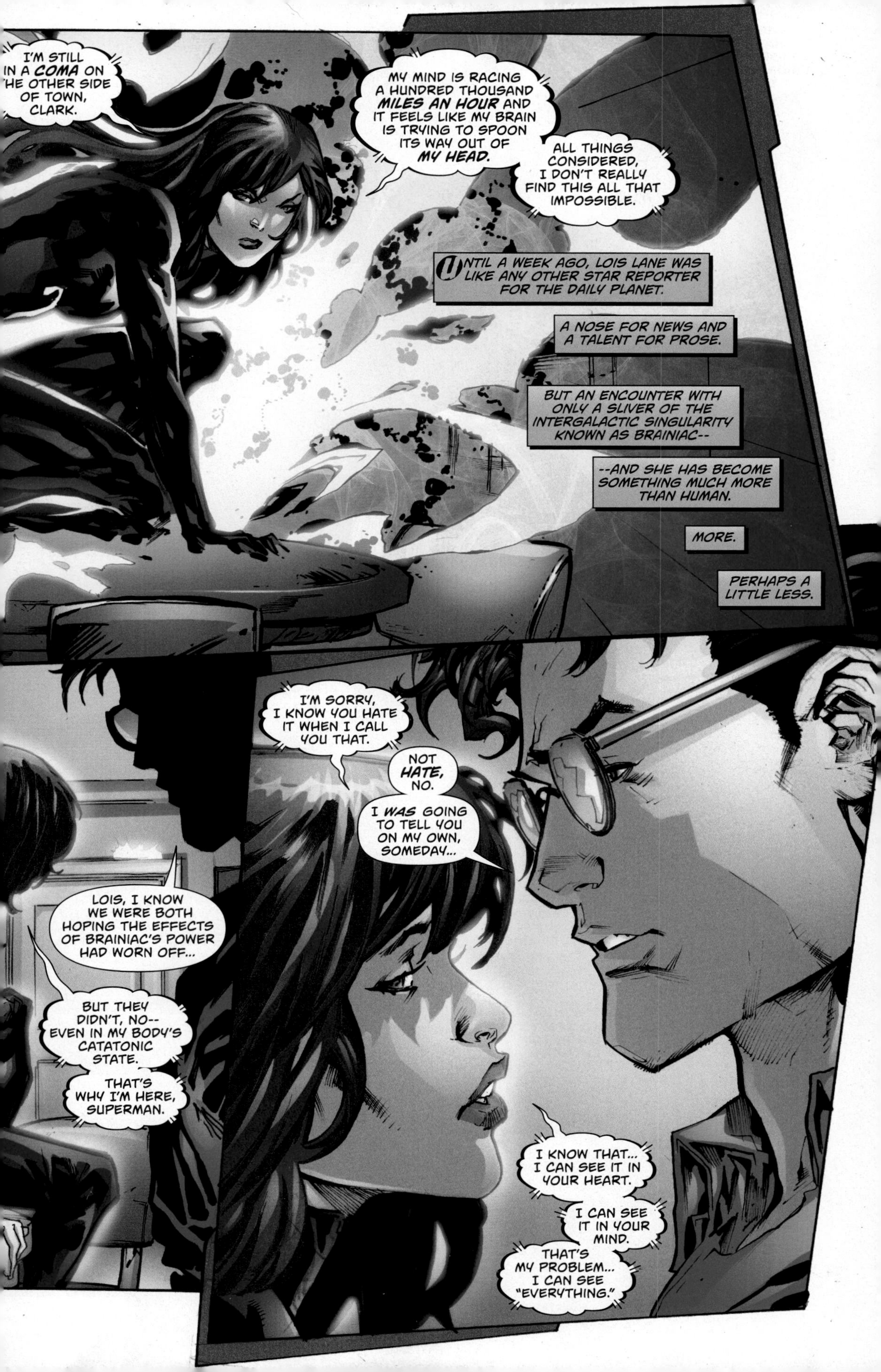

I'M STILL IN A COMA ON THE OTHER SIDE OF TOWN, CLARK.
MY MIND IS RACING A HUNDRED THOUSAND MILES AN HOUR AND IT FEELS LIKE MY BRAIN IS TRYING TO SPOON ITS WAY OUT OF MY HEAD.
ALL THINGS CONSIDERED, I DON'T REALLY FIND THIS ALL THAT IMPOSSIBLE.
UNTIL A WEEK AGO, LOIS LANE WAS LIKE ANY OTHER STAR REPORTER FOR THE DAILY PLANET.
A NOSE FOR NEWS AND A TALENT FOR PROSE.
BUT AN ENCOUNTER WITH ONLY A SLIVER OF THE INTERGALACTIC SINGULARITY KNOWN AS BRAINIAC--
--AND SHE HAS BECOME SOMETHING MUCH MORE THAN HUMAN.
MORE.
PERHAPS A LITTLE LESS.
LOIS, I KNOW WE WERE BOTH HOPING THE EFFECTS OF BRAINIAC'S POWER HAD WORN OFF...
BUT THEY DIDN'T, NO-- EVEN IN MY BODY'S CATATONIC STATE.
THAT'S WHY I'M HERE, SUPERMAN.
I'M SORRY, I KNOW YOU HATE IT WHEN I CALL YOU THAT.
NOT HATE, NO.
I WAS GOING TO TELL YOU ON MY OWN, SOMEDAY...
I KNOW THAT... I CAN SEE IT IN YOUR HEART.
I CAN SEE IT IN YOUR MIND.
THAT'S MY PROBLEM... I CAN SEE "EVERYTHING."

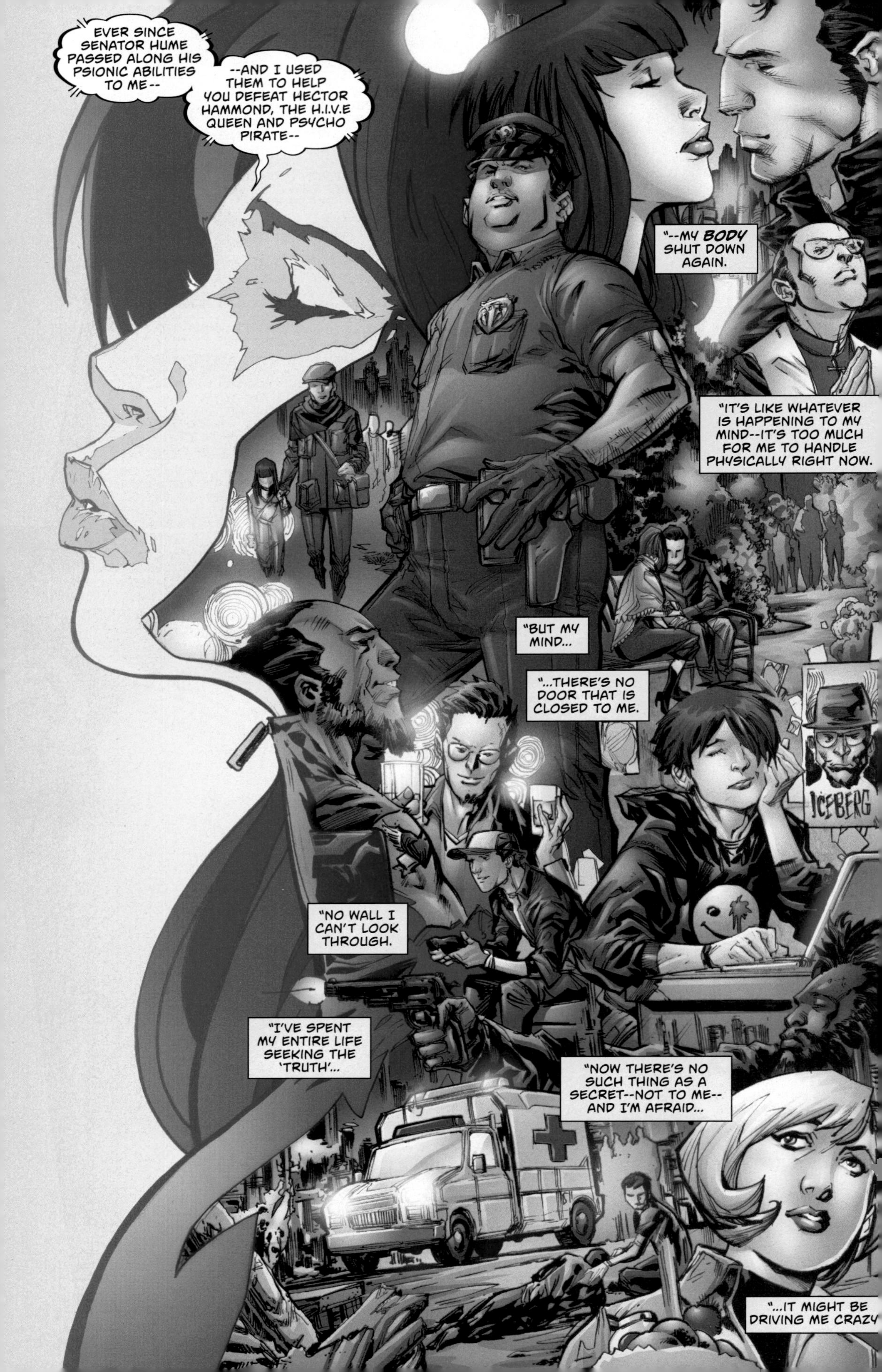
EVER SINCE SENATOR HUME PASSED ALONG HIS PSIONIC ABILITIES TO ME--
--AND I USED THEM TO HELP YOU DEFEAT HECTOR HAMMOND, THE H.I.V.E QUEEN AND PSYCHO PIRATE--
"--MY BODY SHUT DOWN AGAIN.
"IT'S LIKE WHATEVER IS HAPPENING TO MY MIND--IT'S TOO MUCH FOR ME TO HANDLE PHYSICALLY RIGHT NOW.
"BUT MY MIND...
"...THERE'S NO DOOR THAT IS CLOSED TO ME.
ICEBERG
"NO WALL I CAN'T LOOK THROUGH.
"I'VE SPENT MY ENTIRE LIFE SEEKING THE 'TRUTH'...
"NOW THERE'S NO SUCH THING AS A SECRET--NOT TO ME--AND I'M AFRAID...
"...IT MIGHT BE DRIVING ME CRAZY

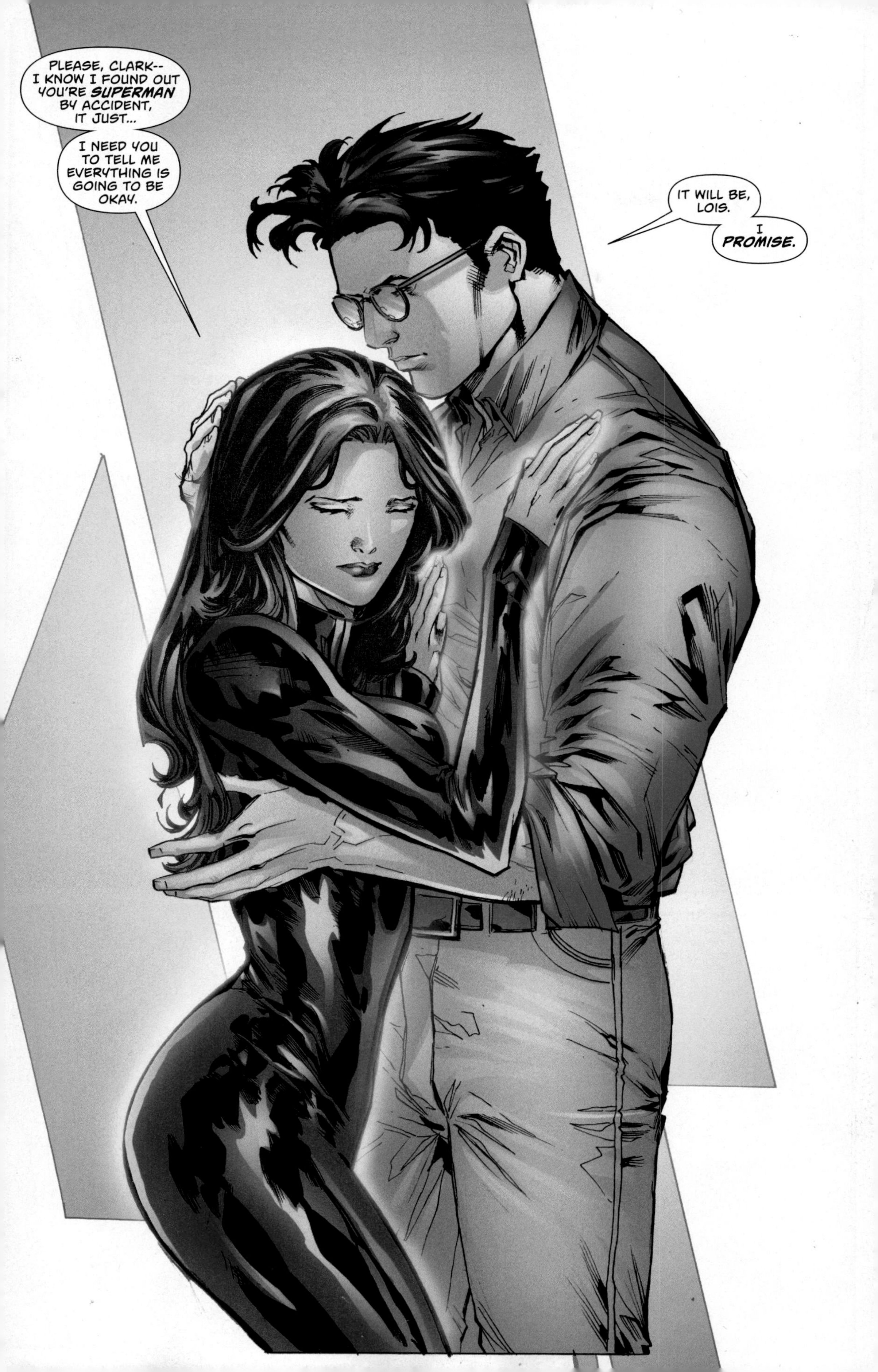
PLEASE, CLARK-- I KNOW I FOUND OUT YOU'RE *SUPERMAN* BY ACCIDENT, IT JUST...
I NEED YOU TO TELL ME EVERYTHING IS GOING TO BE OKAY.
IT WILL BE, LOIS.
I *PROMISE.*

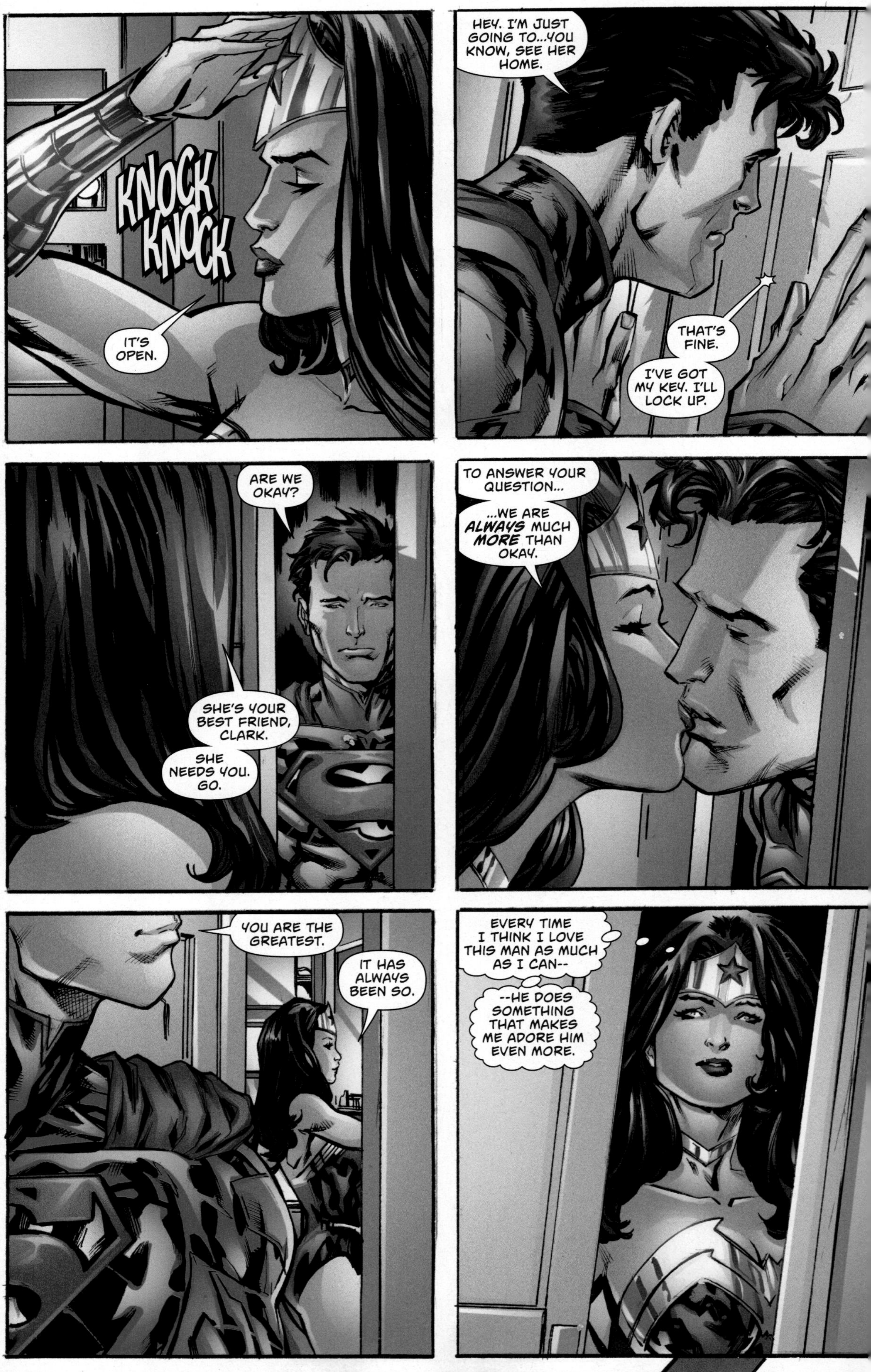
KNOCK KNOCK
IT'S OPEN.
HEY. I'M JUST GOING TO...YOU KNOW, SEE HER HOME.
THAT'S FINE.
I'VE GOT MY KEY. I'LL LOCK UP.
ARE WE OKAY?
SHE'S YOUR BEST FRIEND, CLARK.
SHE NEEDS YOU. GO.
TO ANSWER YOUR QUESTION...
...WE ARE ALWAYS MUCH MORE THAN OKAY.
YOU ARE THE GREATEST.
IT HAS ALWAYS BEEN SO.
EVERY TIME I THINK I LOVE THIS MAN AS MUCH AS I CAN--
--HE DOES SOMETHING THAT MAKES ME ADORE HIM EVEN MORE.

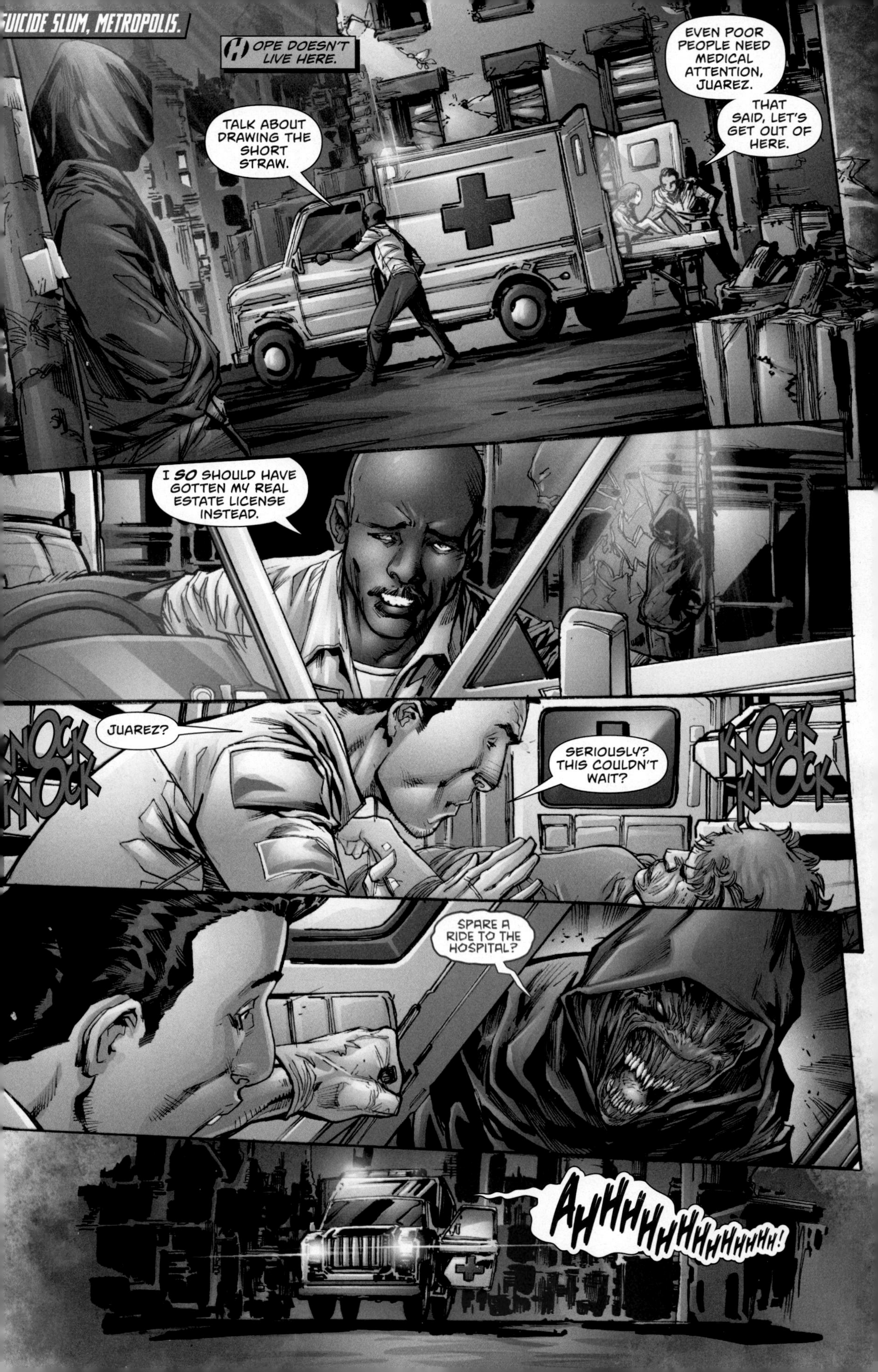
SUICIDE SLUM, METROPOLIS.
HOPE DOESN'T LIVE HERE.
TALK ABOUT DRAWING THE SHORT STRAW.
EVEN POOR PEOPLE NEED MEDICAL ATTENTION, JUAREZ.
THAT SAID, LET'S GET OUT OF HERE.
I SO SHOULD HAVE GOTTEN MY REAL ESTATE LICENSE INSTEAD.
KNOCK KNOCK
JUAREZ?
SERIOUSLY? THIS COULDN'T WAIT?
KNOCK KNOCK
SPARE A RIDE TO THE HOSPITAL?
AHHHHHHHHHHHHHH!

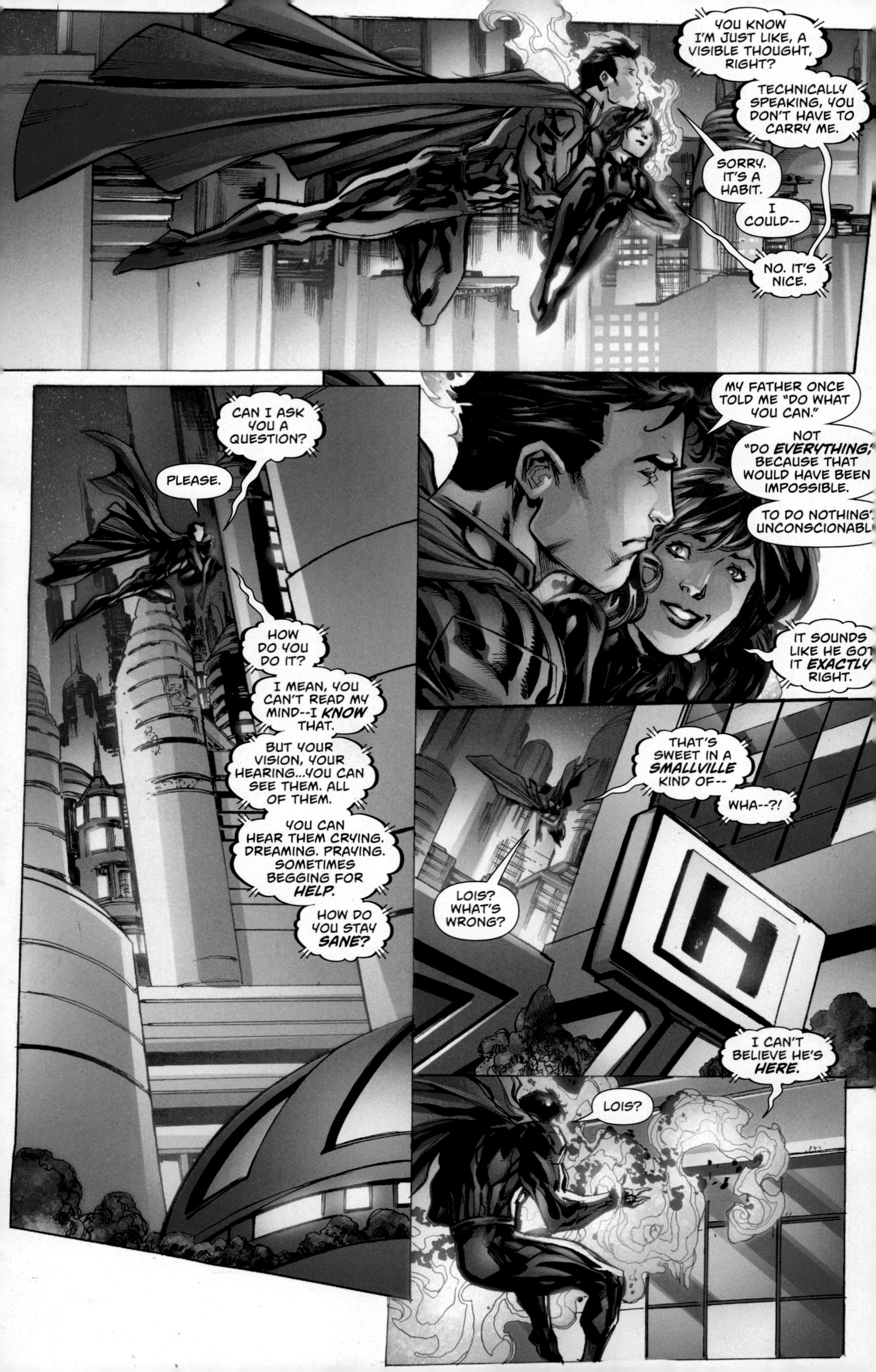
YOU KNOW I'M JUST LIKE, A VISIBLE THOUGHT, RIGHT?
TECHNICALLY SPEAKING, YOU DON'T HAVE TO CARRY ME.
SORRY. IT'S A HABIT.
I COULD--
NO. IT'S NICE.
CAN I ASK YOU A QUESTION?
PLEASE.
HOW DO YOU DO IT?
I MEAN, YOU CAN'T READ MY MIND--I KNOW THAT.
BUT YOUR VISION, YOUR HEARING...YOU CAN SEE THEM. ALL OF THEM.
YOU CAN HEAR THEM CRYING. DREAMING. PRAYING. SOMETIMES BEGGING FOR HELP.
HOW DO YOU STAY SANE?
MY FATHER ONCE TOLD ME "DO WHAT YOU CAN."
NOT "DO EVERYTHING," BECAUSE THAT WOULD HAVE BEEN IMPOSSIBLE.
TO DO NOTHING? UNCONSCIONABLE.
IT SOUNDS LIKE HE GOT IT EXACTLY RIGHT.
THAT'S SWEET IN A SMALLVILLE KIND OF--
WHA--?!
LOIS? WHAT'S WRONG?
H
I CAN'T BELIEVE HE'S HERE.
LOIS?

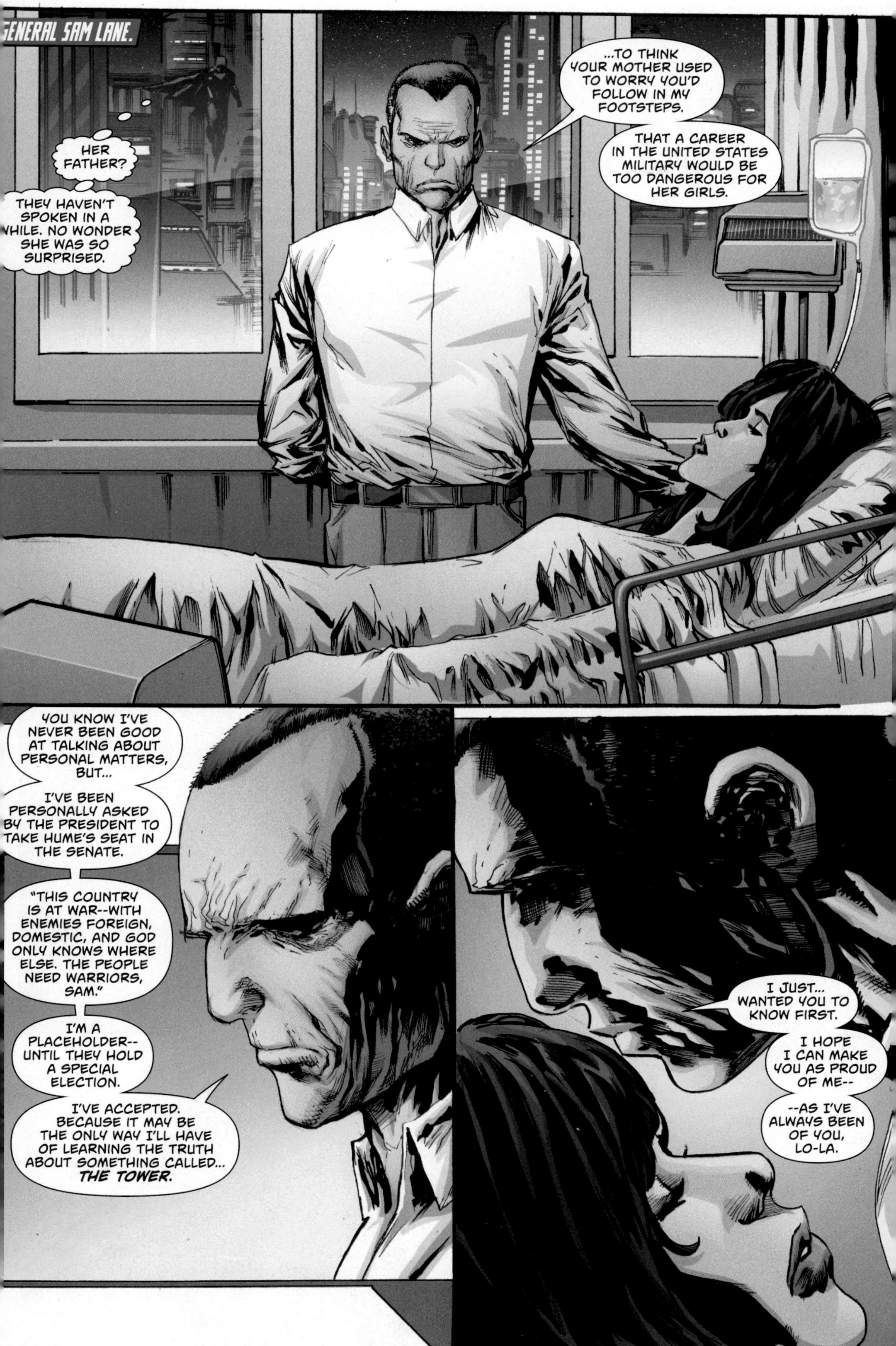
GENERAL SAM LANE.
HER FATHER?
THEY HAVEN'T SPOKEN IN A WHILE. NO WONDER SHE WAS SO SURPRISED.
...TO THINK YOUR MOTHER USED TO WORRY YOU'D FOLLOW IN MY FOOTSTEPS.
THAT A CAREER IN THE UNITED STATES MILITARY WOULD BE TOO DANGEROUS FOR HER GIRLS.
YOU KNOW I'VE NEVER BEEN GOOD AT TALKING ABOUT PERSONAL MATTERS, BUT...
I'VE BEEN PERSONALLY ASKED BY THE PRESIDENT TO TAKE HUME'S SEAT IN THE SENATE.
"THIS COUNTRY IS AT WAR--WITH ENEMIES FOREIGN, DOMESTIC, AND GOD ONLY KNOWS WHERE ELSE. THE PEOPLE NEED WARRIORS, SAM."
I'M A PLACEHOLDER--UNTIL THEY HOLD A SPECIAL ELECTION.
I'VE ACCEPTED. BECAUSE IT MAY BE THE ONLY WAY I'LL HAVE OF LEARNING THE TRUTH ABOUT SOMETHING CALLED... THE TOWER.
I JUST... WANTED YOU TO KNOW FIRST.
I HOPE I CAN MAKE YOU AS PROUD OF ME--
--AS I'VE ALWAYS BEEN OF YOU, LO-LA.

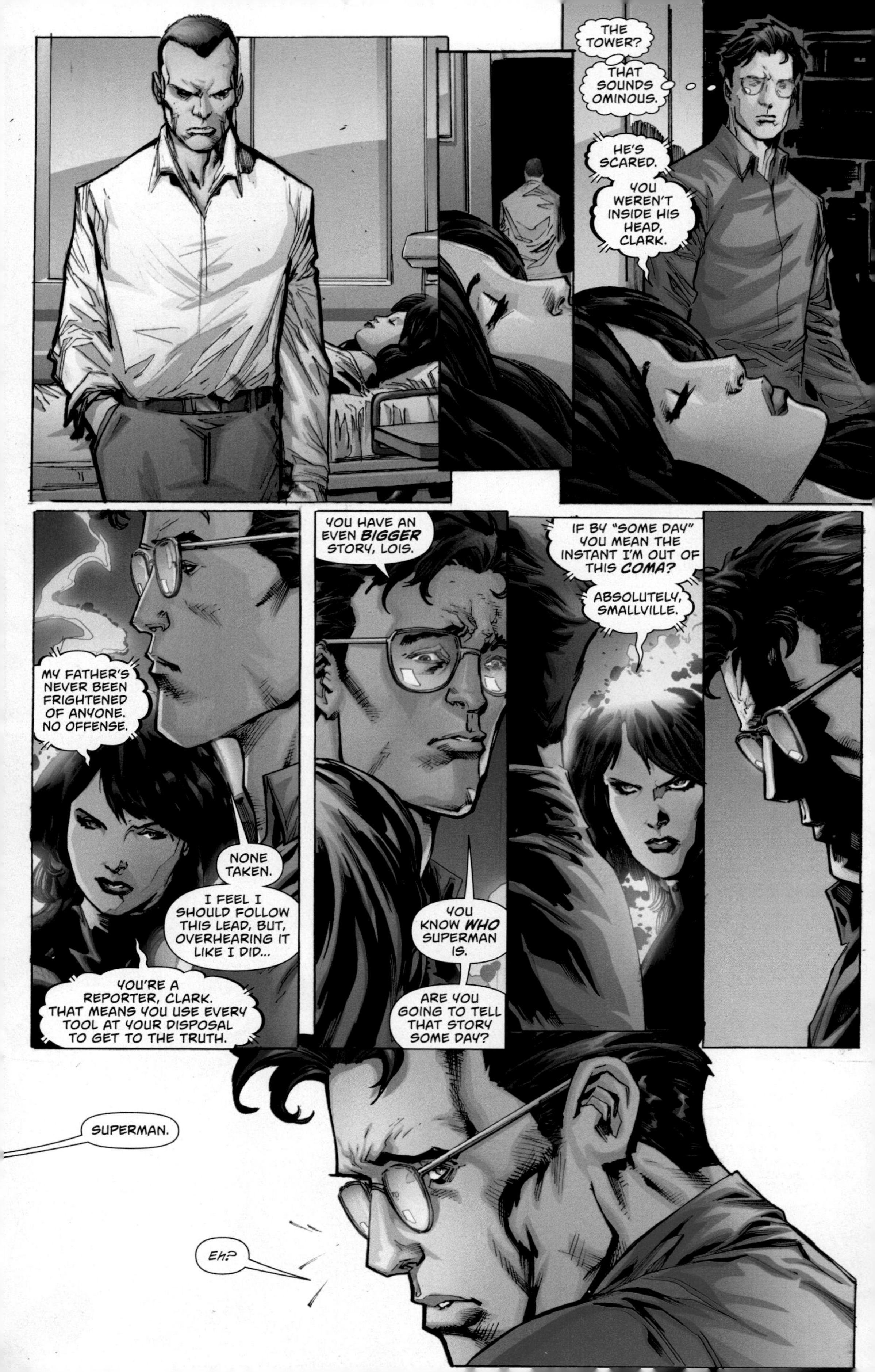
THE TOWER?
THAT SOUNDS OMINOUS.
HE'S SCARED.
YOU WEREN'T INSIDE HIS HEAD, CLARK.
MY FATHER'S NEVER BEEN FRIGHTENED OF ANYONE. NO OFFENSE.
NONE TAKEN.
I FEEL I SHOULD FOLLOW THIS LEAD, BUT, OVERHEARING IT LIKE I DID...
YOU'RE A REPORTER, CLARK. THAT MEANS YOU USE EVERY TOOL AT YOUR DISPOSAL TO GET TO THE TRUTH.
YOU HAVE AN EVEN BIGGER STORY, LOIS.
YOU KNOW WHO SUPERMAN IS.
ARE YOU GOING TO TELL THAT STORY SOME DAY?
IF BY "SOME DAY" YOU MEAN THE INSTANT I'M OUT OF THIS COMA?
ABSOLUTELY, SMALLVILLE.
SUPERMAN.
Eh?

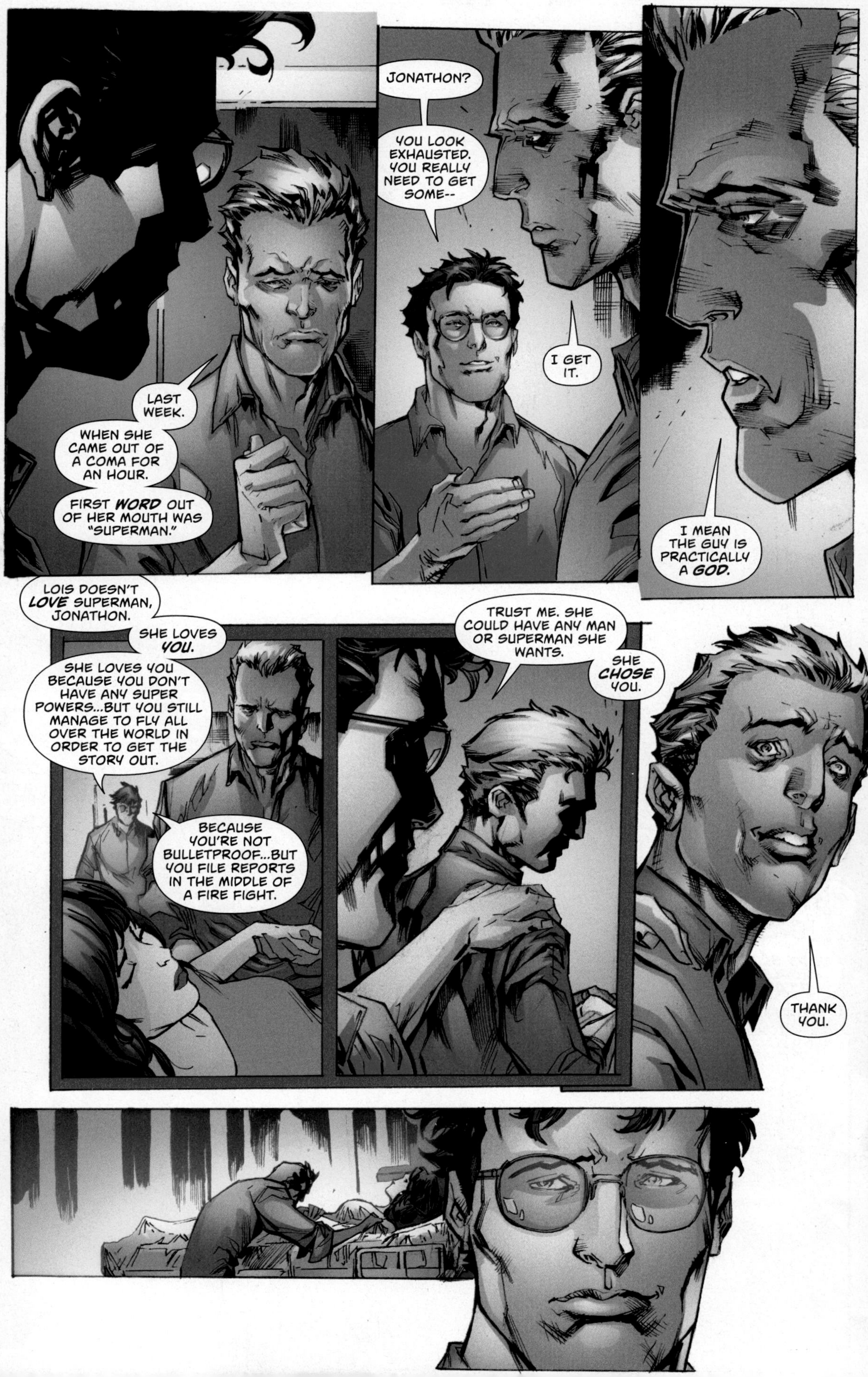
LAST WEEK.
WHEN SHE CAME OUT OF A COMA FOR AN HOUR.
FIRST **WORD** OUT OF HER MOUTH WAS "SUPERMAN."
JONATHON?
YOU LOOK EXHAUSTED. YOU REALLY NEED TO GET SOME--
I GET IT.
I MEAN THE GUY IS PRACTICALLY A **GOD.**
LOIS DOESN'T **LOVE** SUPERMAN, JONATHON.
SHE LOVES **YOU.**
SHE LOVES YOU BECAUSE YOU DON'T HAVE ANY SUPER POWERS...BUT YOU STILL MANAGE TO FLY ALL OVER THE WORLD IN ORDER TO GET THE STORY OUT.
BECAUSE YOU'RE NOT BULLETPROOF...BUT YOU FILE REPORTS IN THE MIDDLE OF A FIRE FIGHT.
TRUST ME. SHE COULD HAVE ANY MAN OR SUPERMAN SHE WANTS.
SHE **CHOSE** YOU.
THANK YOU.

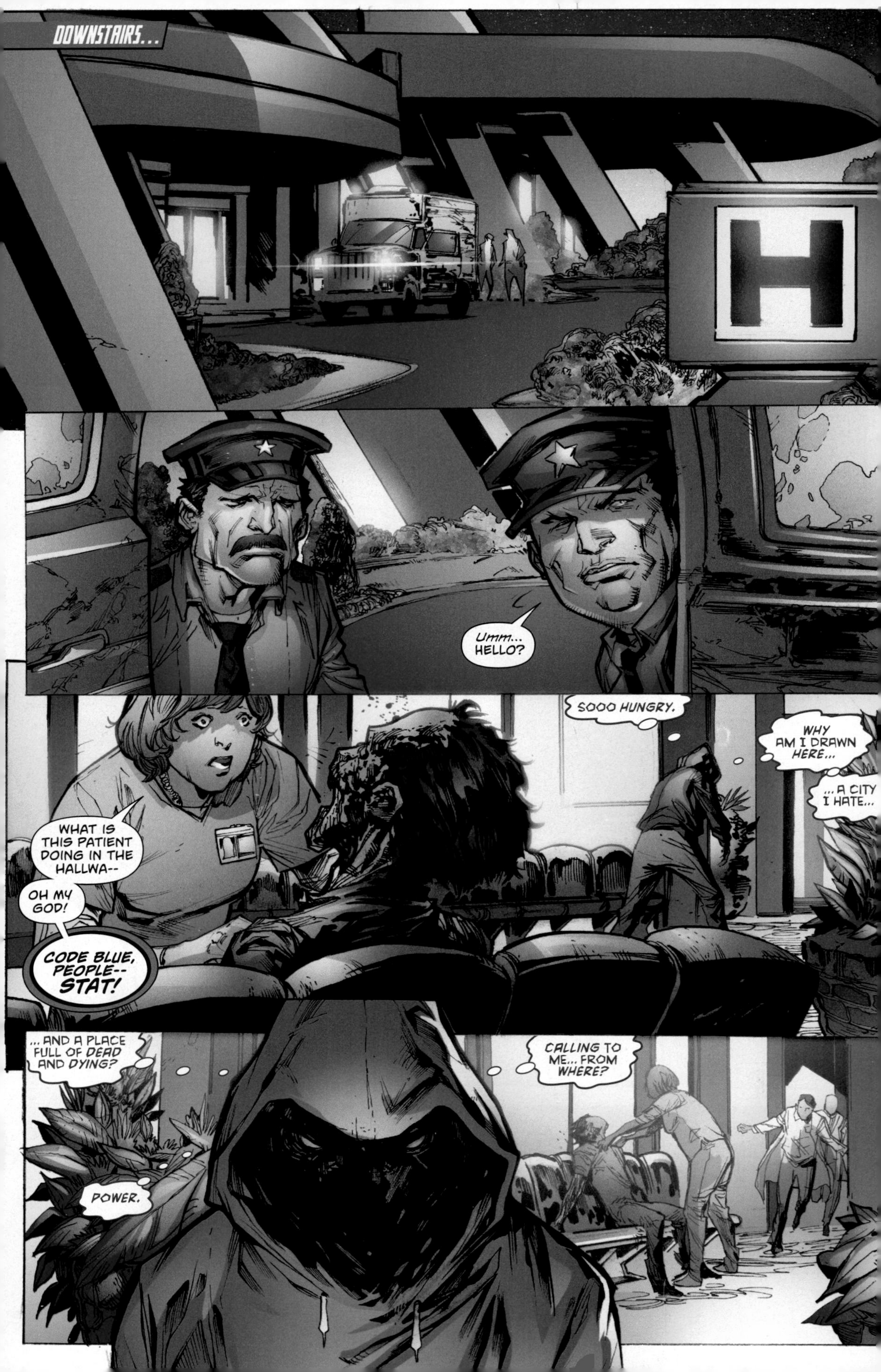
DOWNSTAIRS...
UMM... HELLO?
SOOO HUNGRY.
WHY AM I DRAWN HERE...
...A CITY I HATE...
WHAT IS THIS PATIENT DOING IN THE HALLWA--
OH MY GOD!
CODE BLUE, PEOPLE-- STAT!
...AND A PLACE FULL OF DEAD AND DYING?
CALLING TO ME... FROM WHERE?
POWER.

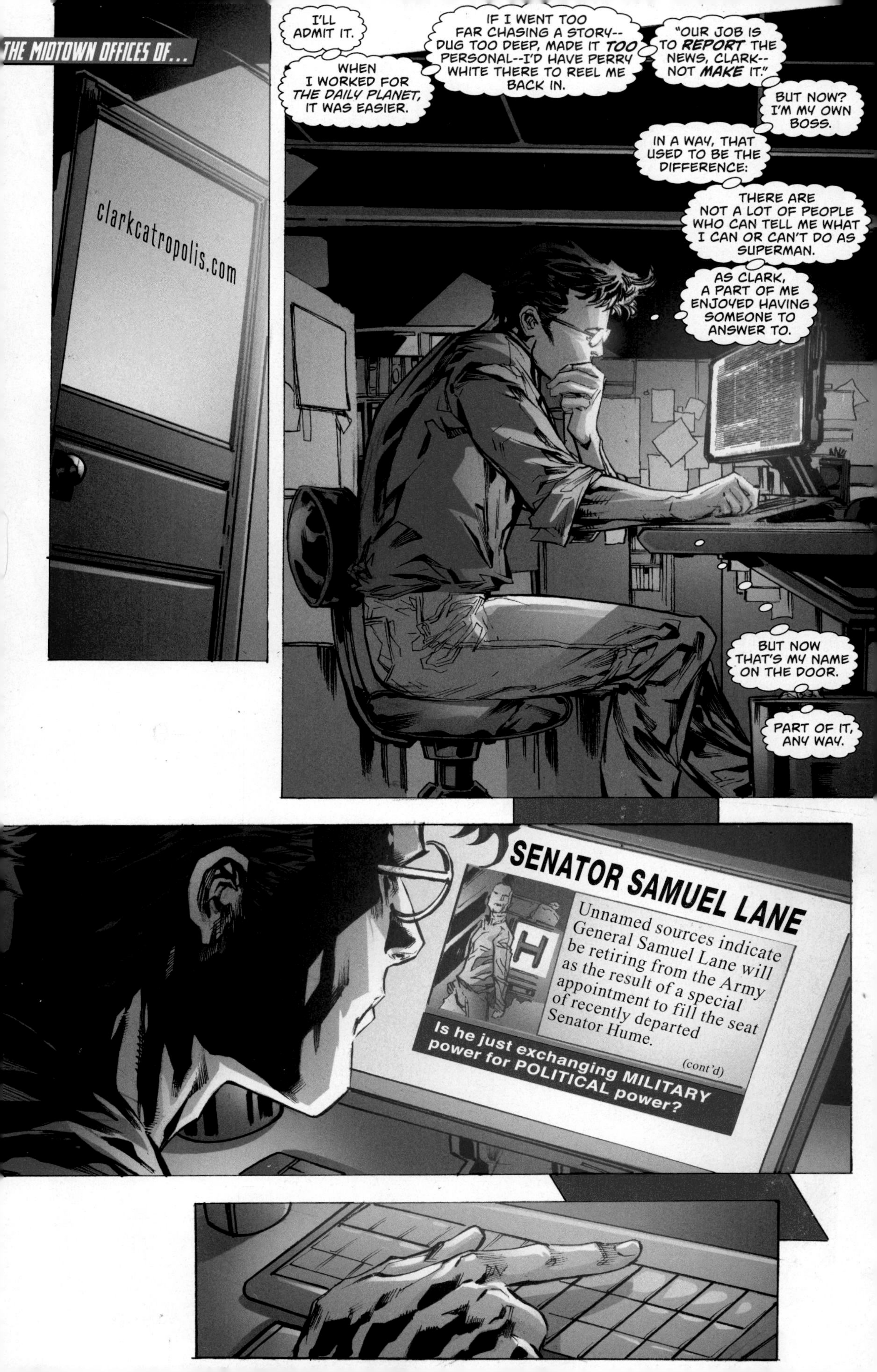
THE MIDTOWN OFFICES OF...
clarkcatropolis.com
I'LL ADMIT IT.
WHEN I WORKED FOR THE DAILY PLANET, IT WAS EASIER.
IF I WENT TOO FAR CHASING A STORY--DUG TOO DEEP, MADE IT TOO PERSONAL--I'D HAVE PERRY WHITE THERE TO REEL ME BACK IN.
"OUR JOB IS TO REPORT THE NEWS, CLARK--NOT MAKE IT."
BUT NOW? I'M MY OWN BOSS.
IN A WAY, THAT USED TO BE THE DIFFERENCE:
THERE ARE NOT A LOT OF PEOPLE WHO CAN TELL ME WHAT I CAN OR CAN'T DO AS SUPERMAN.
AS CLARK, A PART OF ME ENJOYED HAVING SOMEONE TO ANSWER TO.
BUT NOW THAT'S MY NAME ON THE DOOR.
PART OF IT, ANY WAY.
SENATOR SAMUEL LANE
Unnamed sources indicate General Samuel Lane will be retiring from the Army as the result of a special appointment to fill the seat of recently departed Senator Hume.
(cont'd)
Is he just exchanging MILITARY power for POLITICAL power?

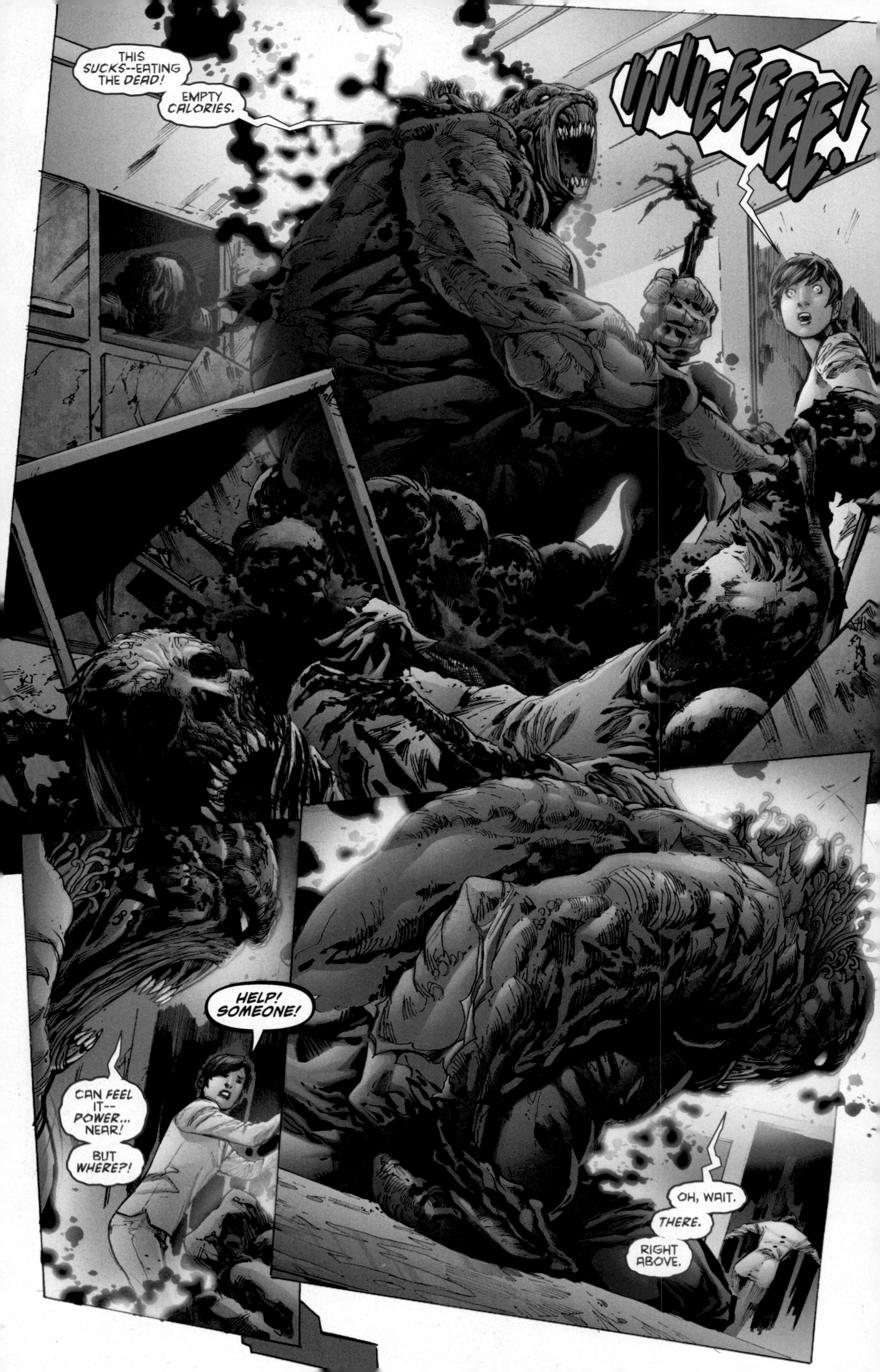
THIS SUCKS--EATING THE DEAD!
EMPTY CALORIES.
IIIIIEEEEEE!
HELP! SOMEONE!
CAN FEEL IT-- POWER... NEAR!
BUT WHERE?!
OH, WAIT.
THERE.
RIGHT ABOVE.

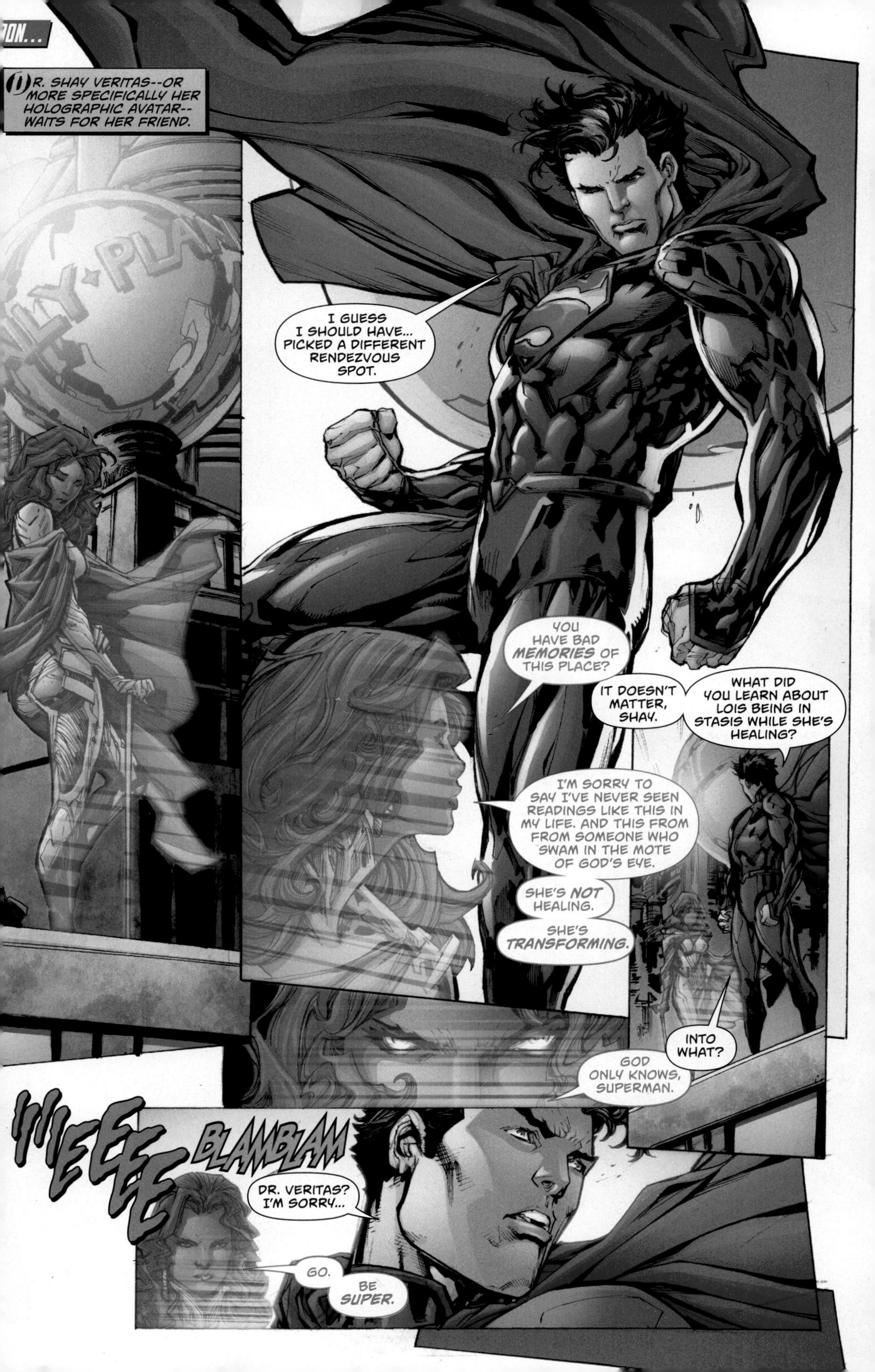
...ON...
DR. SHAY VERITAS--OR MORE SPECIFICALLY HER HOLOGRAPHIC AVATAR--WAITS FOR HER FRIEND.
I GUESS I SHOULD HAVE... PICKED A DIFFERENT RENDEZVOUS SPOT.
YOU HAVE BAD MEMORIES OF THIS PLACE?
IT DOESN'T MATTER, SHAY.
WHAT DID YOU LEARN ABOUT LOIS BEING IN STASIS WHILE SHE'S HEALING?
I'M SORRY TO SAY I'VE NEVER SEEN READINGS LIKE THIS IN MY LIFE. AND THIS FROM FROM SOMEONE WHO SWAM IN THE MOTE OF GOD'S EYE.
SHE'S NOT HEALING.
SHE'S TRANSFORMING.
INTO WHAT?
GOD ONLY KNOWS, SUPERMAN.
IIIEEEE
BLAMBLAM
DR. VERITAS? I'M SORRY...
GO.
BE SUPER.

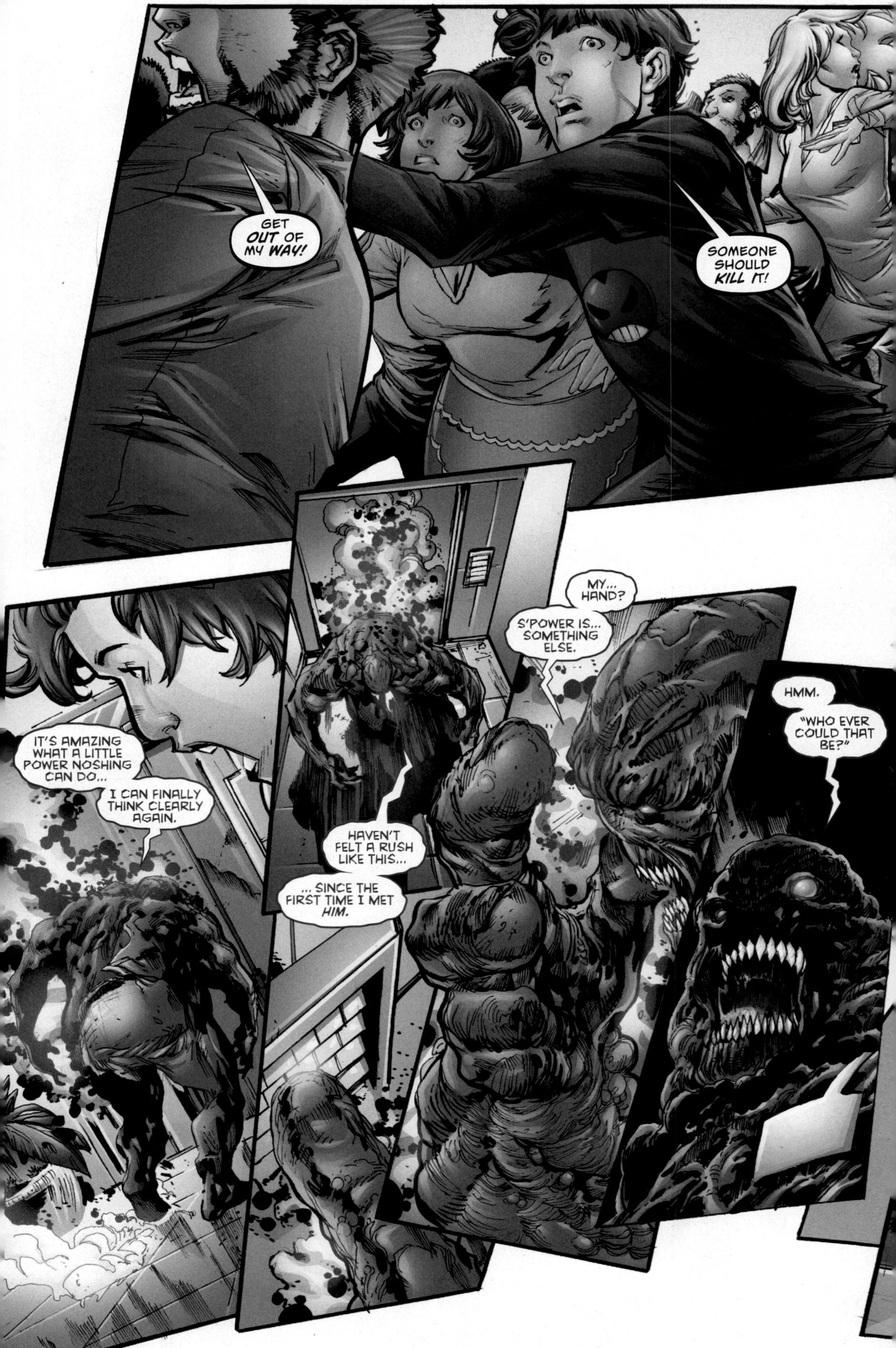
GET OUT OF MY WAY!
SOMEONE SHOULD KILL IT!
IT'S AMAZING WHAT A LITTLE POWER NOSHING CAN DO...
I CAN FINALLY THINK CLEARLY AGAIN.
HAVEN'T FELT A RUSH LIKE THIS...
... SINCE THE FIRST TIME I MET HIM.
MY... HAND?
S'POWER IS... SOMETHING ELSE.
HMM.
"WHO EVER COULD THAT BE?"

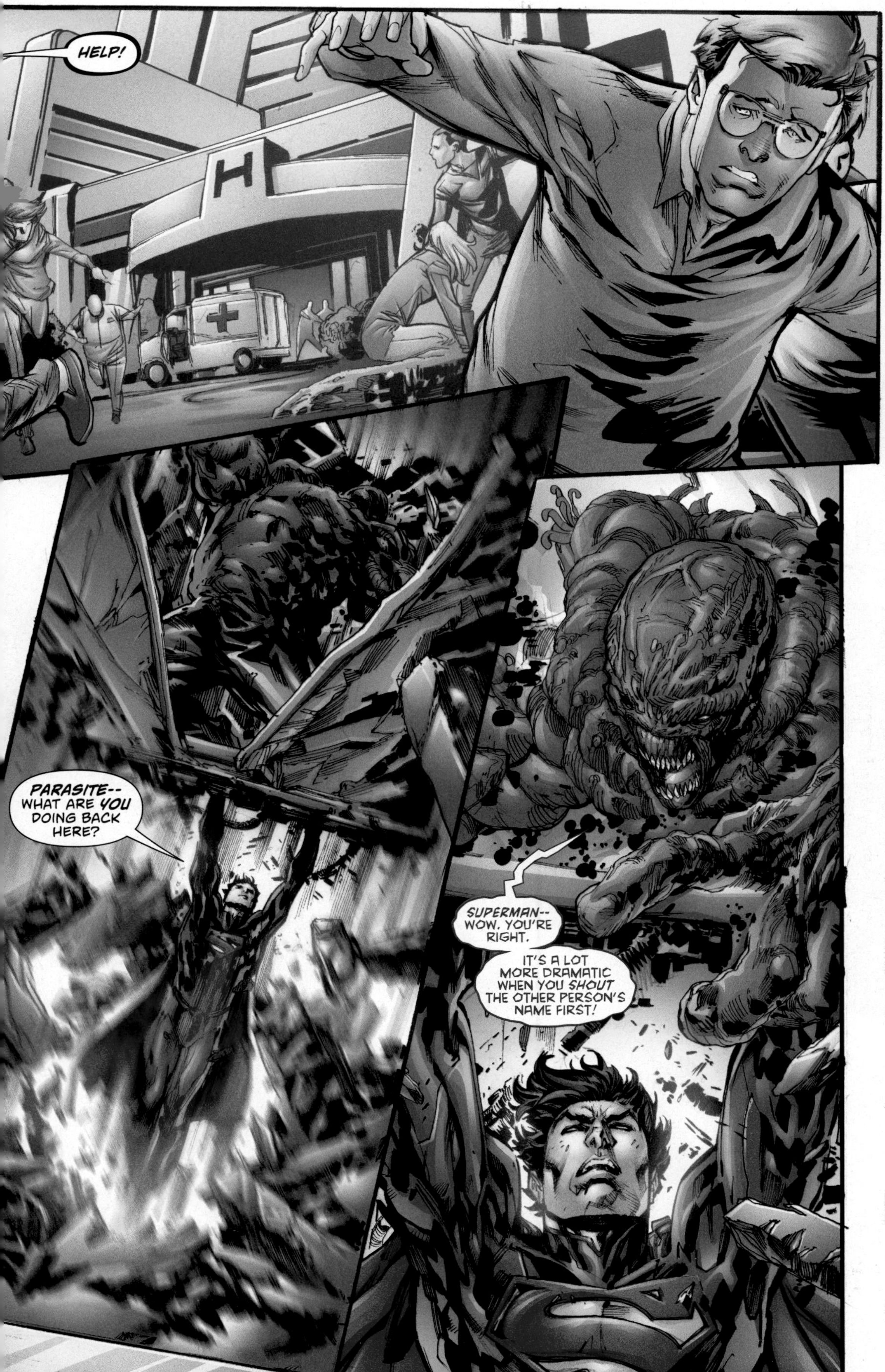
HELP!
PARASITE-- WHAT ARE YOU DOING BACK HERE?
SUPERMAN-- WOW. YOU'RE RIGHT.
IT'S A LOT MORE DRAMATIC WHEN YOU SHOUT THE OTHER PERSON'S NAME FIRST!

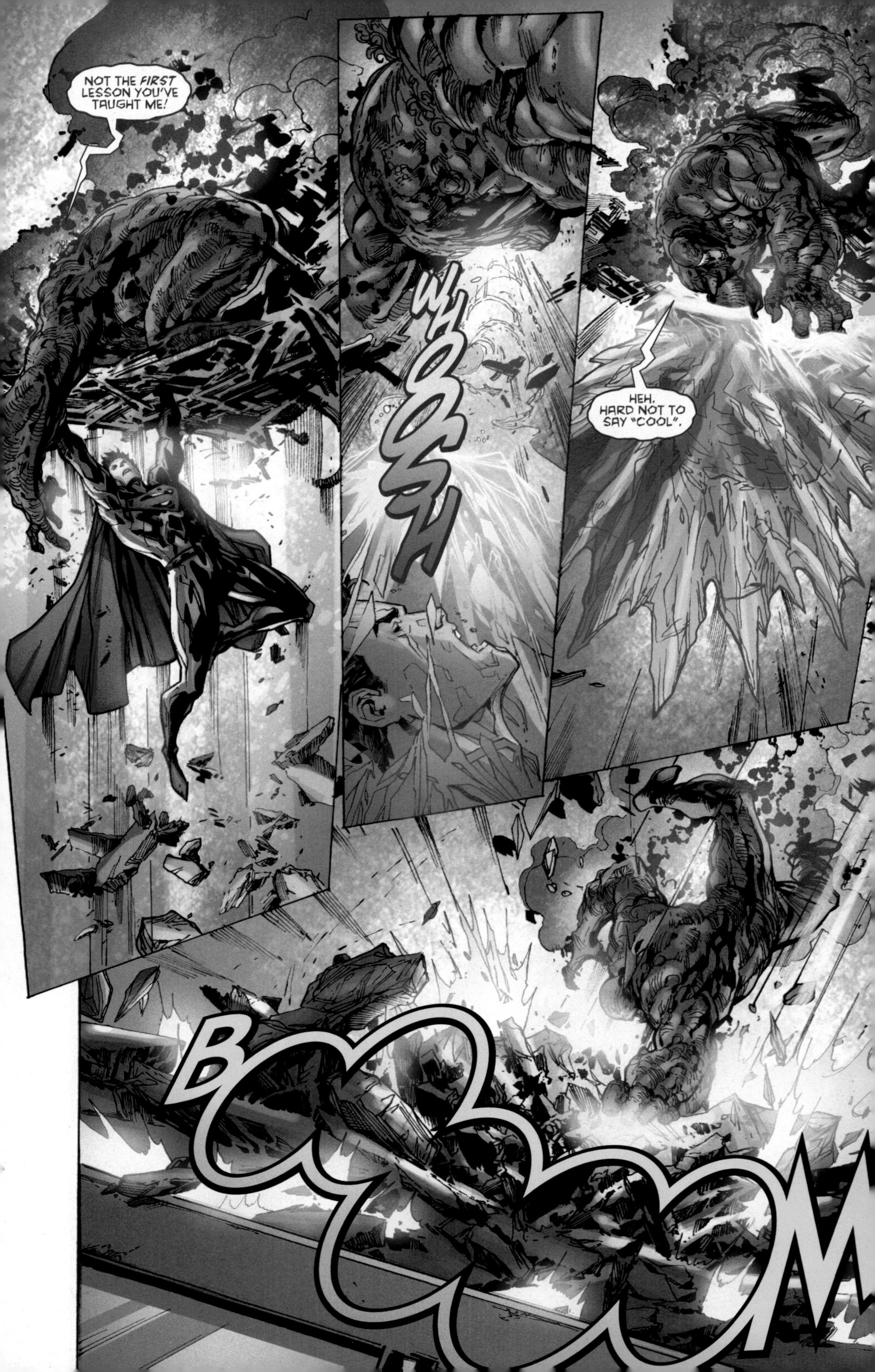
NOT THE *FIRST* LESSON YOU'VE TAUGHT ME!
WHOOSH
HEH. HARD NOT TO SAY "COOL".
BOOOM

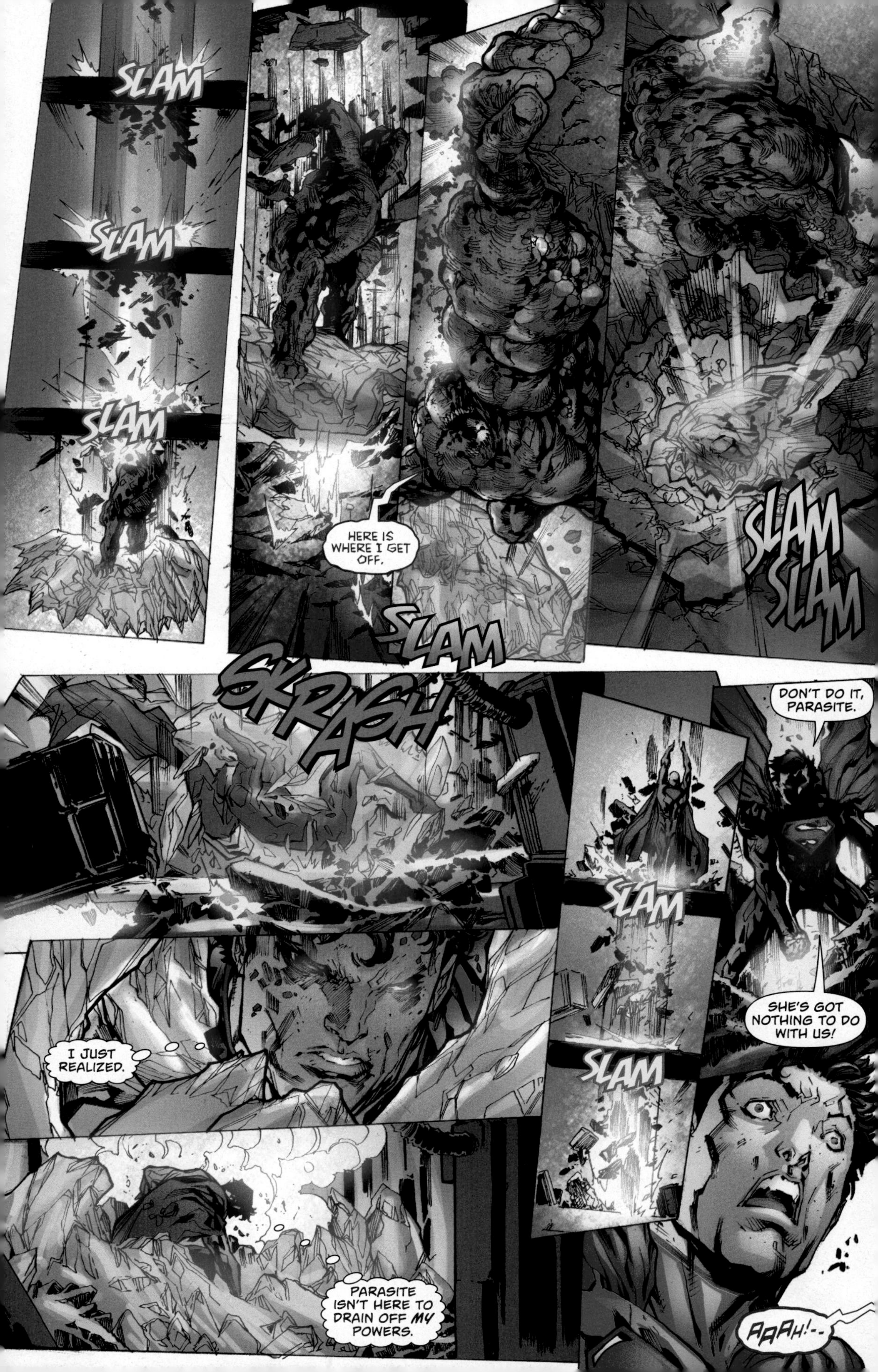
SLAM
SLAM
SLAM
HERE IS WHERE I GET OFF.
SLAM
SLAM SLAM
SKRASH
I JUST REALIZED.
PARASITE ISN'T HERE TO DRAIN OFF MY POWERS.
SLAM
SLAM
DON'T DO IT, PARASITE.
SHE'S GOT NOTHING TO DO WITH US!
AAAH!--

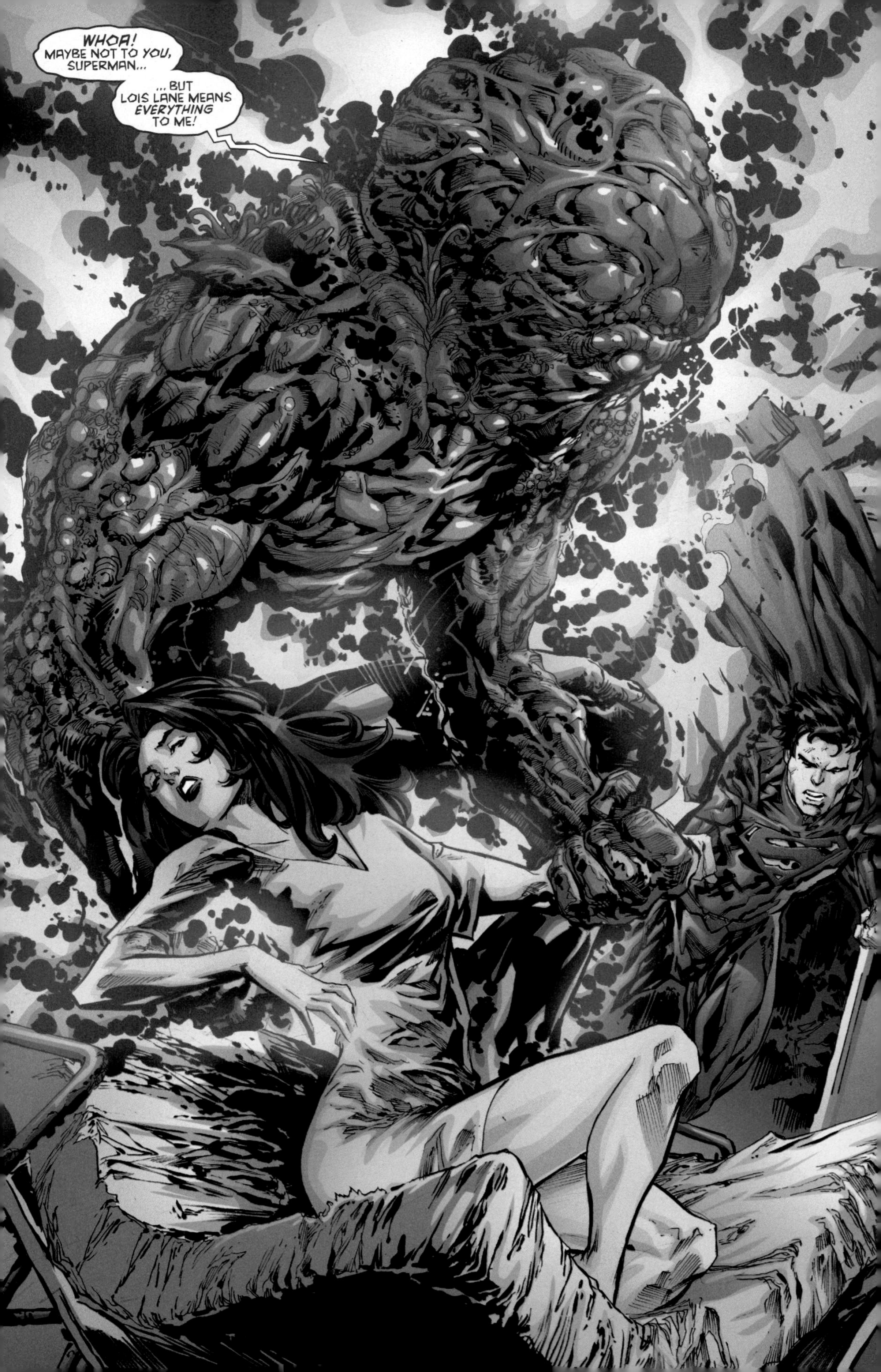
WHOA! MAYBE NOT TO YOU, SUPERMAN...
...BUT LOIS LANE MEANS EVERYTHING TO ME!

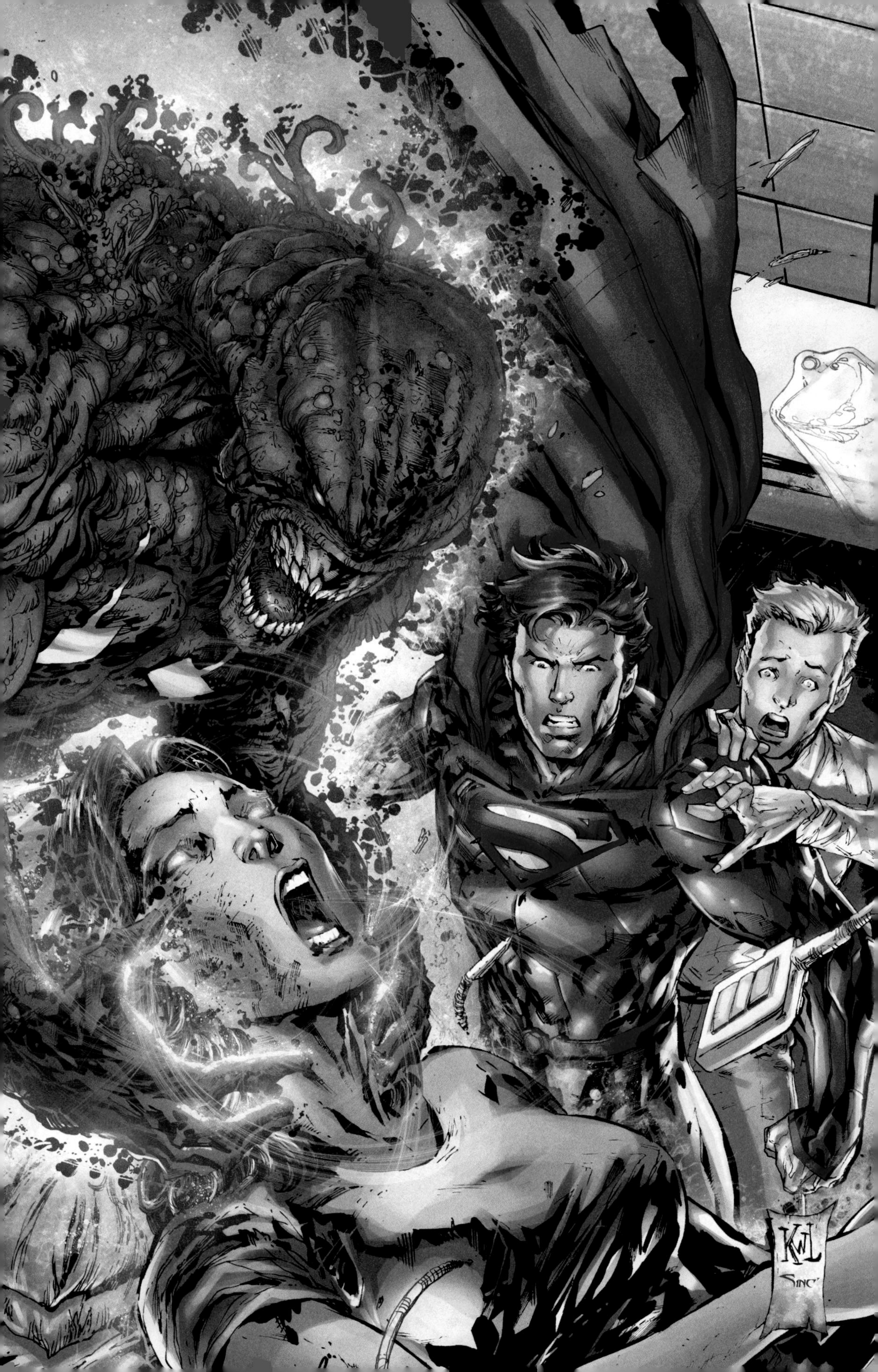

FEEDING FRENZY

SCOTT LOBDELL writer ED BENES artist PETE PANTAZIS colorist cover art by KEN LASHLEY and ALEX SINCLAIR

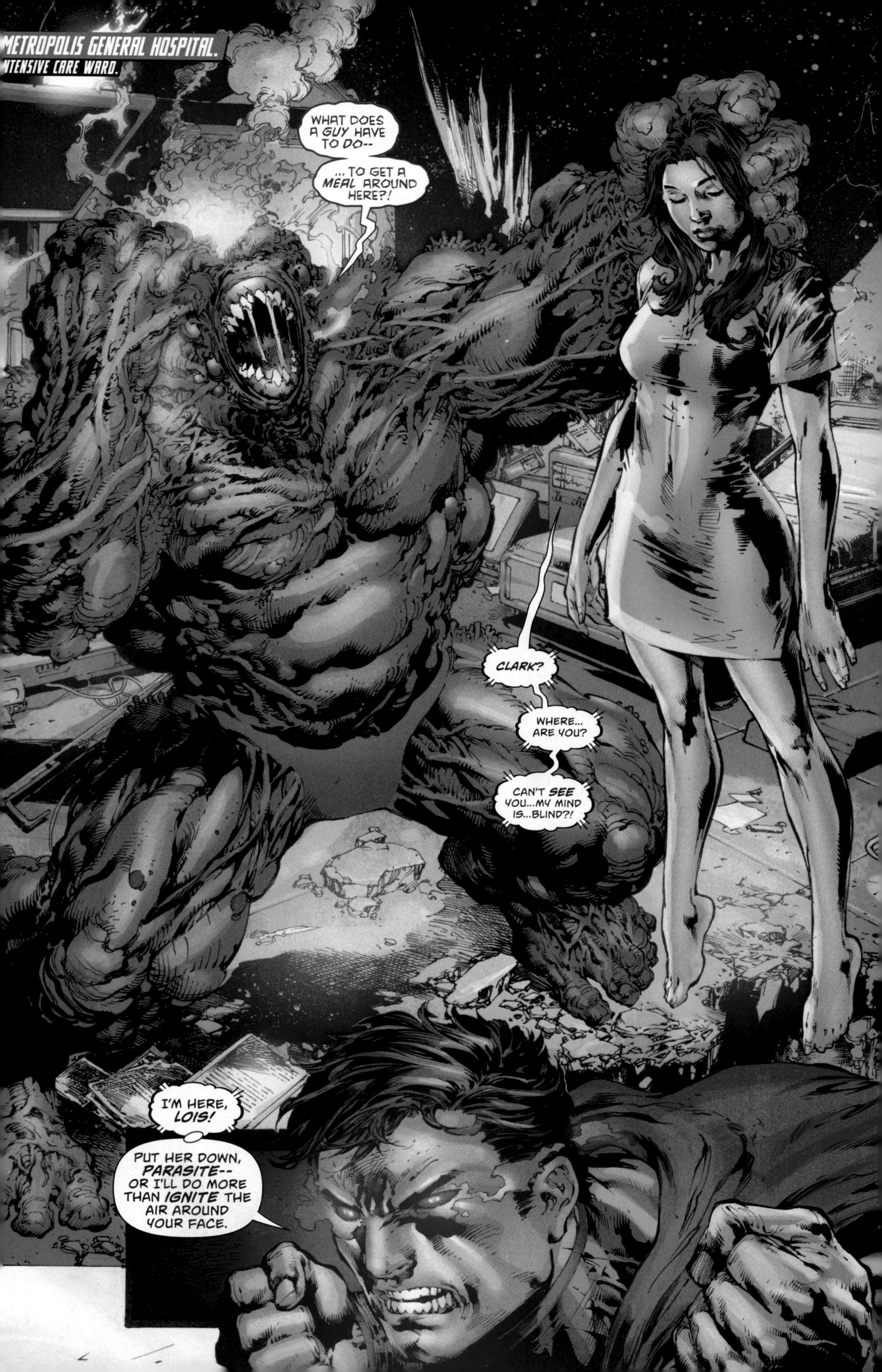
METROPOLIS GENERAL HOSPITAL.
NTENSIVE CARE WARD.
WHAT DOES A GUY HAVE TO DO--
...TO GET A MEAL AROUND HERE?!
CLARK?
WHERE... ARE YOU?
CAN'T SEE YOU...MY MIND IS...BLIND?!
I'M HERE, LOIS!
PUT HER DOWN, PARASITE-- OR I'LL DO MORE THAN IGNITE THE AIR AROUND YOUR FACE.

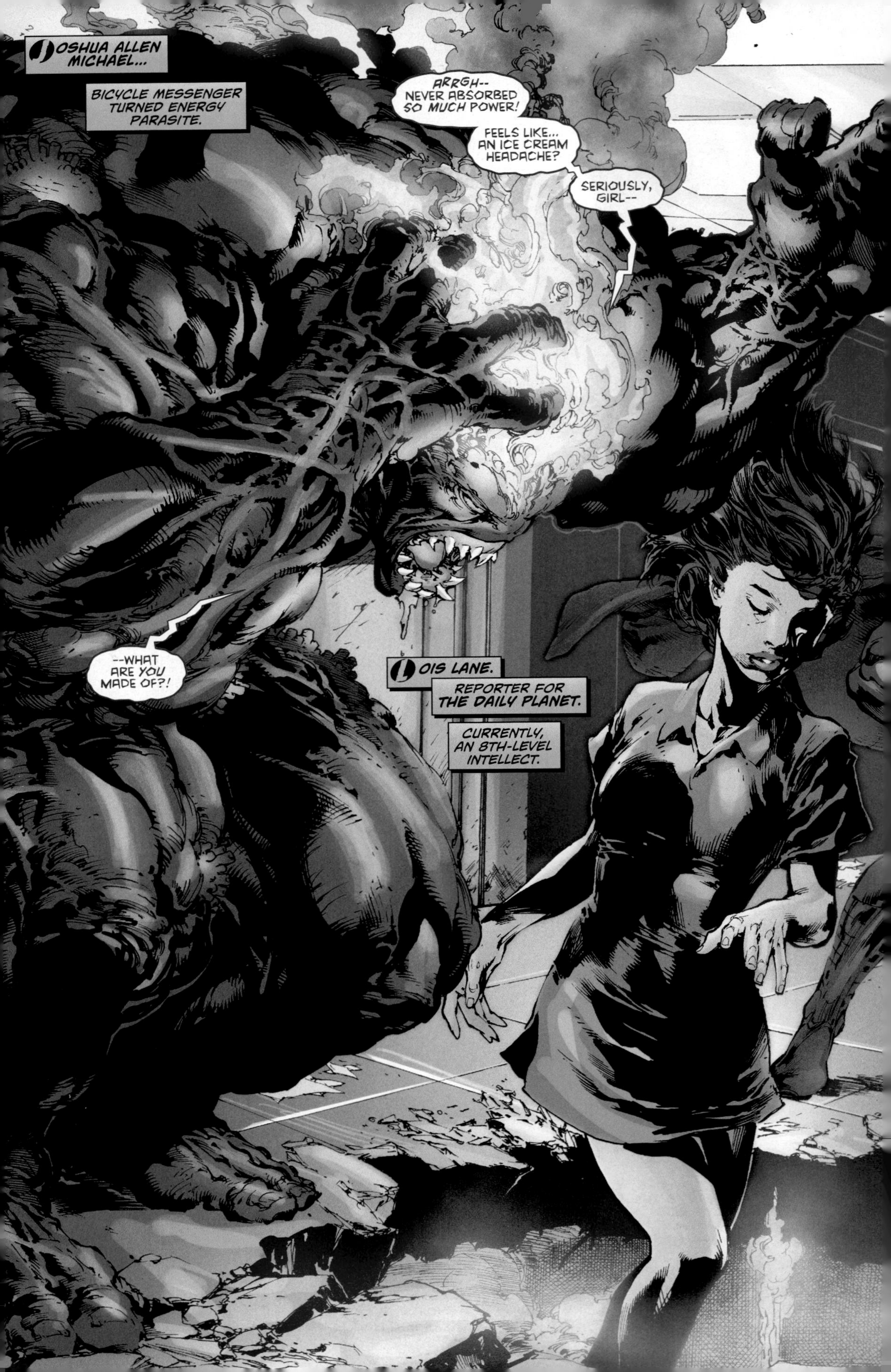
JOSHUA ALLEN MICHAEL...
BICYCLE MESSENGER TURNED ENERGY PARASITE.
ARRGH-- NEVER ABSORBED SO MUCH POWER!
FEELS LIKE... AN ICE CREAM HEADACHE?
SERIOUSLY, GIRL--
--WHAT ARE YOU MADE OF?!
LOIS LANE.
REPORTER FOR THE DAILY PLANET.
CURRENTLY, AN 8TH-LEVEL INTELLECT.

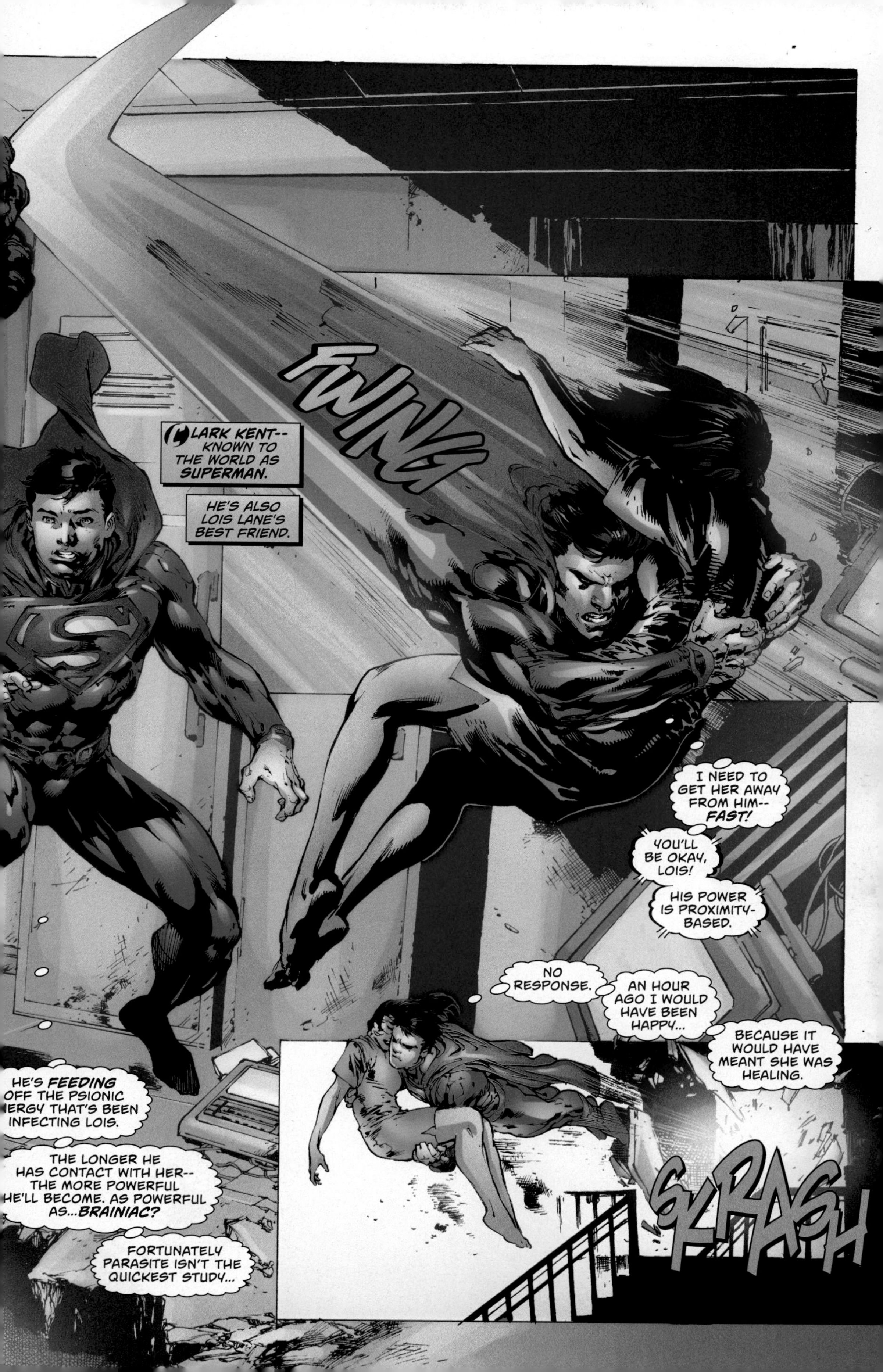
FWING
CLARK KENT-- KNOWN TO THE WORLD AS SUPERMAN.
HE'S ALSO LOIS LANE'S BEST FRIEND.
I NEED TO GET HER AWAY FROM HIM-- FAST!
YOU'LL BE OKAY, LOIS!
HIS POWER IS PROXIMITY-BASED.
HE'S FEEDING OFF THE PSIONIC ENERGY THAT'S BEEN INFECTING LOIS.
THE LONGER HE HAS CONTACT WITH HER-- THE MORE POWERFUL HE'LL BECOME. AS POWERFUL AS...BRAINIAC?
FORTUNATELY PARASITE ISN'T THE QUICKEST STUDY...
NO RESPONSE.
AN HOUR AGO I WOULD HAVE BEEN HAPPY...
BECAUSE IT WOULD HAVE MEANT SHE WAS HEALING.
SKRASH

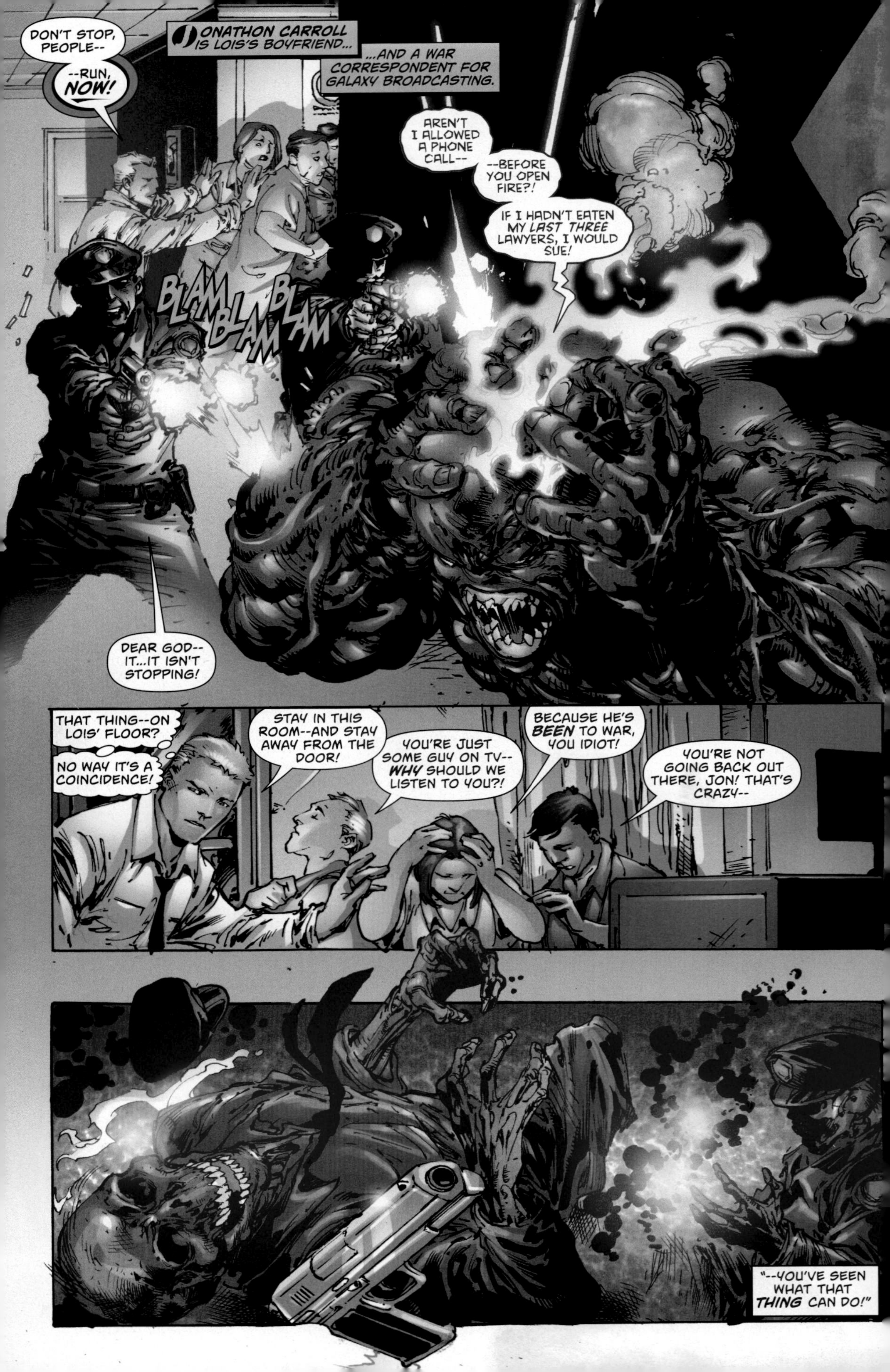
DON'T STOP, PEOPLE--
--RUN, NOW!
JONATHON CARROLL IS LOIS'S BOYFRIEND...
...AND A WAR CORRESPONDENT FOR GALAXY BROADCASTING.
AREN'T I ALLOWED A PHONE CALL--
--BEFORE YOU OPEN FIRE?!
IF I HADN'T EATEN MY LAST THREE LAWYERS, I WOULD SUE!
BLAM BLAM BLAM BLAM
DEAR GOD--IT...IT ISN'T STOPPING!
THAT THING--ON LOIS' FLOOR?
NO WAY IT'S A COINCIDENCE!
STAY IN THIS ROOM--AND STAY AWAY FROM THE DOOR!
YOU'RE JUST SOME GUY ON TV--WHY SHOULD WE LISTEN TO YOU?!
BECAUSE HE'S BEEN TO WAR, YOU IDIOT!
YOU'RE NOT GOING BACK OUT THERE, JON! THAT'S CRAZY--
"--YOU'VE SEEN WHAT THAT THING CAN DO!"

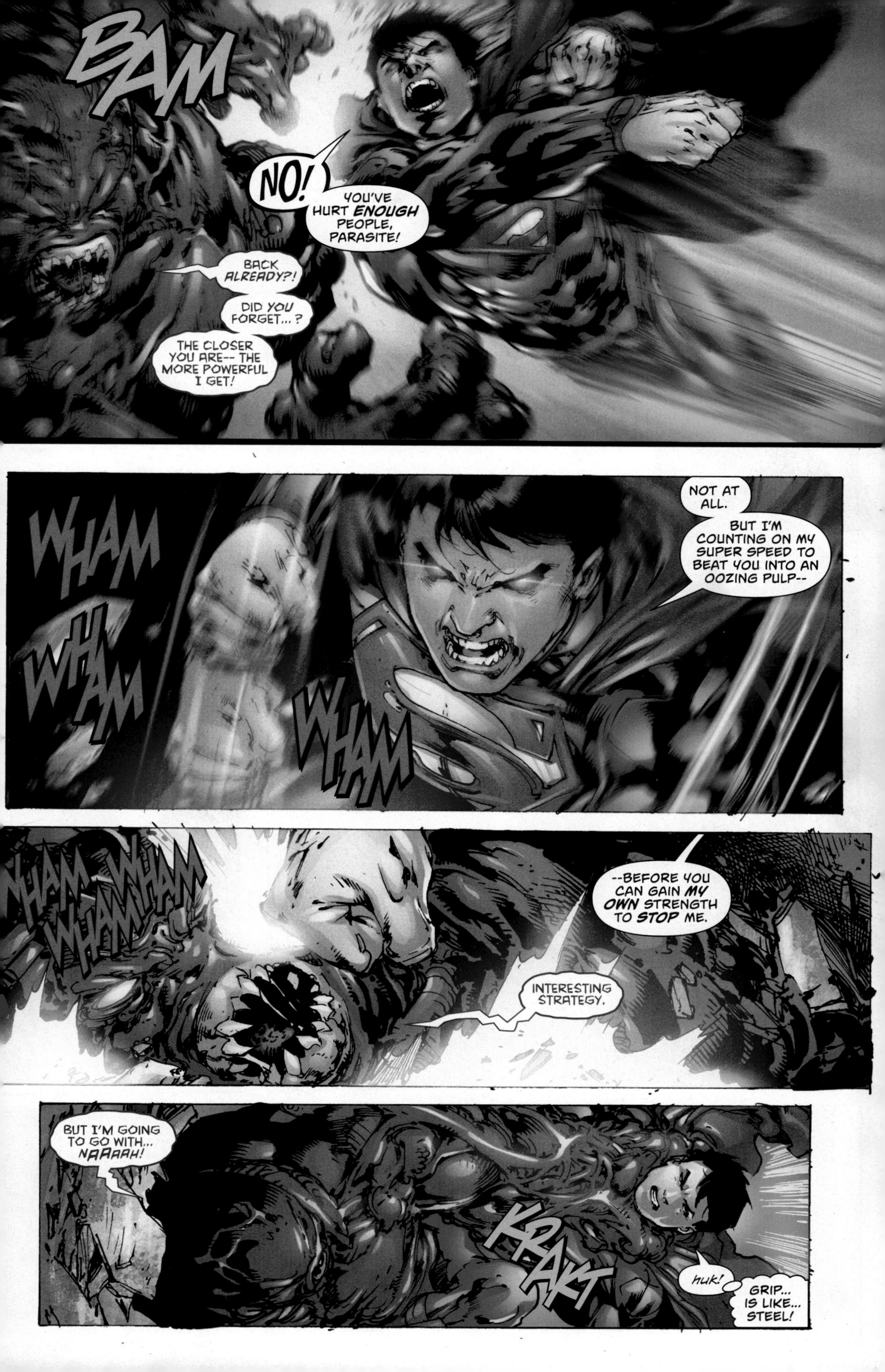
BAM
NO!
YOU'VE HURT ENOUGH PEOPLE, PARASITE!
BACK ALREADY?!
DID YOU FORGET...?
THE CLOSER YOU ARE-- THE MORE POWERFUL I GET!
WHAM
WHAM
WHAM
NOT AT ALL.
BUT I'M COUNTING ON MY SUPER SPEED TO BEAT YOU INTO AN OOZING PULP--
WHAM WHAM WHAM WHAM
--BEFORE YOU CAN GAIN MY OWN STRENGTH TO STOP ME.
INTERESTING STRATEGY.
BUT I'M GOING TO GO WITH... NAAaah!
KRAKT
huk!
GRIP... IS LIKE... STEEL!

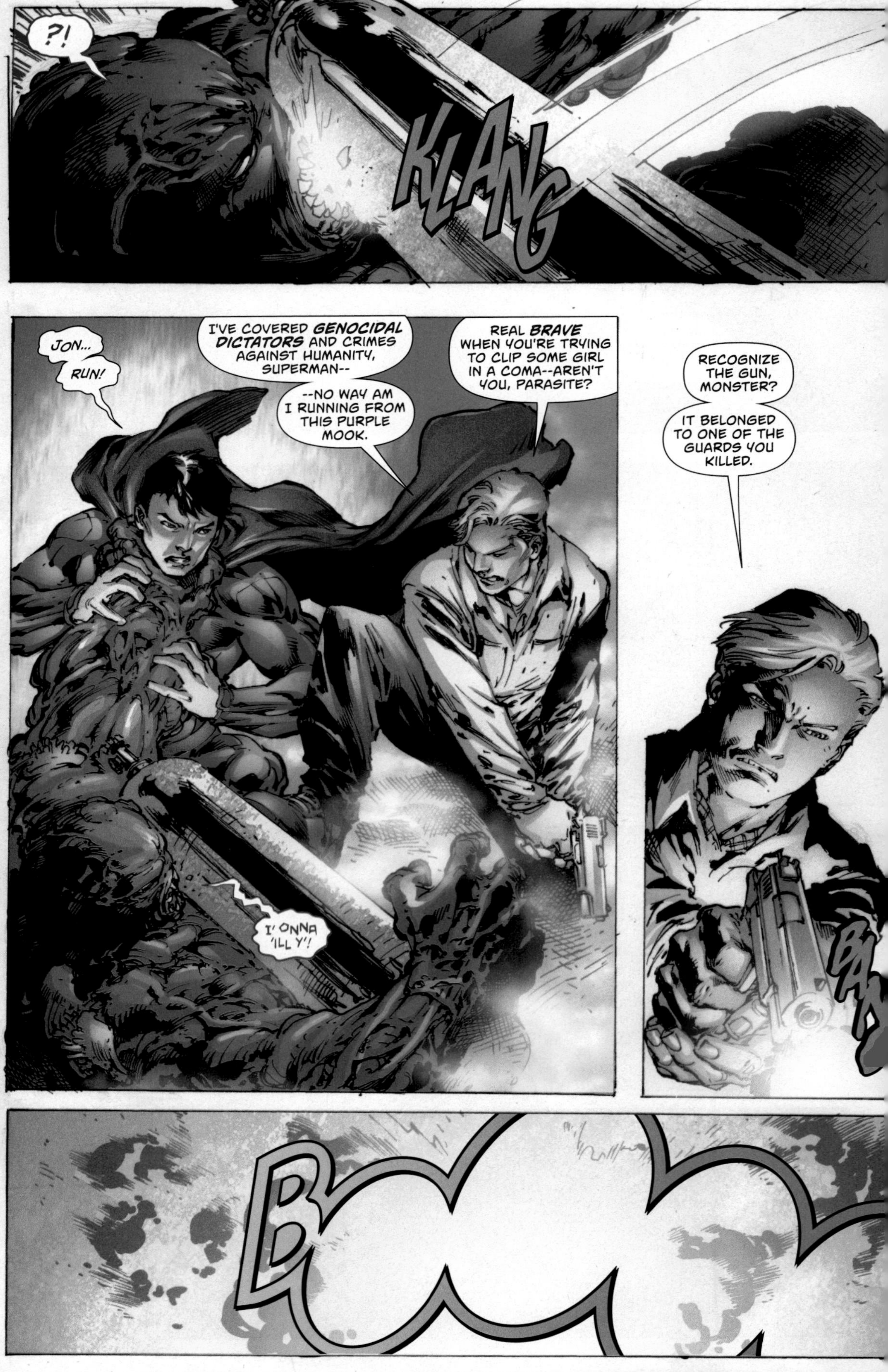
?!
KLANG
JON... RUN!
I'VE COVERED GENOCIDAL DICTATORS AND CRIMES AGAINST HUMANITY, SUPERMAN--
--NO WAY AM I RUNNING FROM THIS PURPLE MOOK.
REAL BRAVE WHEN YOU'RE TRYING TO CLIP SOME GIRL IN A COMA--AREN'T YOU, PARASITE?
I' ONNA 'ILL Y'!
RECOGNIZE THE GUN, MONSTER?
IT BELONGED TO ONE OF THE GUARDS YOU KILLED.
BOO

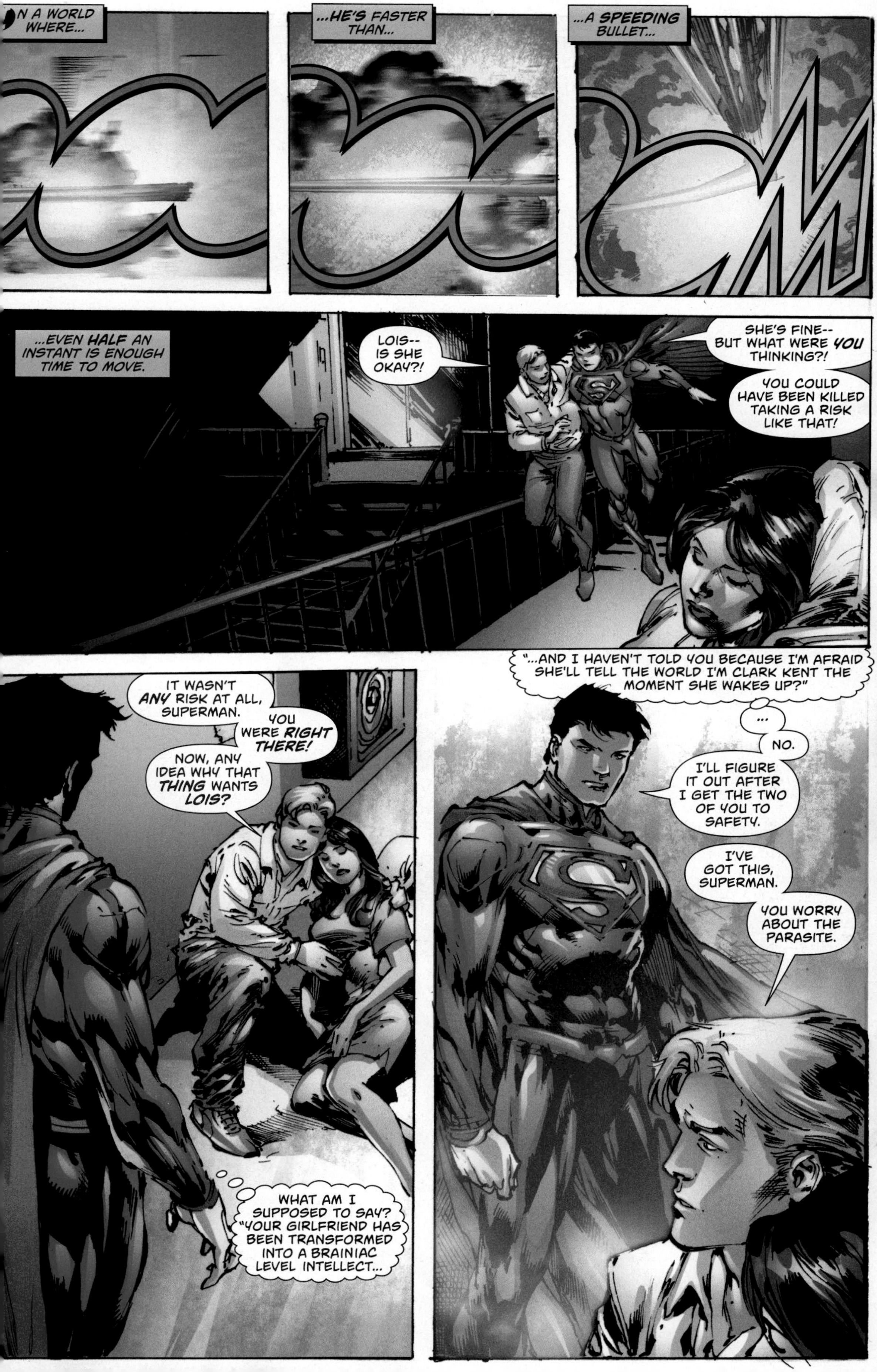
N A WORLD WHERE...
...HE'S FASTER THAN...
...A SPEEDING BULLET...
...EVEN HALF AN INSTANT IS ENOUGH TIME TO MOVE.
LOIS-- IS SHE OKAY?!
SHE'S FINE-- BUT WHAT WERE YOU THINKING?!
YOU COULD HAVE BEEN KILLED TAKING A RISK LIKE THAT!
IT WASN'T ANY RISK AT ALL, SUPERMAN.
YOU WERE RIGHT THERE!
NOW, ANY IDEA WHY THAT THING WANTS LOIS?
WHAT AM I SUPPOSED TO SAY? "YOUR GIRLFRIEND HAS BEEN TRANSFORMED INTO A BRAINIAC LEVEL INTELLECT...
"...AND I HAVEN'T TOLD YOU BECAUSE I'M AFRAID SHE'LL TELL THE WORLD I'M CLARK KENT THE MOMENT SHE WAKES UP?"
...
NO.
I'LL FIGURE IT OUT AFTER I GET THE TWO OF YOU TO SAFETY.
I'VE GOT THIS, SUPERMAN.
YOU WORRY ABOUT THE PARASITE.

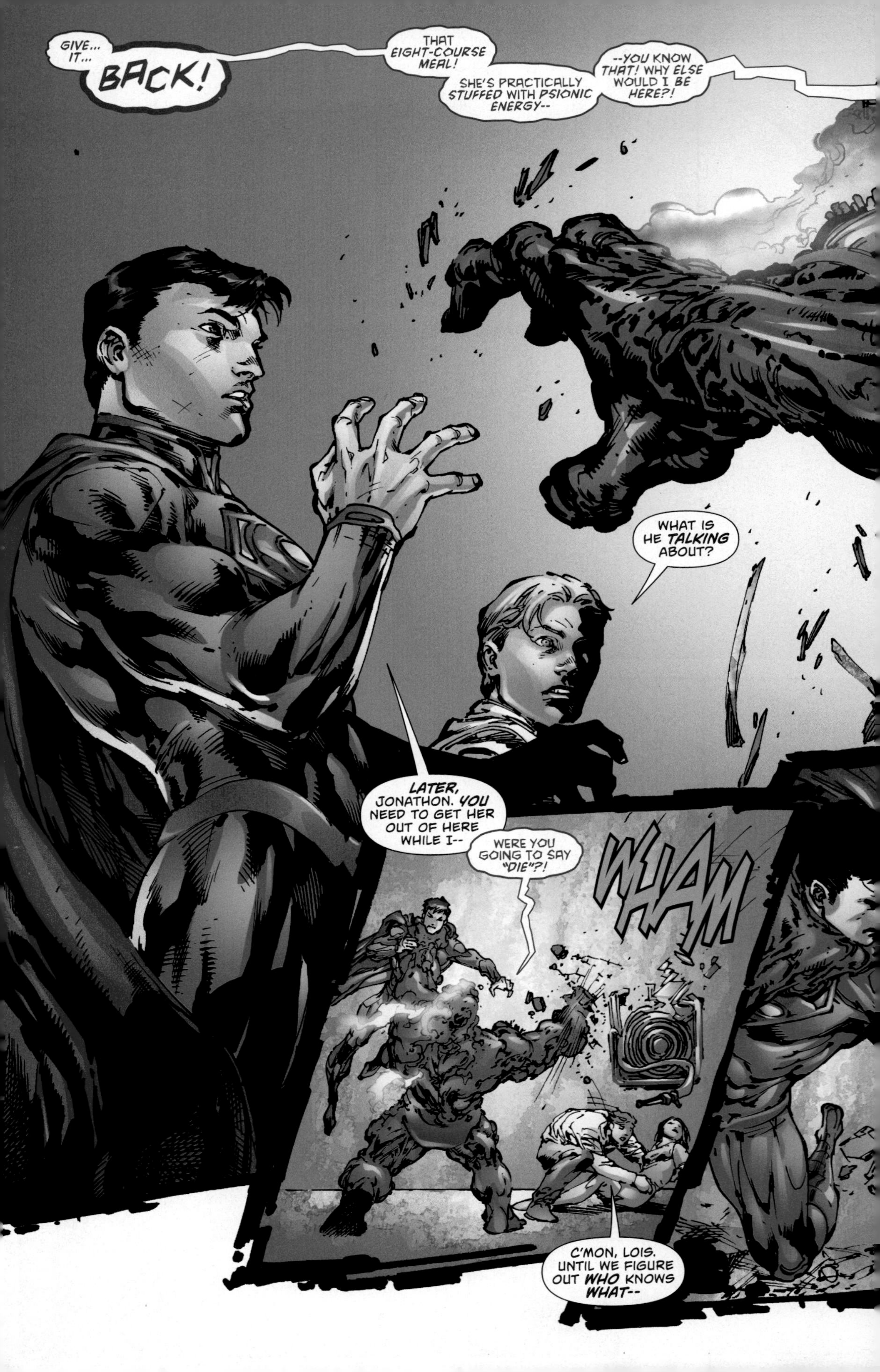

GIVE... IT... BACK!
THAT EIGHT-COURSE MEAL!
SHE'S PRACTICALLY STUFFED WITH PSIONIC ENERGY--
--YOU KNOW THAT! WHY ELSE WOULD I BE HERE?!
WHAT IS HE TALKING ABOUT?
LATER, JONATHON. YOU NEED TO GET HER OUT OF HERE WHILE I--
WERE YOU GOING TO SAY "DIE"?!
WHAM
C'MON, LOIS. UNTIL WE FIGURE OUT WHO KNOWS WHAT--

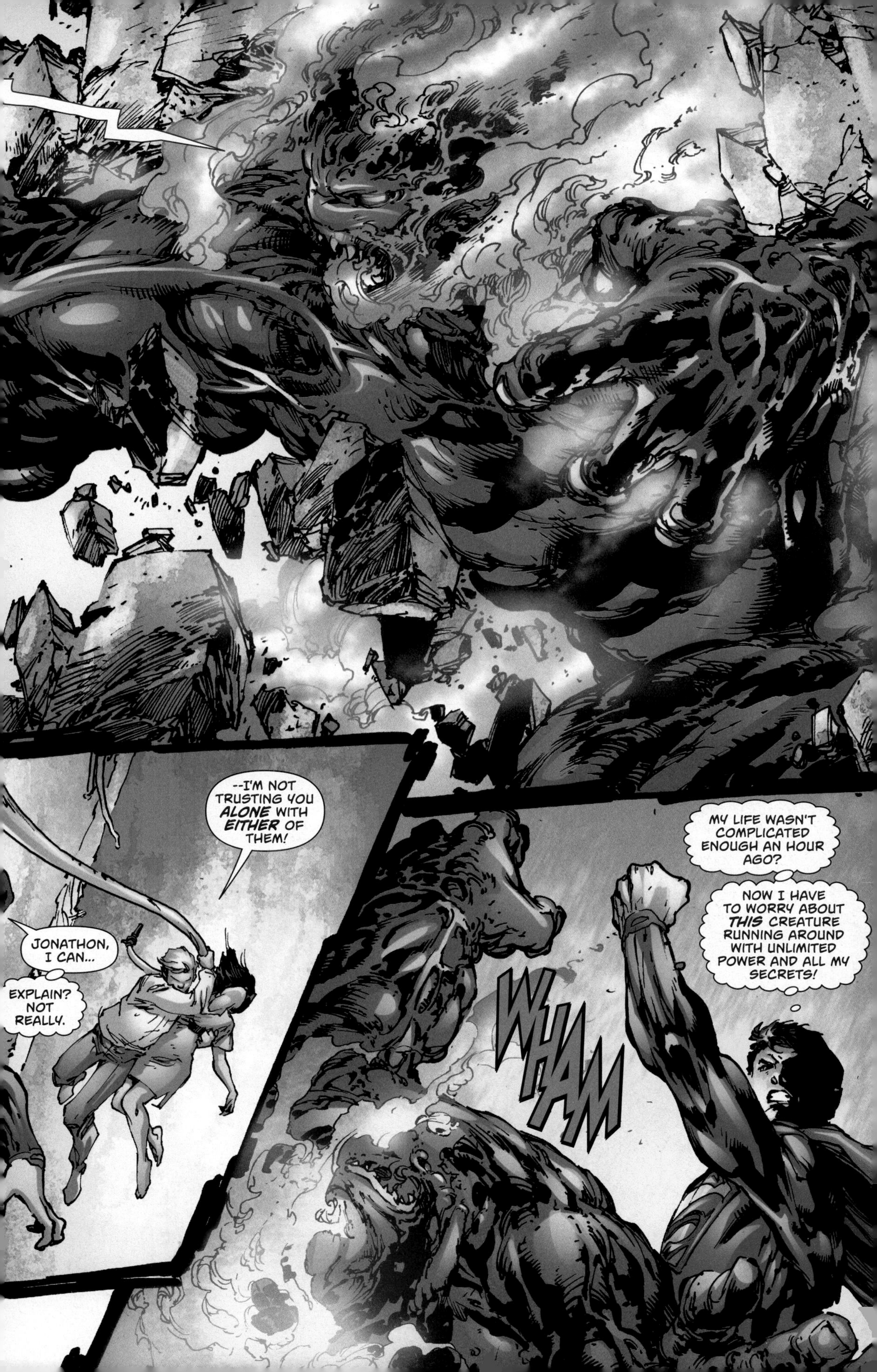
--I'M NOT TRUSTING YOU ALONE WITH EITHER OF THEM!
JONATHON, I CAN...
EXPLAIN? NOT REALLY.
MY LIFE WASN'T COMPLICATED ENOUGH AN HOUR AGO?
NOW I HAVE TO WORRY ABOUT THIS CREATURE RUNNING AROUND WITH UNLIMITED POWER AND ALL MY SECRETS!
WHAM

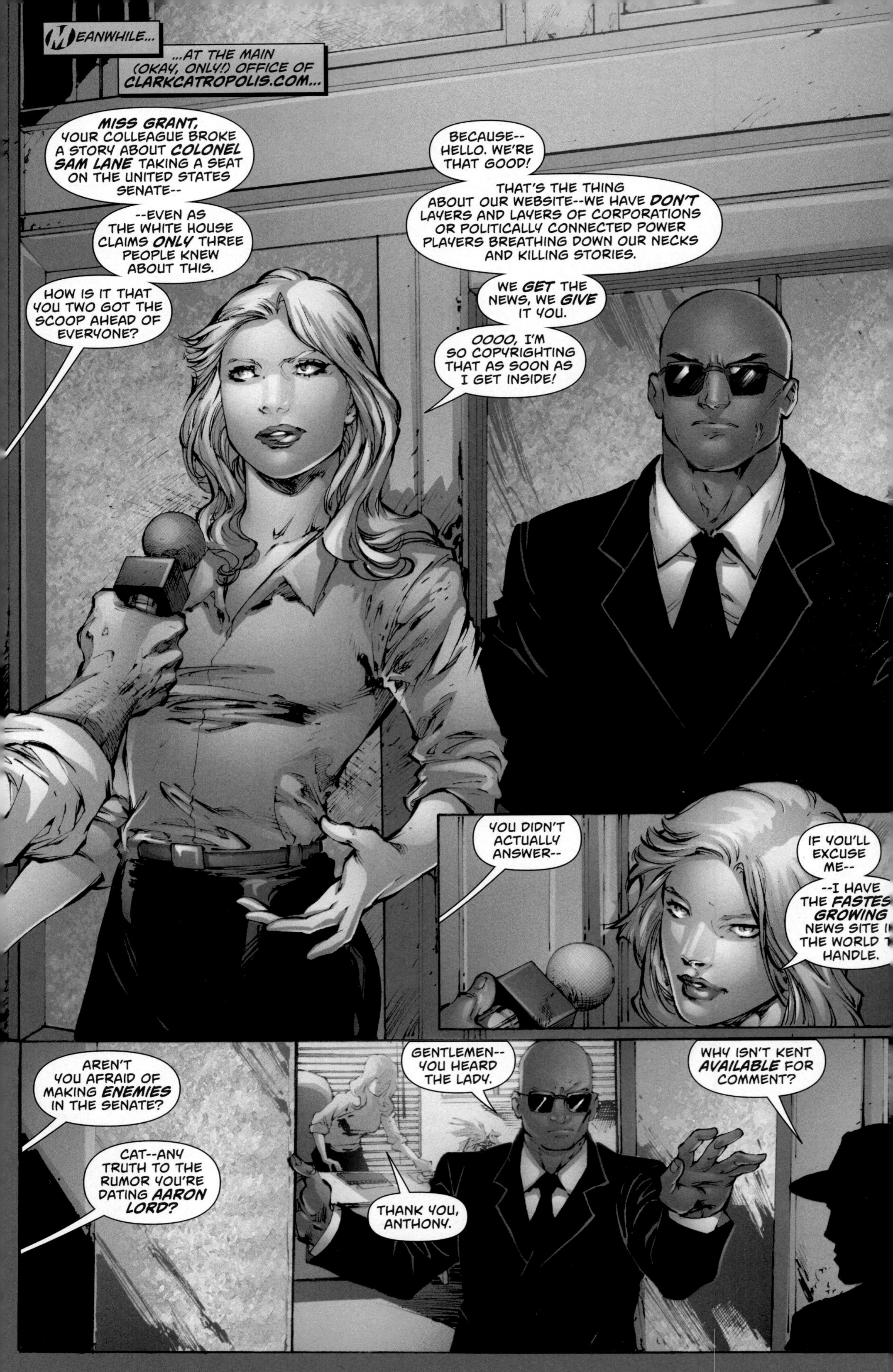
MEANWHILE...
...AT THE MAIN (OKAY, ONLY!) OFFICE OF CLARKCATROPOLIS.COM...
MISS GRANT, YOUR COLLEAGUE BROKE A STORY ABOUT COLONEL SAM LANE TAKING A SEAT ON THE UNITED STATES SENATE--
--EVEN AS THE WHITE HOUSE CLAIMS ONLY THREE PEOPLE KNEW ABOUT THIS.
HOW IS IT THAT YOU TWO GOT THE SCOOP AHEAD OF EVERYONE?
BECAUSE-- HELLO. WE'RE THAT GOOD!
THAT'S THE THING ABOUT OUR WEBSITE--WE HAVE DON'T LAYERS AND LAYERS OF CORPORATIONS OR POLITICALLY CONNECTED POWER PLAYERS BREATHING DOWN OUR NECKS AND KILLING STORIES.
WE GET THE NEWS, WE GIVE IT YOU.
OOOO, I'M SO COPYRIGHTING THAT AS SOON AS I GET INSIDE!
YOU DIDN'T ACTUALLY ANSWER--
IF YOU'LL EXCUSE ME--
--I HAVE THE FASTES GROWING NEWS SITE I THE WORLD HANDLE.
AREN'T YOU AFRAID OF MAKING ENEMIES IN THE SENATE?
CAT--ANY TRUTH TO THE RUMOR YOU'RE DATING AARON LORD?
GENTLEMEN-- YOU HEARD THE LADY.
THANK YOU, ANTHONY.
WHY ISN'T KENT AVAILABLE FOR COMMENT?

I'VE BEEN ASKING MYSELF THAT SAME QUESTION. SERIOUSLY, CLARK--*WHERE* ARE YOU?

HEY, C.K.--ME, AGAIN.

AGAIN.

I'M OVER THE MOON ABOUT ALL THE WEB TRAFFIC--YOU SCOOPED EVERY WONK IN WASHINGTON AND BOTH COASTS.

BUT I REALLY NEED YOU TO CALL ME BACK BEFORE THE FEDS RETURN. THANKS.

TROUBLE IN PARADISE?

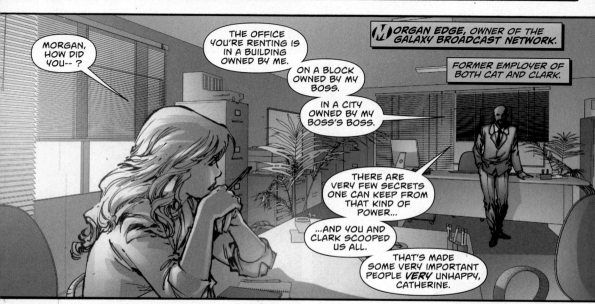

MORGAN, HOW DID YOU--?

THE OFFICE YOU'RE RENTING IS IN A BUILDING OWNED BY ME.

ON A BLOCK OWNED BY MY BOSS.

IN A CITY OWNED BY MY BOSS'S BOSS.

THERE ARE VERY FEW SECRETS ONE CAN KEEP FROM THAT KIND OF POWER...

...AND YOU AND CLARK SCOOPED US ALL.

THAT'S MADE SOME VERY IMPORTANT PEOPLE *VERY* UNHAPPY, CATHERINE.

MORGAN EDGE, OWNER OF THE GALAXY BROADCAST NETWORK.

FORMER EMPLOYER OF BOTH CAT AND CLARK.

MY GREAT-AUNT'S NAME WAS CATHERINE.

AND WE DON'T REVEAL OUR SOURCES, MORGAN, CERTAINLY NOT TO THE BRICK AND MORTAR COMPETITION.

I'M NOT HERE FOR YOUR SOURCES.

I'M HERE FOR YOUR COMPANY.

THE SAME ONE THAT BROKE THE SUPERMAN AND WONDER WOMAN RELATIONSHIP.

I CAN SEE THE WRITING ON THE WALL...

...WHICH IS WHY I'M OFFERING TO BUY YOUR COMPANY FOR *THIRTEEN MILLION DOLLARS.*

CASH.

...

CAT?

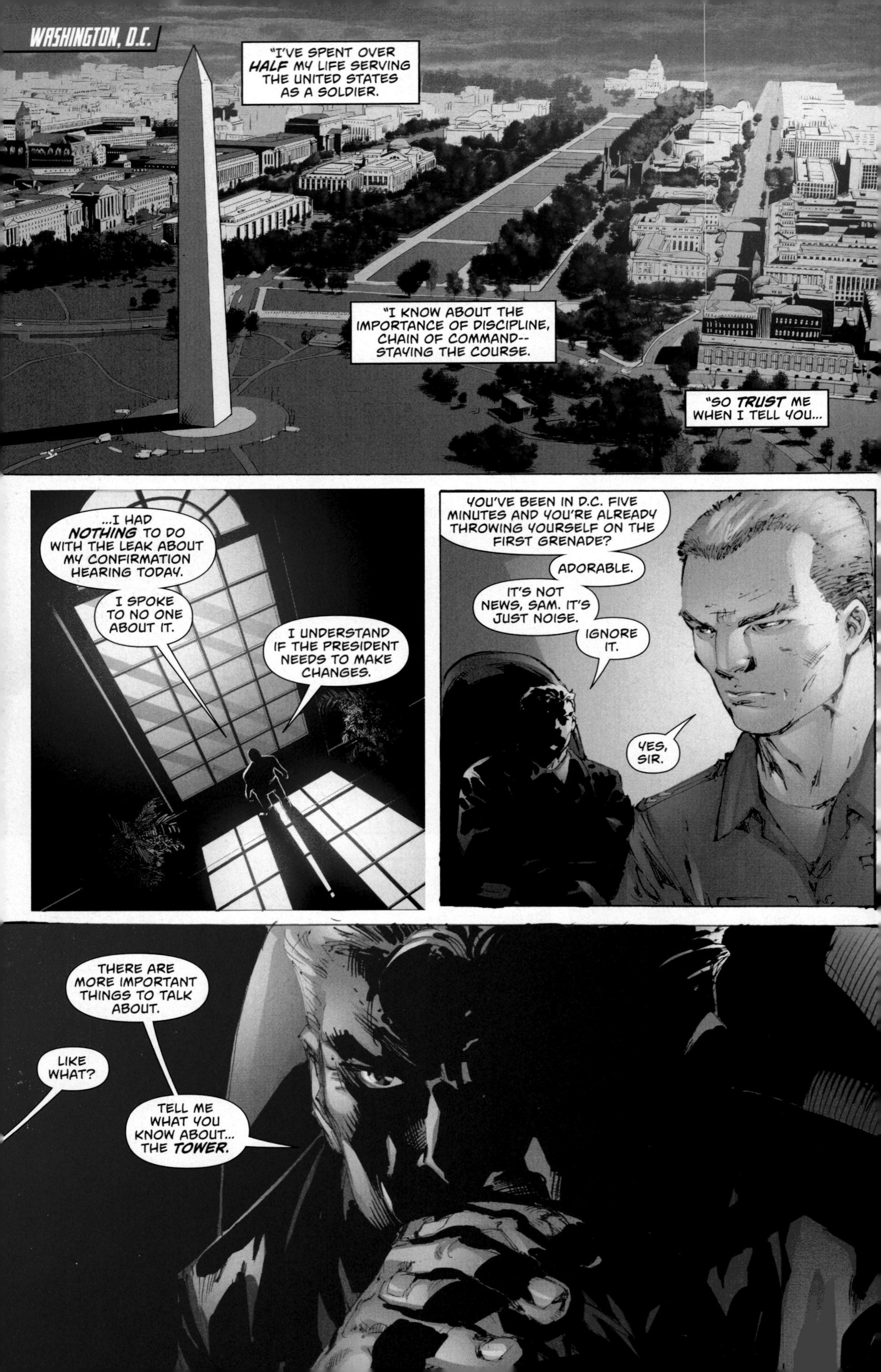
WASHINGTON, D.C.
"I'VE SPENT OVER HALF MY LIFE SERVING THE UNITED STATES AS A SOLDIER.
"I KNOW ABOUT THE IMPORTANCE OF DISCIPLINE, CHAIN OF COMMAND-- STAYING THE COURSE.
"SO TRUST ME WHEN I TELL YOU...
...I HAD NOTHING TO DO WITH THE LEAK ABOUT MY CONFIRMATION HEARING TODAY.
I SPOKE TO NO ONE ABOUT IT.
I UNDERSTAND IF THE PRESIDENT NEEDS TO MAKE CHANGES.
YOU'VE BEEN IN D.C. FIVE MINUTES AND YOU'RE ALREADY THROWING YOURSELF ON THE FIRST GRENADE?
ADORABLE.
IT'S NOT NEWS, SAM. IT'S JUST NOISE.
IGNORE IT.
YES, SIR.
THERE ARE MORE IMPORTANT THINGS TO TALK ABOUT.
LIKE WHAT?
TELL ME WHAT YOU KNOW ABOUT... THE TOWER.

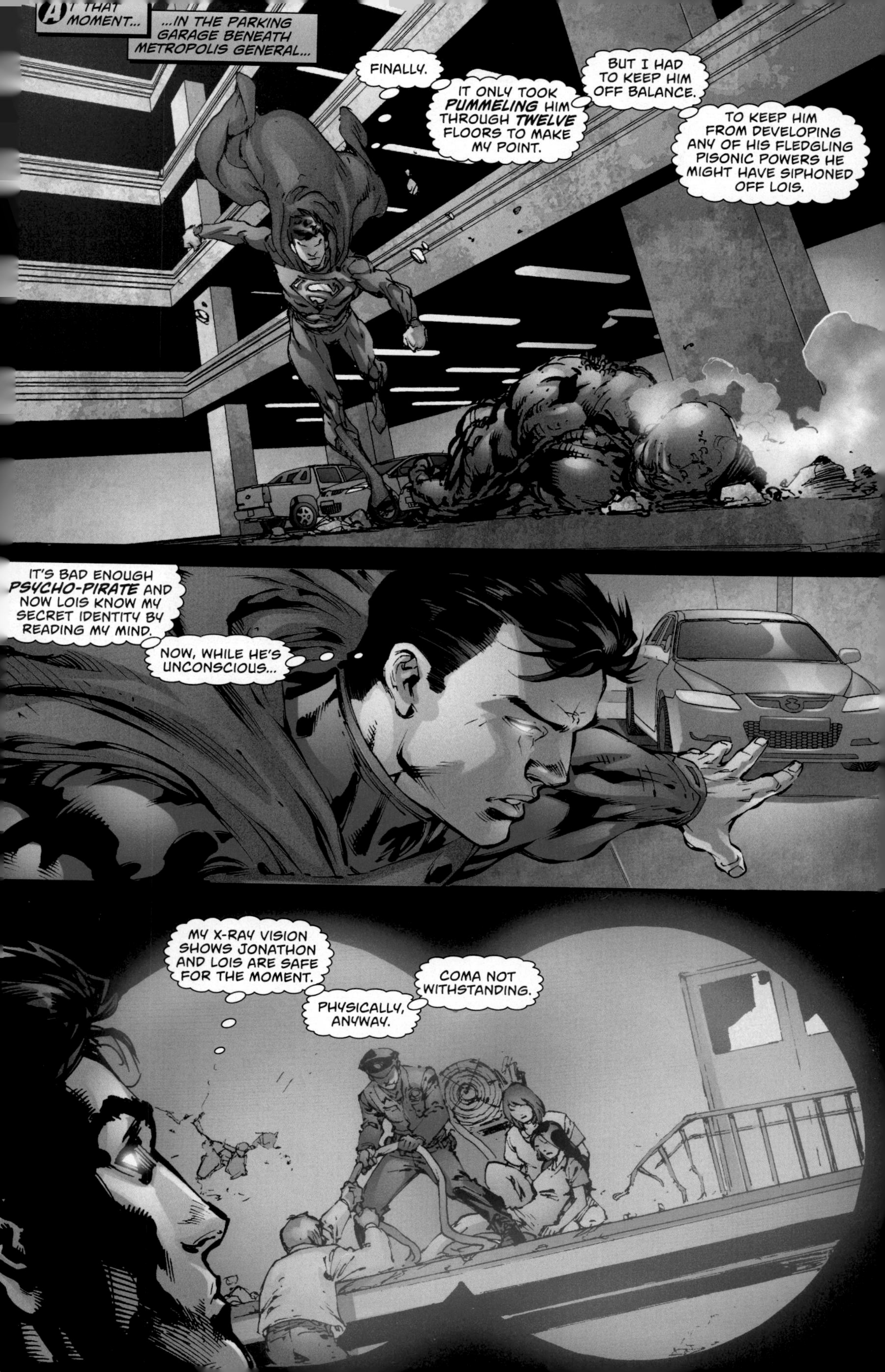
AT THAT MOMENT...
...IN THE PARKING GARAGE BENEATH METROPOLIS GENERAL...
FINALLY.
IT ONLY TOOK PUMMELING HIM THROUGH TWELVE FLOORS TO MAKE MY POINT.
BUT I HAD TO KEEP HIM OFF BALANCE.
TO KEEP HIM FROM DEVELOPING ANY OF HIS FLEDGLING PISONIC POWERS HE MIGHT HAVE SIPHONED OFF LOIS.
IT'S BAD ENOUGH PSYCHO-PIRATE AND NOW LOIS KNOW MY SECRET IDENTITY BY READING MY MIND.
NOW, WHILE HE'S UNCONSCIOUS...
MY X-RAY VISION SHOWS JONATHON AND LOIS ARE SAFE FOR THE MOMENT.
PHYSICALLY, ANYWAY.
COMA NOT WITHSTANDING.

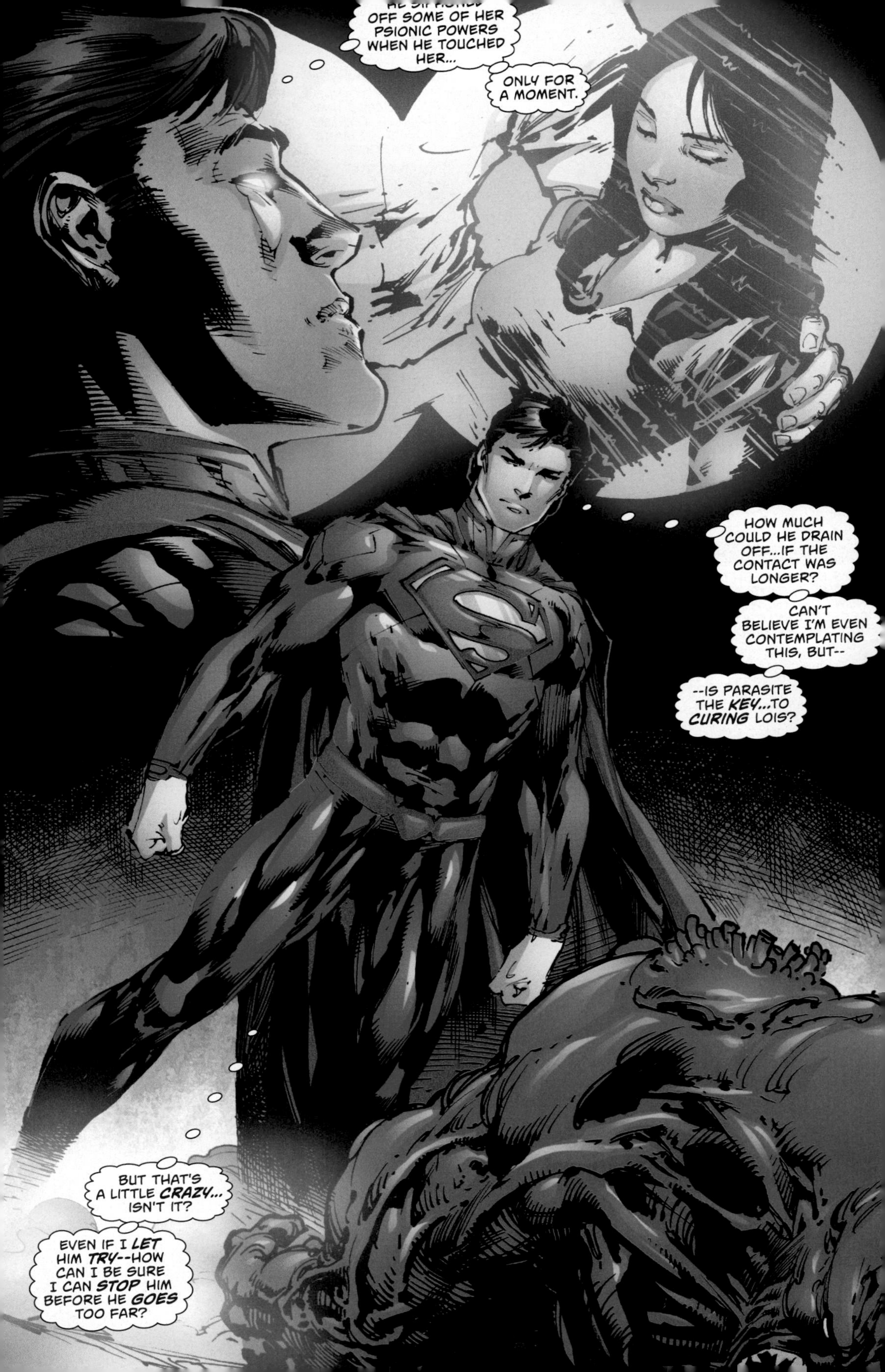
OFF SOME OF HER PSIONIC POWERS WHEN HE TOUCHED HER...
ONLY FOR A MOMENT.
HOW MUCH COULD HE DRAIN OFF...IF THE CONTACT WAS LONGER?
CAN'T BELIEVE I'M EVEN CONTEMPLATING THIS, BUT--
--IS PARASITE THE KEY...TO CURING LOIS?
BUT THAT'S A LITTLE CRAZY... ISN'T IT?
EVEN IF I LET HIM TRY--HOW CAN I BE SURE I CAN STOP HIM BEFORE HE GOES TOO FAR?

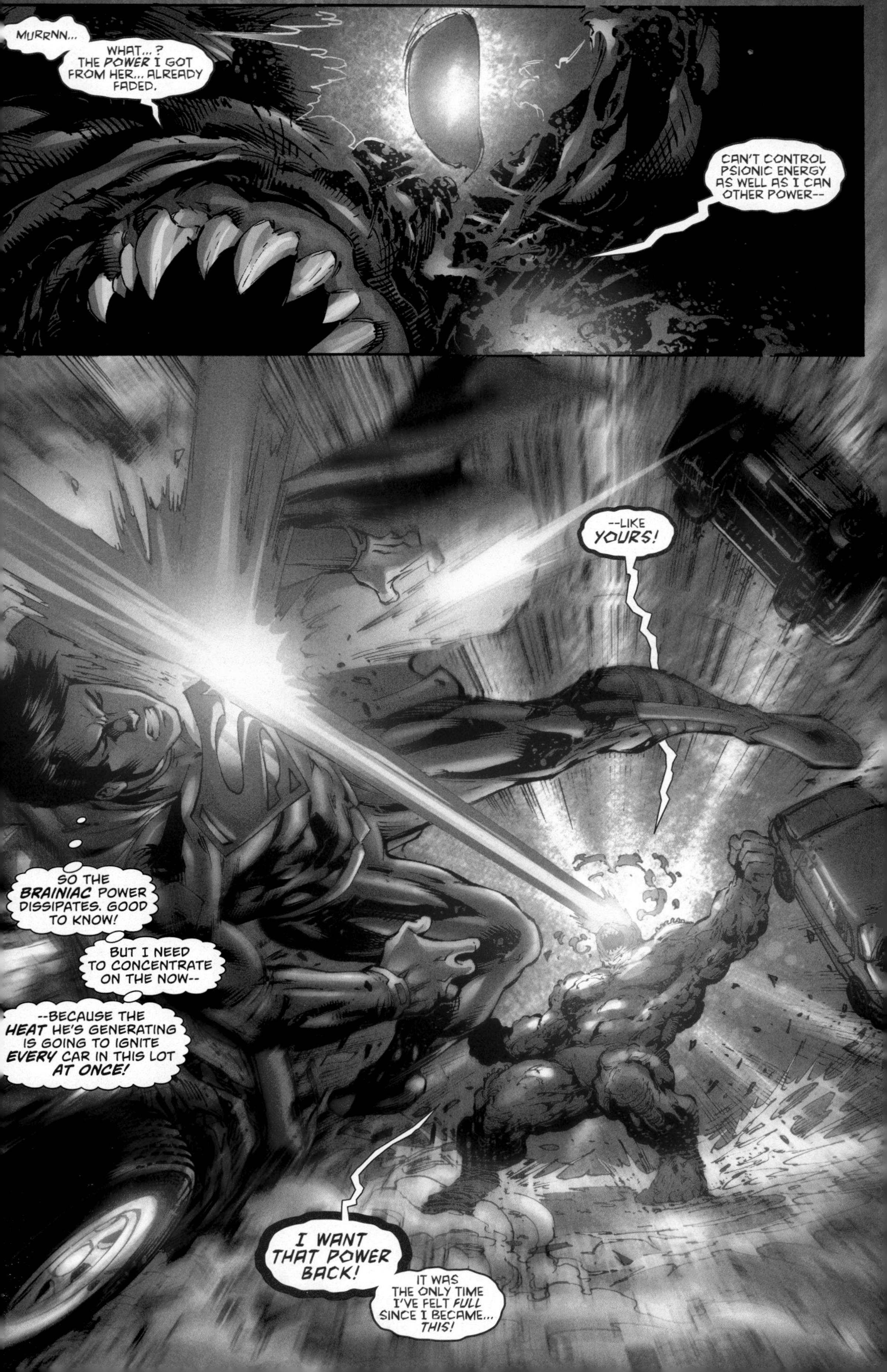
MURRNN...
WHAT...? THE POWER I GOT FROM HER... ALREADY FADED.
CAN'T CONTROL PSIONIC ENERGY AS WELL AS I CAN OTHER POWER--
--LIKE YOURS!
SO THE BRAINIAC POWER DISSIPATES. GOOD TO KNOW!
BUT I NEED TO CONCENTRATE ON THE NOW--
--BECAUSE THE HEAT HE'S GENERATING IS GOING TO IGNITE EVERY CAR IN THIS LOT AT ONCE!
I WANT THAT POWER BACK!
IT WAS THE ONLY TIME I'VE FELT FULL SINCE I BECAME... THIS!

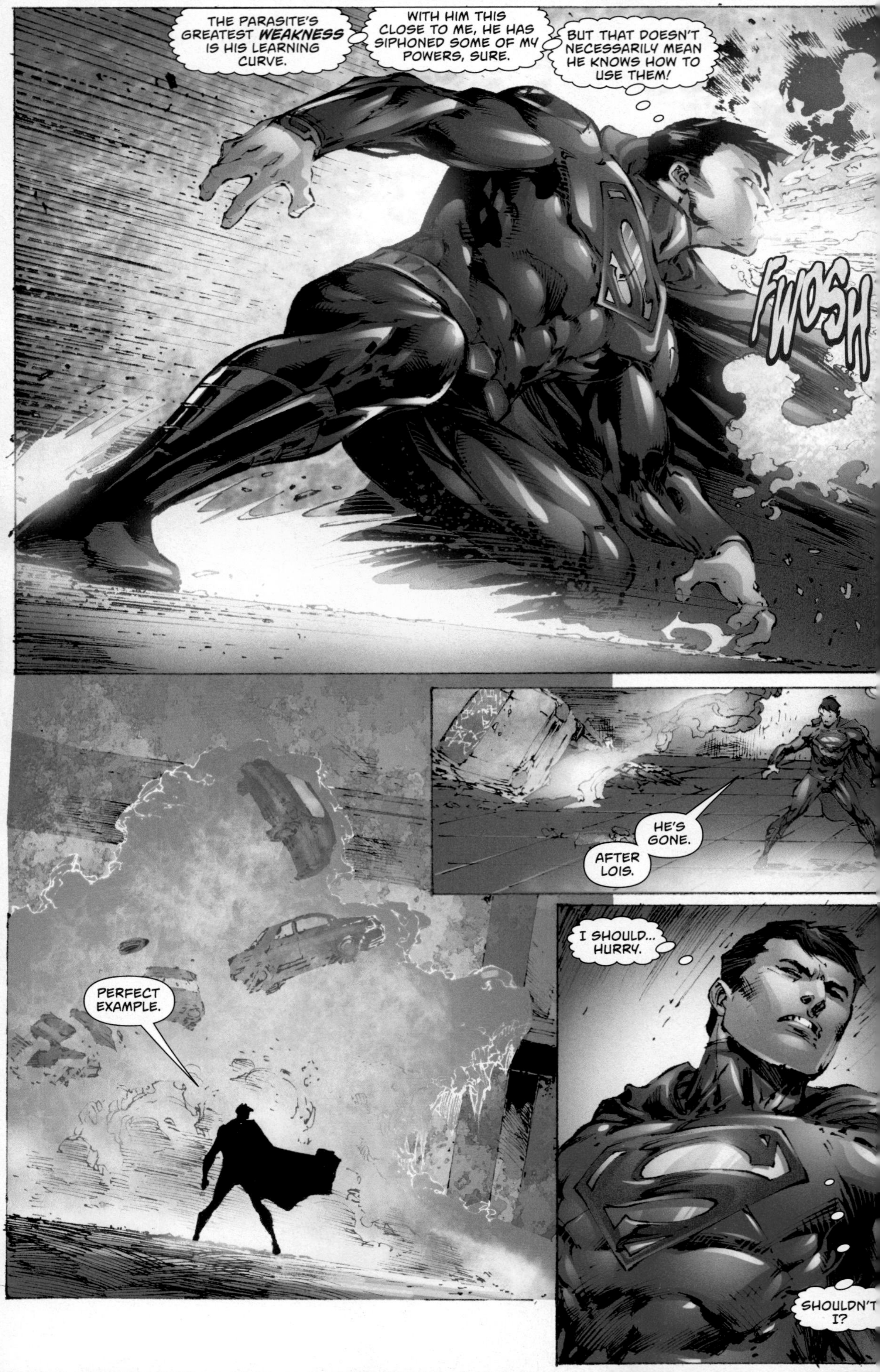
THE PARASITE'S GREATEST **WEAKNESS** IS HIS LEARNING CURVE.
WITH HIM THIS CLOSE TO ME, HE HAS SIPHONED SOME OF MY POWERS, SURE.
BUT THAT DOESN'T NECESSARILY MEAN HE KNOWS HOW TO USE THEM!
FWOSH
HE'S GONE.
AFTER LOIS.
PERFECT EXAMPLE.
I SHOULD... HURRY.
SHOULDN'T I?

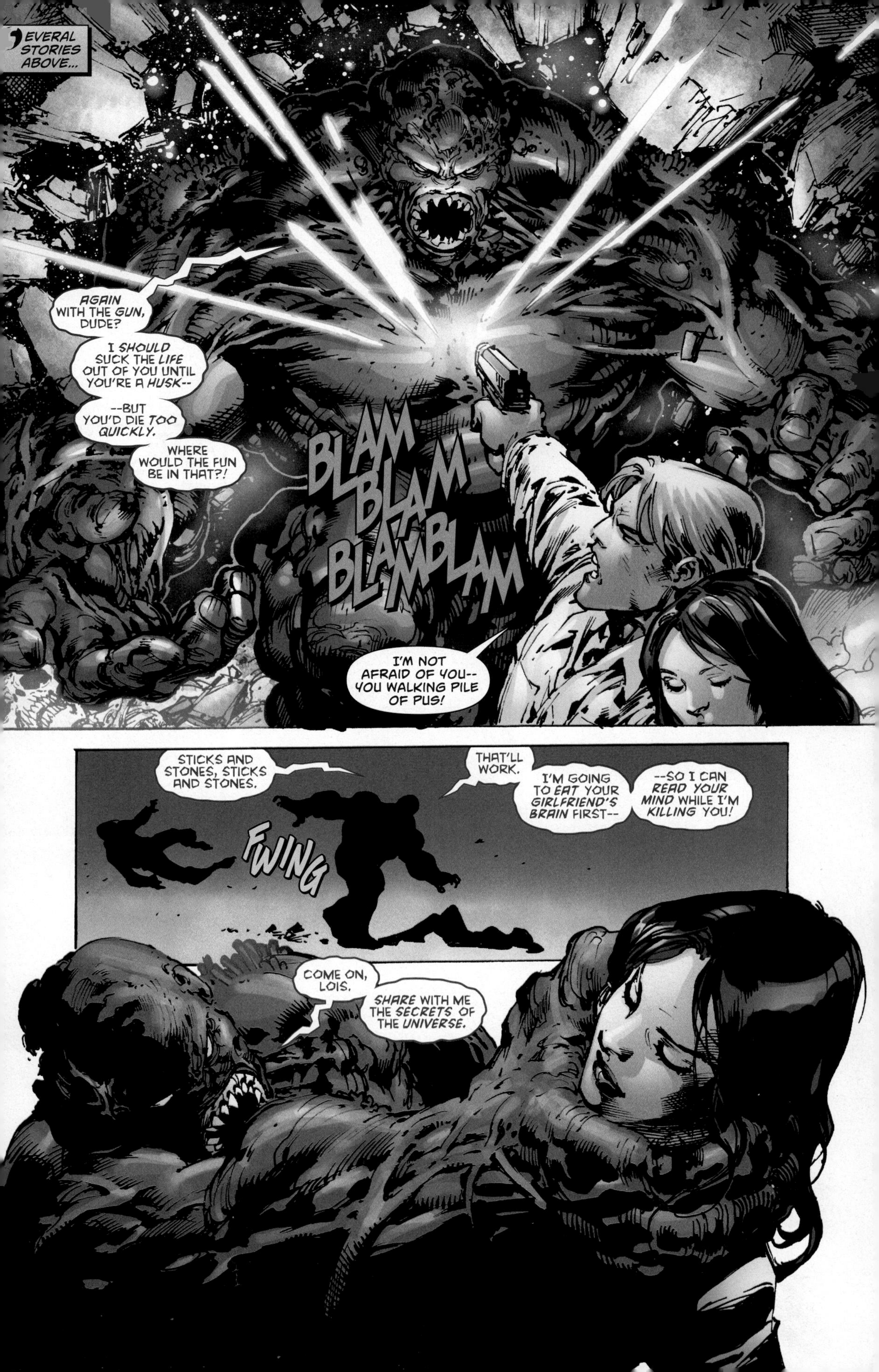
SEVERAL STORIES ABOVE...
AGAIN WITH THE GUN, DUDE?
I SHOULD SUCK THE LIFE OUT OF YOU UNTIL YOU'RE A HUSK--
--BUT YOU'D DIE TOO QUICKLY.
WHERE WOULD THE FUN BE IN THAT?!
BLAM BLAM BLAM BLAM BLAM
I'M NOT AFRAID OF YOU-- YOU WALKING PILE OF PUS!
STICKS AND STONES, STICKS AND STONES.
FWING
THAT'LL WORK.
I'M GOING TO EAT YOUR GIRLFRIEND'S BRAIN FIRST--
--SO I CAN READ YOUR MIND WHILE I'M KILLING YOU!
COME ON, LOIS.
SHARE WITH ME THE SECRETS OF THE UNIVERSE.

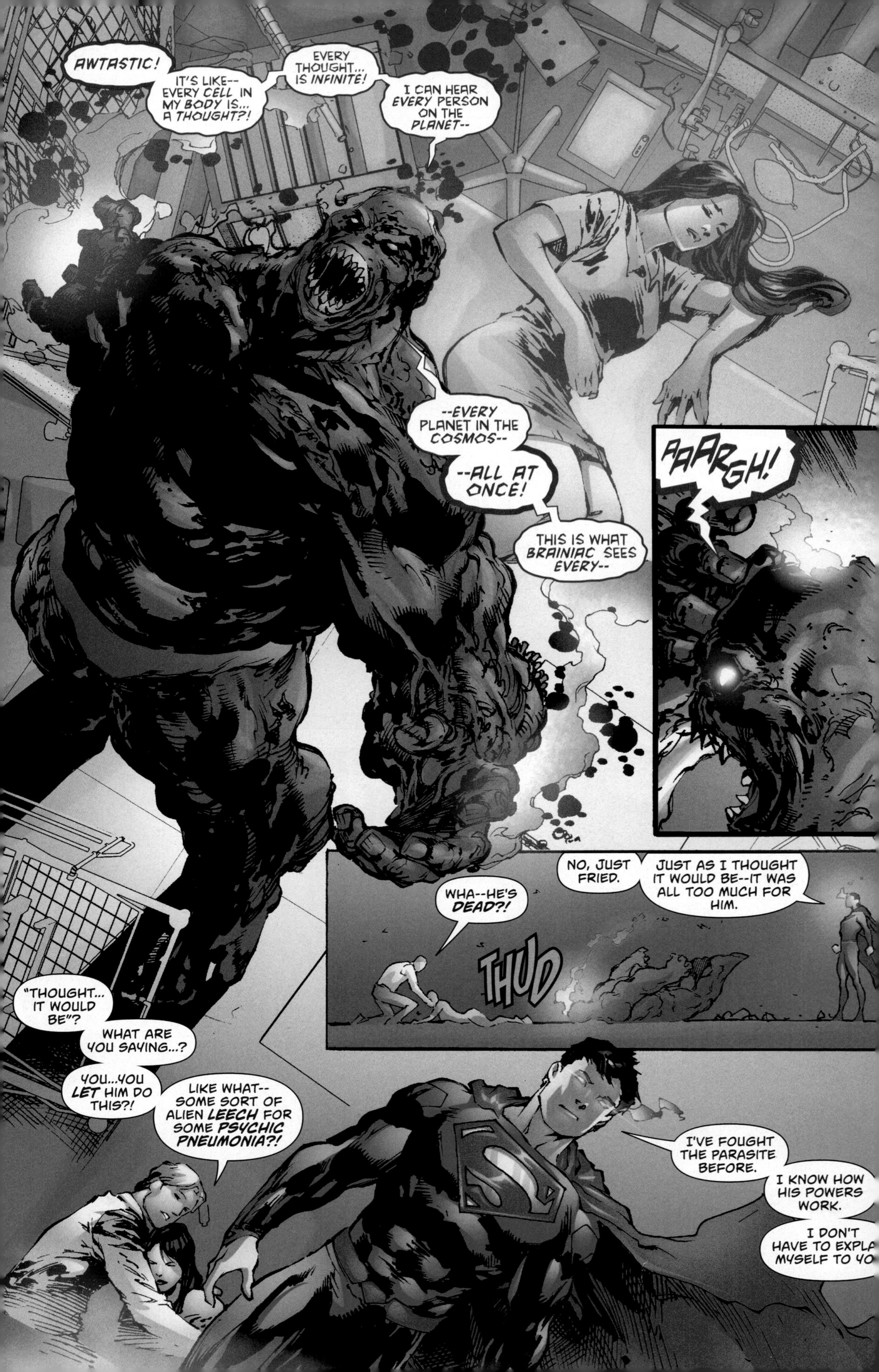

AWTASTIC!
IT'S LIKE-- EVERY CELL IN MY BODY IS... A THOUGHT?!
EVERY THOUGHT... IS INFINITE!
I CAN HEAR EVERY PERSON ON THE PLANET--
--EVERY PLANET IN THE COSMOS--
--ALL AT ONCE!
THIS IS WHAT BRAINIAC SEES EVERY--
AAARGH!
THUD
WHA--HE'S DEAD?!
NO, JUST FRIED.
JUST AS I THOUGHT IT WOULD BE--IT WAS ALL TOO MUCH FOR HIM.
"THOUGHT... IT WOULD BE"?
WHAT ARE YOU SAYING...?
YOU...YOU LET HIM DO THIS?!
LIKE WHAT-- SOME SORT OF ALIEN LEECH FOR SOME PSYCHIC PNEUMONIA?!
I'VE FOUGHT THE PARASITE BEFORE.
I KNOW HOW HIS POWERS WORK.
I DON'T HAVE TO EXPLA MYSELF TO YO

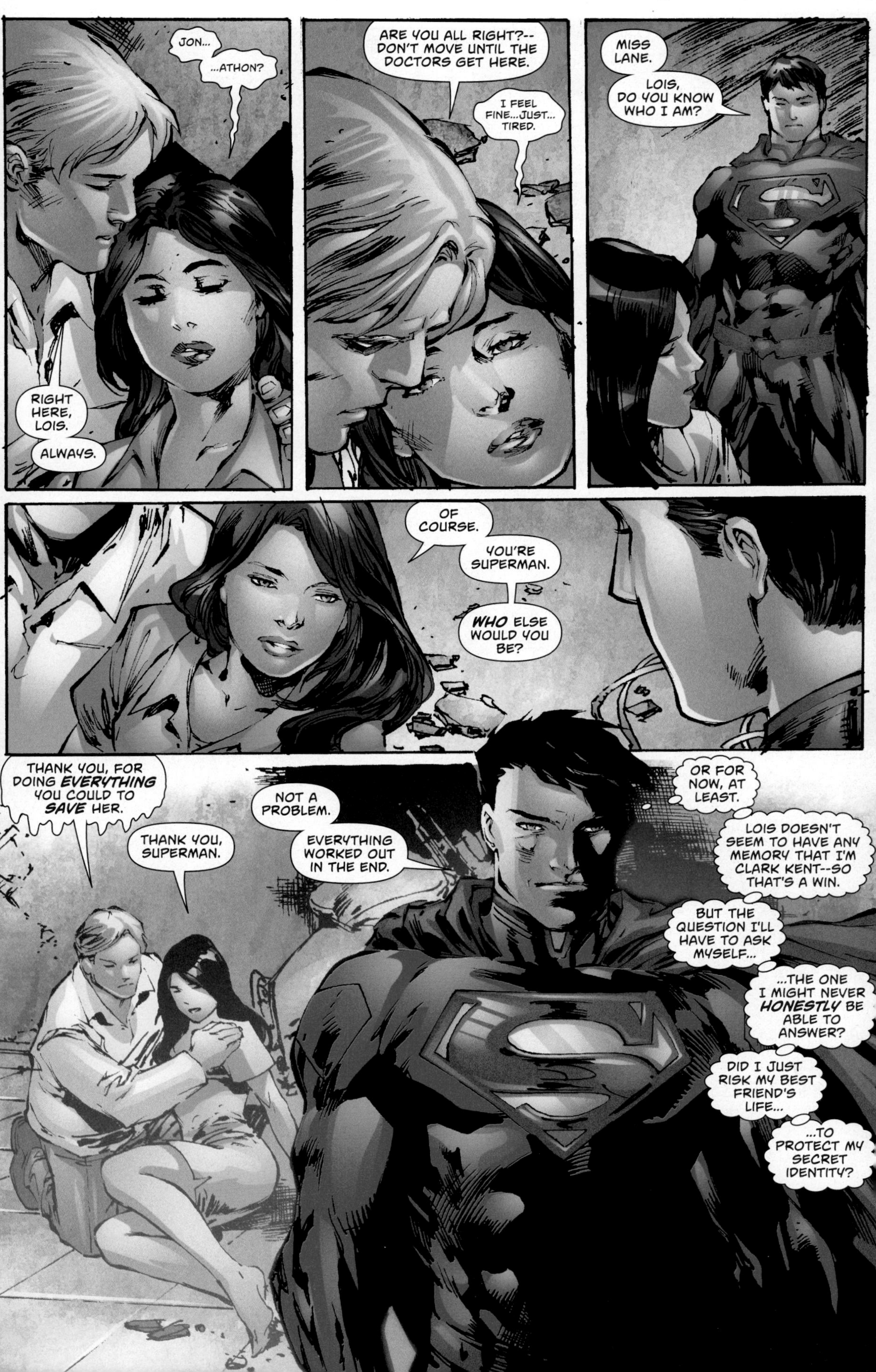
JON...
...ATHON?
RIGHT HERE, LOIS.
ALWAYS.
ARE YOU ALL RIGHT?--DON'T MOVE UNTIL THE DOCTORS GET HERE.
I FEEL FINE...JUST...TIRED.
MISS LANE.
LOIS, DO YOU KNOW WHO I AM?
OF COURSE.
YOU'RE SUPERMAN.
WHO ELSE WOULD YOU BE?
THANK YOU, FOR DOING EVERYTHING YOU COULD TO SAVE HER.
THANK YOU, SUPERMAN.
NOT A PROBLEM.
EVERYTHING WORKED OUT IN THE END.
OR FOR NOW, AT LEAST.
LOIS DOESN'T SEEM TO HAVE ANY MEMORY THAT I'M CLARK KENT--SO THAT'S A WIN.
BUT THE QUESTION I'LL HAVE TO ASK MYSELF...
...THE ONE I MIGHT NEVER HONESTLY BE ABLE TO ANSWER?
DID I JUST RISK MY BEST FRIEND'S LIFE...
...TO PROTECT MY SECRET IDENTITY?

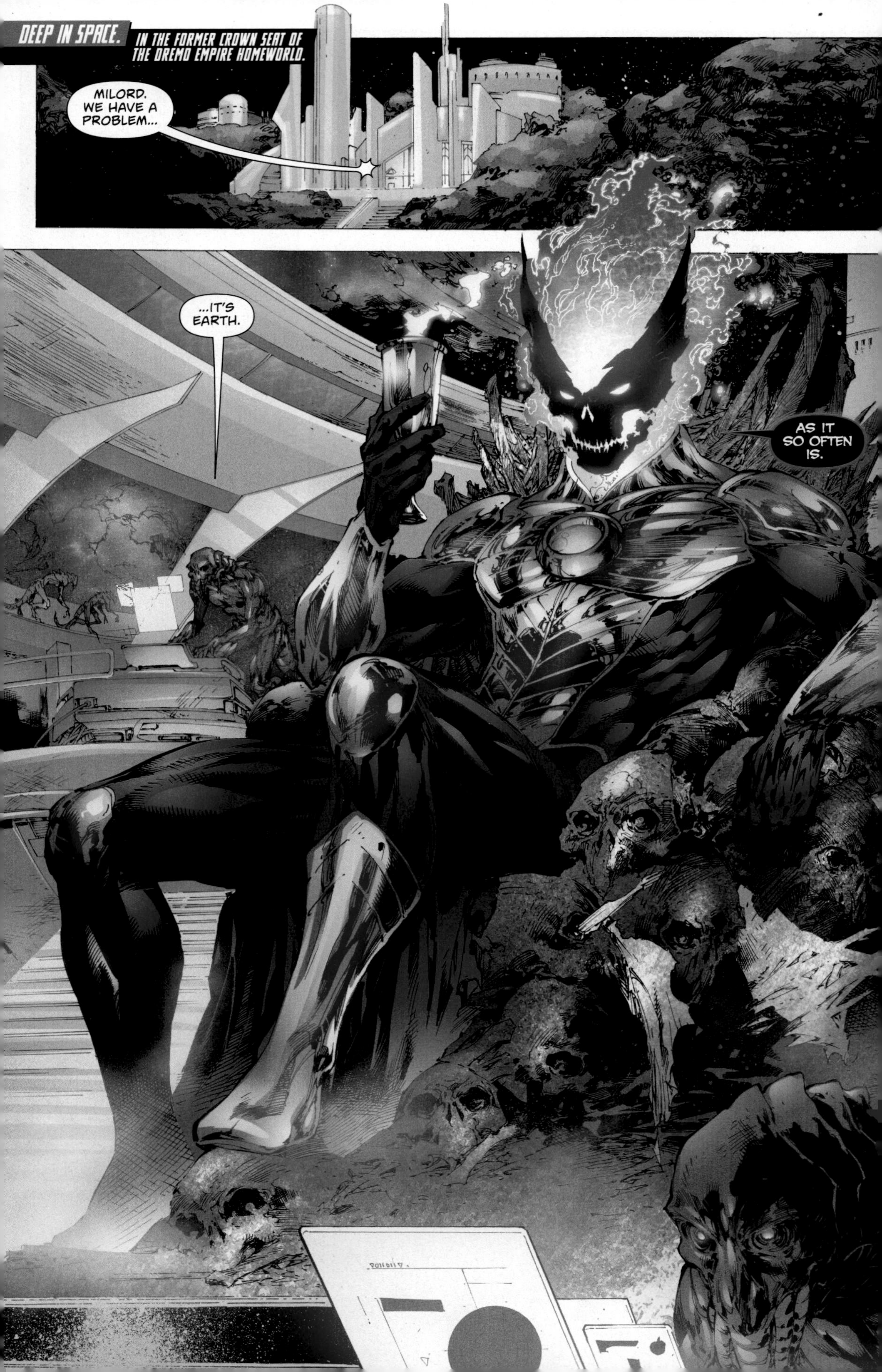
DEEP IN SPACE.
IN THE FORMER CROWN SEAT OF THE DREMO EMPIRE HOMEWORLD.
MILORD. WE HAVE A PROBLEM...
...IT'S EARTH.
AS IT SO OFTEN IS.

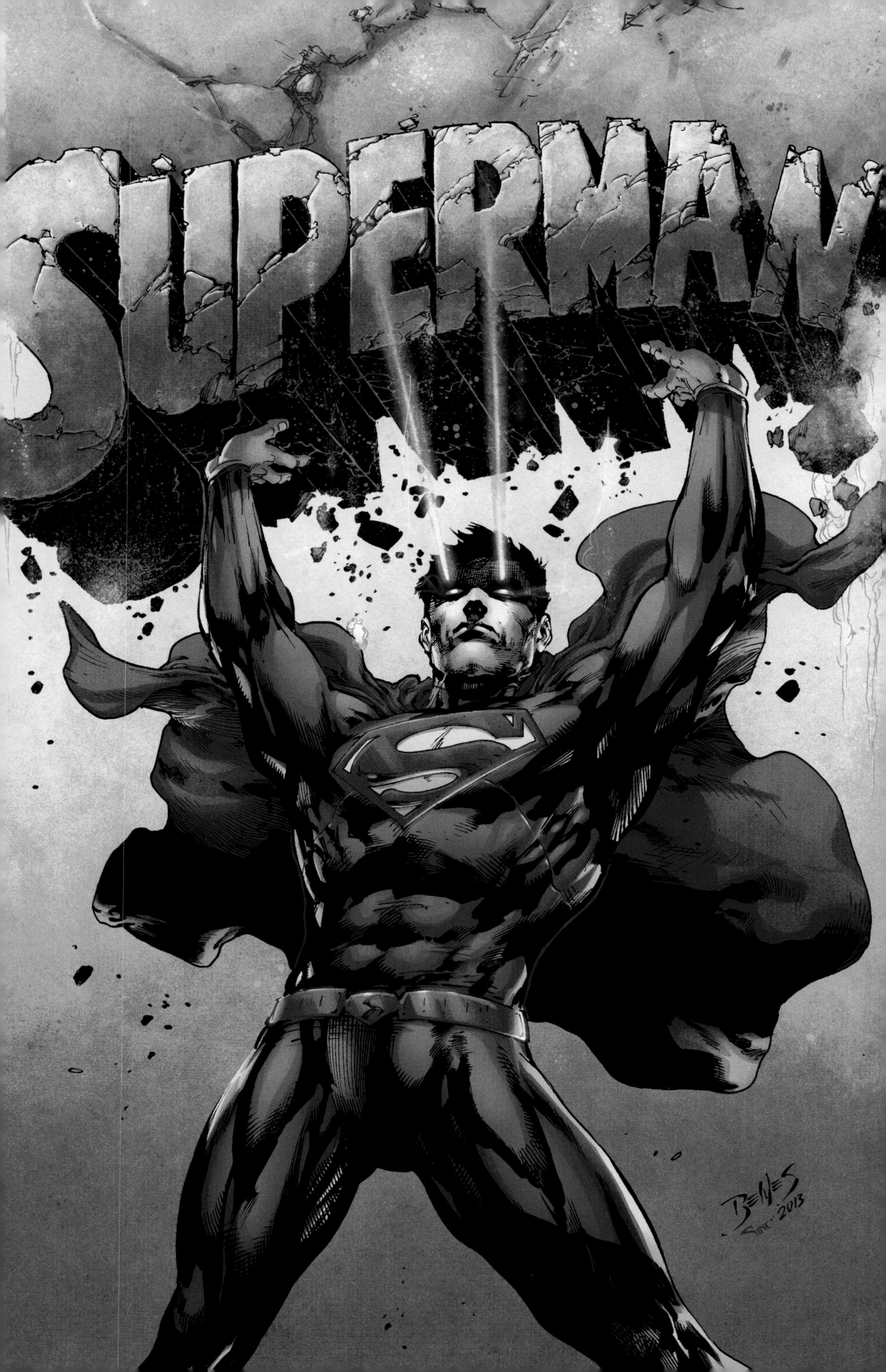
SUPERMAN

UNDER FIRE

SCOTT LOBDELL writer **BRETT BOOTH** penciller **NORM RAPMUND** inker **ANDREW DALHOUSE** colorist
cover art by **ED BENES** and **ALEX SINCLAIR**

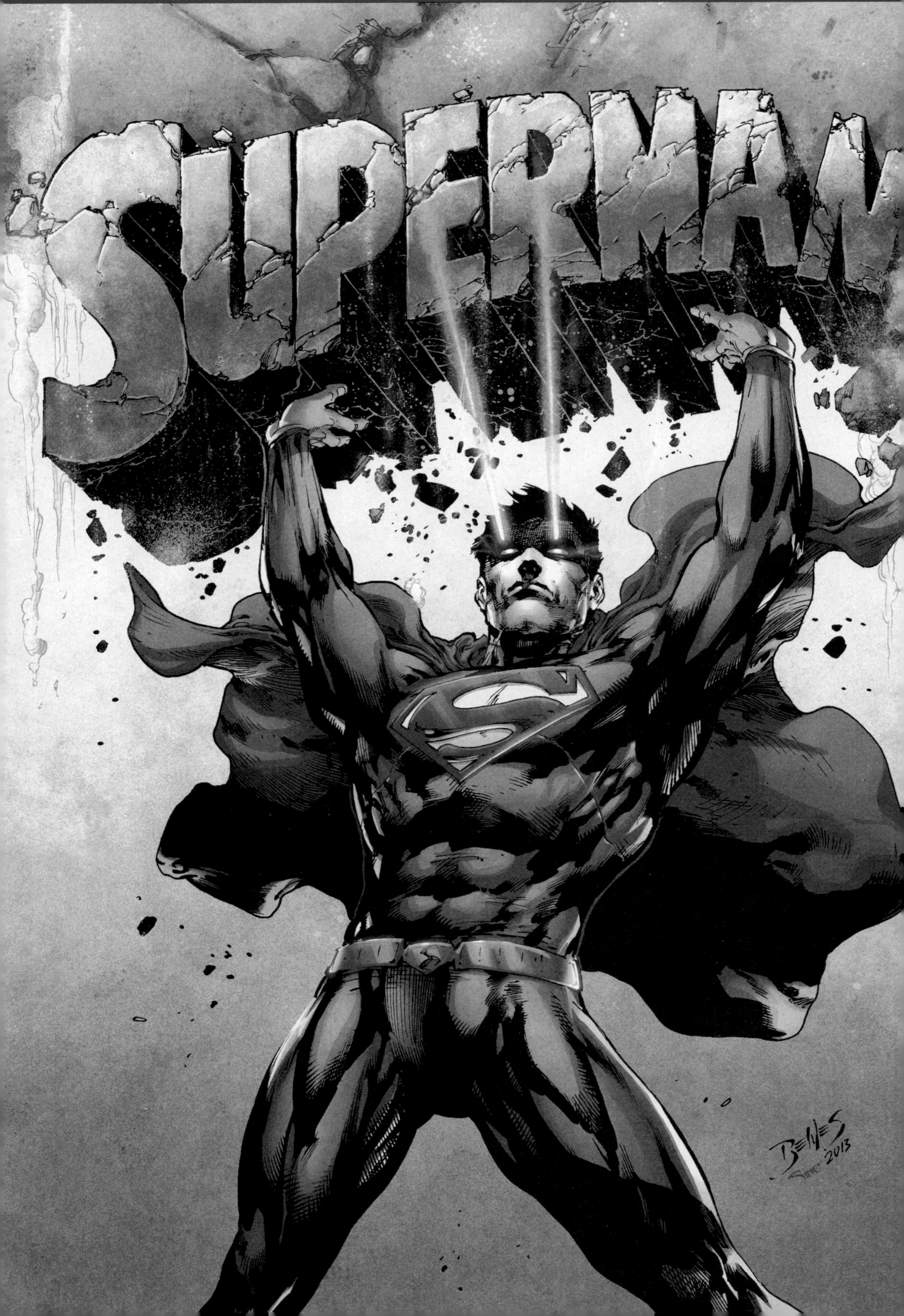

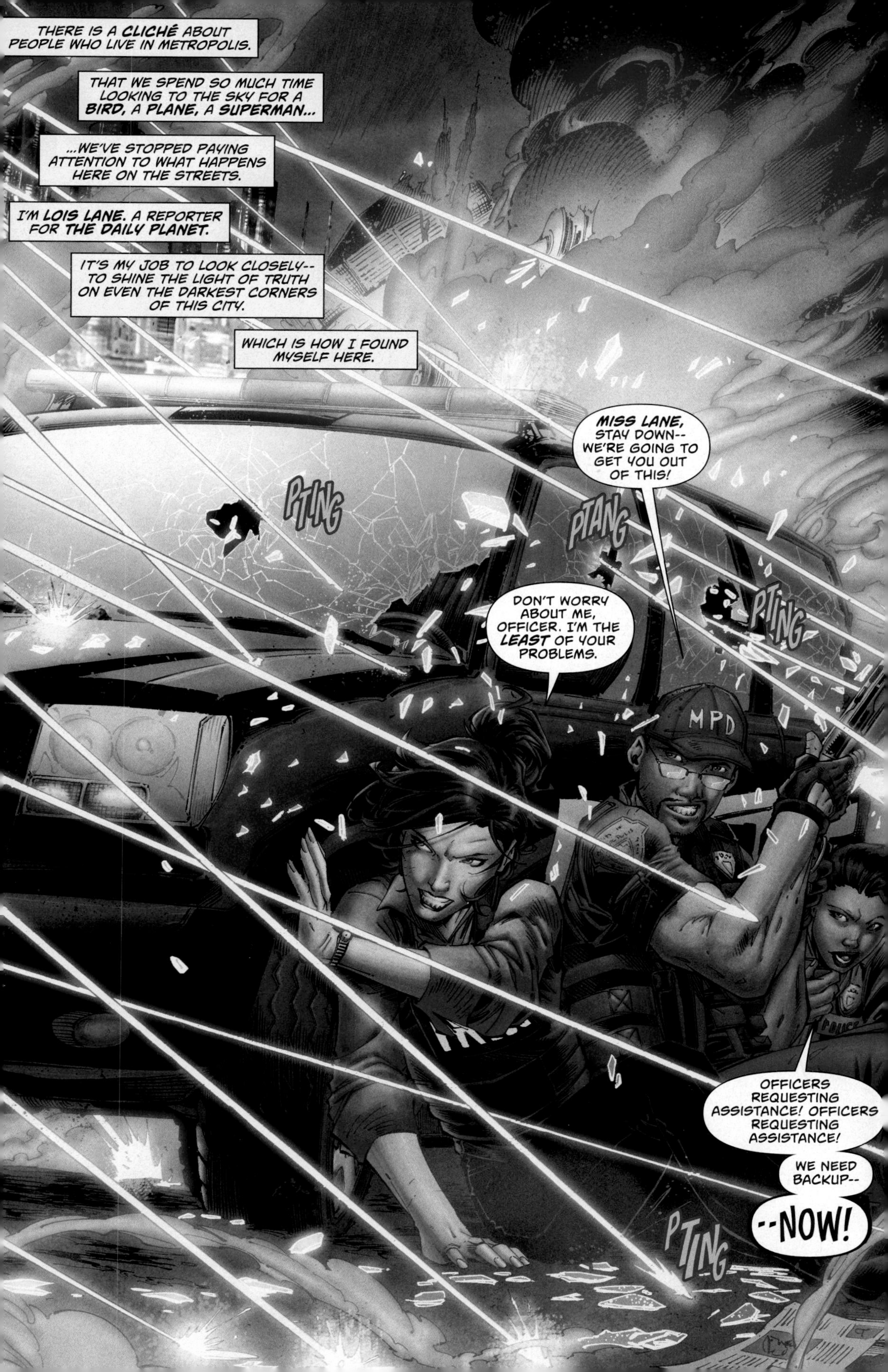
THERE IS A CLICHÉ ABOUT PEOPLE WHO LIVE IN METROPOLIS.
THAT WE SPEND SO MUCH TIME LOOKING TO THE SKY FOR A BIRD, A PLANE, A SUPERMAN...
...WE'VE STOPPED PAYING ATTENTION TO WHAT HAPPENS HERE ON THE STREETS.
I'M LOIS LANE. A REPORTER FOR THE DAILY PLANET.
IT'S MY JOB TO LOOK CLOSELY-- TO SHINE THE LIGHT OF TRUTH ON EVEN THE DARKEST CORNERS OF THIS CITY.
WHICH IS HOW I FOUND MYSELF HERE.
PTING
PTANG
MISS LANE, STAY DOWN-- WE'RE GOING TO GET YOU OUT OF THIS!
PTING
DON'T WORRY ABOUT ME, OFFICER. I'M THE LEAST OF YOUR PROBLEMS.
MPD
OFFICERS REQUESTING ASSISTANCE! OFFICERS REQUESTING ASSISTANCE!
WE NEED BACKUP--
--NOW!
PTING

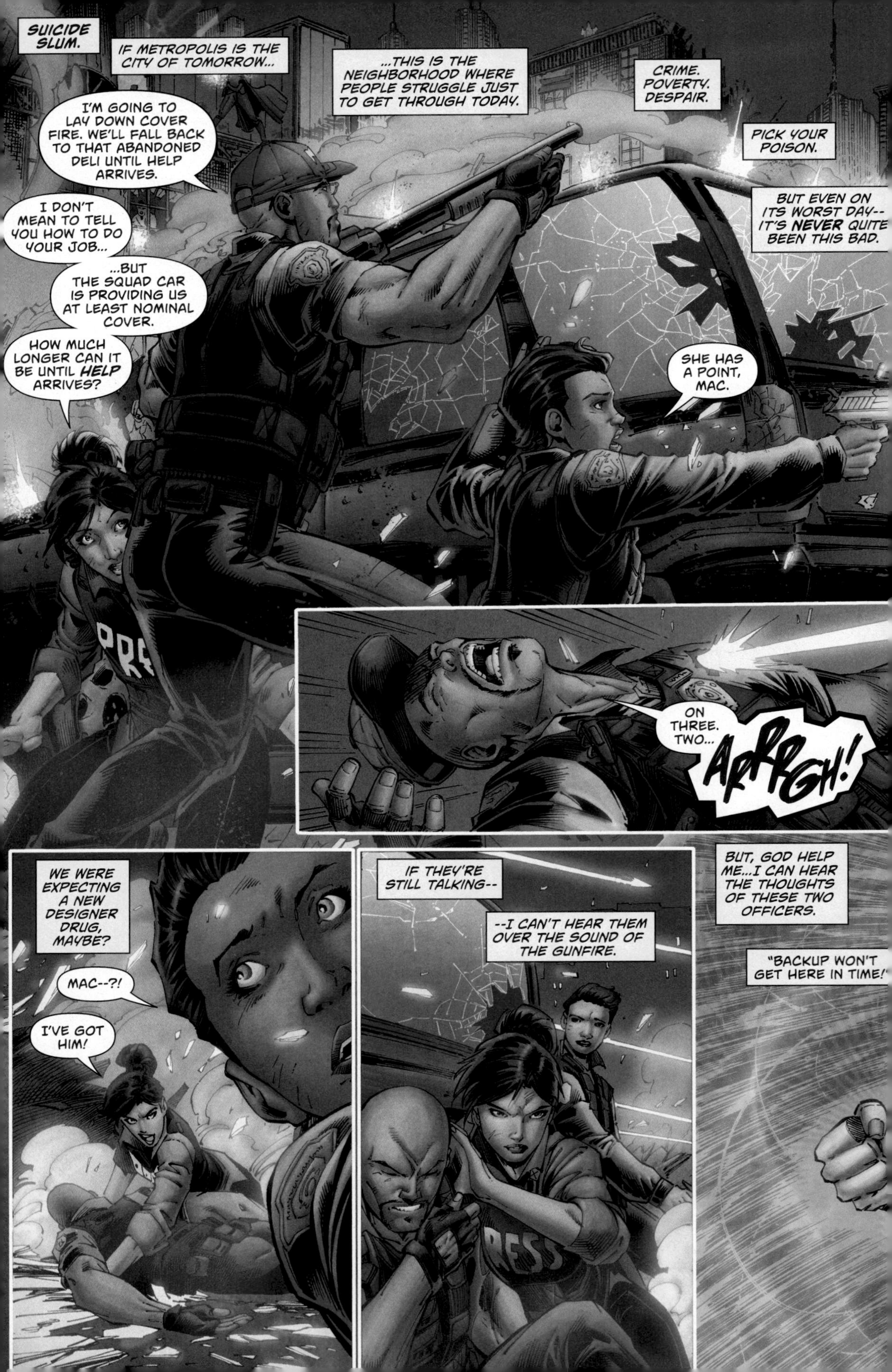
SUICIDE SLUM.
IF METROPOLIS IS THE CITY OF TOMORROW...
...THIS IS THE NEIGHBORHOOD WHERE PEOPLE STRUGGLE JUST TO GET THROUGH TODAY.
CRIME. POVERTY. DESPAIR.
PICK YOUR POISON.
BUT EVEN ON ITS WORST DAY--IT'S NEVER QUITE BEEN THIS BAD.
I'M GOING TO LAY DOWN COVER FIRE. WE'LL FALL BACK TO THAT ABANDONED DELI UNTIL HELP ARRIVES.
I DON'T MEAN TO TELL YOU HOW TO DO YOUR JOB...
...BUT THE SQUAD CAR IS PROVIDING US AT LEAST NOMINAL COVER.
HOW MUCH LONGER CAN IT BE UNTIL HELP ARRIVES?
SHE HAS A POINT, MAC.
ON THREE. TWO...
ARRRGH!
WE WERE EXPECTING A NEW DESIGNER DRUG, MAYBE?
MAC--?!
I'VE GOT HIM!
IF THEY'RE STILL TALKING--
--I CAN'T HEAR THEM OVER THE SOUND OF THE GUNFIRE.
BUT, GOD HELP ME...I CAN HEAR THE THOUGHTS OF THESE TWO OFFICERS.
"BACKUP WON'T GET HERE IN TIME!"

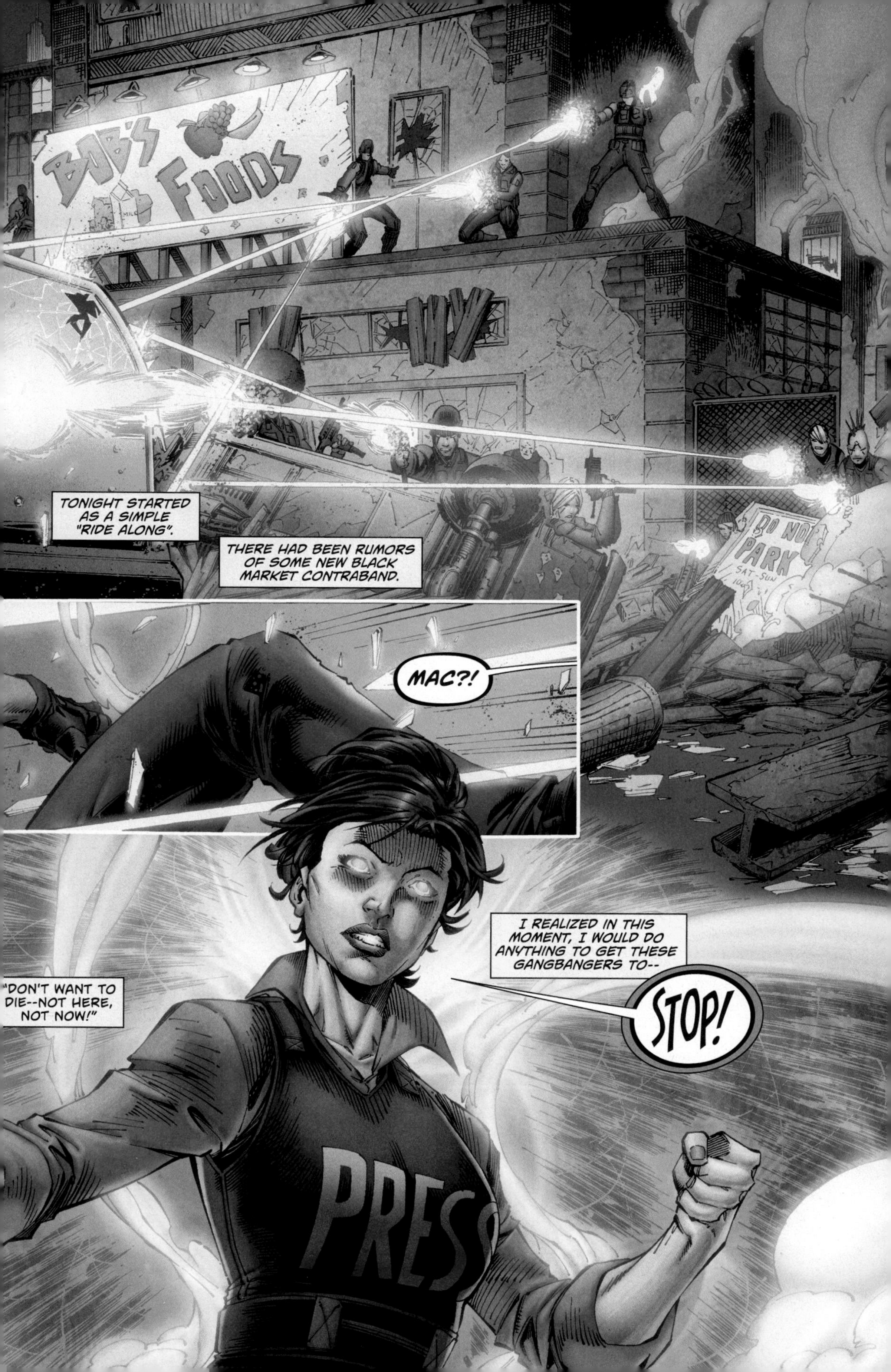
BOB'S
FOODS
MILK
TONIGHT STARTED AS A SIMPLE "RIDE ALONG".
THERE HAD BEEN RUMORS OF SOME NEW BLACK MARKET CONTRABAND.
DO NOT PARK
SAT-SUN
MAC?!
"DON'T WANT TO DIE--NOT HERE, NOT NOW!"
I REALIZED IN THIS MOMENT, I WOULD DO ANYTHING TO GET THESE GANGBANGERS TO--
STOP!
PRES

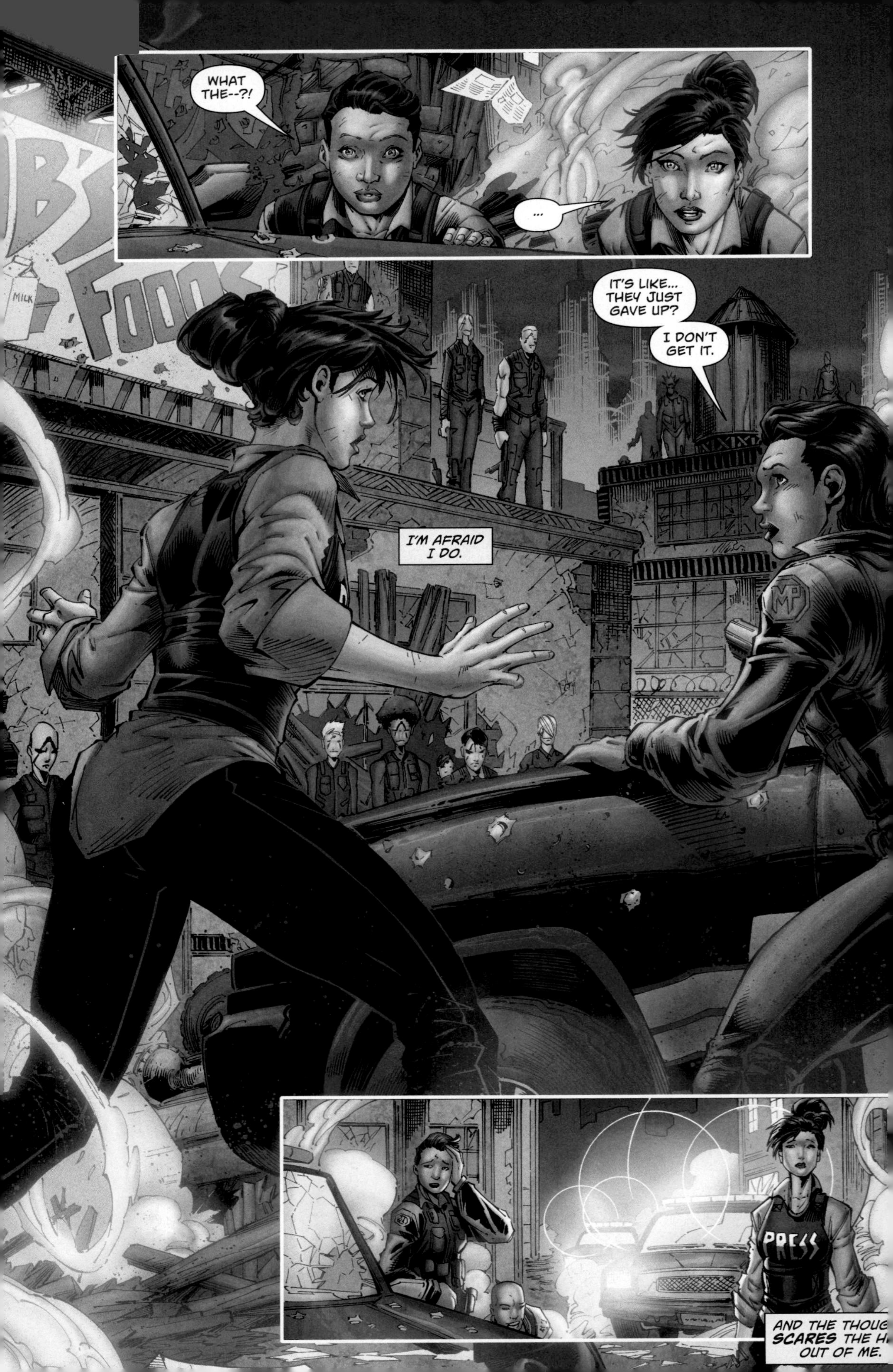
WHAT THE--?!
...
IT'S LIKE... THEY JUST GAVE UP?
I DON'T GET IT.
I'M AFRAID I DO.
MILK
AND THE THOUG SCARES THE H OUT OF ME.

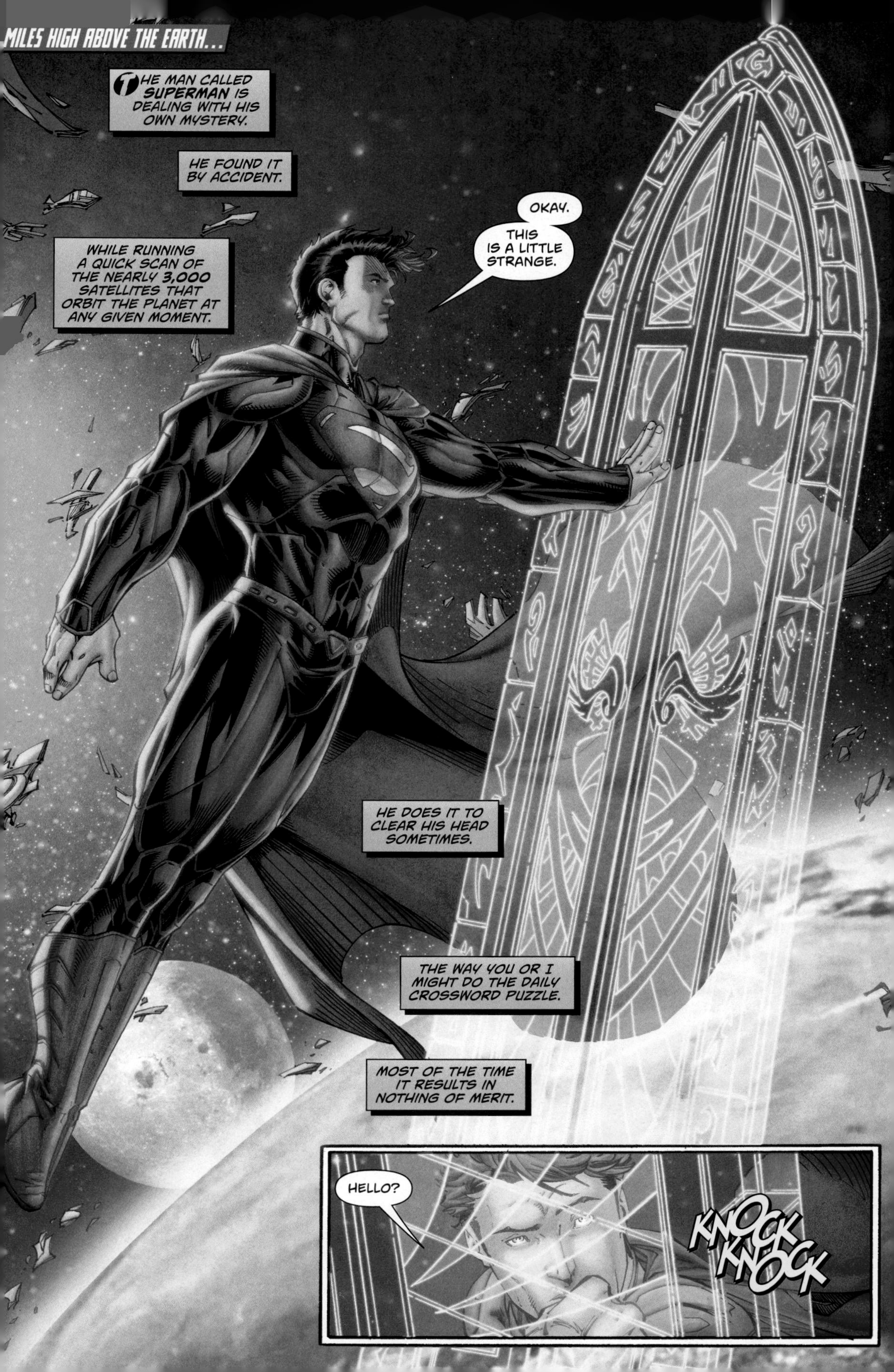
MILES HIGH ABOVE THE EARTH...
THE MAN CALLED SUPERMAN IS DEALING WITH HIS OWN MYSTERY.
HE FOUND IT BY ACCIDENT.
WHILE RUNNING A QUICK SCAN OF THE NEARLY 3,000 SATELLITES THAT ORBIT THE PLANET AT ANY GIVEN MOMENT.
OKAY.
THIS IS A LITTLE STRANGE.
HE DOES IT TO CLEAR HIS HEAD SOMETIMES.
THE WAY YOU OR I MIGHT DO THE DAILY CROSSWORD PUZZLE.
MOST OF THE TIME IT RESULTS IN NOTHING OF MERIT.
HELLO?
KNOCK KNOCK

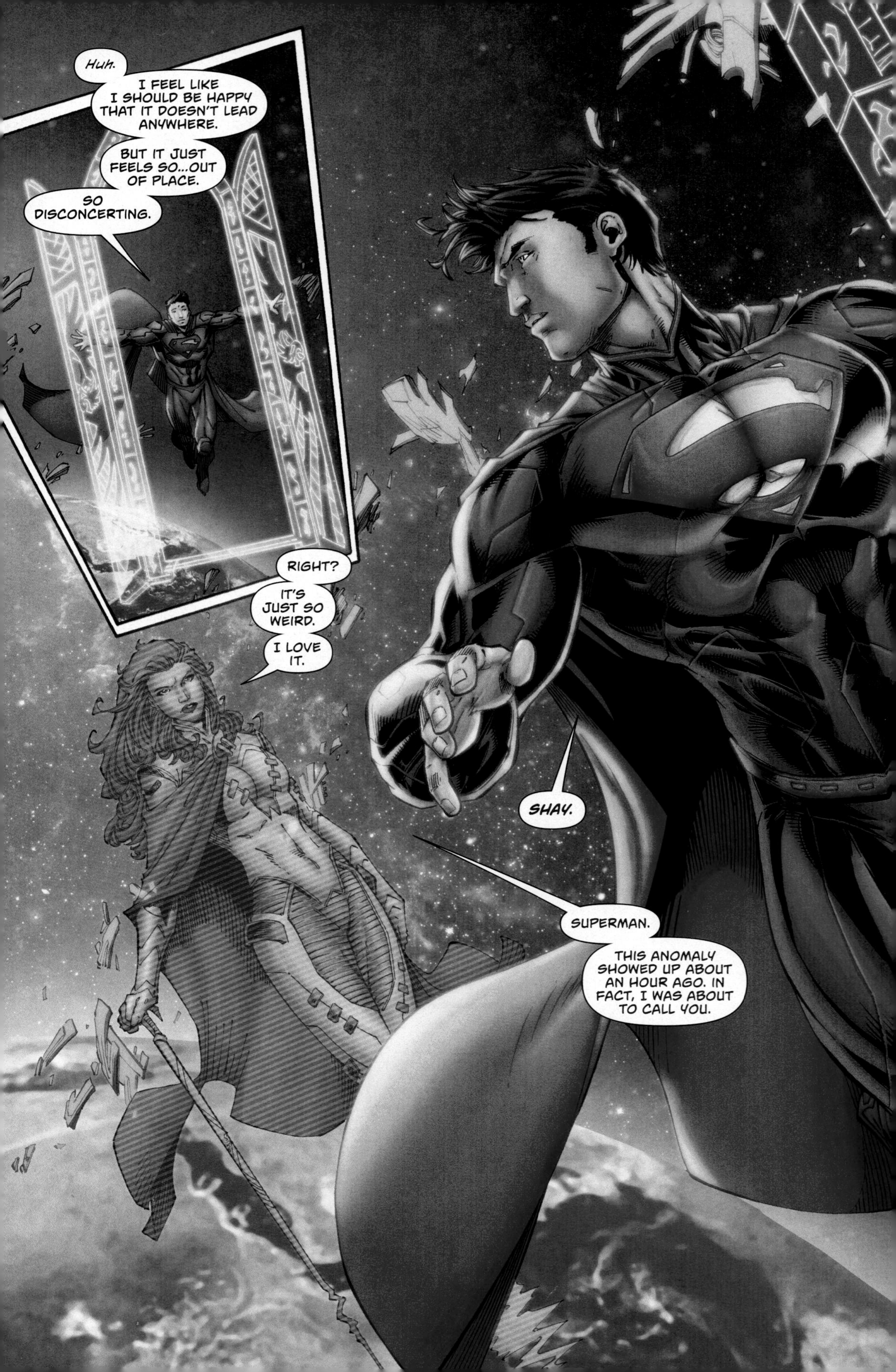

Huh.
I FEEL LIKE I SHOULD BE HAPPY THAT IT DOESN'T LEAD ANYWHERE.
BUT IT JUST FEELS SO...OUT OF PLACE.
SO DISCONCERTING.
RIGHT?
IT'S JUST SO WEIRD.
I LOVE IT.
SHAY.
SUPERMAN.
THIS ANOMALY SHOWED UP ABOUT AN HOUR AGO. IN FACT, I WAS ABOUT TO CALL YOU.

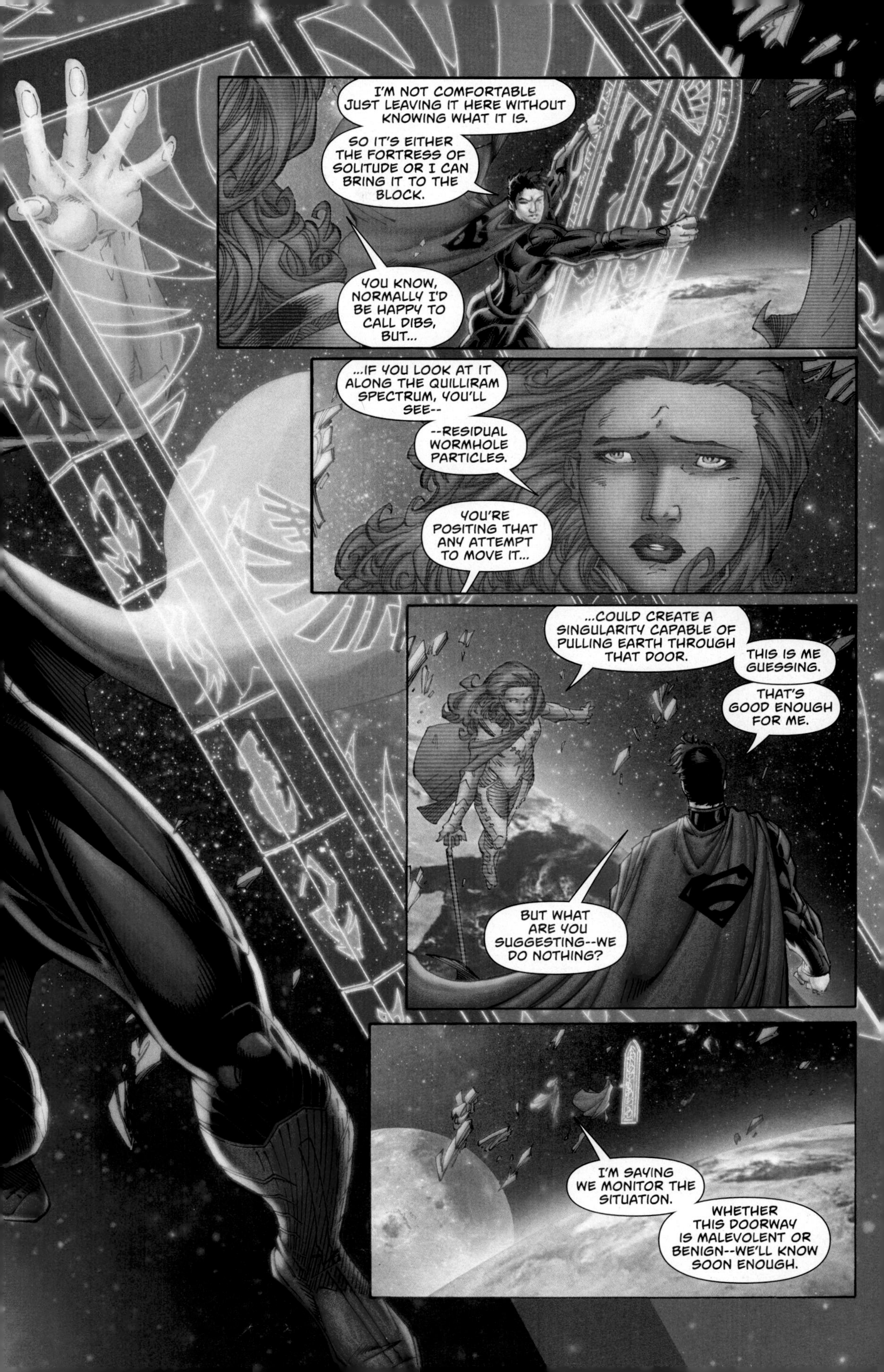
I'M NOT COMFORTABLE JUST LEAVING IT HERE WITHOUT KNOWING WHAT IT IS.
SO IT'S EITHER THE FORTRESS OF SOLITUDE OR I CAN BRING IT TO THE BLOCK.
YOU KNOW, NORMALLY I'D BE HAPPY TO CALL DIBS, BUT...
...IF YOU LOOK AT IT ALONG THE QUILLIRAM SPECTRUM, YOU'LL SEE--
--RESIDUAL WORMHOLE PARTICLES.
YOU'RE POSITING THAT ANY ATTEMPT TO MOVE IT...
...COULD CREATE A SINGULARITY CAPABLE OF PULLING EARTH THROUGH THAT DOOR.
THIS IS ME GUESSING.
THAT'S GOOD ENOUGH FOR ME.
BUT WHAT ARE YOU SUGGESTING--WE DO NOTHING?
I'M SAYING WE MONITOR THE SITUATION.
WHETHER THIS DOORWAY IS MALEVOLENT OR BENIGN--WE'LL KNOW SOON ENOUGH.

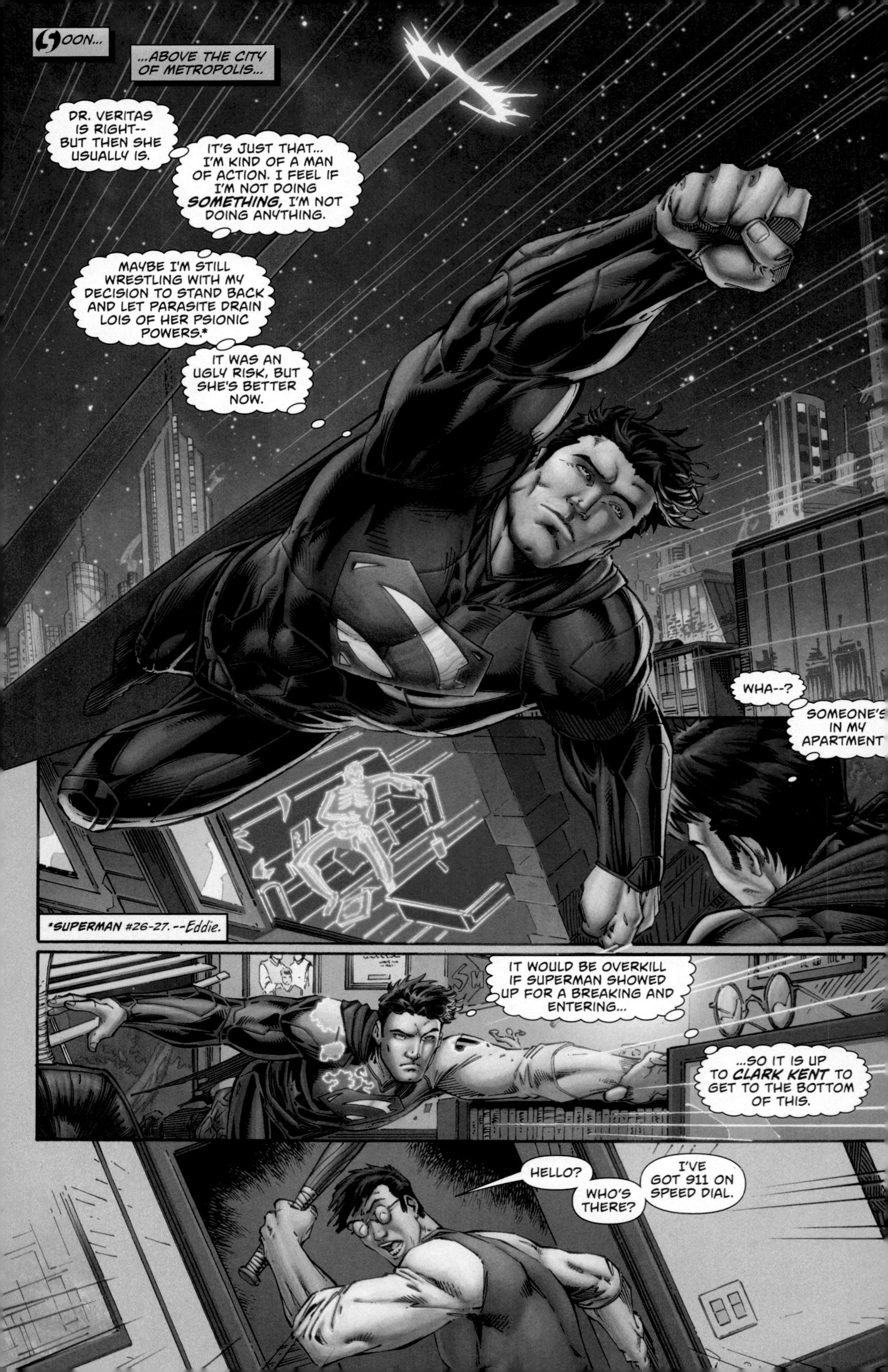
SOON...
...ABOVE THE CITY OF METROPOLIS...
DR. VERITAS IS RIGHT-- BUT THEN SHE USUALLY IS.
IT'S JUST THAT... I'M KIND OF A MAN OF ACTION. I FEEL IF I'M NOT DOING SOMETHING, I'M NOT DOING ANYTHING.
MAYBE I'M STILL WRESTLING WITH MY DECISION TO STAND BACK AND LET PARASITE DRAIN LOIS OF HER PSIONIC POWERS.*
IT WAS AN UGLY RISK, BUT SHE'S BETTER NOW.
WHA--?
SOMEONE'S IN MY APARTMENT
*SUPERMAN #26-27. --Eddie.
IT WOULD BE OVERKILL IF SUPERMAN SHOWED UP FOR A BREAKING AND ENTERING...
...SO IT IS UP TO CLARK KENT TO GET TO THE BOTTOM OF THIS.
HELLO?
WHO'S THERE?
I'VE GOT 911 ON SPEED DIAL.

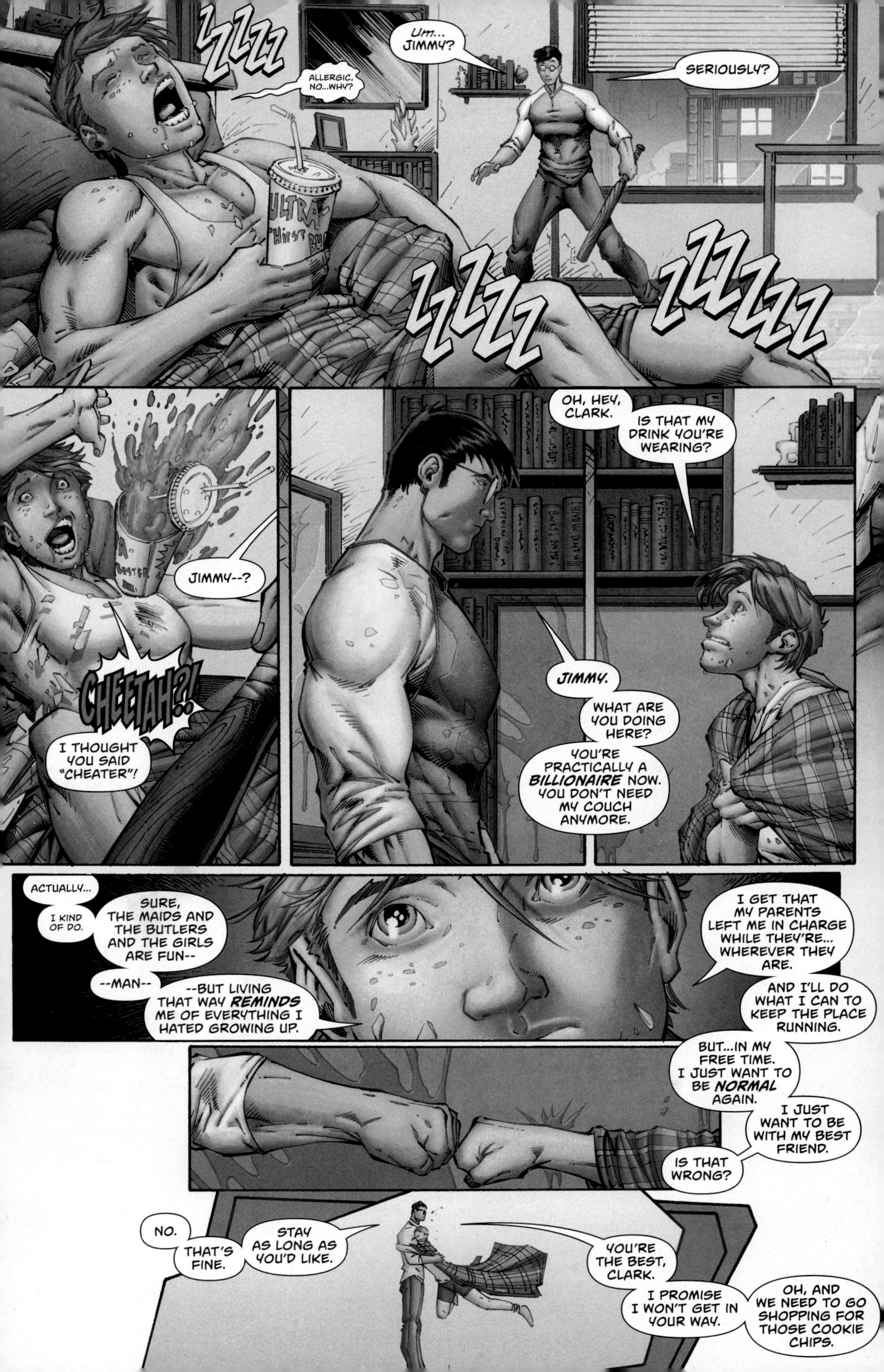

ZZZZZ
ALLERGIC, NO...WHY?
Um... JIMMY?
SERIOUSLY?
ZZZZZ
ZZZZZZZ
JIMMY--?
CHEETAH?!
I THOUGHT YOU SAID "CHEATER"!
OH, HEY, CLARK.
IS THAT MY DRINK YOU'RE WEARING?
JIMMY.
WHAT ARE YOU DOING HERE?
YOU'RE PRACTICALLY A BILLIONAIRE NOW. YOU DON'T NEED MY COUCH ANYMORE.
ACTUALLY...
I KIND OF DO.
SURE, THE MAIDS AND THE BUTLERS AND THE GIRLS ARE FUN--
--MAN--
--BUT LIVING THAT WAY REMINDS ME OF EVERYTHING I HATED GROWING UP.
I GET THAT MY PARENTS LEFT ME IN CHARGE WHILE THEY'RE... WHEREVER THEY ARE.
AND I'LL DO WHAT I CAN TO KEEP THE PLACE RUNNING.
BUT...IN MY FREE TIME. I JUST WANT TO BE NORMAL AGAIN.
I JUST WANT TO BE WITH MY BEST FRIEND.
IS THAT WRONG?
NO.
THAT'S FINE.
STAY AS LONG AS YOU'D LIKE.
YOU'RE THE BEST, CLARK.
I PROMISE I WON'T GET IN YOUR WAY.
OH, AND WE NEED TO GO SHOPPING FOR THOSE COOKIE CHIPS.

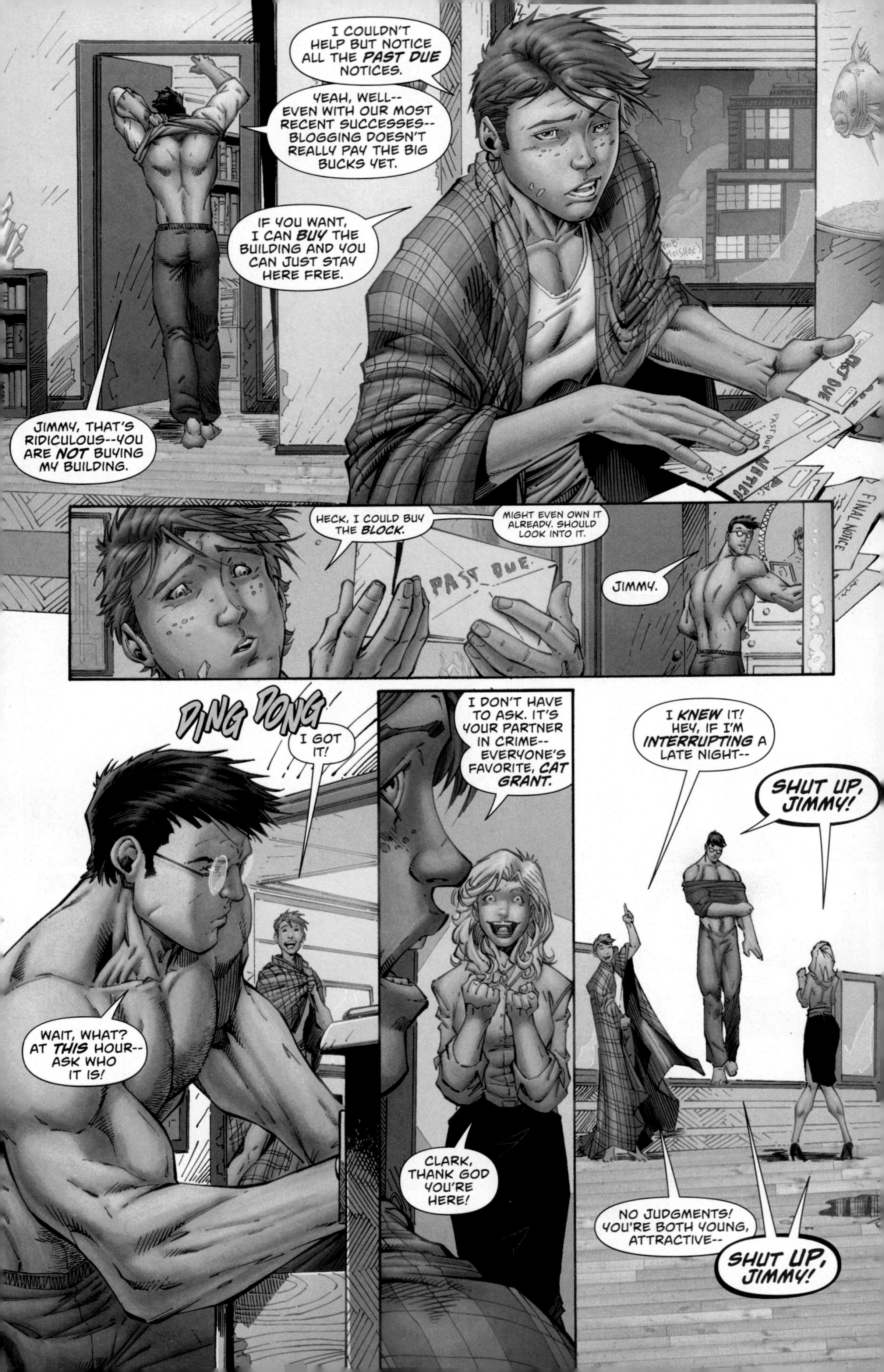
I COULDN'T HELP BUT NOTICE ALL THE PAST DUE NOTICES.
YEAH, WELL-- EVEN WITH OUR MOST RECENT SUCCESSES-- BLOGGING DOESN'T REALLY PAY THE BIG BUCKS YET.
IF YOU WANT, I CAN BUY THE BUILDING AND YOU CAN JUST STAY HERE FREE.
JIMMY, THAT'S RIDICULOUS--YOU ARE NOT BUYING MY BUILDING.
PAST DUE
FINAL NOTICE
HECK, I COULD BUY THE BLOCK.
MIGHT EVEN OWN IT ALREADY. SHOULD LOOK INTO IT.
PAST DUE
JIMMY.
DING DONG
I GOT IT!
WAIT, WHAT? AT THIS HOUR-- ASK WHO IT IS!
I DON'T HAVE TO ASK. IT'S YOUR PARTNER IN CRIME-- EVERYONE'S FAVORITE, CAT GRANT.
CLARK, THANK GOD YOU'RE HERE!
I KNEW IT! HEY, IF I'M INTERRUPTING A LATE NIGHT--
SHUT UP, JIMMY!
NO JUDGMENTS! YOU'RE BOTH YOUNG, ATTRACTIVE--
SHUT UP, JIMMY!

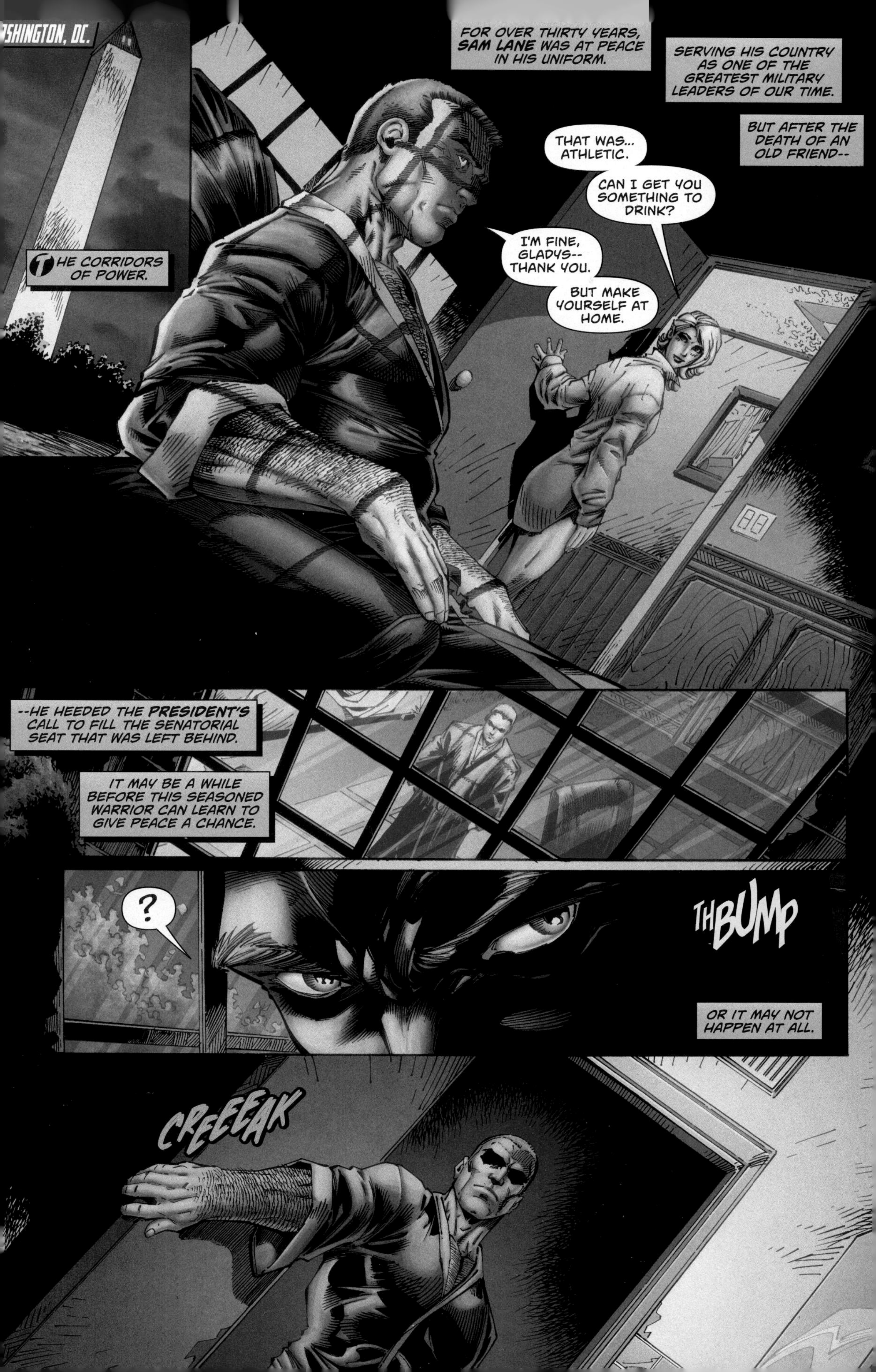

SHINGTON, DC.
THE CORRIDORS OF POWER.
FOR OVER THIRTY YEARS, SAM LANE WAS AT PEACE IN HIS UNIFORM.
SERVING HIS COUNTRY AS ONE OF THE GREATEST MILITARY LEADERS OF OUR TIME.
BUT AFTER THE DEATH OF AN OLD FRIEND--
THAT WAS... ATHLETIC.
CAN I GET YOU SOMETHING TO DRINK?
I'M FINE, GLADYS-- THANK YOU.
BUT MAKE YOURSELF AT HOME.
--HE HEEDED THE PRESIDENT'S CALL TO FILL THE SENATORIAL SEAT THAT WAS LEFT BEHIND.
IT MAY BE A WHILE BEFORE THIS SEASONED WARRIOR CAN LEARN TO GIVE PEACE A CHANCE.
?
THBUMP
OR IT MAY NOT HAPPEN AT ALL.
CREEEAK

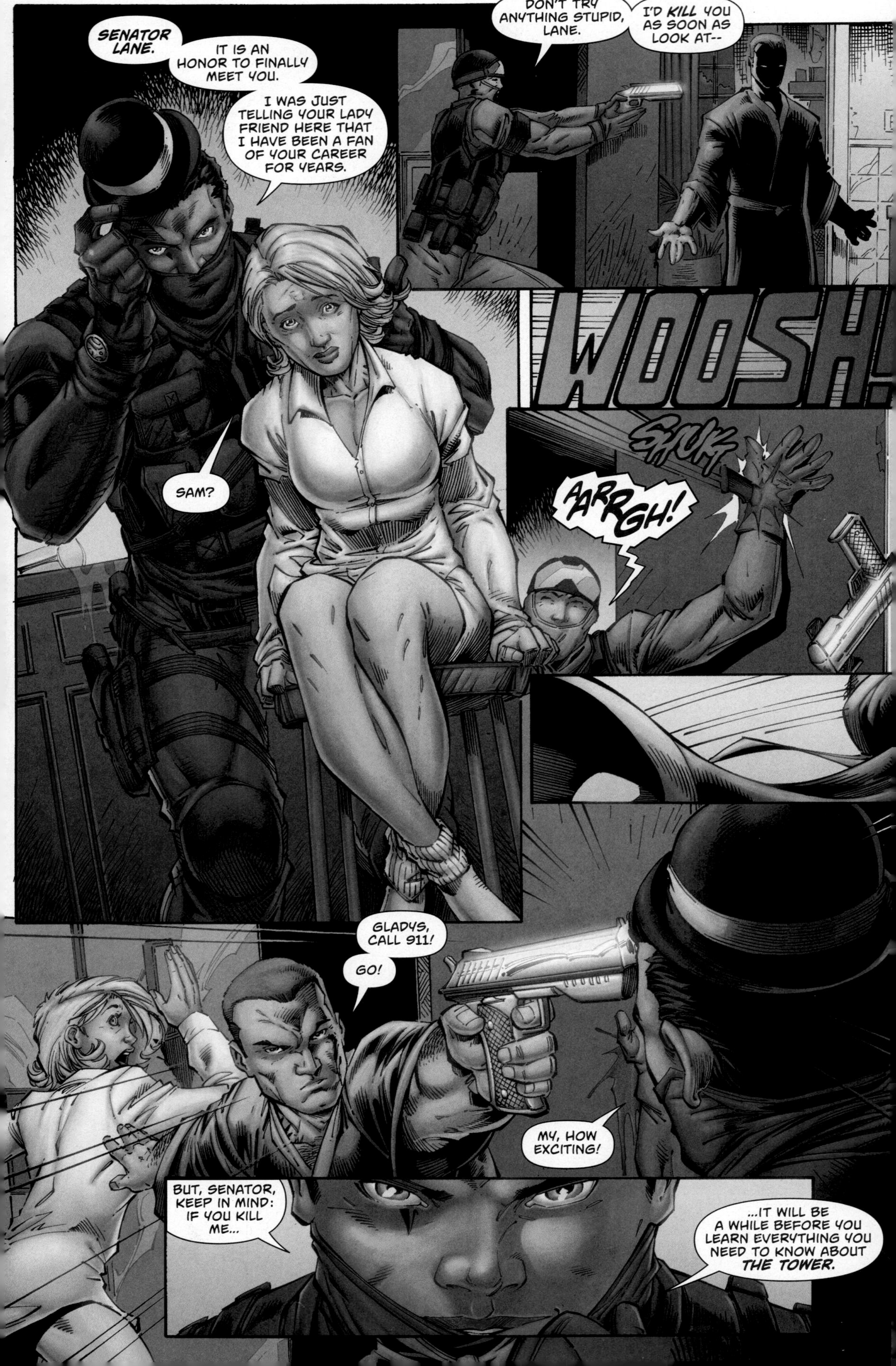
SENATOR LANE.
IT IS AN HONOR TO FINALLY MEET YOU.
I WAS JUST TELLING YOUR LADY FRIEND HERE THAT I HAVE BEEN A FAN OF YOUR CAREER FOR YEARS.
SAM?
DON'T TRY ANYTHING STUPID, LANE.
I'D KILL YOU AS SOON AS LOOK AT--
WOOSH!
SHUK
AARRGH!
GLADYS, CALL 911!
GO!
MY, HOW EXCITING!
BUT, SENATOR, KEEP IN MIND: IF YOU KILL ME...
...IT WILL BE A WHILE BEFORE YOU LEARN EVERYTHING YOU NEED TO KNOW ABOUT THE TOWER.

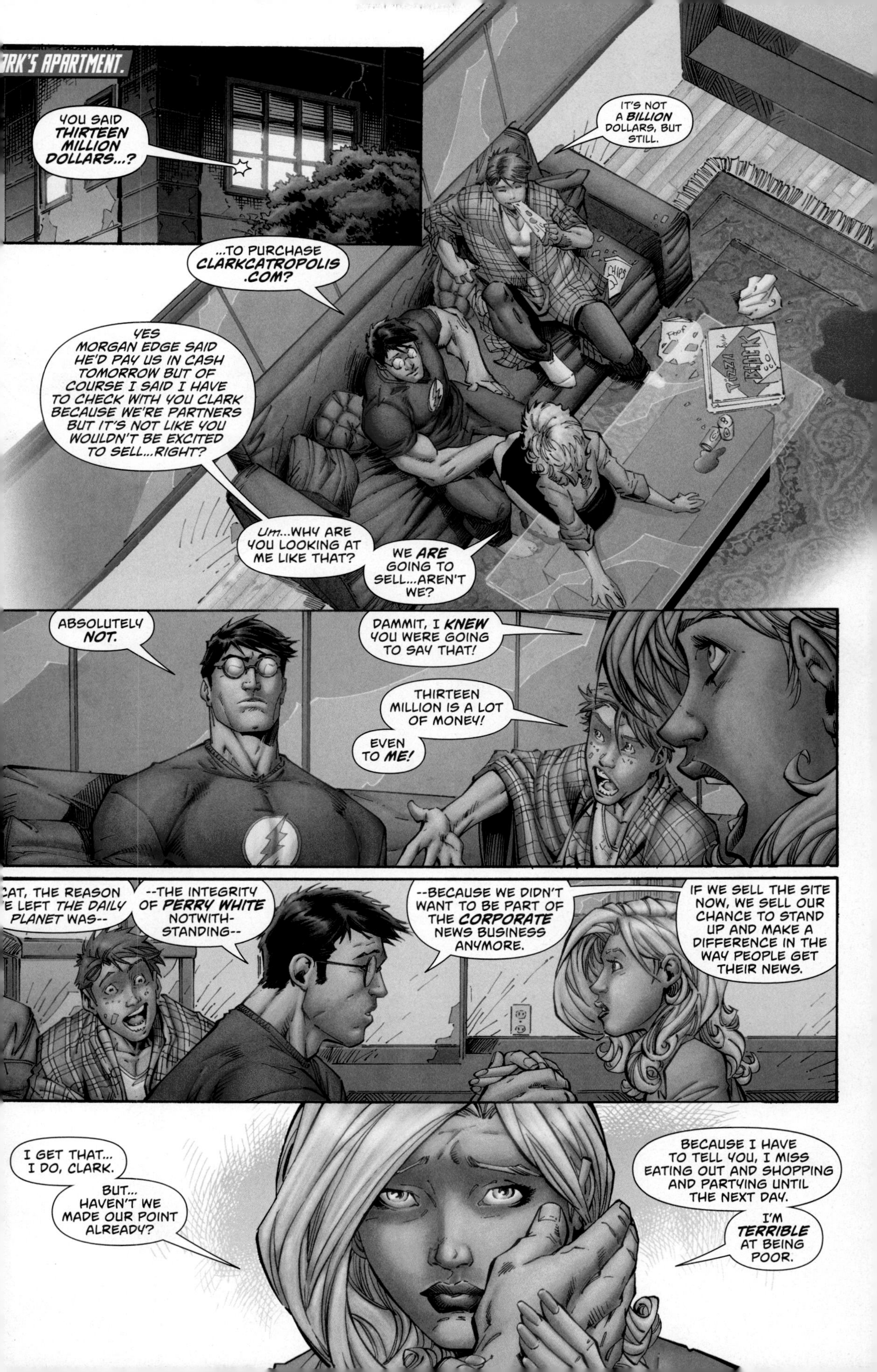
ARK'S APARTMENT.
YOU SAID THIRTEEN MILLION DOLLARS...?
IT'S NOT A BILLION DOLLARS, BUT STILL.
...TO PURCHASE CLARKCATROPOLIS.COM?
YES MORGAN EDGE SAID HE'D PAY US IN CASH TOMORROW BUT OF COURSE I SAID I HAVE TO CHECK WITH YOU CLARK BECAUSE WE'RE PARTNERS BUT IT'S NOT LIKE YOU WOULDN'T BE EXCITED TO SELL...RIGHT?
UM...WHY ARE YOU LOOKING AT ME LIKE THAT?
WE ARE GOING TO SELL...AREN'T WE?
CHIPS
ABSOLUTELY NOT.
DAMMIT, I KNEW YOU WERE GOING TO SAY THAT!
THIRTEEN MILLION IS A LOT OF MONEY!
EVEN TO ME!
CAT, THE REASON E LEFT THE DAILY PLANET WAS--
--THE INTEGRITY OF PERRY WHITE NOTWITH-STANDING--
--BECAUSE WE DIDN'T WANT TO BE PART OF THE CORPORATE NEWS BUSINESS ANYMORE.
IF WE SELL THE SITE NOW, WE SELL OUR CHANCE TO STAND UP AND MAKE A DIFFERENCE IN THE WAY PEOPLE GET THEIR NEWS.
I GET THAT... I DO, CLARK.
BUT... HAVEN'T WE MADE OUR POINT ALREADY?
BECAUSE I HAVE TO TELL YOU, I MISS EATING OUT AND SHOPPING AND PARTYING UNTIL THE NEXT DAY.
I'M TERRIBLE AT BEING POOR.

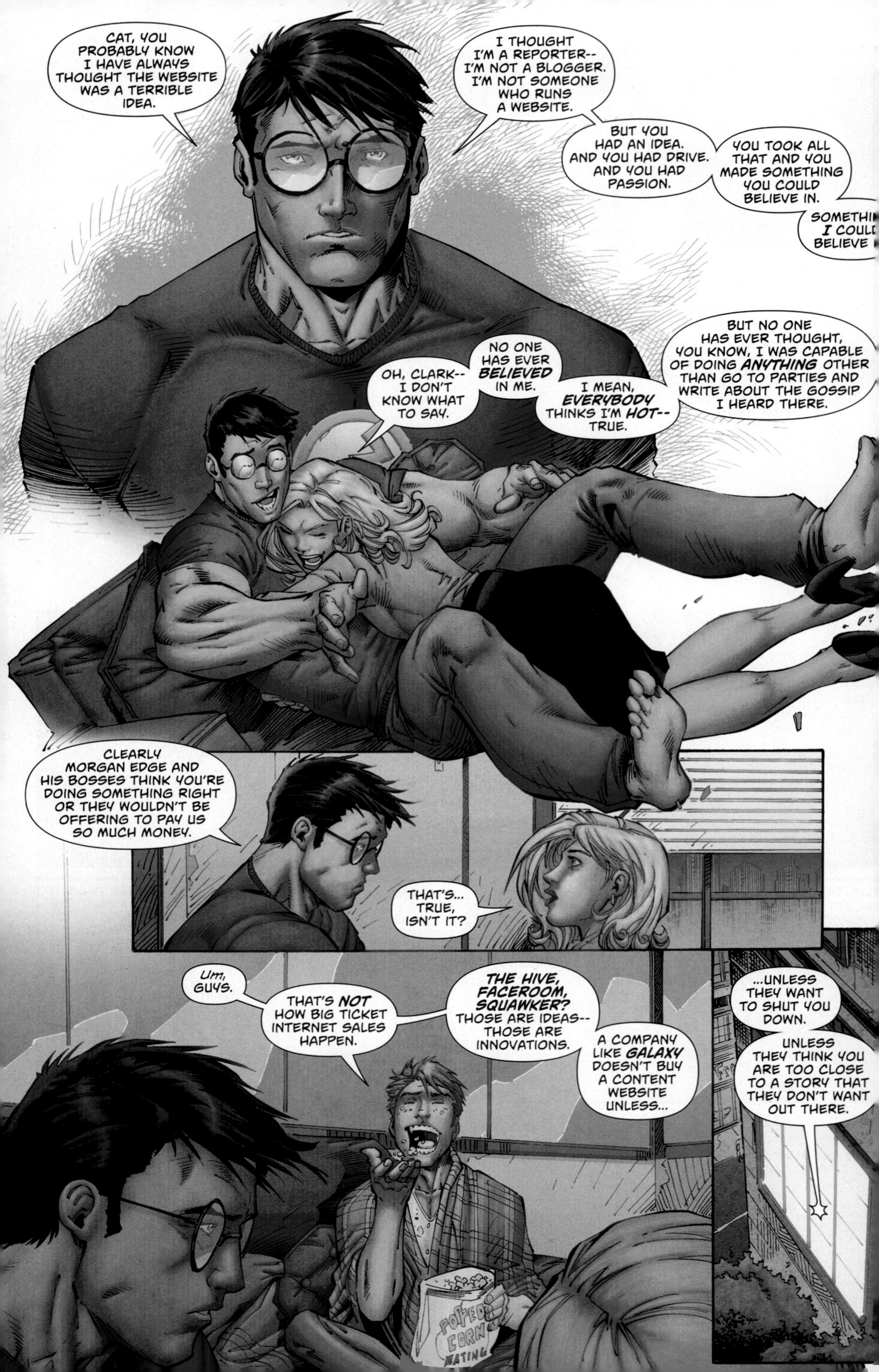
CAT, YOU PROBABLY KNOW I HAVE ALWAYS THOUGHT THE WEBSITE WAS A TERRIBLE IDEA.
I THOUGHT I'M A REPORTER-- I'M NOT A BLOGGER. I'M NOT SOMEONE WHO RUNS A WEBSITE.
BUT YOU HAD AN IDEA. AND YOU HAD DRIVE. AND YOU HAD PASSION.
YOU TOOK ALL THAT AND YOU MADE SOMETHING YOU COULD BELIEVE IN.
SOMETHI I COULD BELIEVE
OH, CLARK-- I DON'T KNOW WHAT TO SAY.
NO ONE HAS EVER BELIEVED IN ME.
I MEAN, EVERYBODY THINKS I'M HOT-- TRUE.
BUT NO ONE HAS EVER THOUGHT, YOU KNOW, I WAS CAPABLE OF DOING ANYTHING OTHER THAN GO TO PARTIES AND WRITE ABOUT THE GOSSIP I HEARD THERE.
CLEARLY MORGAN EDGE AND HIS BOSSES THINK YOU'RE DOING SOMETHING RIGHT OR THEY WOULDN'T BE OFFERING TO PAY US SO MUCH MONEY.
THAT'S... TRUE, ISN'T IT?
Um, GUYS.
THAT'S NOT HOW BIG TICKET INTERNET SALES HAPPEN.
THE HIVE, FACEROOM, SQUAWKER? THOSE ARE IDEAS-- THOSE ARE INNOVATIONS.
A COMPANY LIKE GALAXY DOESN'T BUY A CONTENT WEBSITE UNLESS...
...UNLESS THEY WANT TO SHUT YOU DOWN.
UNLESS THEY THINK YOU ARE TOO CLOSE TO A STORY THAT THEY DON'T WANT OUT THERE.
POPPED CORN EATING

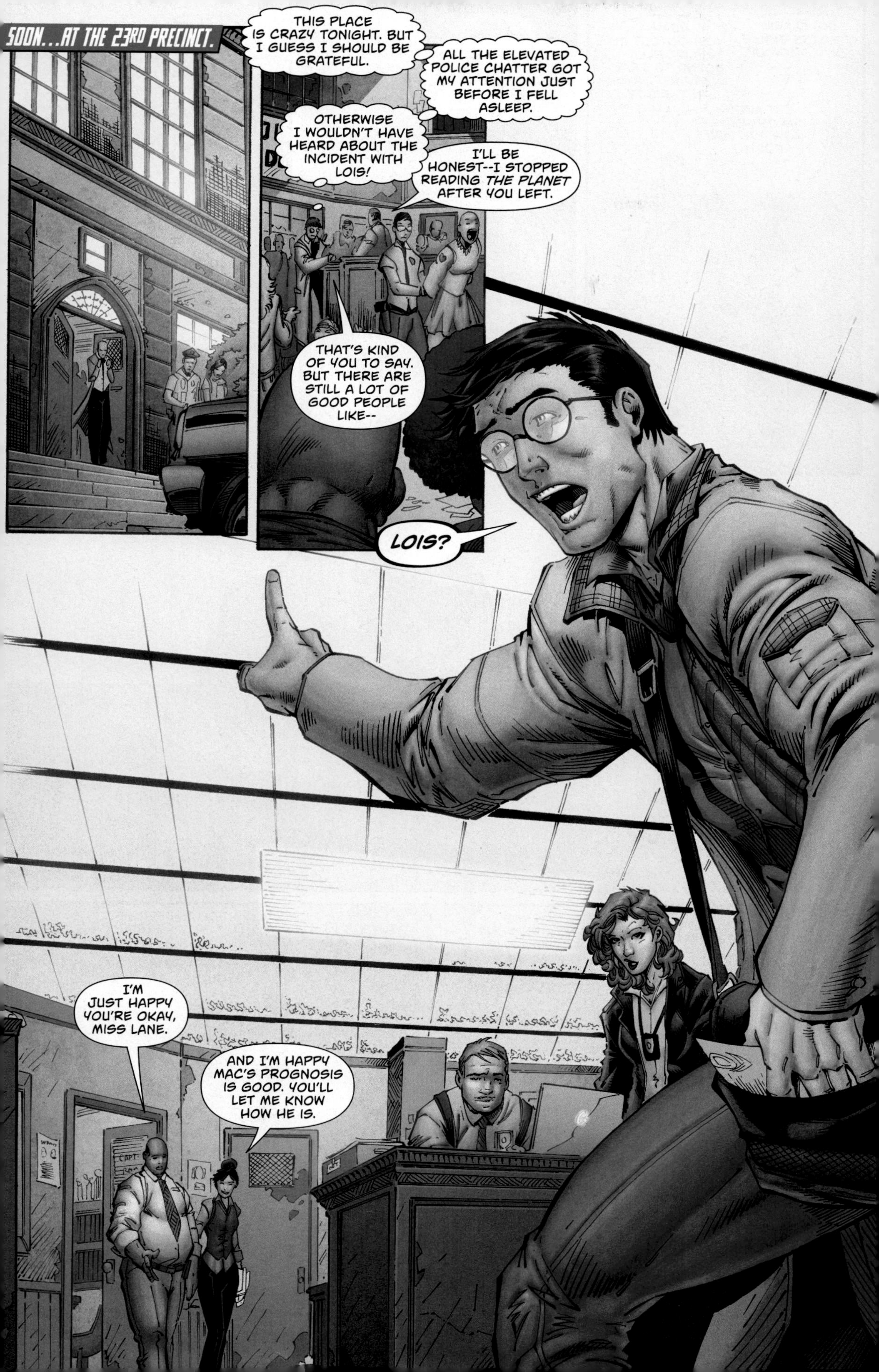
SOON...AT THE 23RD PRECINCT.
THIS PLACE IS CRAZY TONIGHT. BUT I GUESS I SHOULD BE GRATEFUL.
ALL THE ELEVATED POLICE CHATTER GOT MY ATTENTION JUST BEFORE I FELL ASLEEP.
OTHERWISE I WOULDN'T HAVE HEARD ABOUT THE INCIDENT WITH LOIS!
I'LL BE HONEST--I STOPPED READING *THE PLANET* AFTER YOU LEFT.
THAT'S KIND OF YOU TO SAY. BUT THERE ARE STILL A LOT OF GOOD PEOPLE LIKE--
LOIS?
I'M JUST HAPPY YOU'RE OKAY, MISS LANE.
AND I'M HAPPY MAC'S PROGNOSIS IS GOOD. YOU'LL LET ME KNOW HOW HE IS.

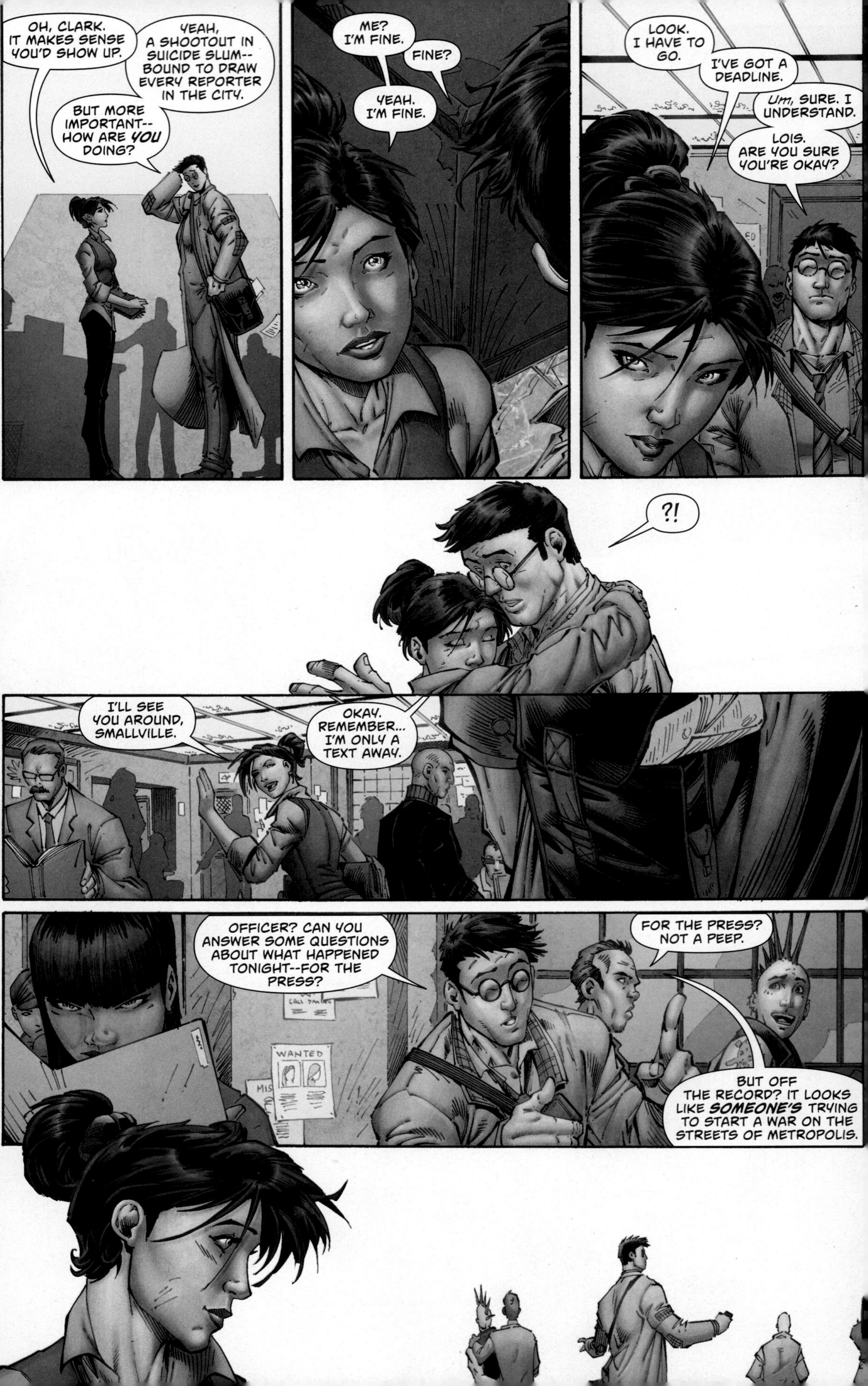
OH, CLARK. IT MAKES SENSE YOU'D SHOW UP.
YEAH, A SHOOTOUT IN SUICIDE SLUM-- BOUND TO DRAW EVERY REPORTER IN THE CITY.
BUT MORE IMPORTANT-- HOW ARE *YOU* DOING?
ME? I'M FINE.
FINE?
YEAH. I'M FINE.
LOOK. I HAVE TO GO.
I'VE GOT A DEADLINE.
UM, SURE. I UNDERSTAND.
LOIS. ARE YOU SURE YOU'RE OKAY?
?!
I'LL SEE YOU AROUND, SMALLVILLE.
OKAY. REMEMBER... I'M ONLY A TEXT AWAY.
OFFICER? CAN YOU ANSWER SOME QUESTIONS ABOUT WHAT HAPPENED TONIGHT--FOR THE PRESS?
FOR THE PRESS? NOT A PEEP.
BUT OFF THE RECORD? IT LOOKS LIKE **SOMEONE'S** TRYING TO START A WAR ON THE STREETS OF METROPOLIS.
WANTED

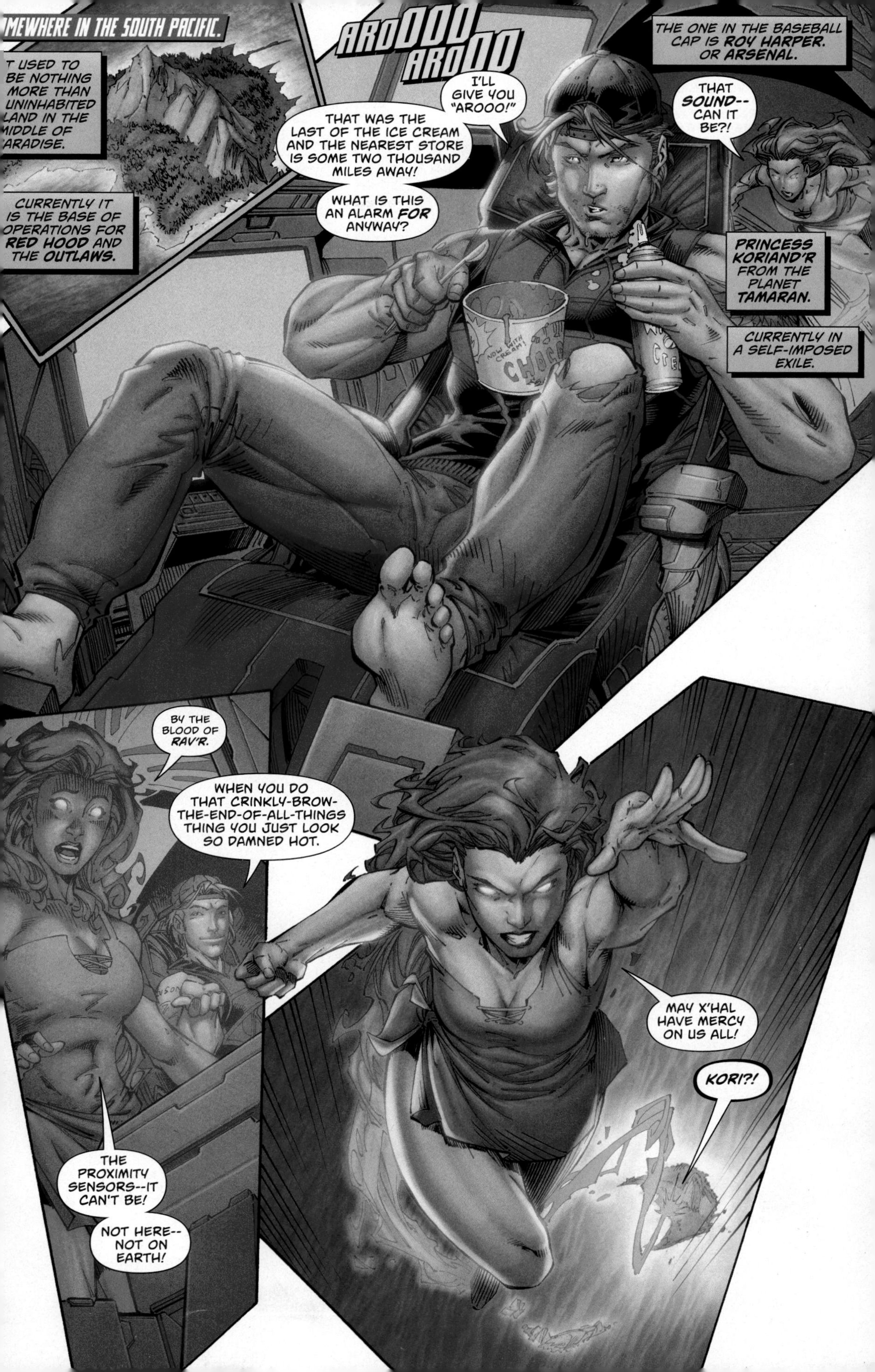

MEWHERE IN THE SOUTH PACIFIC.
T USED TO BE NOTHING MORE THAN UNINHABITED LAND IN THE MIDDLE OF ARADISE.
CURRENTLY IT IS THE BASE OF OPERATIONS FOR RED HOOD AND THE OUTLAWS.
AROOOO AROOO
I'LL GIVE YOU "AROOO!"
THAT WAS THE LAST OF THE ICE CREAM AND THE NEAREST STORE IS SOME TWO THOUSAND MILES AWAY!
WHAT IS THIS AN ALARM FOR ANYWAY?
THE ONE IN THE BASEBALL CAP IS ROY HARPER. OR ARSENAL.
THAT SOUND-- CAN IT BE?!
PRINCESS KORIAND'R FROM THE PLANET TAMARAN.
CURRENTLY IN A SELF-IMPOSED EXILE.
CHOCO
BY THE BLOOD OF RAV'R.
WHEN YOU DO THAT CRINKLY-BROW-THE-END-OF-ALL-THINGS THING YOU JUST LOOK SO DAMNED HOT.
THE PROXIMITY SENSORS--IT CAN'T BE!
NOT HERE-- NOT ON EARTH!
MAY X'HAL HAVE MERCY ON US ALL!
KORI?!

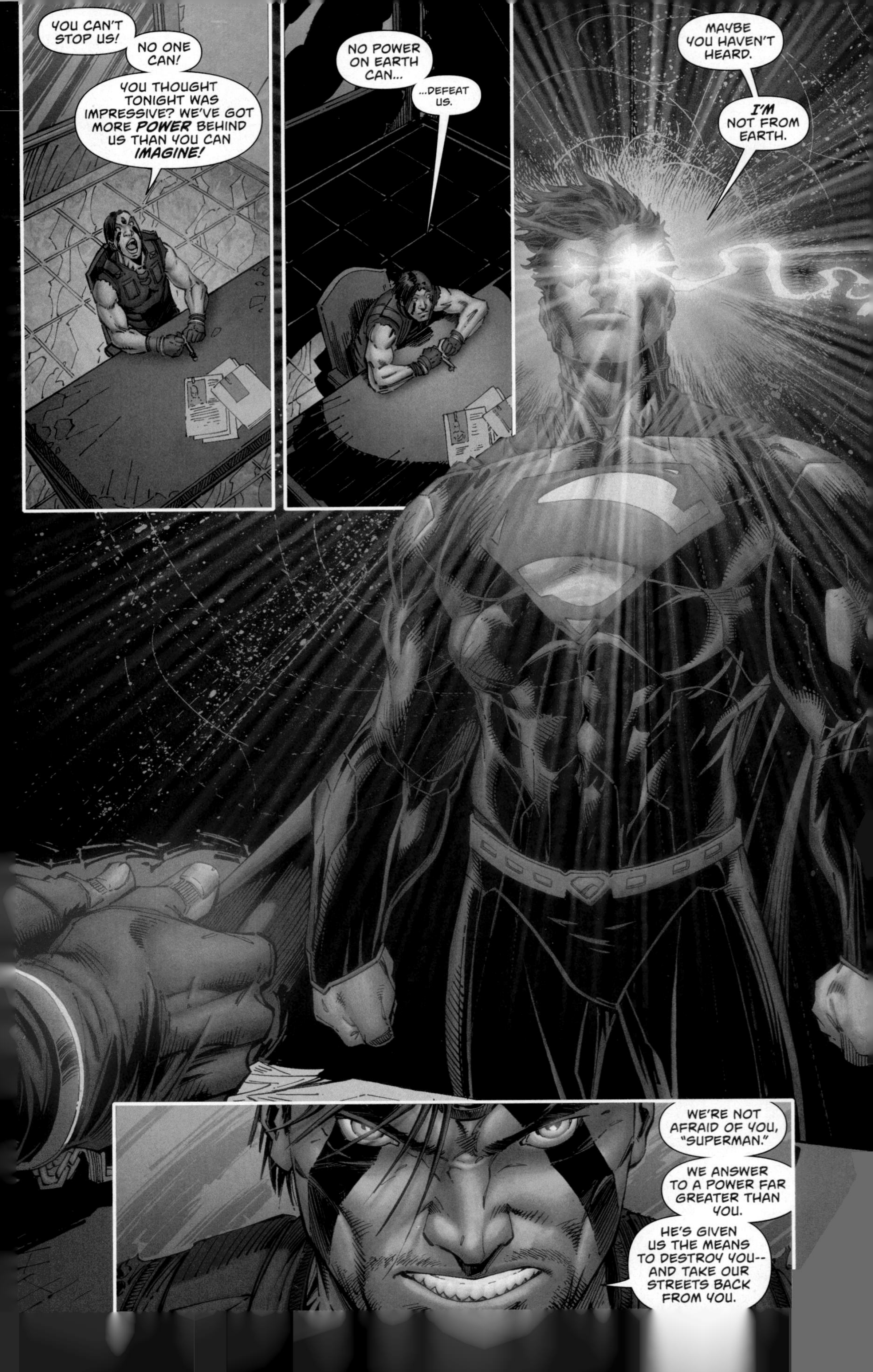
YOU CAN'T STOP US!
NO ONE CAN!
YOU THOUGHT TONIGHT WAS IMPRESSIVE? WE'VE GOT MORE POWER BEHIND US THAN YOU CAN IMAGINE!
NO POWER ON EARTH CAN...
...DEFEAT US.
MAYBE YOU HAVEN'T HEARD.
I'M NOT FROM EARTH.
WE'RE NOT AFRAID OF YOU, "SUPERMAN."
WE ANSWER TO A POWER FAR GREATER THAN YOU.
HE'S GIVEN US THE MEANS TO DESTROY YOU--AND TAKE OUR STREETS BACK FROM YOU.

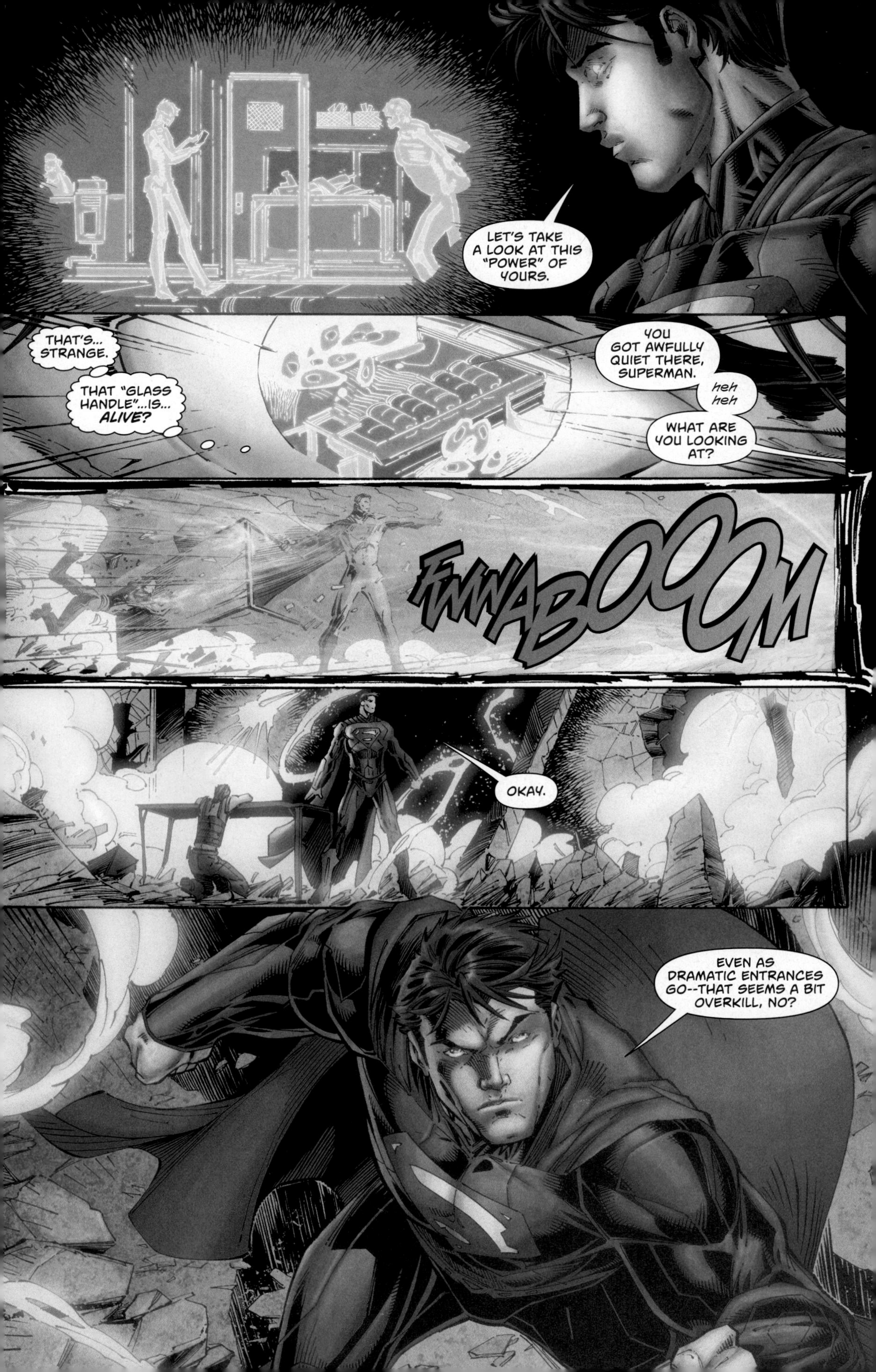

LET'S TAKE A LOOK AT THIS "POWER" OF YOURS.
THAT'S... STRANGE.
THAT "GLASS HANDLE"...IS... ALIVE?
YOU GOT AWFULLY QUIET THERE, SUPERMAN.
heh heh
WHAT ARE YOU LOOKING AT?
FWWABOOOOM
OKAY.
EVEN AS DRAMATIC ENTRANCES GO--THAT SEEMS A BIT OVERKILL, NO?

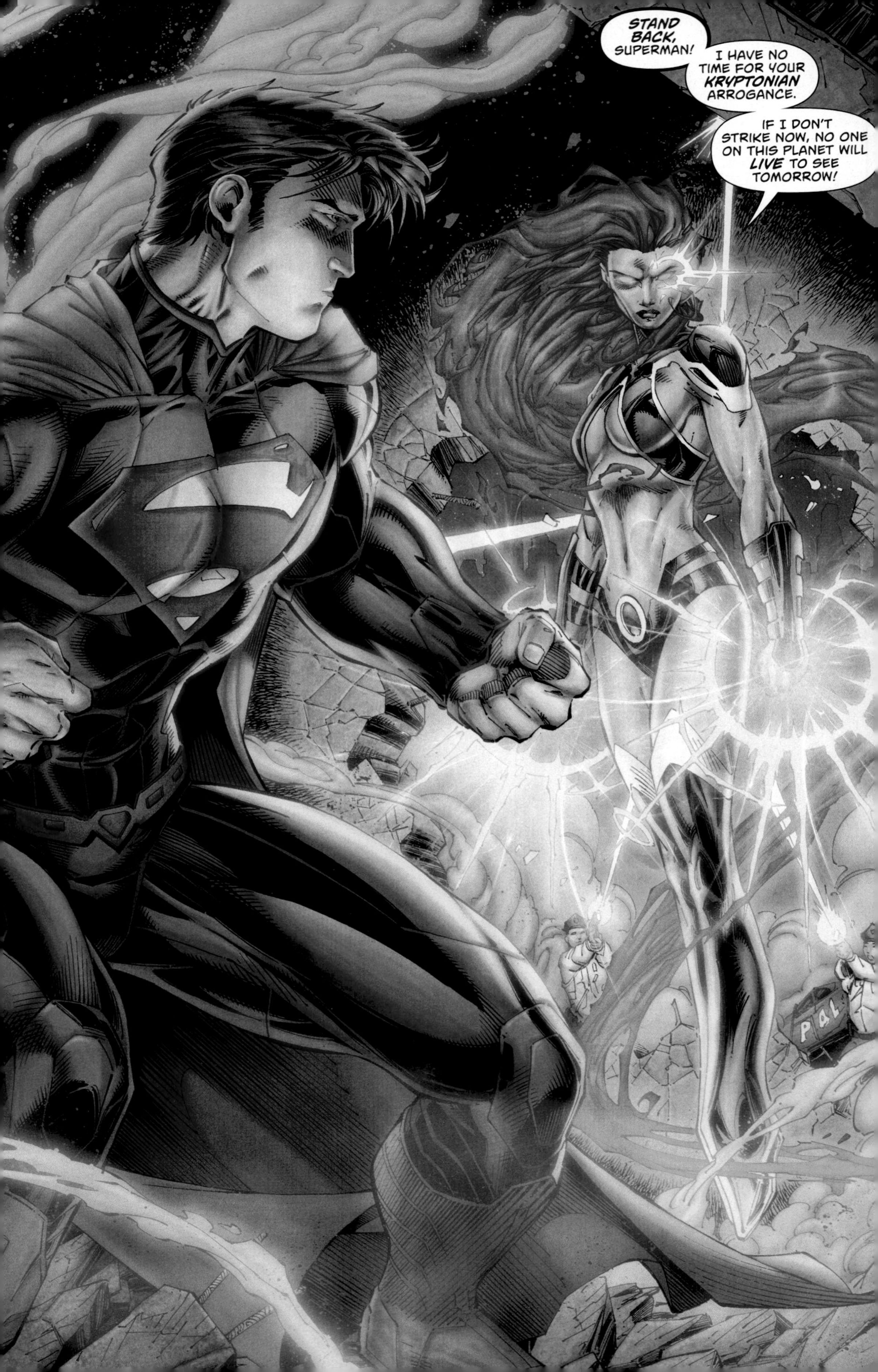

STAND BACK, SUPERMAN!
I HAVE NO TIME FOR YOUR KRYPTONIAN ARROGANCE.
IF I DON'T STRIKE NOW, NO ONE ON THIS PLANET WILL LIVE TO SEE TOMORROW!

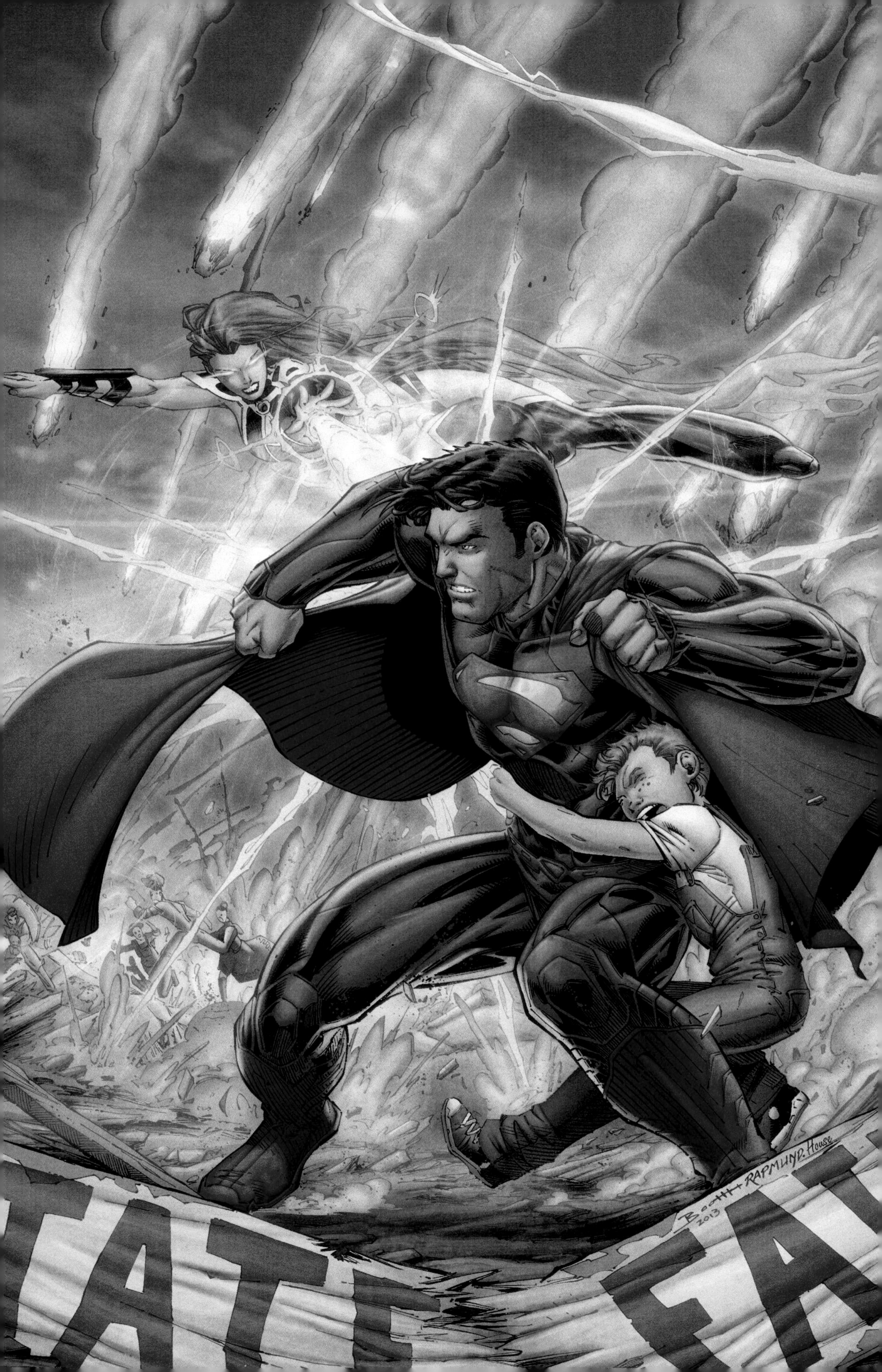
BOOTH + RAPMUND. House
2013

1,000 DEGREES IN THE SHADE

SCOTT LOBDELL writer **ED BENES** penciller **JONATHAN GLAPION** and **NORM RAPMUND** inkers **PETE PANTAZIS** colorist
cover art by **BRETT BOOTH, NORM RAPMUND** and **ANDREW DALHOUSE**

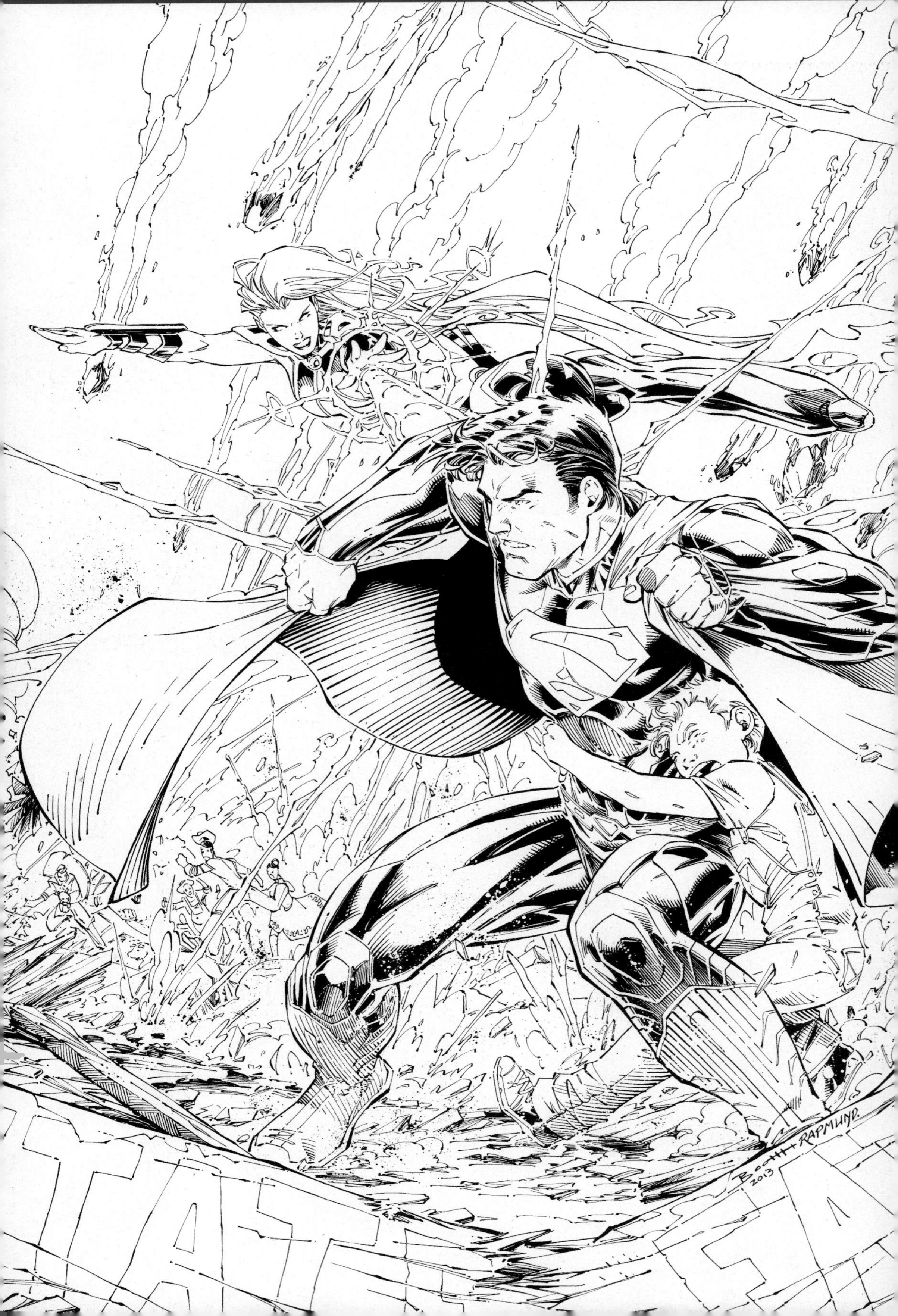
BOOTH + RAPMUND.
2013

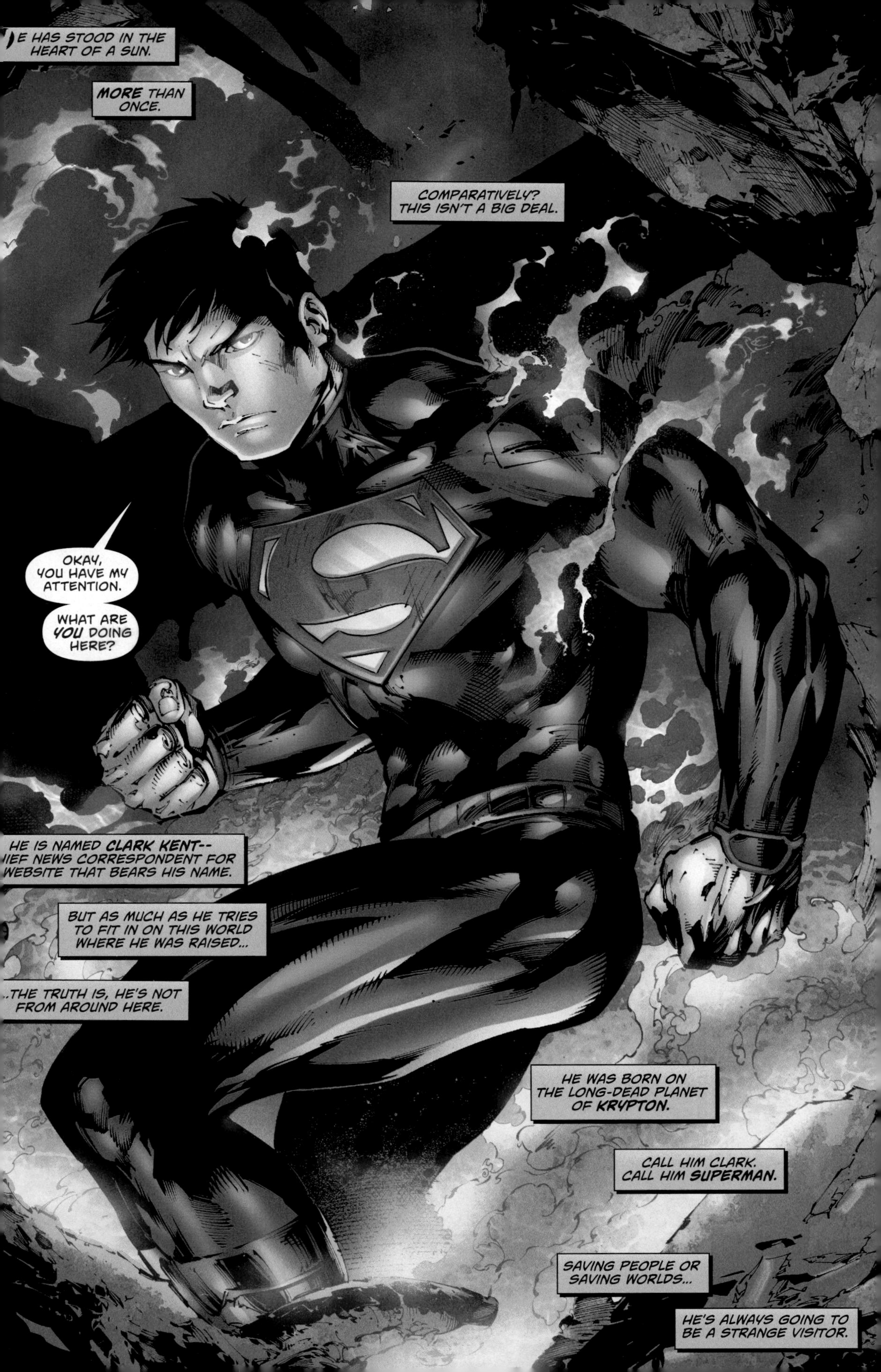

E HAS STOOD IN THE HEART OF A SUN.
MORE THAN ONCE.
COMPARATIVELY? THIS ISN'T A BIG DEAL.
OKAY, YOU HAVE MY ATTENTION.
WHAT ARE YOU DOING HERE?
HE IS NAMED CLARK KENT-- IEF NEWS CORRESPONDENT FOR WEBSITE THAT BEARS HIS NAME.
BUT AS MUCH AS HE TRIES TO FIT IN ON THIS WORLD WHERE HE WAS RAISED...
..THE TRUTH IS, HE'S NOT FROM AROUND HERE.
HE WAS BORN ON THE LONG-DEAD PLANET OF KRYPTON.
CALL HIM CLARK. CALL HIM SUPERMAN.
SAVING PEOPLE OR SAVING WORLDS...
HE'S ALWAYS GOING TO BE A STRANGE VISITOR.

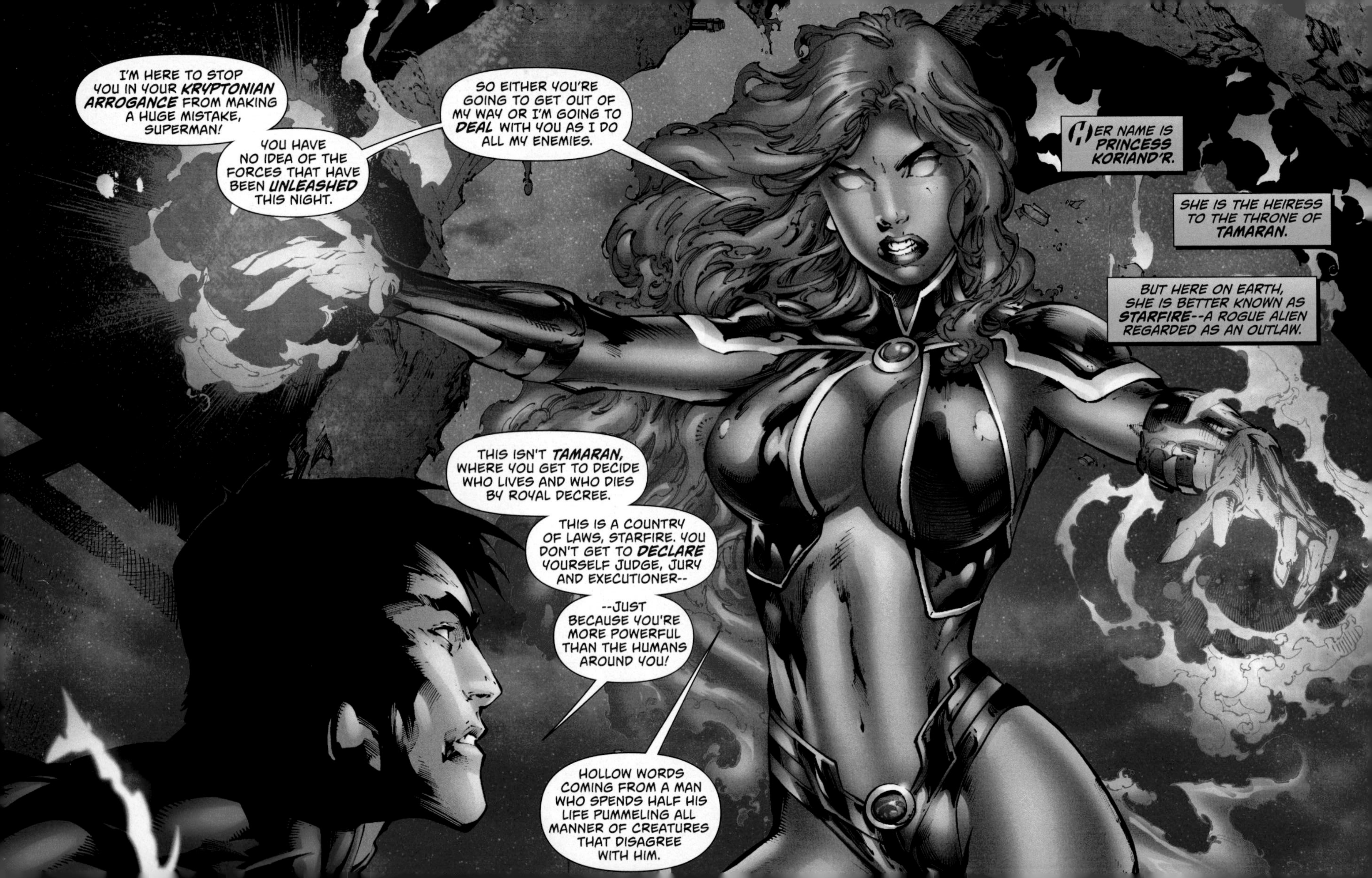
HER NAME IS PRINCESS KORIAND'R.
SHE IS THE HEIRESS TO THE THRONE OF TAMARAN.
BUT HERE ON EARTH, SHE IS BETTER KNOWN AS STARFIRE--A ROGUE ALIEN REGARDED AS AN OUTLAW.
I'M HERE TO STOP YOU IN YOUR KRYPTONIAN ARROGANCE FROM MAKING A HUGE MISTAKE, SUPERMAN!
YOU HAVE NO IDEA OF THE FORCES THAT HAVE BEEN UNLEASHED THIS NIGHT.
SO EITHER YOU'RE GOING TO GET OUT OF MY WAY OR I'M GOING TO DEAL WITH YOU AS I DO ALL MY ENEMIES.
THIS ISN'T TAMARAN, WHERE YOU GET TO DECIDE WHO LIVES AND WHO DIES BY ROYAL DECREE.
THIS IS A COUNTRY OF LAWS, STARFIRE. YOU DON'T GET TO DECLARE YOURSELF JUDGE, JURY AND EXECUTIONER--
--JUST BECAUSE YOU'RE MORE POWERFUL THAN THE HUMANS AROUND YOU!
HOLLOW WORDS COMING FROM A MAN WHO SPENDS HALF HIS LIFE PUMMELING ALL MANNER OF CREATURES THAT DISAGREE WITH HIM.

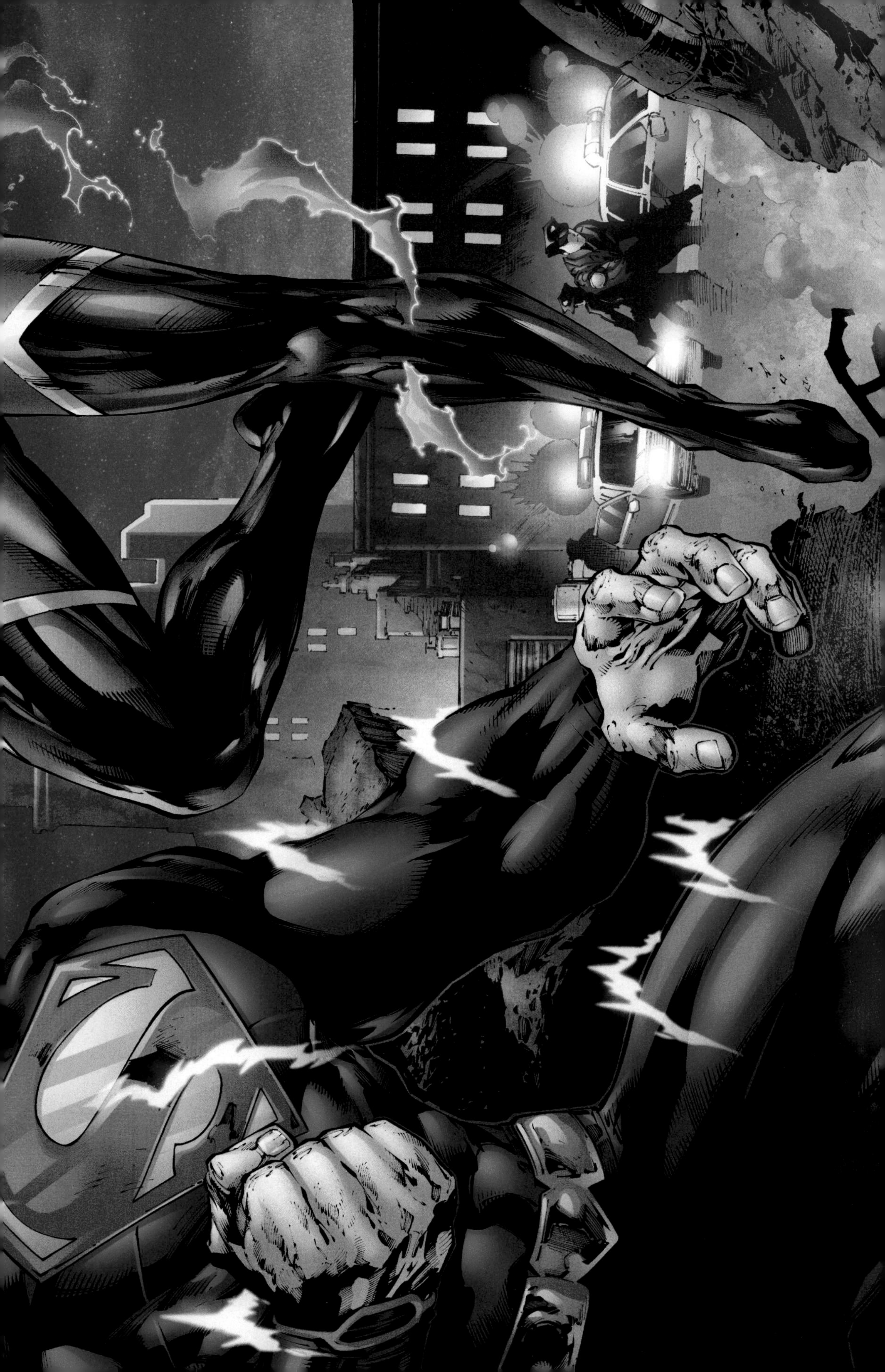

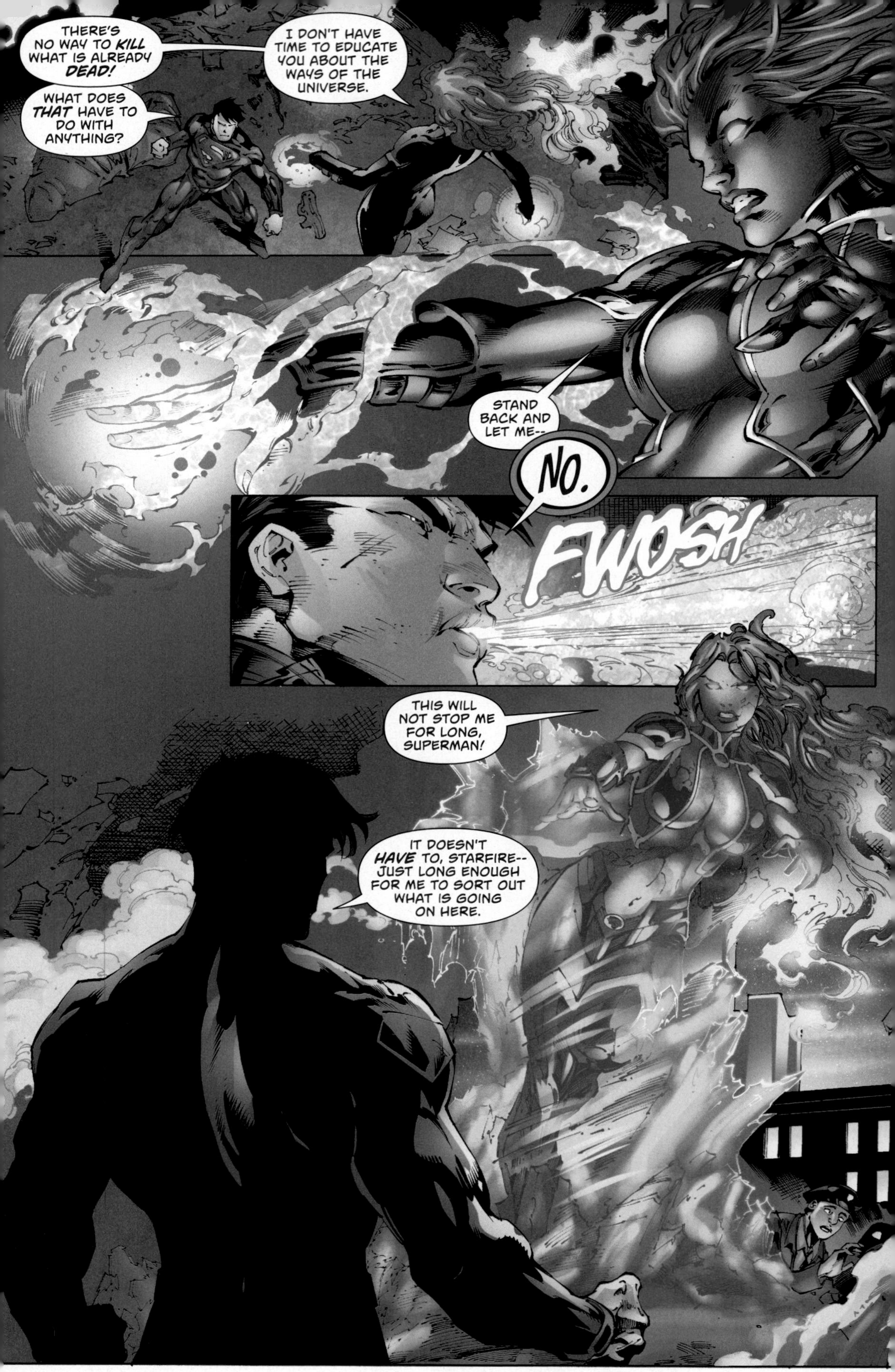
THERE'S NO WAY TO KILL WHAT IS ALREADY DEAD!
I DON'T HAVE TIME TO EDUCATE YOU ABOUT THE WAYS OF THE UNIVERSE.
WHAT DOES THAT HAVE TO DO WITH ANYTHING?
STAND BACK AND LET ME--
NO.
FWOSH
THIS WILL NOT STOP ME FOR LONG, SUPERMAN!
IT DOESN'T HAVE TO, STARFIRE-- JUST LONG ENOUGH FOR ME TO SORT OUT WHAT IS GOING ON HERE.

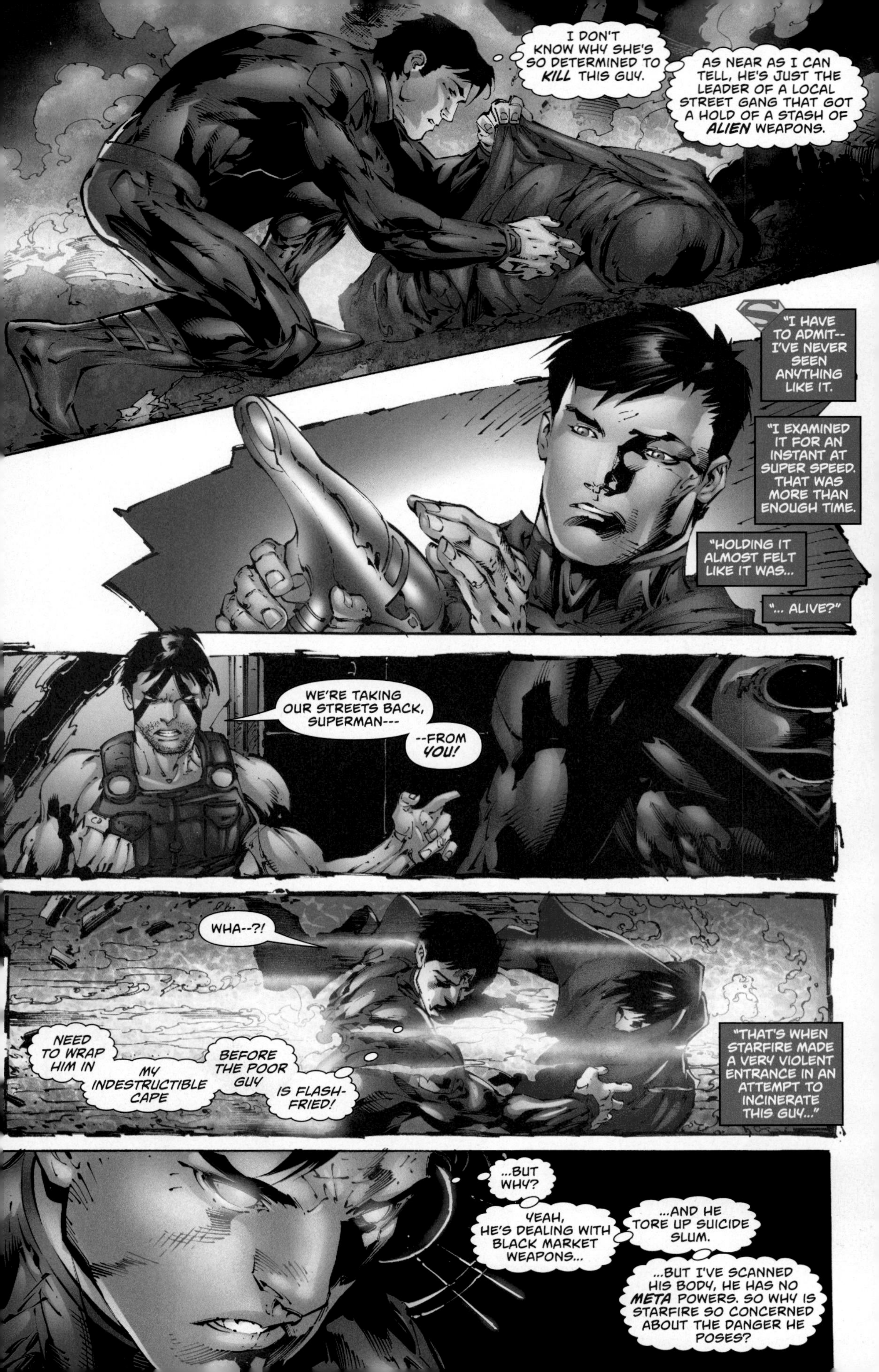

I DON'T KNOW WHY SHE'S SO DETERMINED TO KILL THIS GUY.
AS NEAR AS I CAN TELL, HE'S JUST THE LEADER OF A LOCAL STREET GANG THAT GOT A HOLD OF A STASH OF ALIEN WEAPONS.
"I HAVE TO ADMIT-- I'VE NEVER SEEN ANYTHING LIKE IT.
"I EXAMINED IT FOR AN INSTANT AT SUPER SPEED. THAT WAS MORE THAN ENOUGH TIME.
"HOLDING IT ALMOST FELT LIKE IT WAS...
"... ALIVE?"
WE'RE TAKING OUR STREETS BACK, SUPERMAN---
--FROM YOU!
WHA--?!
NEED TO WRAP HIM IN
MY INDESTRUCTIBLE CAPE
BEFORE THE POOR GUY
IS FLASH-FRIED!
"THAT'S WHEN STARFIRE MADE A VERY VIOLENT ENTRANCE IN AN ATTEMPT TO INCINERATE THIS GUY..."
...BUT WHY?
YEAH, HE'S DEALING WITH BLACK MARKET WEAPONS...
...AND HE TORE UP SUICIDE SLUM.
...BUT I'VE SCANNED HIS BODY, HE HAS NO META POWERS. SO WHY IS STARFIRE SO CONCERNED ABOUT THE DANGER HE POSES?

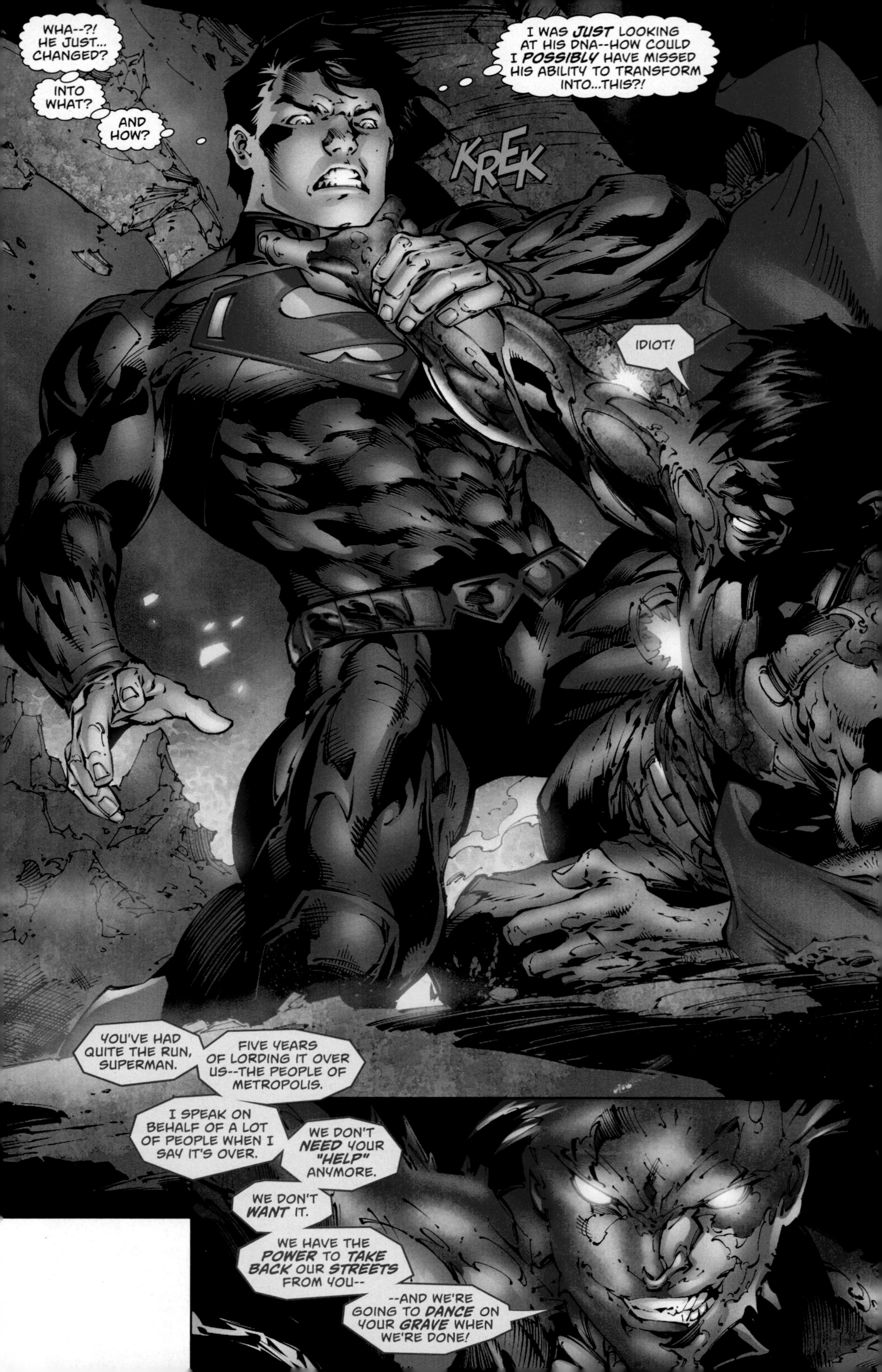
WHA--?! HE JUST... CHANGED?
INTO WHAT?
AND HOW?
I WAS JUST LOOKING AT HIS DNA--HOW COULD I POSSIBLY HAVE MISSED HIS ABILITY TO TRANSFORM INTO...THIS?!
KREK
IDIOT!
YOU'VE HAD QUITE THE RUN, SUPERMAN.
FIVE YEARS OF LORDING IT OVER US--THE PEOPLE OF METROPOLIS.
I SPEAK ON BEHALF OF A LOT OF PEOPLE WHEN I SAY IT'S OVER.
WE DON'T NEED YOUR "HELP" ANYMORE.
WE DON'T WANT IT.
WE HAVE THE POWER TO TAKE BACK OUR STREETS FROM YOU--
--AND WE'RE GOING TO DANCE ON YOUR GRAVE WHEN WE'RE DONE!

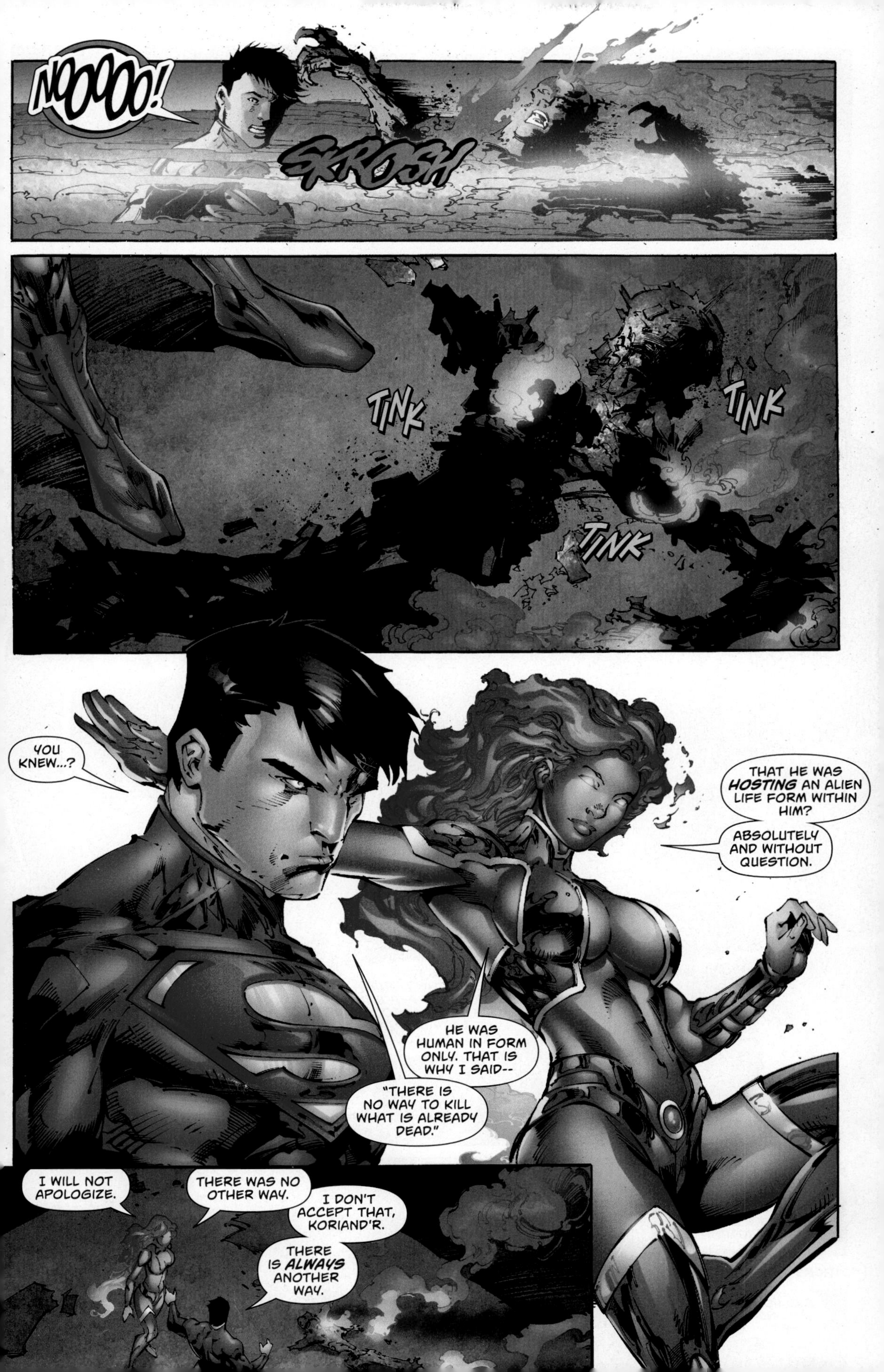
NOOOOO!
SKROSH
TINK
TINK
TINK
YOU KNEW...?
THAT HE WAS HOSTING AN ALIEN LIFE FORM WITHIN HIM?
ABSOLUTELY AND WITHOUT QUESTION.
HE WAS HUMAN IN FORM ONLY. THAT IS WHY I SAID--
"THERE IS NO WAY TO KILL WHAT IS ALREADY DEAD."
I WILL NOT APOLOGIZE.
THERE WAS NO OTHER WAY.
I DON'T ACCEPT THAT, KORIAND'R.
THERE IS ALWAYS ANOTHER WAY.

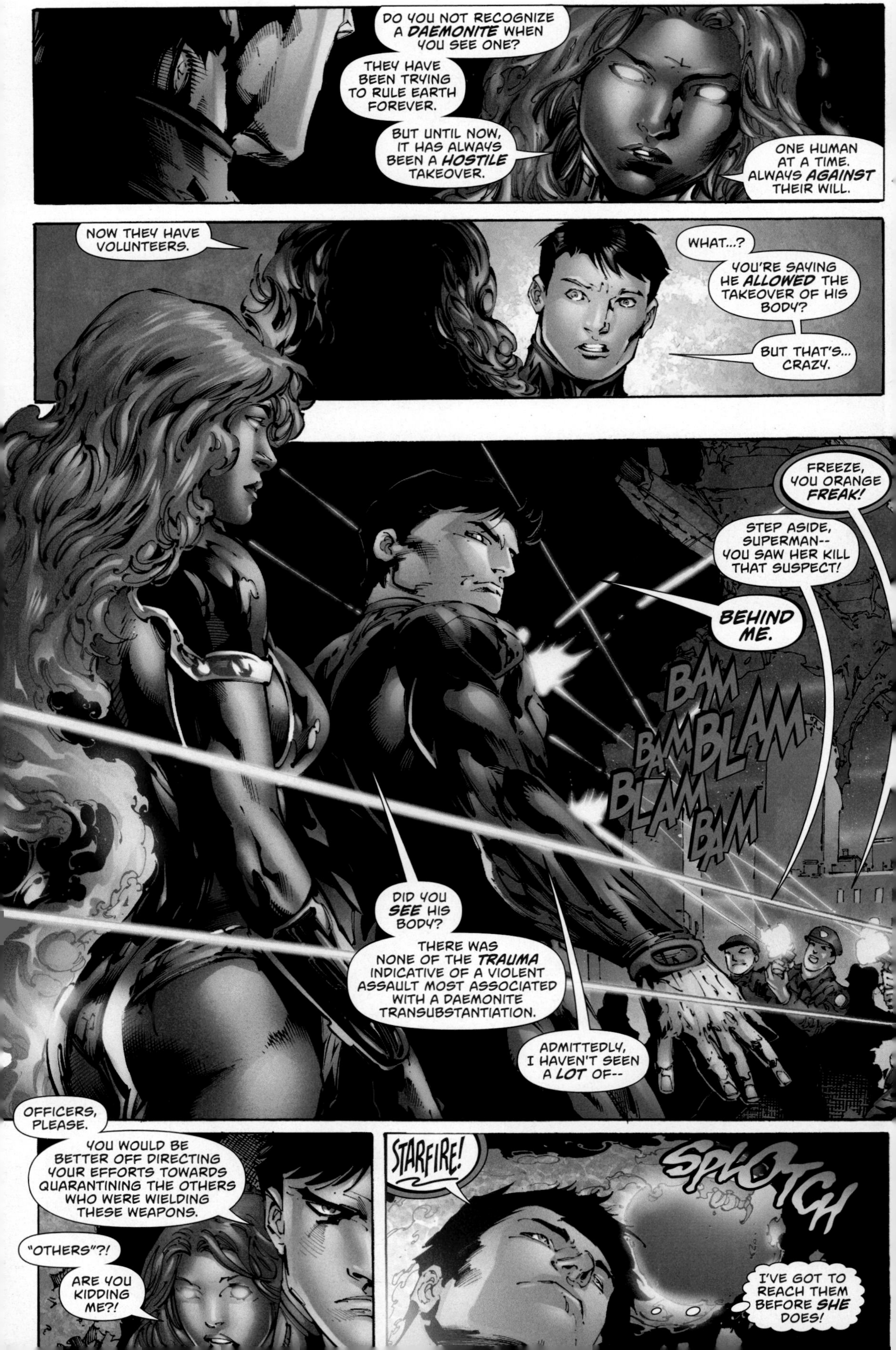
DO YOU NOT RECOGNIZE A DAEMONITE WHEN YOU SEE ONE?
THEY HAVE BEEN TRYING TO RULE EARTH FOREVER.
BUT UNTIL NOW, IT HAS ALWAYS BEEN A HOSTILE TAKEOVER.
ONE HUMAN AT A TIME. ALWAYS AGAINST THEIR WILL.
NOW THEY HAVE VOLUNTEERS.
WHAT...?
YOU'RE SAYING HE ALLOWED THE TAKEOVER OF HIS BODY?
BUT THAT'S... CRAZY.
FREEZE, YOU ORANGE FREAK!
STEP ASIDE, SUPERMAN-- YOU SAW HER KILL THAT SUSPECT!
BEHIND ME.
BAM BAM BLAM BLAM BAM
DID YOU SEE HIS BODY?
THERE WAS NONE OF THE TRAUMA INDICATIVE OF A VIOLENT ASSAULT MOST ASSOCIATED WITH A DAEMONITE TRANSUBSTANTIATION.
ADMITTEDLY, I HAVEN'T SEEN A LOT OF--
OFFICERS, PLEASE.
YOU WOULD BE BETTER OFF DIRECTING YOUR EFFORTS TOWARDS QUARANTINING THE OTHERS WHO WERE WIELDING THESE WEAPONS.
"OTHERS"?!
ARE YOU KIDDING ME?!
STARFIRE!
SPLOTCH
I'VE GOT TO REACH THEM BEFORE SHE DOES!

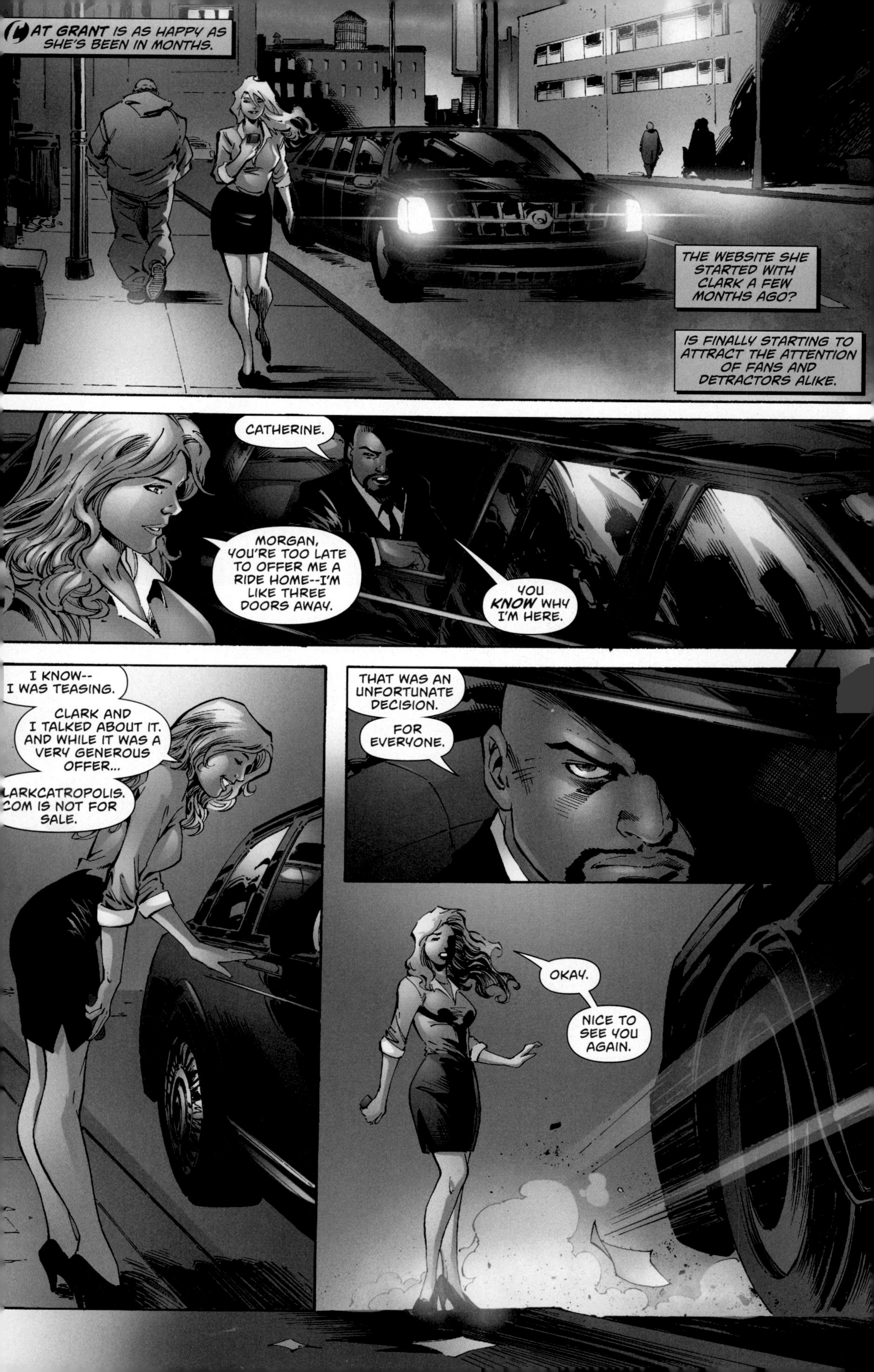
CAT GRANT IS AS HAPPY AS SHE'S BEEN IN MONTHS.
THE WEBSITE SHE STARTED WITH CLARK A FEW MONTHS AGO?
IS FINALLY STARTING TO ATTRACT THE ATTENTION OF FANS AND DETRACTORS ALIKE.
CATHERINE.
MORGAN, YOU'RE TOO LATE TO OFFER ME A RIDE HOME--I'M LIKE THREE DOORS AWAY.
YOU KNOW WHY I'M HERE.
I KNOW-- I WAS TEASING.
CLARK AND I TALKED ABOUT IT. AND WHILE IT WAS A VERY GENEROUS OFFER...
LARKCATROPOLIS.COM IS NOT FOR SALE.
THAT WAS AN UNFORTUNATE DECISION.
FOR EVERYONE.
OKAY.
NICE TO SEE YOU AGAIN.

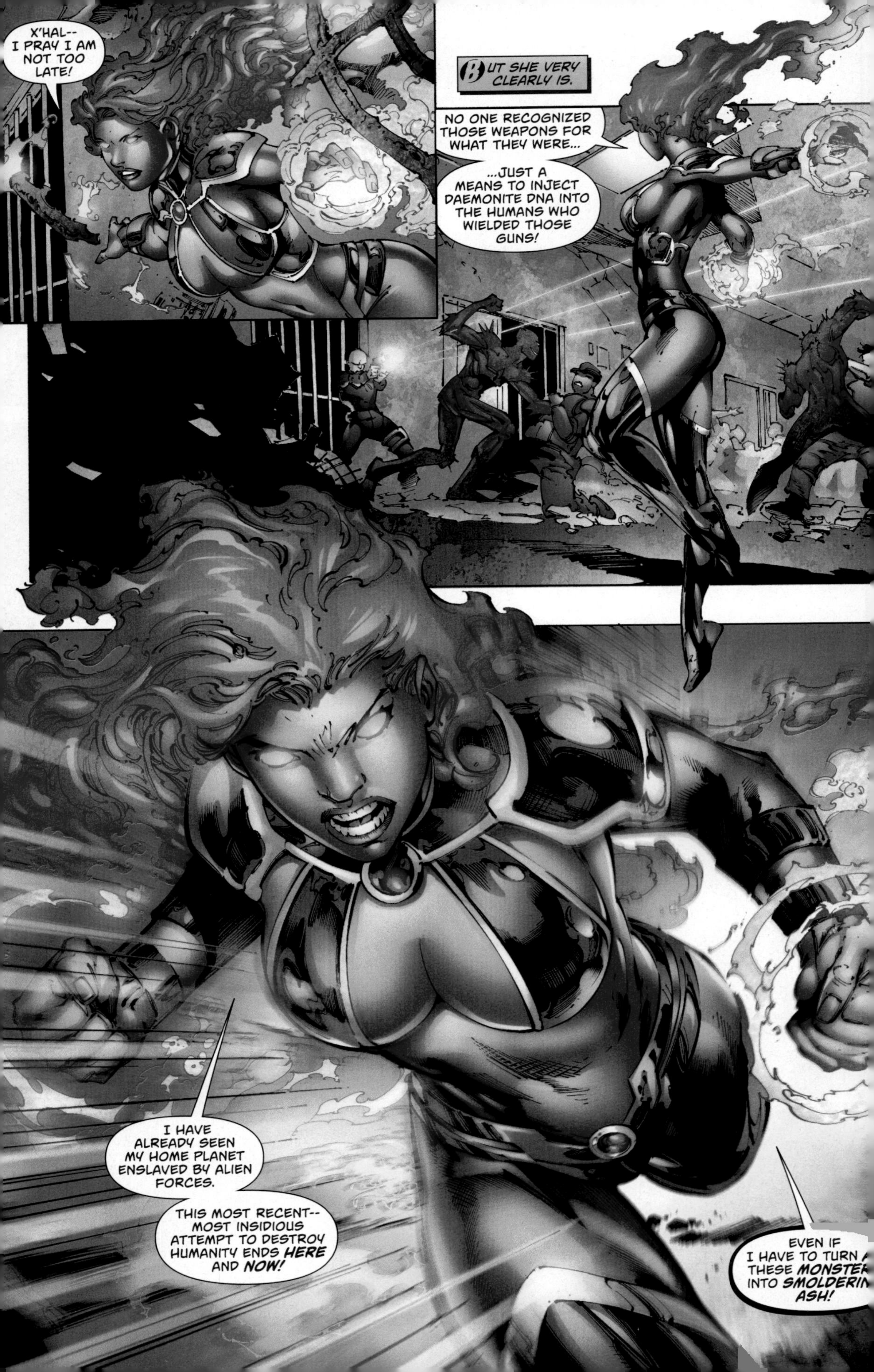
X'HAL-- I PRAY I AM NOT TOO LATE!
BUT SHE VERY CLEARLY IS.
NO ONE RECOGNIZED THOSE WEAPONS FOR WHAT THEY WERE...
...JUST A MEANS TO INJECT DAEMONITE DNA INTO THE HUMANS WHO WIELDED THOSE GUNS!
I HAVE ALREADY SEEN MY HOME PLANET ENSLAVED BY ALIEN FORCES.
THIS MOST RECENT-- MOST INSIDIOUS ATTEMPT TO DESTROY HUMANITY ENDS HERE AND NOW!
EVEN IF I HAVE TO TURN THESE MONSTER INTO SMOLDERIN ASH!

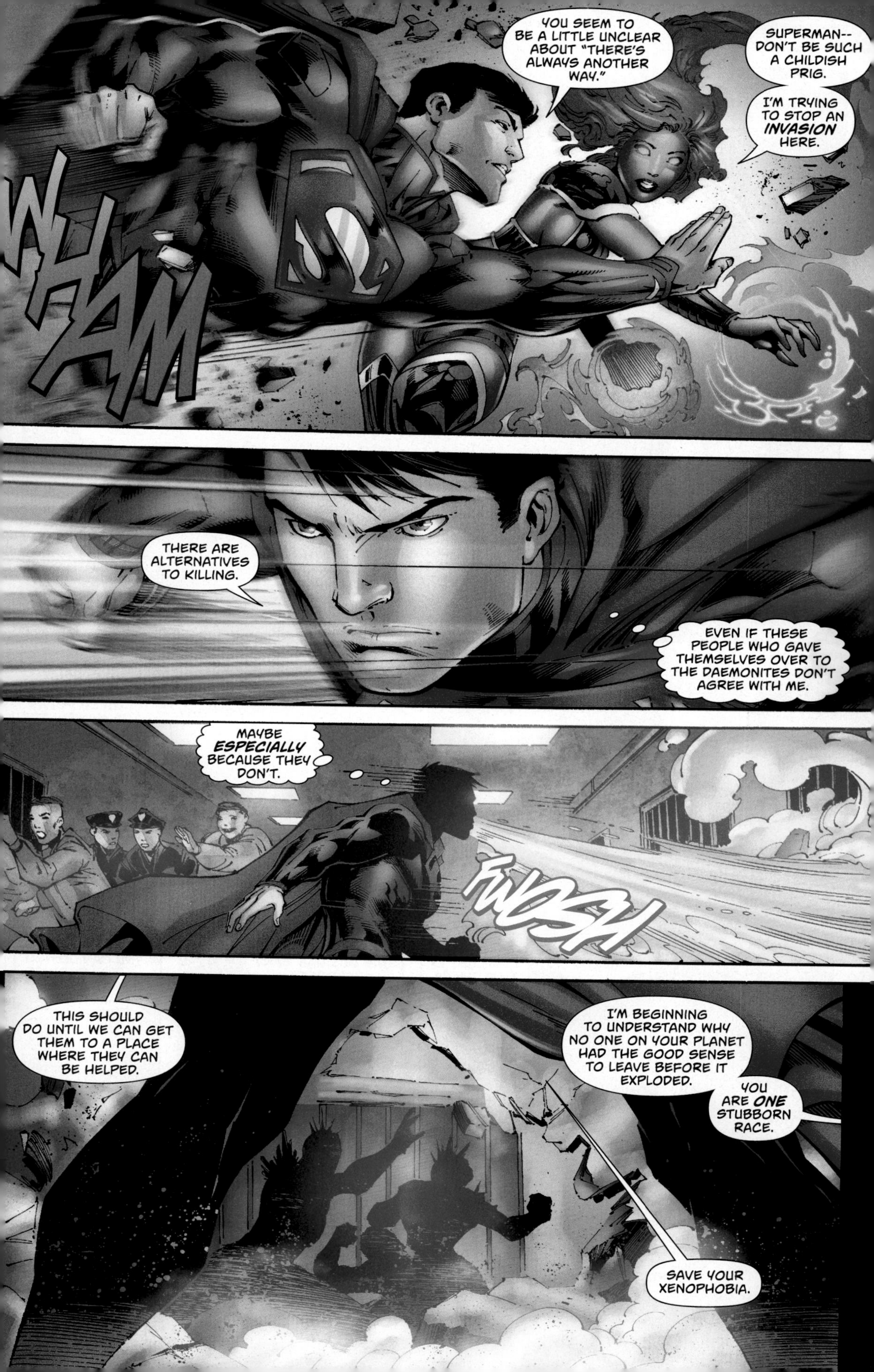
YOU SEEM TO BE A LITTLE UNCLEAR ABOUT "THERE'S ALWAYS ANOTHER WAY."
SUPERMAN-- DON'T BE SUCH A CHILDISH PRIG.
I'M TRYING TO STOP AN INVASION HERE.
WHAM
THERE ARE ALTERNATIVES TO KILLING.
EVEN IF THESE PEOPLE WHO GAVE THEMSELVES OVER TO THE DAEMONITES DON'T AGREE WITH ME.
MAYBE ESPECIALLY BECAUSE THEY DON'T.
FWOSH
THIS SHOULD DO UNTIL WE CAN GET THEM TO A PLACE WHERE THEY CAN BE HELPED.
I'M BEGINNING TO UNDERSTAND WHY NO ONE ON YOUR PLANET HAD THE GOOD SENSE TO LEAVE BEFORE IT EXPLODED.
YOU ARE ONE STUBBORN RACE.
SAVE YOUR XENOPHOBIA.

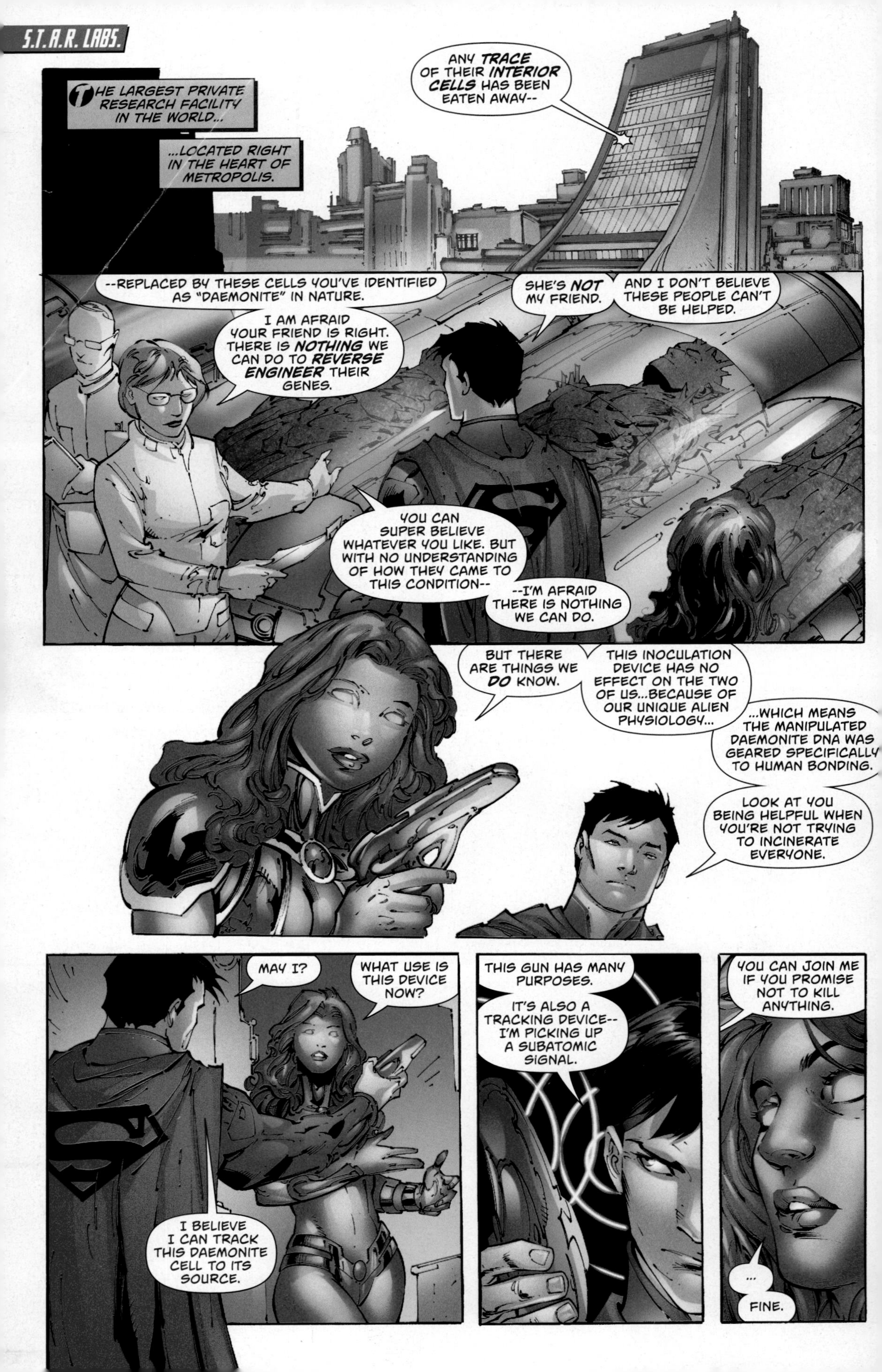
S.T.A.R. LABS.
THE LARGEST PRIVATE RESEARCH FACILITY IN THE WORLD...
...LOCATED RIGHT IN THE HEART OF METROPOLIS.
ANY TRACE OF THEIR INTERIOR CELLS HAS BEEN EATEN AWAY--
--REPLACED BY THESE CELLS YOU'VE IDENTIFIED AS "DAEMONITE" IN NATURE.
I AM AFRAID YOUR FRIEND IS RIGHT. THERE IS NOTHING WE CAN DO TO REVERSE ENGINEER THEIR GENES.
SHE'S NOT MY FRIEND.
AND I DON'T BELIEVE THESE PEOPLE CAN'T BE HELPED.
YOU CAN SUPER BELIEVE WHATEVER YOU LIKE. BUT WITH NO UNDERSTANDING OF HOW THEY CAME TO THIS CONDITION--
--I'M AFRAID THERE IS NOTHING WE CAN DO.
BUT THERE ARE THINGS WE DO KNOW.
THIS INOCULATION DEVICE HAS NO EFFECT ON THE TWO OF US...BECAUSE OF OUR UNIQUE ALIEN PHYSIOLOGY...
...WHICH MEANS THE MANIPULATED DAEMONITE DNA WAS GEARED SPECIFICALLY TO HUMAN BONDING.
LOOK AT YOU BEING HELPFUL WHEN YOU'RE NOT TRYING TO INCINERATE EVERYONE.
MAY I?
WHAT USE IS THIS DEVICE NOW?
I BELIEVE I CAN TRACK THIS DAEMONITE CELL TO ITS SOURCE.
THIS GUN HAS MANY PURPOSES.
IT'S ALSO A TRACKING DEVICE-- I'M PICKING UP A SUBATOMIC SIGNAL.
YOU CAN JOIN ME IF YOU PROMISE NOT TO KILL ANYTHING.
...
FINE.

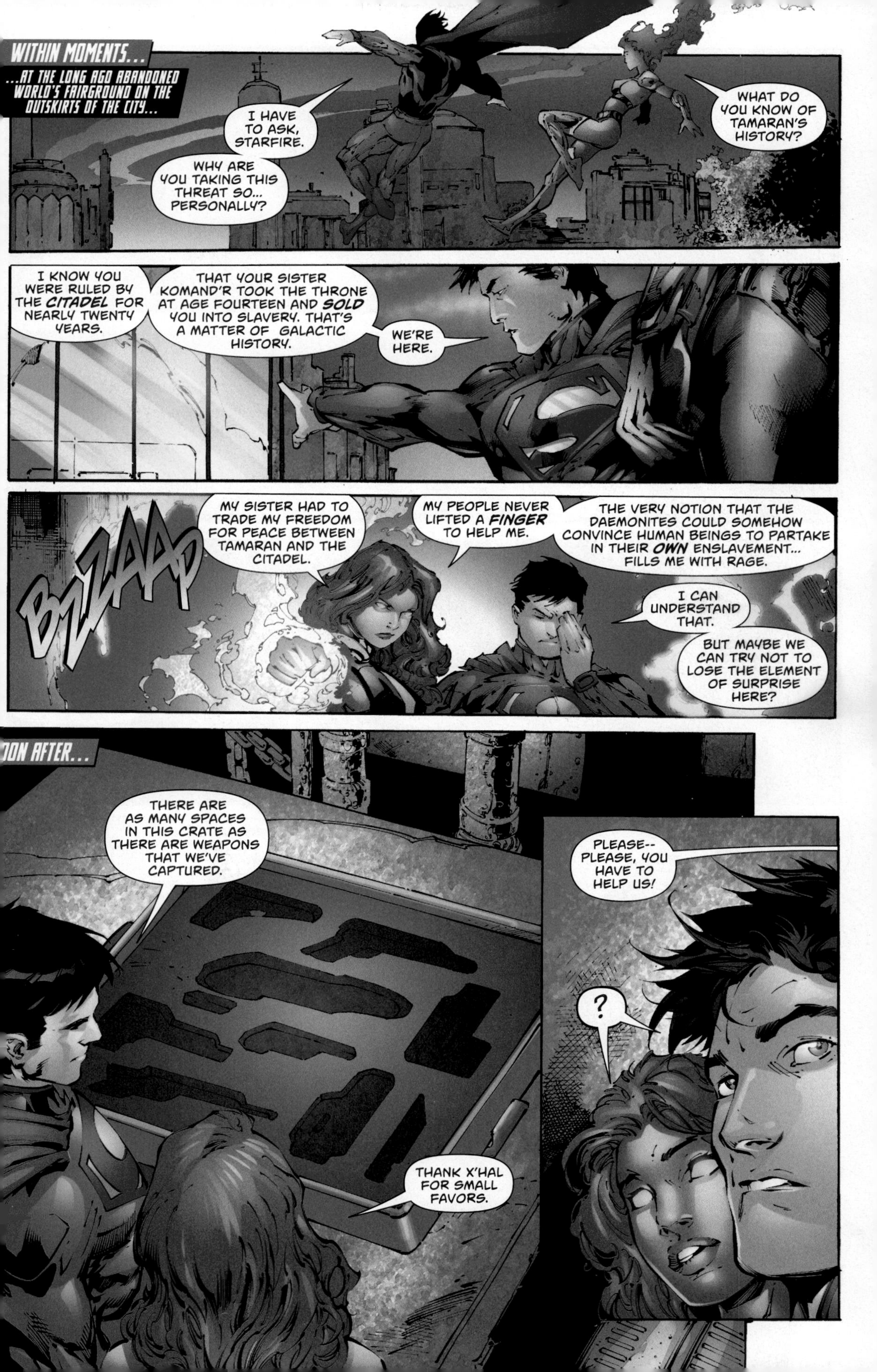
WITHIN MOMENTS...
...AT THE LONG AGO ABANDONED WORLD'S FAIRGROUND ON THE OUTSKIRTS OF THE CITY...
I HAVE TO ASK, STARFIRE.
WHY ARE YOU TAKING THIS THREAT SO... PERSONALLY?
WHAT DO YOU KNOW OF TAMARAN'S HISTORY?
I KNOW YOU WERE RULED BY THE CITADEL FOR NEARLY TWENTY YEARS.
THAT YOUR SISTER KOMAND'R TOOK THE THRONE AT AGE FOURTEEN AND SOLD YOU INTO SLAVERY. THAT'S A MATTER OF GALACTIC HISTORY.
WE'RE HERE.
BZZAAP
MY SISTER HAD TO TRADE MY FREEDOM FOR PEACE BETWEEN TAMARAN AND THE CITADEL.
MY PEOPLE NEVER LIFTED A FINGER TO HELP ME.
THE VERY NOTION THAT THE DAEMONITES COULD SOMEHOW CONVINCE HUMAN BEINGS TO PARTAKE IN THEIR OWN ENSLAVEMENT... FILLS ME WITH RAGE.
I CAN UNDERSTAND THAT.
BUT MAYBE WE CAN TRY NOT TO LOSE THE ELEMENT OF SURPRISE HERE?
OON AFTER...
THERE ARE AS MANY SPACES IN THIS CRATE AS THERE ARE WEAPONS THAT WE'VE CAPTURED.
THANK X'HAL FOR SMALL FAVORS.
PLEASE-- PLEASE, YOU HAVE TO HELP US!
?

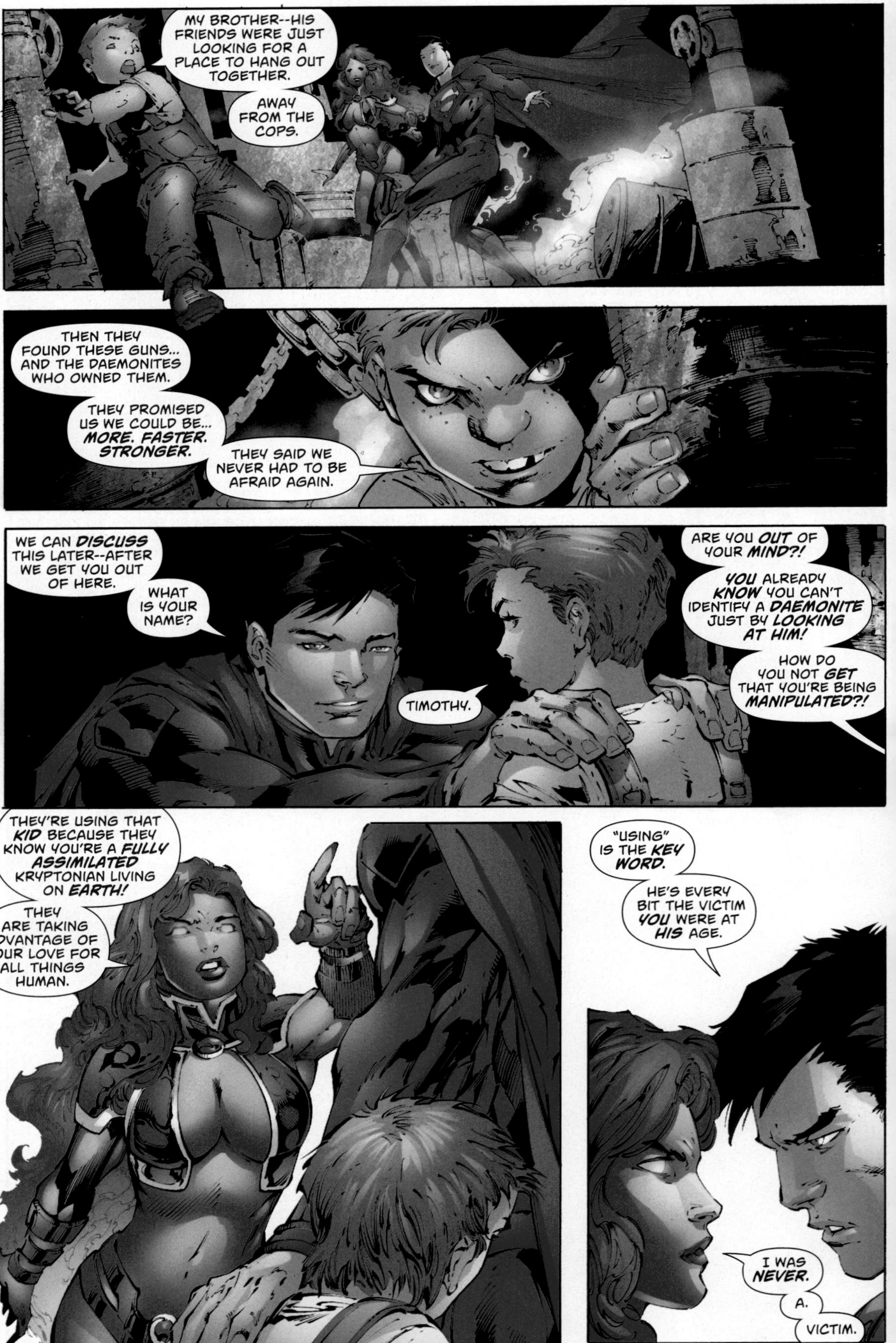
MY BROTHER--HIS FRIENDS WERE JUST LOOKING FOR A PLACE TO HANG OUT TOGETHER.
AWAY FROM THE COPS.
THEN THEY FOUND THESE GUNS... AND THE DAEMONITES WHO OWNED THEM.
THEY PROMISED US WE COULD BE... MORE. FASTER. STRONGER.
THEY SAID WE NEVER HAD TO BE AFRAID AGAIN.
WE CAN DISCUSS THIS LATER--AFTER WE GET YOU OUT OF HERE.
WHAT IS YOUR NAME?
TIMOTHY.
ARE YOU OUT OF YOUR MIND?!
YOU ALREADY KNOW YOU CAN'T IDENTIFY A DAEMONITE JUST BY LOOKING AT HIM!
HOW DO YOU NOT GET THAT YOU'RE BEING MANIPULATED?!
THEY'RE USING THAT KID BECAUSE THEY KNOW YOU'RE A FULLY ASSIMILATED KRYPTONIAN LIVING ON EARTH!
THEY ARE TAKING ADVANTAGE OF YOUR LOVE FOR ALL THINGS HUMAN.
"USING" IS THE KEY WORD.
HE'S EVERY BIT THE VICTIM YOU WERE AT HIS AGE.
I WAS NEVER.
A.
VICTIM.

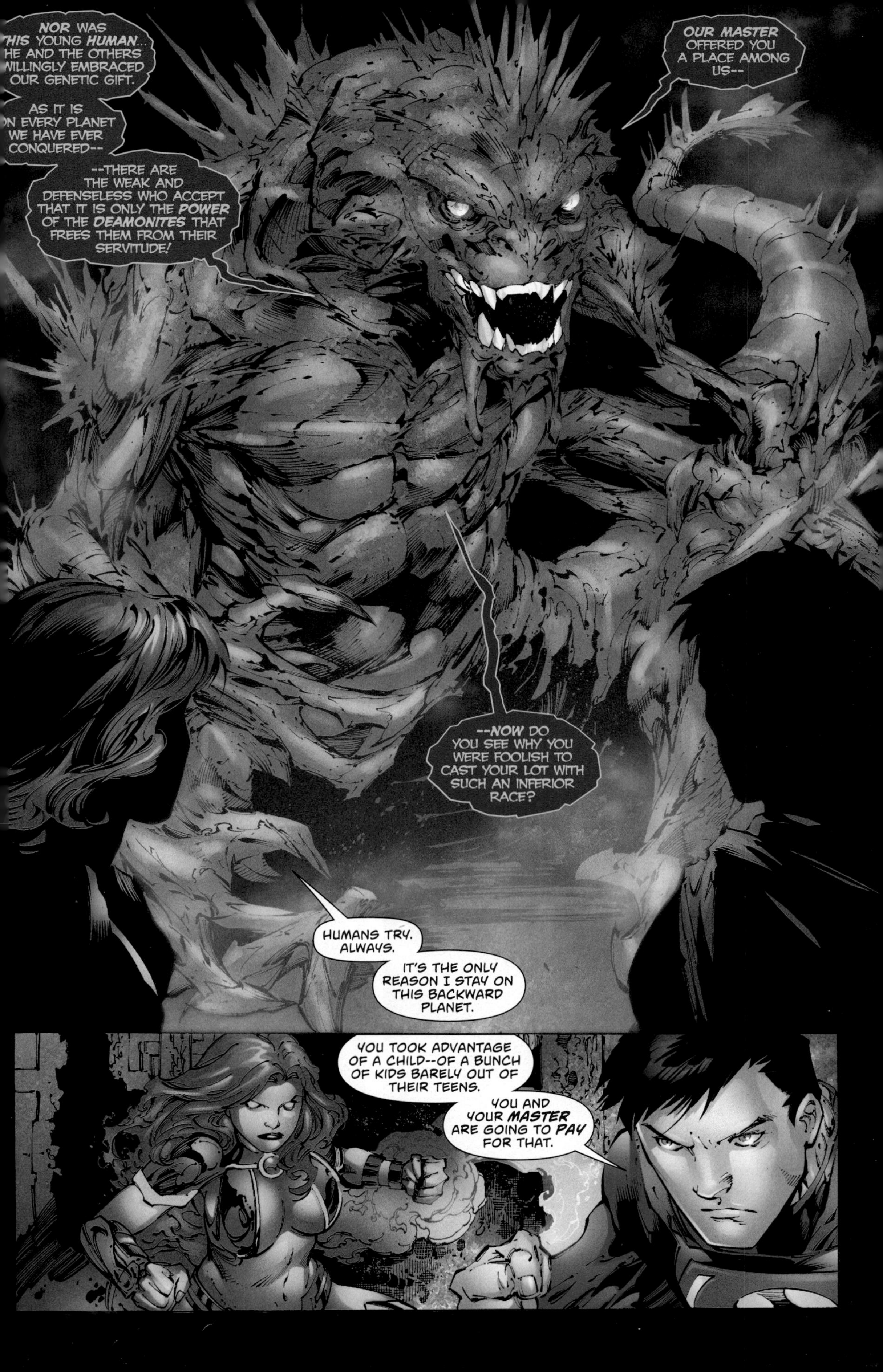
NOR WAS THIS YOUNG HUMAN... HE AND THE OTHERS WILLINGLY EMBRACED OUR GENETIC GIFT.
AS IT IS ON EVERY PLANET WE HAVE EVER CONQUERED--
--THERE ARE THE WEAK AND DEFENSELESS WHO ACCEPT THAT IT IS ONLY THE POWER OF THE DEAMONITES THAT FREES THEM FROM THEIR SERVITUDE!
OUR MASTER OFFERED YOU A PLACE AMONG US--
--NOW DO YOU SEE WHY YOU WERE FOOLISH TO CAST YOUR LOT WITH SUCH AN INFERIOR RACE?
HUMANS TRY. ALWAYS.
IT'S THE ONLY REASON I STAY ON THIS BACKWARD PLANET.
YOU TOOK ADVANTAGE OF A CHILD--OF A BUNCH OF KIDS BARELY OUT OF THEIR TEENS.
YOU AND YOUR MASTER ARE GOING TO PAY FOR THAT.

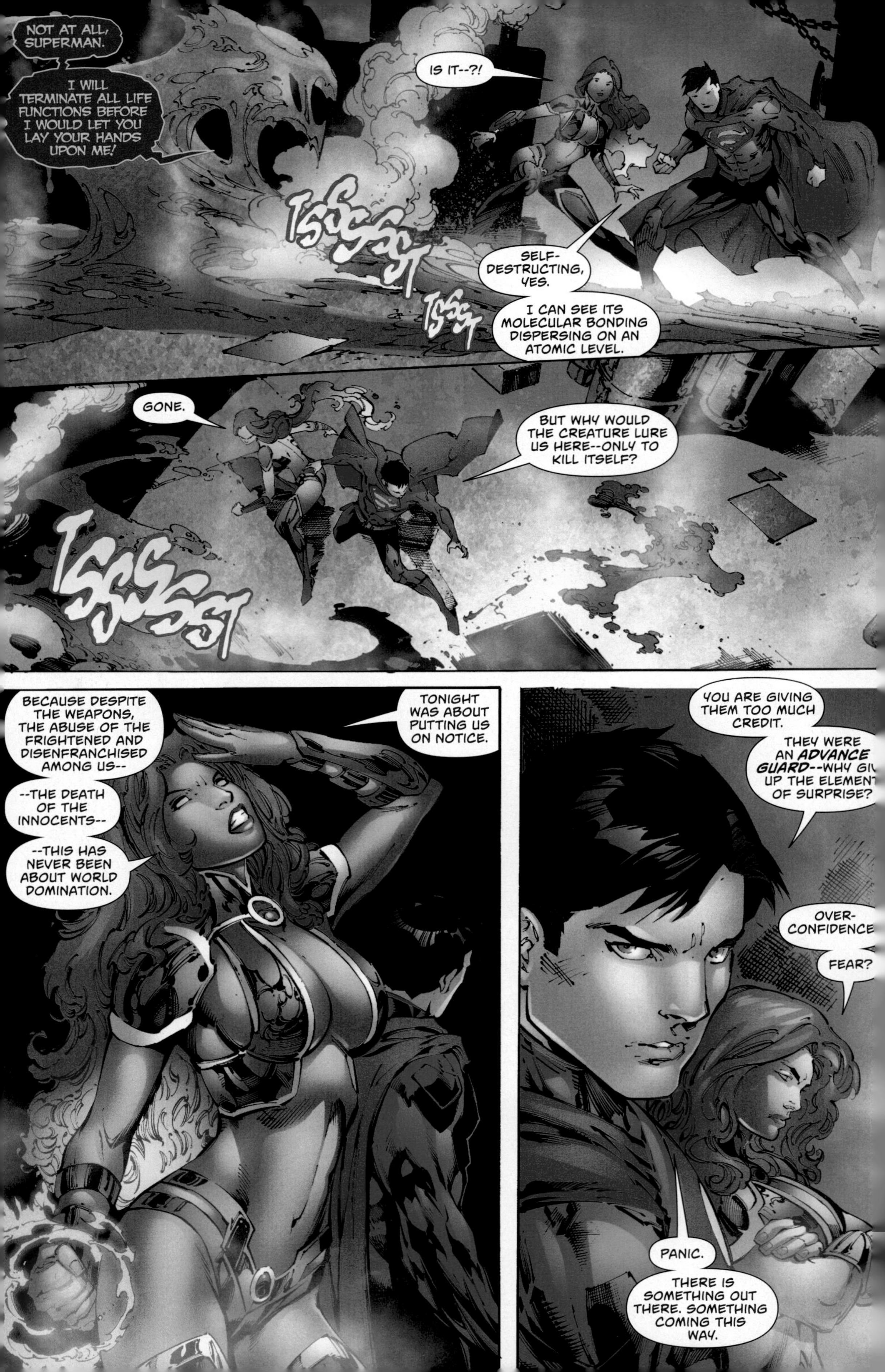

NOT AT ALL, SUPERMAN.
I WILL TERMINATE ALL LIFE FUNCTIONS BEFORE I WOULD LET YOU LAY YOUR HANDS UPON ME!
IS IT--?!
TSSSSST
SELF-DESTRUCTING, YES.
I CAN SEE ITS MOLECULAR BONDING DISPERSING ON AN ATOMIC LEVEL.
TSSST
GONE.
BUT WHY WOULD THE CREATURE LURE US HERE--ONLY TO KILL ITSELF?
TSSSSST
BECAUSE DESPITE THE WEAPONS, THE ABUSE OF THE FRIGHTENED AND DISENFRANCHISED AMONG US--
--THE DEATH OF THE INNOCENTS--
--THIS HAS NEVER BEEN ABOUT WORLD DOMINATION.
TONIGHT WAS ABOUT PUTTING US ON NOTICE.
YOU ARE GIVING THEM TOO MUCH CREDIT.
THEY WERE AN *ADVANCE GUARD*--WHY GIV UP THE ELEMENT OF SURPRISE?
OVER-CONFIDENCE
FEAR?
PANIC.
THERE IS SOMETHING OUT THERE. SOMETHING COMING THIS WAY.

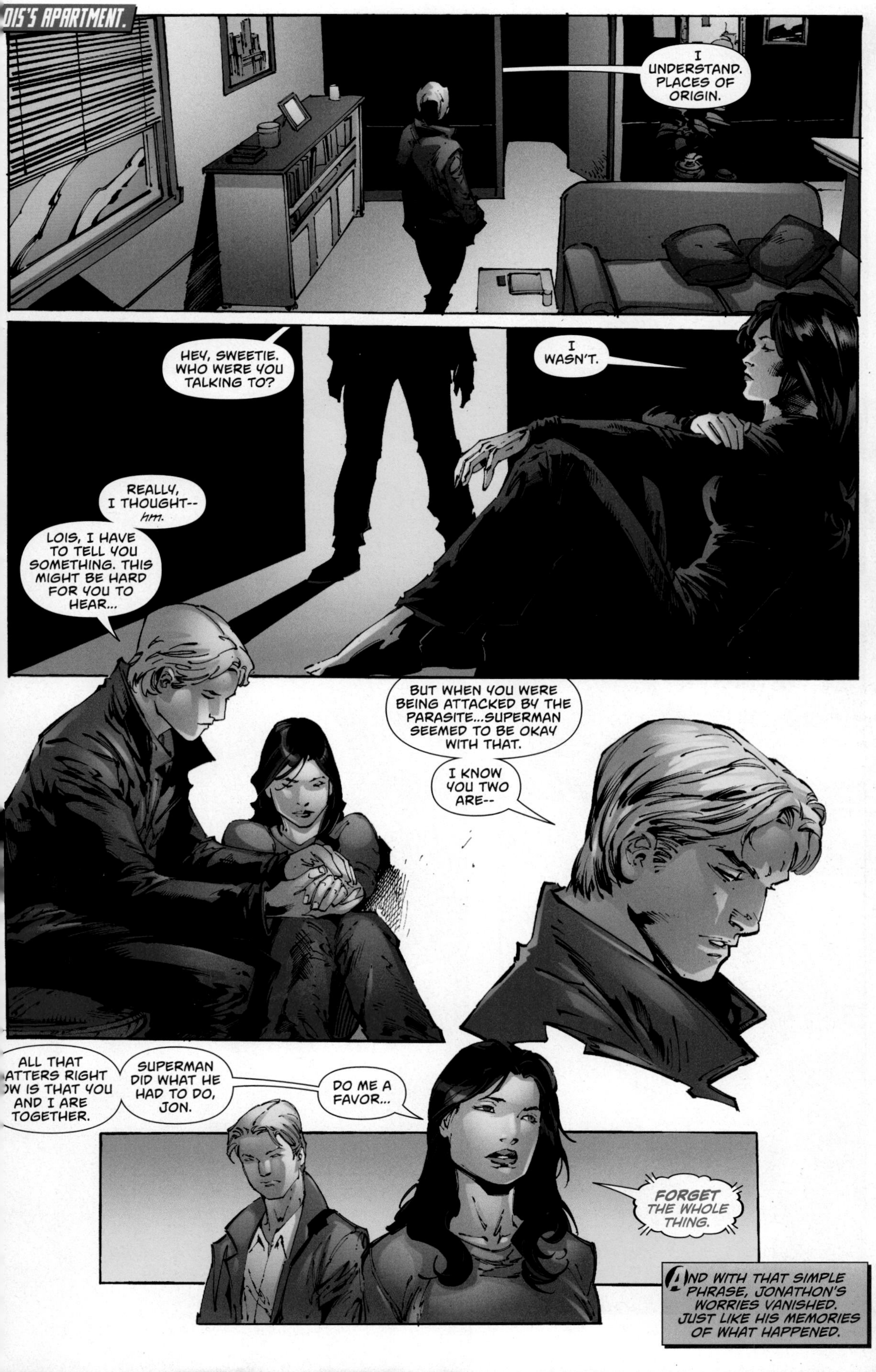
OIS'S APARTMENT.
I UNDERSTAND. PLACES OF ORIGIN.
HEY, SWEETIE. WHO WERE YOU TALKING TO?
I WASN'T.
REALLY, I THOUGHT-- hm.
LOIS, I HAVE TO TELL YOU SOMETHING. THIS MIGHT BE HARD FOR YOU TO HEAR...
BUT WHEN YOU WERE BEING ATTACKED BY THE PARASITE...SUPERMAN SEEMED TO BE OKAY WITH THAT.
I KNOW YOU TWO ARE--
ALL THAT ATTERS RIGHT OW IS THAT YOU AND I ARE TOGETHER.
SUPERMAN DID WHAT HE HAD TO DO, JON.
DO ME A FAVOR...
FORGET THE WHOLE THING.
AND WITH THAT SIMPLE PHRASE, JONATHON'S WORRIES VANISHED. JUST LIKE HIS MEMORIES OF WHAT HAPPENED.

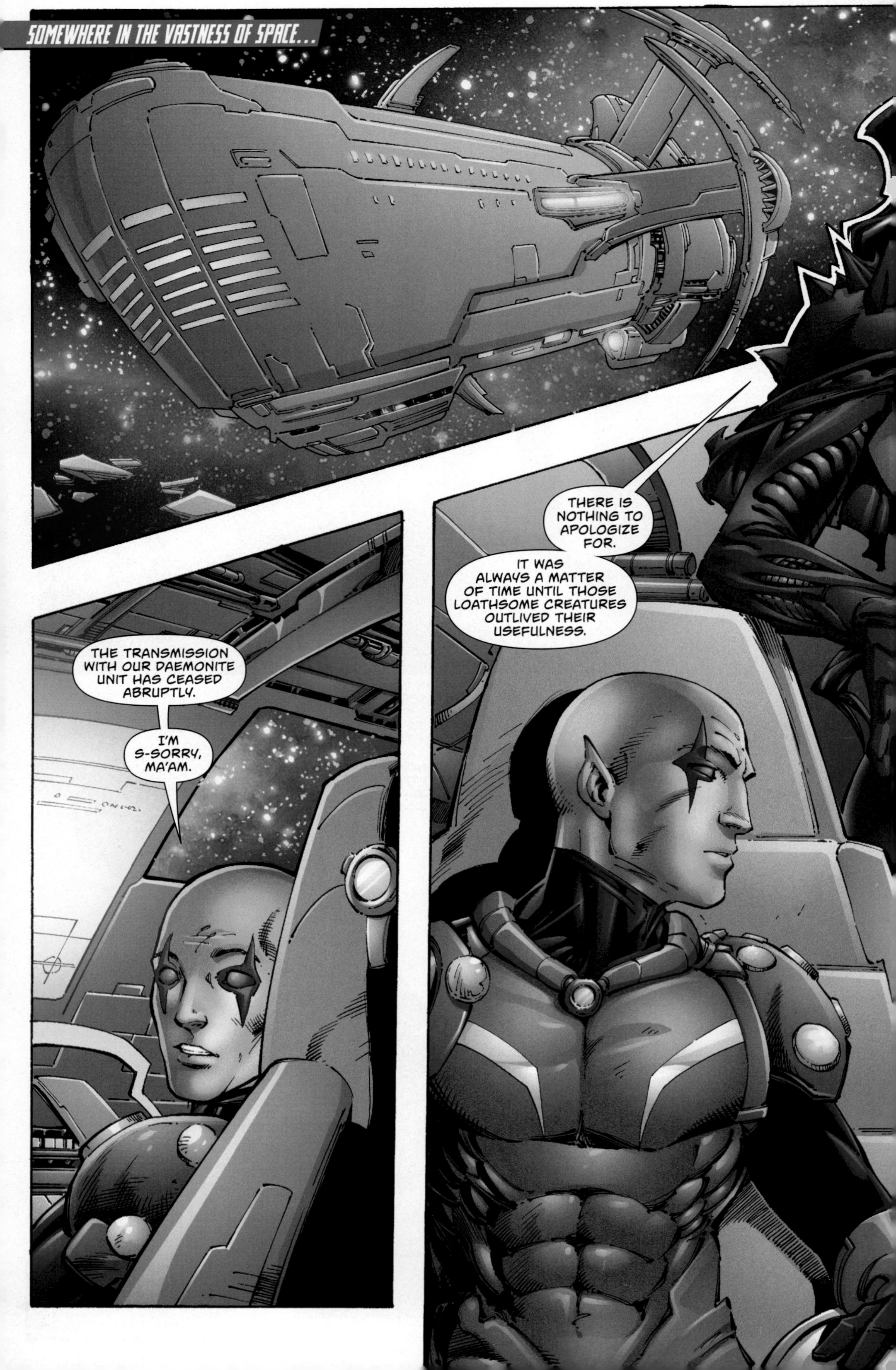
SOMEWHERE IN THE VASTNESS OF SPACE...
THE TRANSMISSION WITH OUR DAEMONITE UNIT HAS CEASED ABRUPTLY.
I'M S-SORRY, MA'AM.
THERE IS NOTHING TO APOLOGIZE FOR.
IT WAS ALWAYS A MATTER OF TIME UNTIL THOSE LOATHSOME CREATURES OUTLIVED THEIR USEFULNESS.

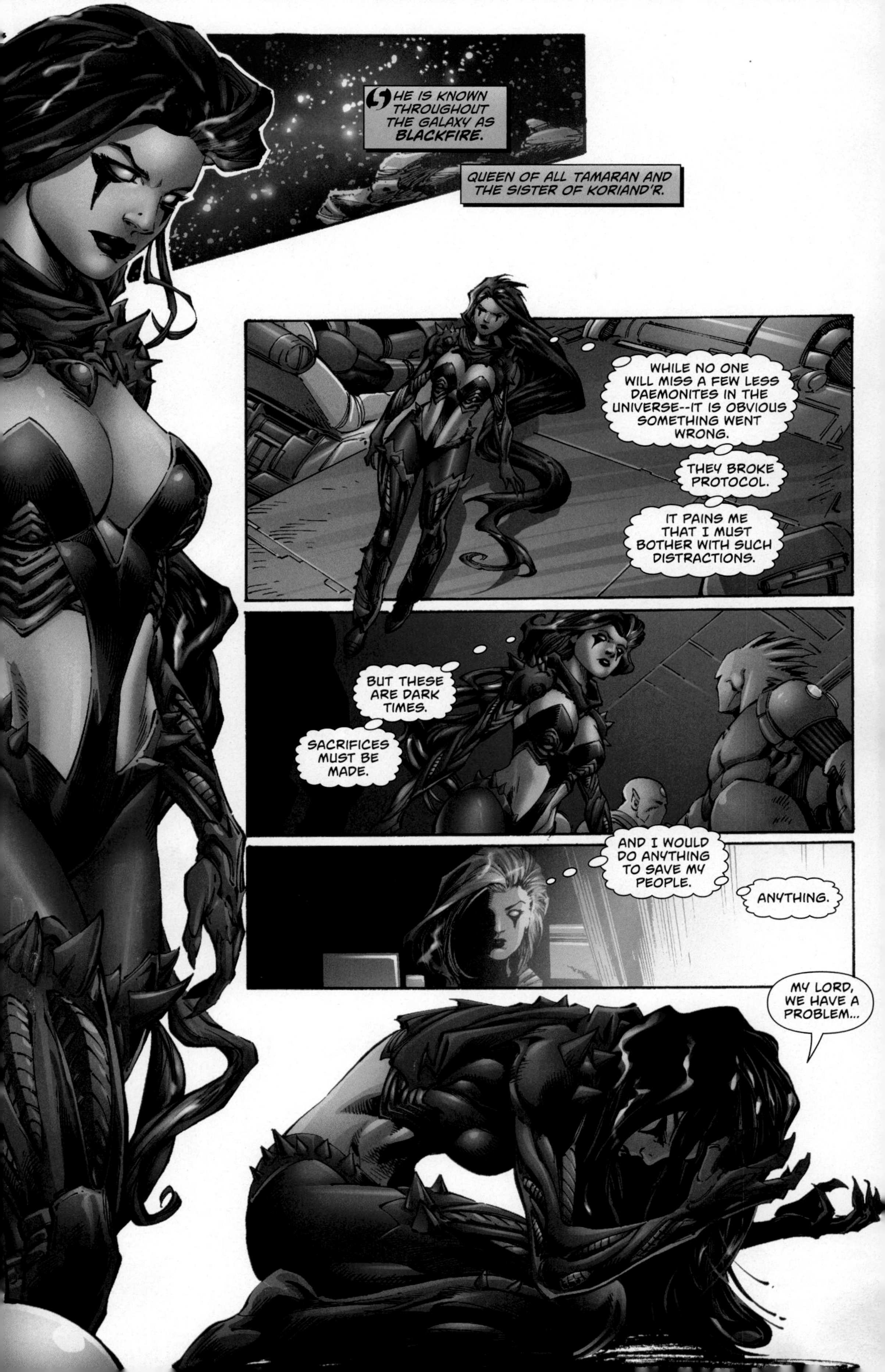
SHE IS KNOWN THROUGHOUT THE GALAXY AS BLACKFIRE.
QUEEN OF ALL TAMARAN AND THE SISTER OF KORIAND'R.
WHILE NO ONE WILL MISS A FEW LESS DAEMONITES IN THE UNIVERSE--IT IS OBVIOUS SOMETHING WENT WRONG.
THEY BROKE PROTOCOL.
IT PAINS ME THAT I MUST BOTHER WITH SUCH DISTRACTIONS.
BUT THESE ARE DARK TIMES.
SACRIFICES MUST BE MADE.
AND I WOULD DO ANYTHING TO SAVE MY PEOPLE.
ANYTHING.
MY LORD, WE HAVE A PROBLEM...

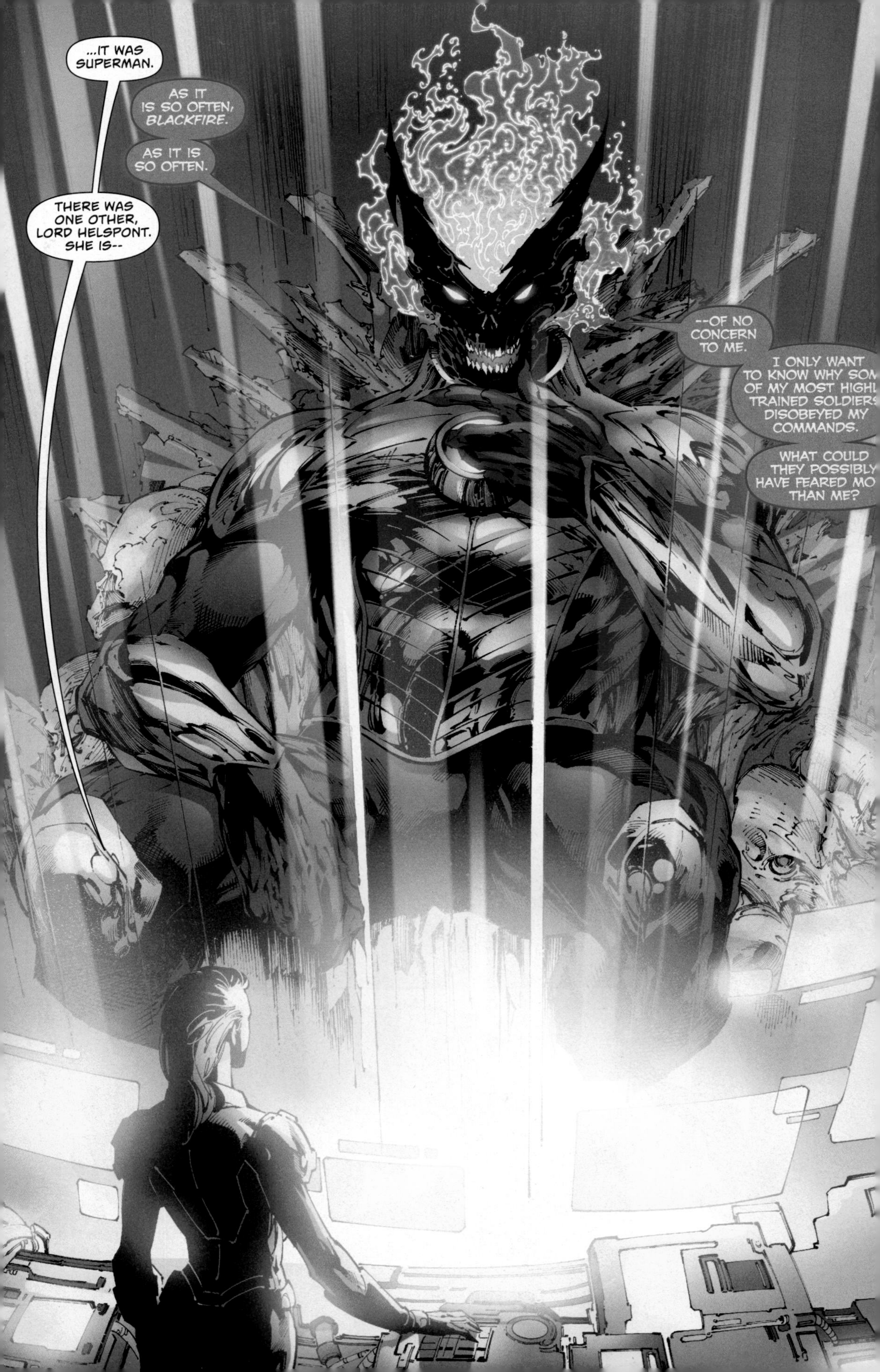
...IT WAS SUPERMAN.
AS IT IS SO OFTEN, BLACKFIRE.
AS IT IS SO OFTEN.
THERE WAS ONE OTHER, LORD HELSPONT. SHE IS--
--OF NO CONCERN TO ME.
I ONLY WANT TO KNOW WHY SOM OF MY MOST HIGHL TRAINED SOLDIERS DISOBEYED MY COMMANDS.
WHAT COULD THEY POSSIBLY HAVE FEARED MO THAN ME?

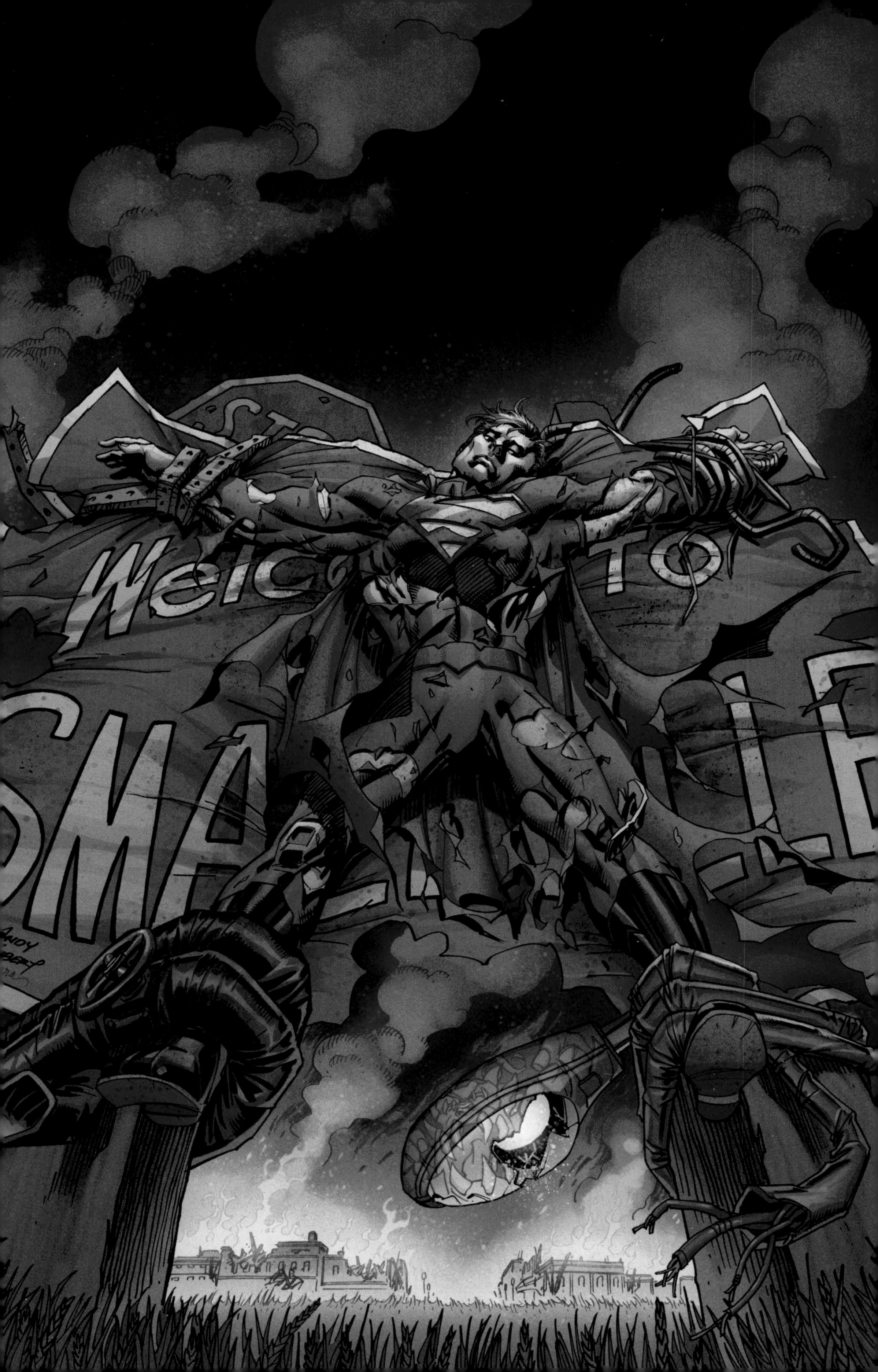
TO

ALL GOOD THINGS MUST END

SCOTT LOBDELL writer **ED BENES** penciller **NORM RAPMUND** inker **PETE PANTAZIS** colorist
cover art by **ANDY KUBERT** and **BRAD ANDERSON**

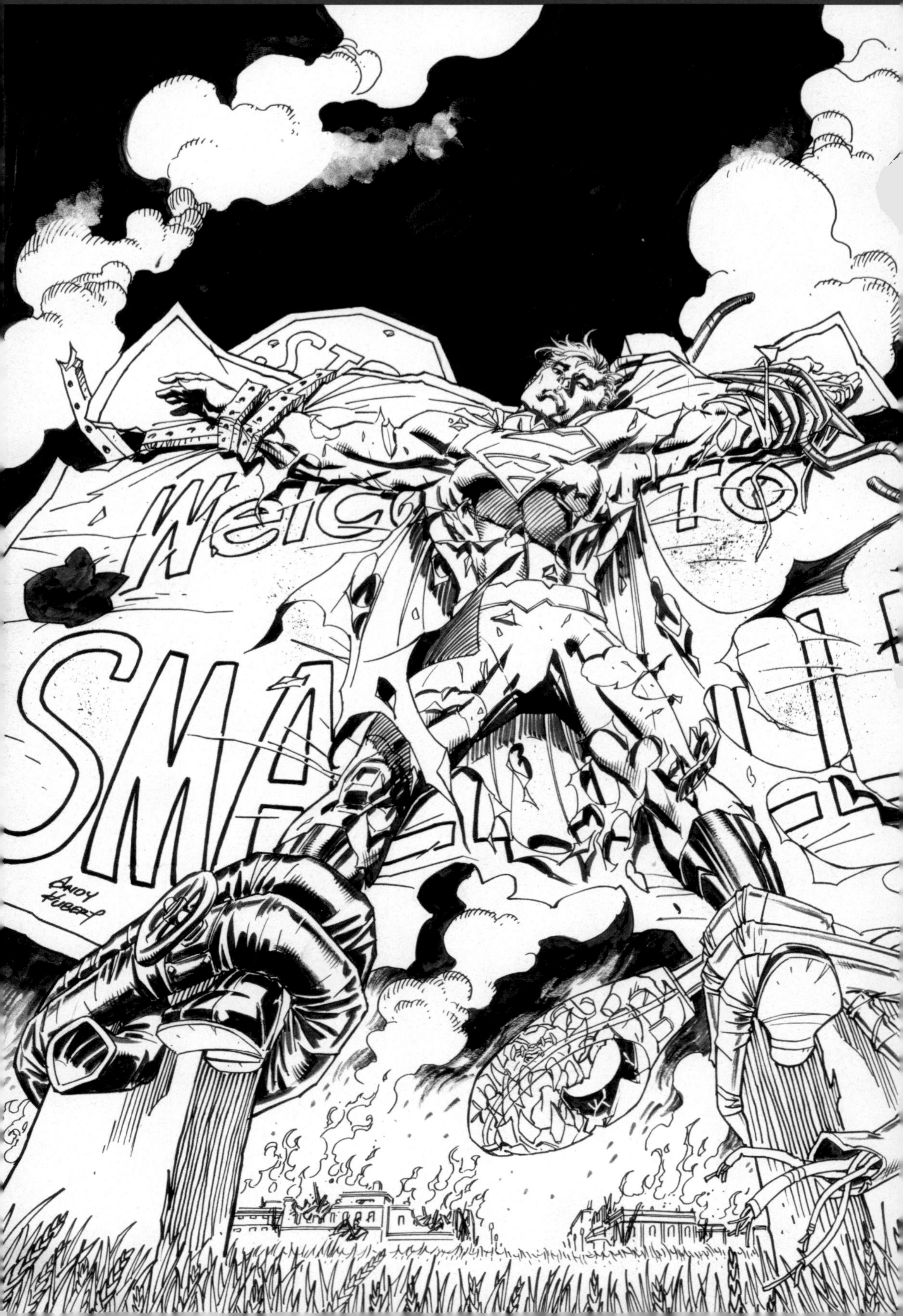
ANDY KUBERT

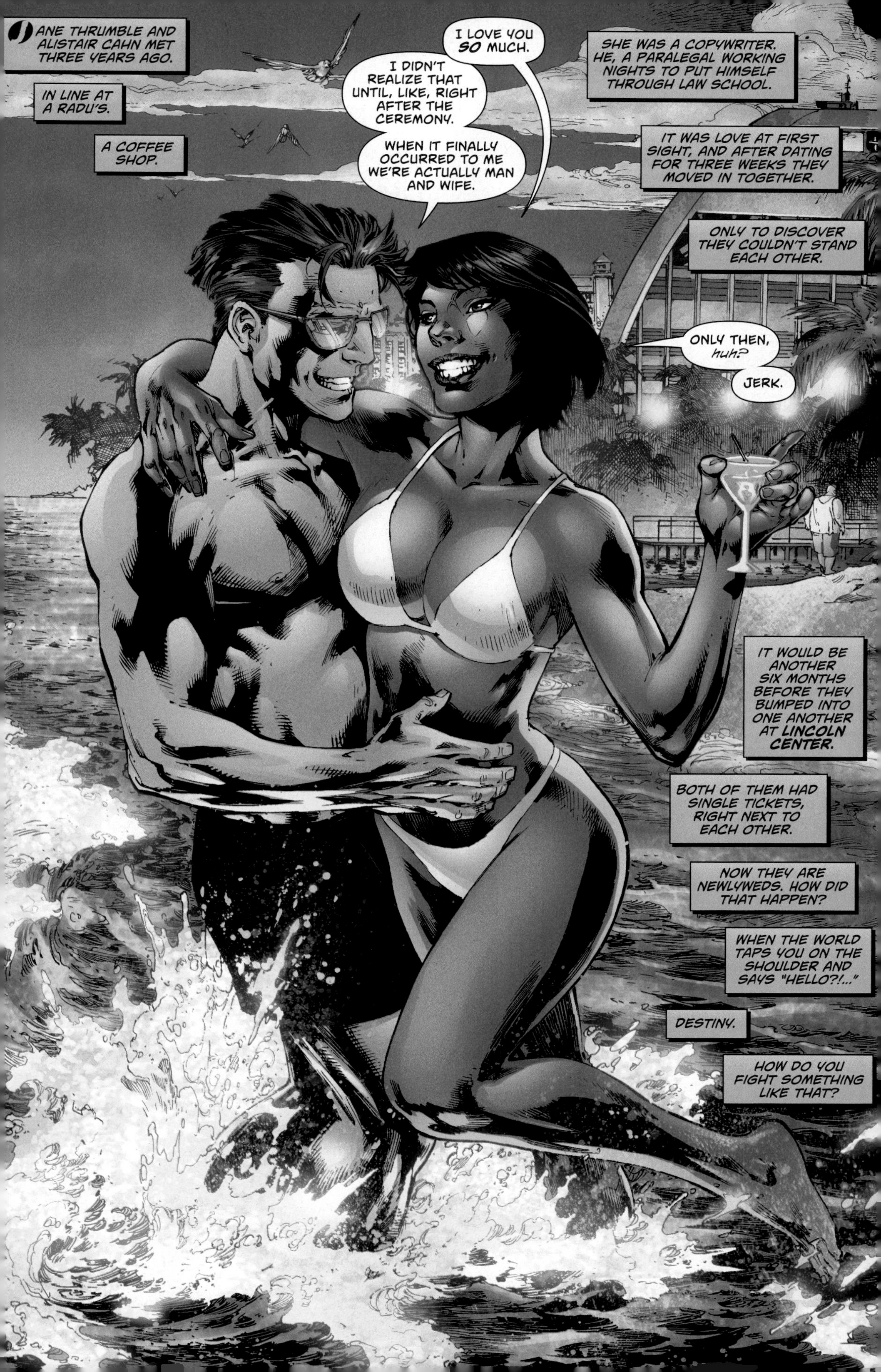
JANE THRUMBLE AND ALISTAIR CAHN MET THREE YEARS AGO.
IN LINE AT A RADU'S.
A COFFEE SHOP.
I LOVE YOU SO MUCH.
I DIDN'T REALIZE THAT UNTIL, LIKE, RIGHT AFTER THE CEREMONY.
WHEN IT FINALLY OCCURRED TO ME WE'RE ACTUALLY MAN AND WIFE.
SHE WAS A COPYWRITER. HE, A PARALEGAL WORKING NIGHTS TO PUT HIMSELF THROUGH LAW SCHOOL.
IT WAS LOVE AT FIRST SIGHT, AND AFTER DATING FOR THREE WEEKS THEY MOVED IN TOGETHER.
ONLY TO DISCOVER THEY COULDN'T STAND EACH OTHER.
ONLY THEN, huh?
JERK.
IT WOULD BE ANOTHER SIX MONTHS BEFORE THEY BUMPED INTO ONE ANOTHER AT LINCOLN CENTER.
BOTH OF THEM HAD SINGLE TICKETS, RIGHT NEXT TO EACH OTHER.
NOW THEY ARE NEWLYWEDS. HOW DID THAT HAPPEN?
WHEN THE WORLD TAPS YOU ON THE SHOULDER AND SAYS "HELLO?!..."
DESTINY.
HOW DO YOU FIGHT SOMETHING LIKE THAT?

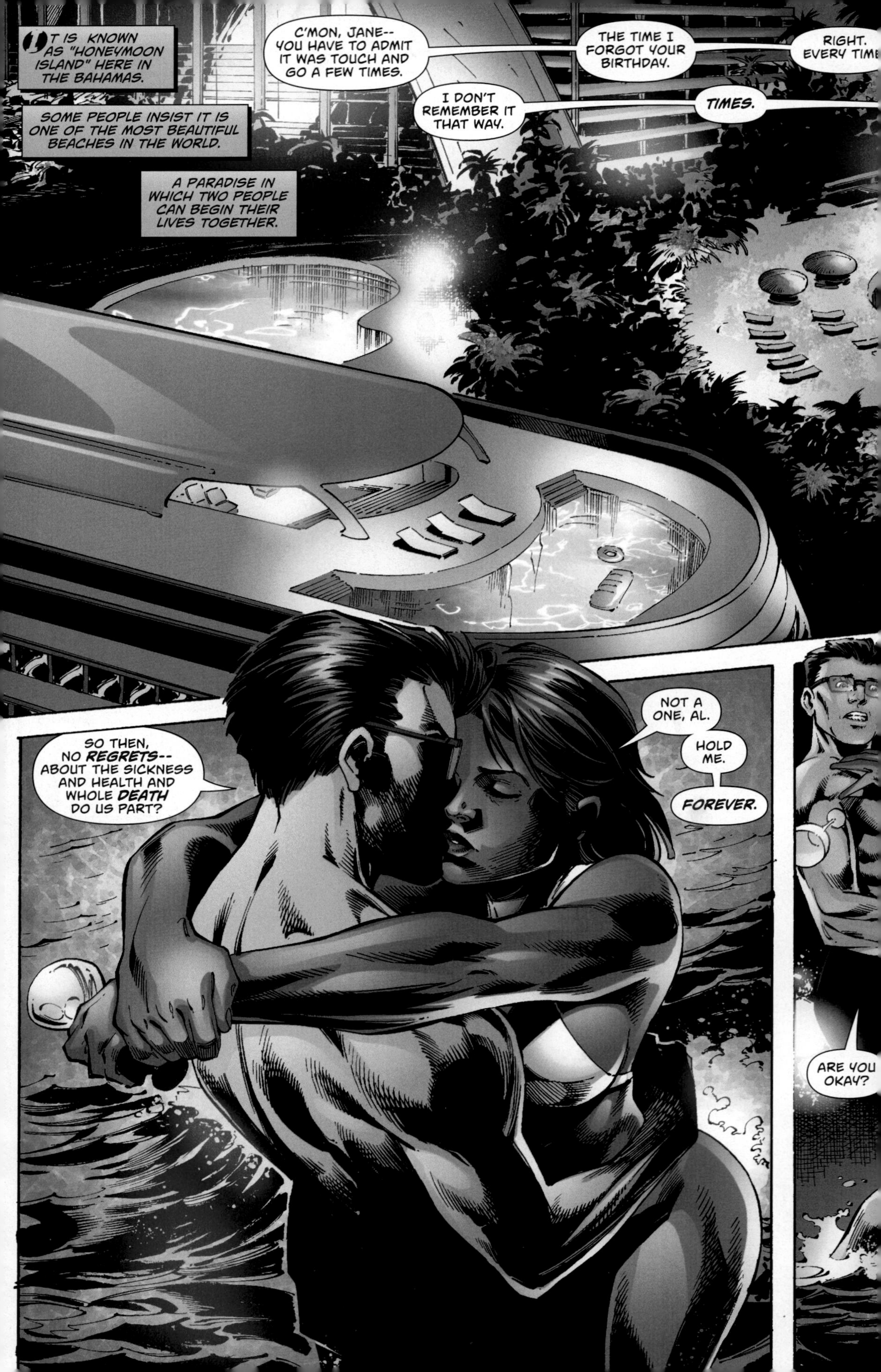
IT IS KNOWN AS "HONEYMOON ISLAND" HERE IN THE BAHAMAS.
SOME PEOPLE INSIST IT IS ONE OF THE MOST BEAUTIFUL BEACHES IN THE WORLD.
A PARADISE IN WHICH TWO PEOPLE CAN BEGIN THEIR LIVES TOGETHER.
C'MON, JANE-- YOU HAVE TO ADMIT IT WAS TOUCH AND GO A FEW TIMES.
I DON'T REMEMBER IT THAT WAY.
THE TIME I FORGOT YOUR BIRTHDAY.
TIMES.
RIGHT. EVERY TIM
SO THEN, NO REGRETS-- ABOUT THE SICKNESS AND HEALTH AND WHOLE DEATH DO US PART?
NOT A ONE, AL.
HOLD ME.
FOREVER.
ARE YOU OKAY?

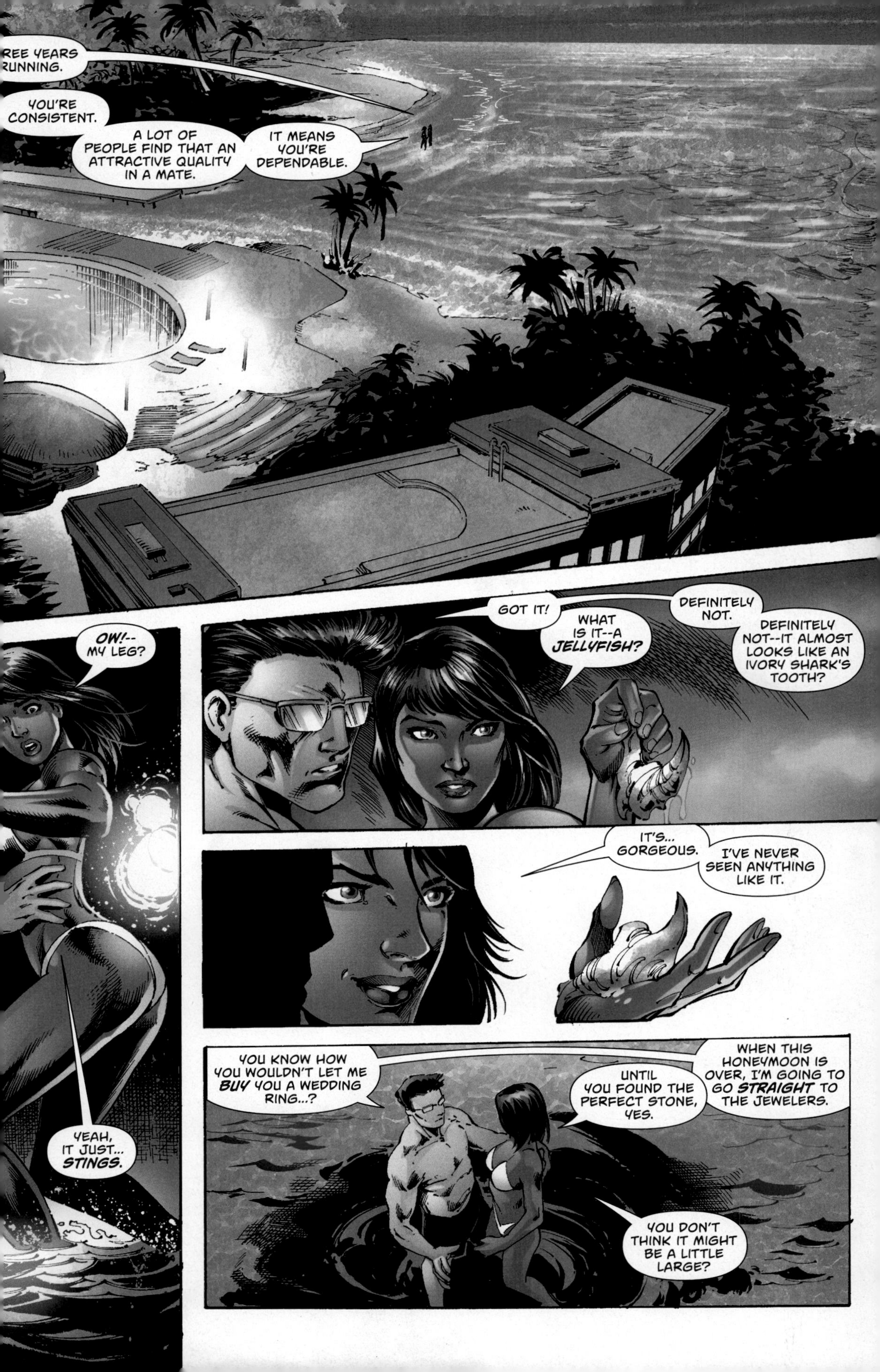
REE YEARS RUNNING.
YOU'RE CONSISTENT.
A LOT OF PEOPLE FIND THAT AN ATTRACTIVE QUALITY IN A MATE.
IT MEANS YOU'RE DEPENDABLE.
OW!-- MY LEG?
GOT IT!
WHAT IS IT--A JELLYFISH?
DEFINITELY NOT.
DEFINITELY NOT--IT ALMOST LOOKS LIKE AN IVORY SHARK'S TOOTH?
IT'S... GORGEOUS.
I'VE NEVER SEEN ANYTHING LIKE IT.
YEAH, IT JUST... STINGS.
YOU KNOW HOW YOU WOULDN'T LET ME BUY YOU A WEDDING RING...?
UNTIL YOU FOUND THE PERFECT STONE, YES.
WHEN THIS HONEYMOON IS OVER, I'M GOING TO GO STRAIGHT TO THE JEWELERS.
YOU DON'T THINK IT MIGHT BE A LITTLE LARGE?

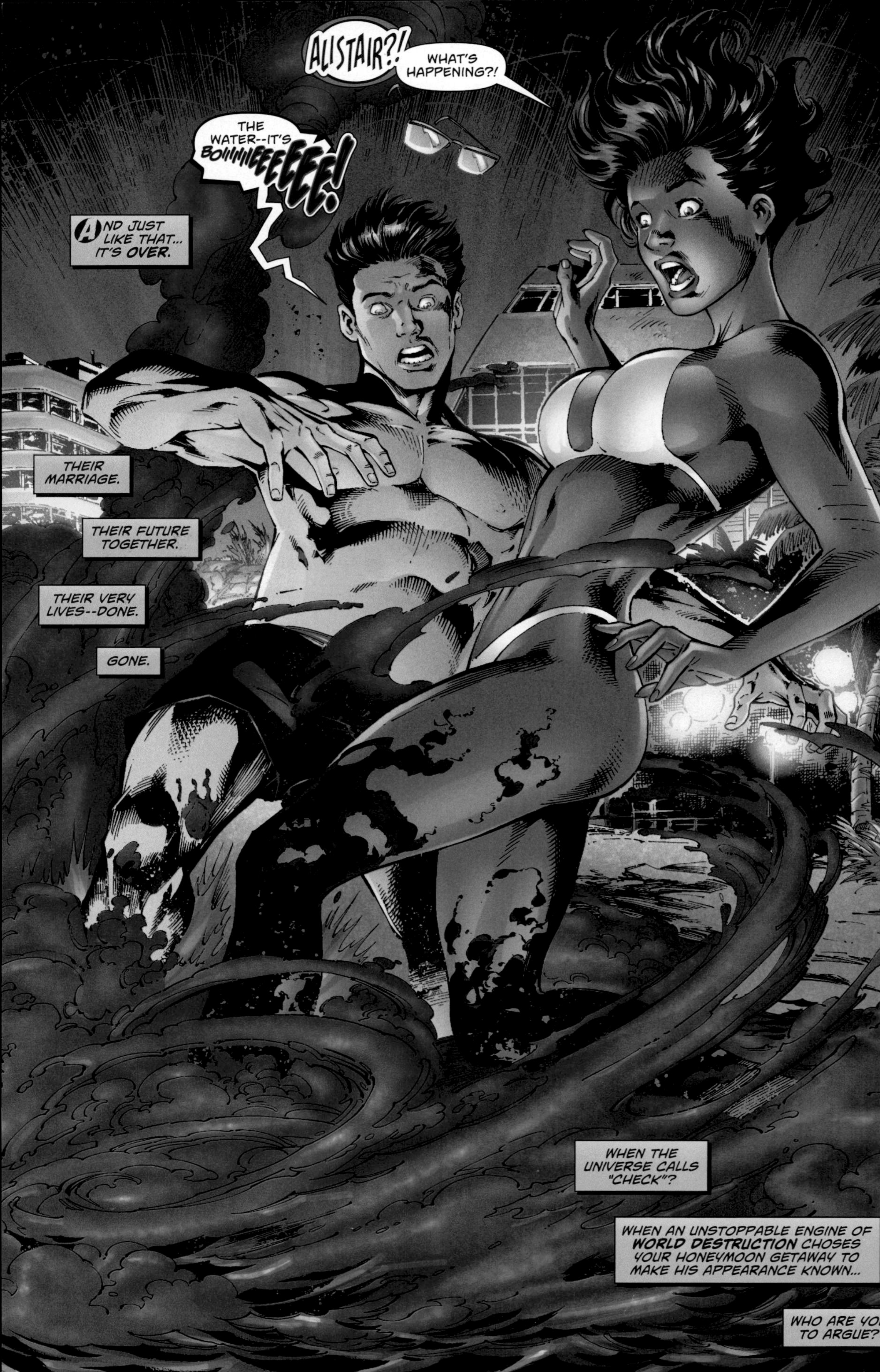
ALISTAIR?!
WHAT'S HAPPENING?!
THE WATER--IT'S BOIIIIIEEEEEE!
AND JUST LIKE THAT... IT'S OVER.
THEIR MARRIAGE.
THEIR FUTURE TOGETHER.
THEIR VERY LIVES--DONE.
GONE.
WHEN THE UNIVERSE CALLS "CHECK"?
WHEN AN UNSTOPPABLE ENGINE OF WORLD DESTRUCTION CHOSES YOUR HONEYMOON GETAWAY TO MAKE HIS APPEARANCE KNOWN...
WHO ARE YO TO ARGUE?

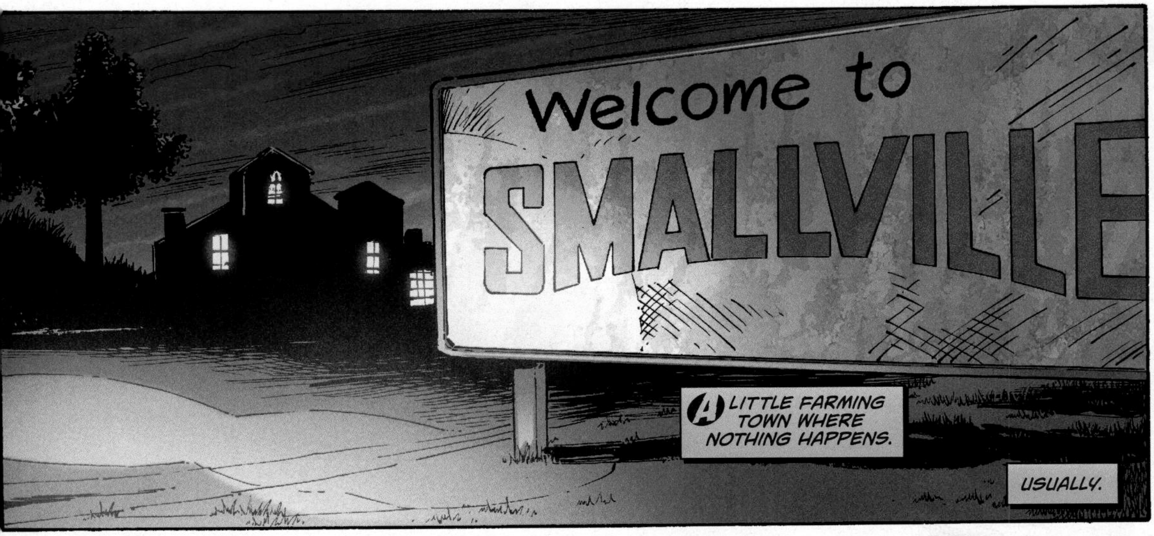
Welcome to
SMALLVILLE
A LITTLE FARMING TOWN WHERE NOTHING HAPPENS.
USUALLY.

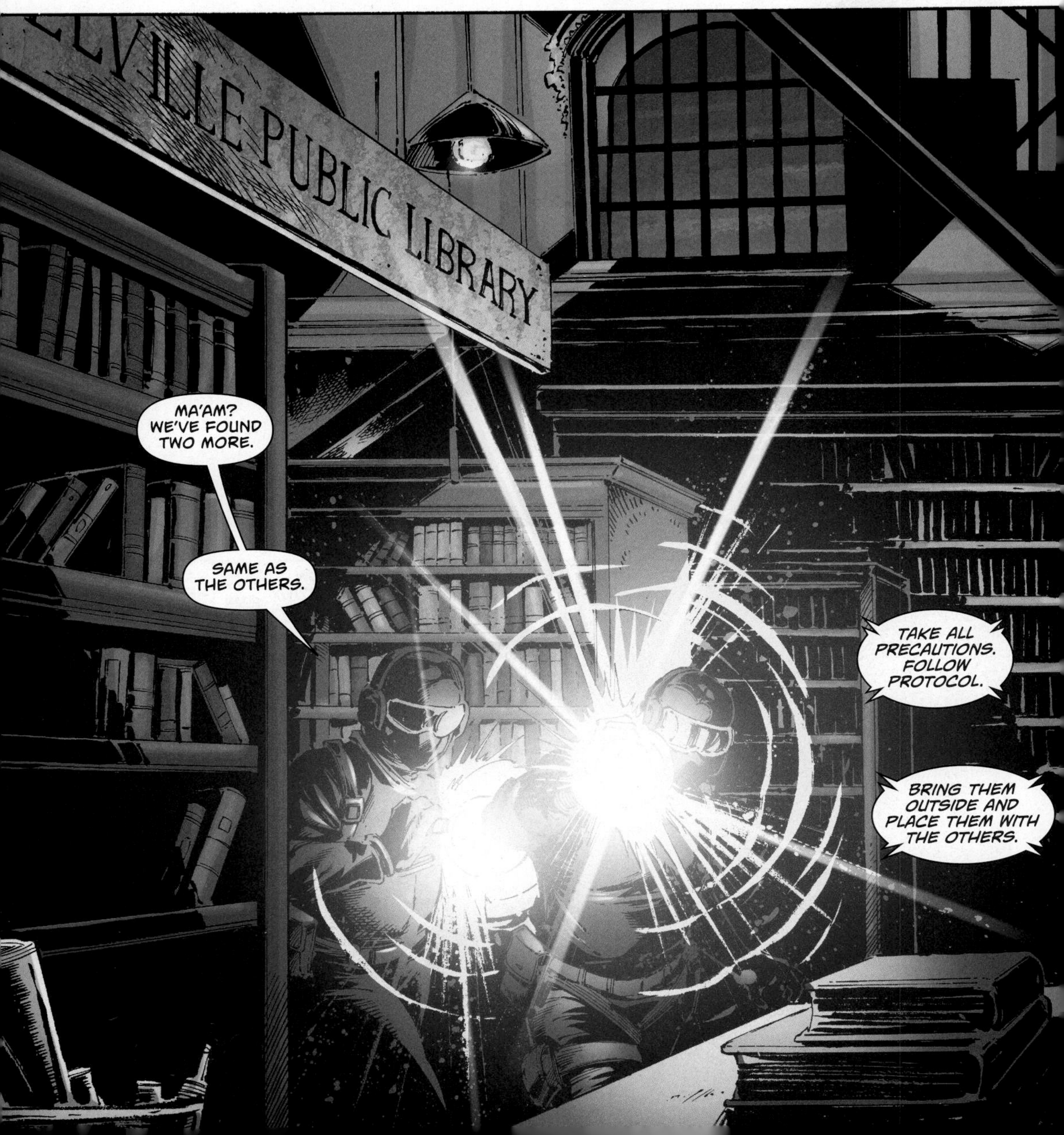
LVILLE PUBLIC LIBRARY
MA'AM? WE'VE FOUND TWO MORE.
SAME AS THE OTHERS.
TAKE ALL PRECAUTIONS. FOLLOW PROTOCOL.
BRING THEM OUTSIDE AND PLACE THEM WITH THE OTHERS.

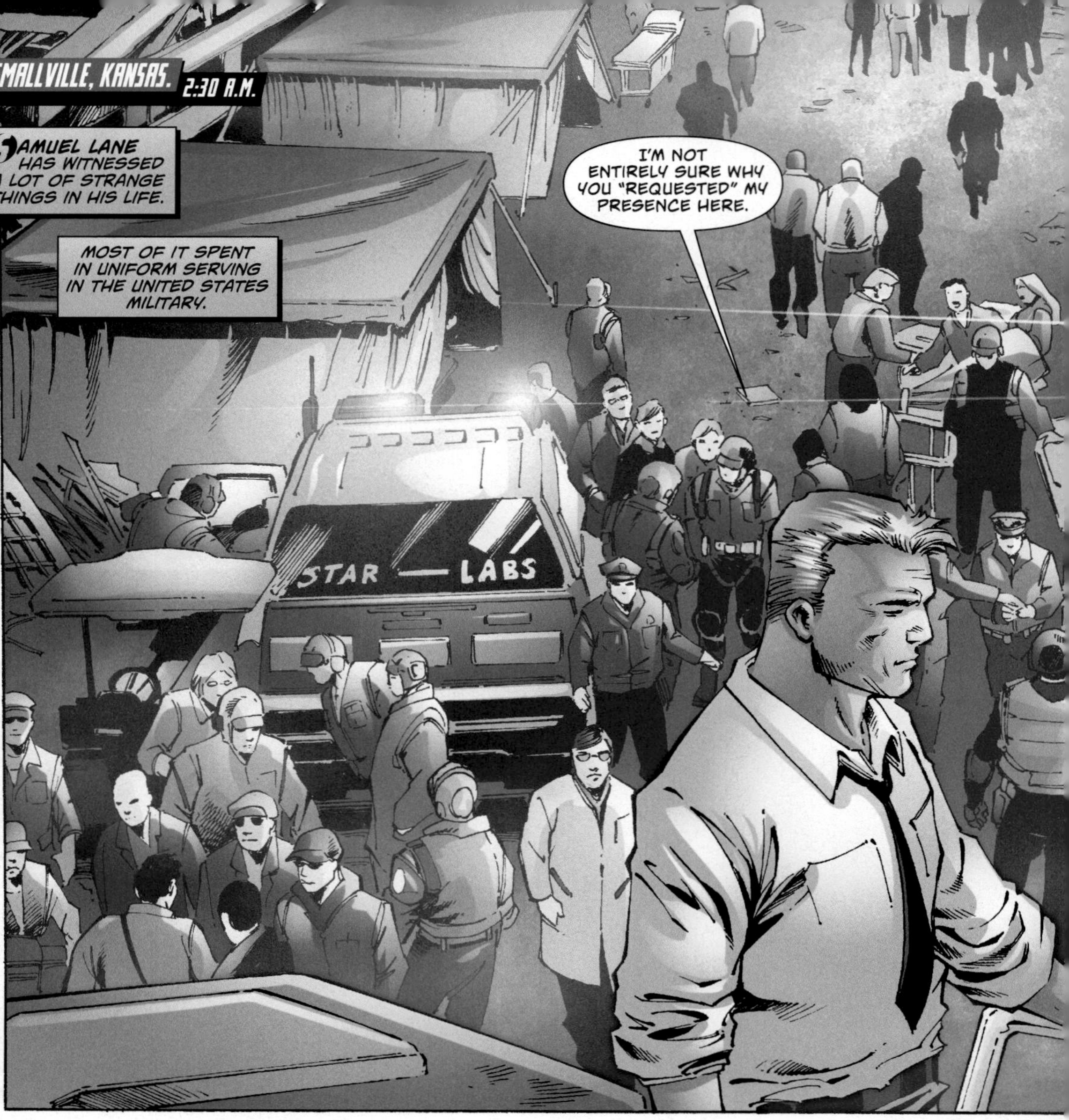
SMALLVILLE, KANSAS.
2:30 A.M.
SAMUEL LANE HAS WITNESSED A LOT OF STRANGE THINGS IN HIS LIFE.
MOST OF IT SPENT IN UNIFORM SERVING IN THE UNITED STATES MILITARY.
I'M NOT ENTIRELY SURE WHY YOU "REQUESTED" MY PRESENCE HERE.
STAR LABS

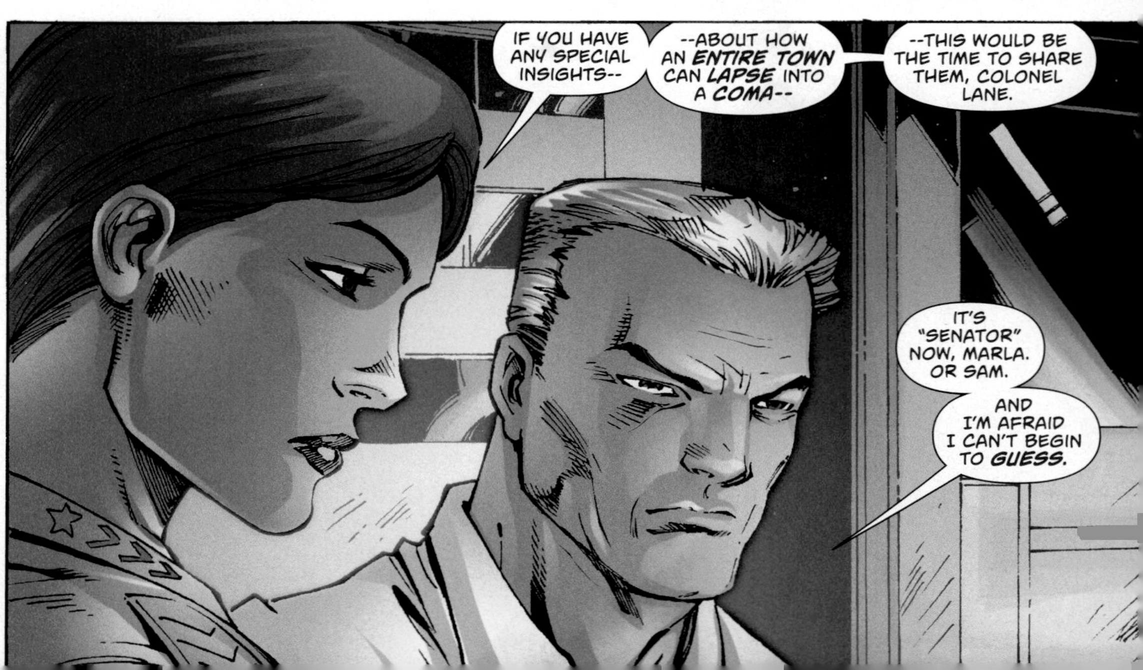
IF YOU HAVE ANY SPECIAL INSIGHTS--
--ABOUT HOW AN ENTIRE TOWN CAN LAPSE INTO A COMA--
--THIS WOULD BE THE TIME TO SHARE THEM, COLONEL LANE.
IT'S "SENATOR" NOW, MARLA. OR SAM.
AND I'M AFRAID I CAN'T BEGIN TO GUESS.

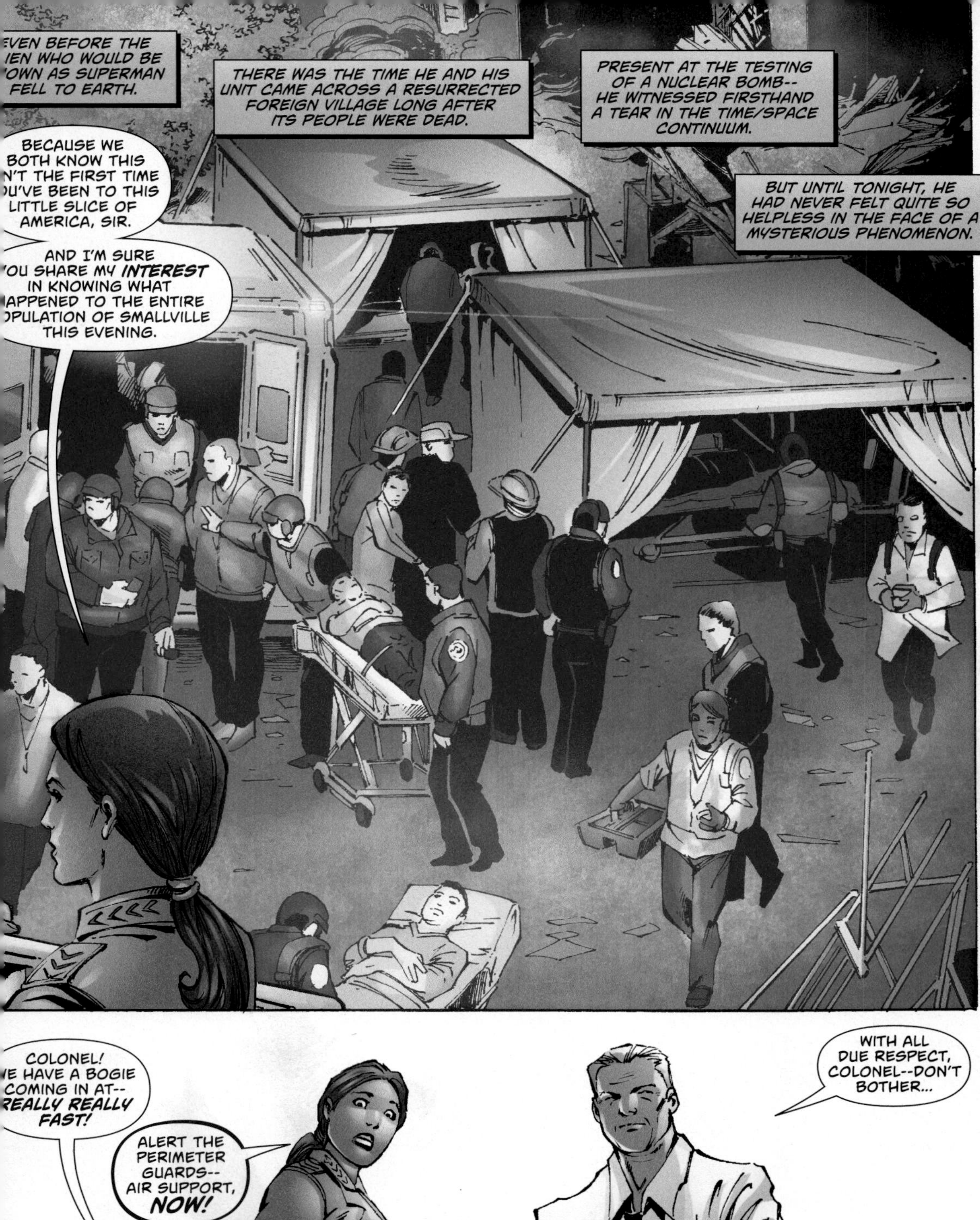
EVEN BEFORE THE IEN WHO WOULD BE OWN AS SUPERMAN FELL TO EARTH.
THERE WAS THE TIME HE AND HIS UNIT CAME ACROSS A RESURRECTED FOREIGN VILLAGE LONG AFTER ITS PEOPLE WERE DEAD.
PRESENT AT THE TESTING OF A NUCLEAR BOMB-- HE WITNESSED FIRSTHAND A TEAR IN THE TIME/SPACE CONTINUUM.
BUT UNTIL TONIGHT, HE HAD NEVER FELT QUITE SO HELPLESS IN THE FACE OF A MYSTERIOUS PHENOMENON.
BECAUSE WE BOTH KNOW THIS N'T THE FIRST TIME OU'VE BEEN TO THIS LITTLE SLICE OF AMERICA, SIR.
AND I'M SURE OU SHARE MY INTEREST IN KNOWING WHAT APPENED TO THE ENTIRE OPULATION OF SMALLVILLE THIS EVENING.

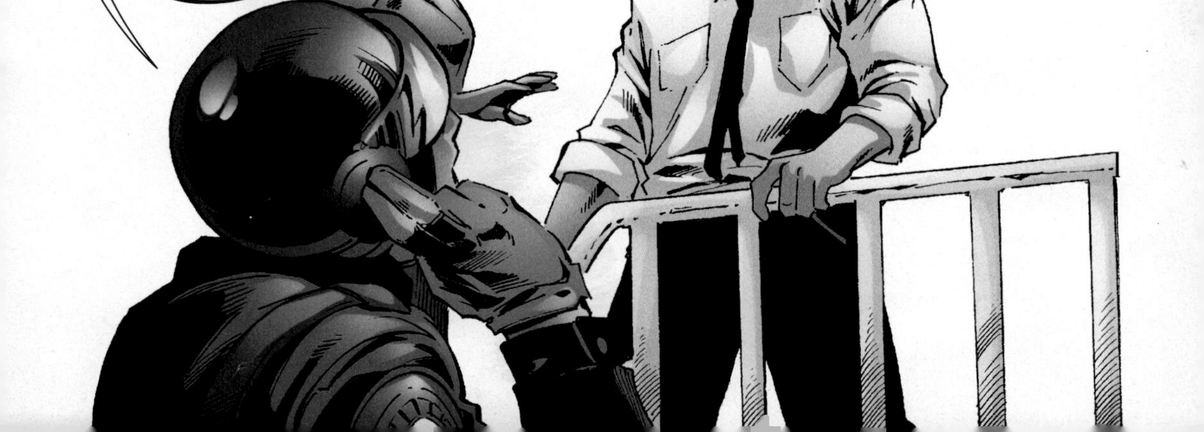
COLONEL! E HAVE A BOGIE COMING IN AT-- REALLY REALLY FAST!
ALERT THE PERIMETER GUARDS-- AIR SUPPORT, NOW!
WITH ALL DUE RESPECT, COLONEL--DON'T BOTHER...

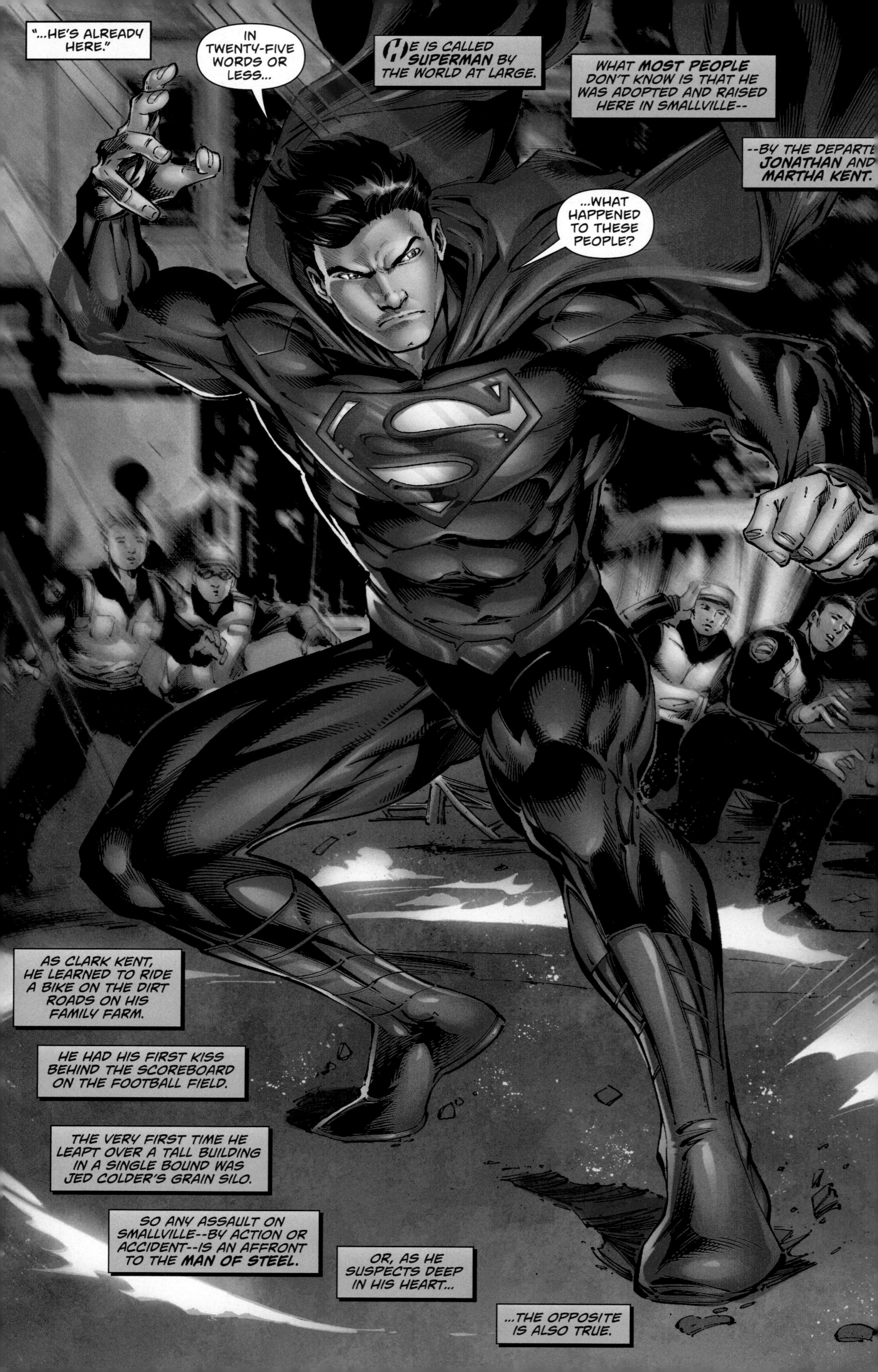
"...HE'S ALREADY HERE."
IN TWENTY-FIVE WORDS OR LESS...
HE IS CALLED SUPERMAN BY THE WORLD AT LARGE.
WHAT MOST PEOPLE DON'T KNOW IS THAT HE WAS ADOPTED AND RAISED HERE IN SMALLVILLE--
--BY THE DEPARTE JONATHAN AND MARTHA KENT.
...WHAT HAPPENED TO THESE PEOPLE?
AS CLARK KENT, HE LEARNED TO RIDE A BIKE ON THE DIRT ROADS ON HIS FAMILY FARM.
HE HAD HIS FIRST KISS BEHIND THE SCOREBOARD ON THE FOOTBALL FIELD.
THE VERY FIRST TIME HE LEAPT OVER A TALL BUILDING IN A SINGLE BOUND WAS JED COLDER'S GRAIN SILO.
SO ANY ASSAULT ON SMALLVILLE--BY ACTION OR ACCIDENT--IS AN AFFRONT TO THE MAN OF STEEL.
OR, AS HE SUSPECTS DEEP IN HIS HEART...
...THE OPPOSITE IS ALSO TRUE.

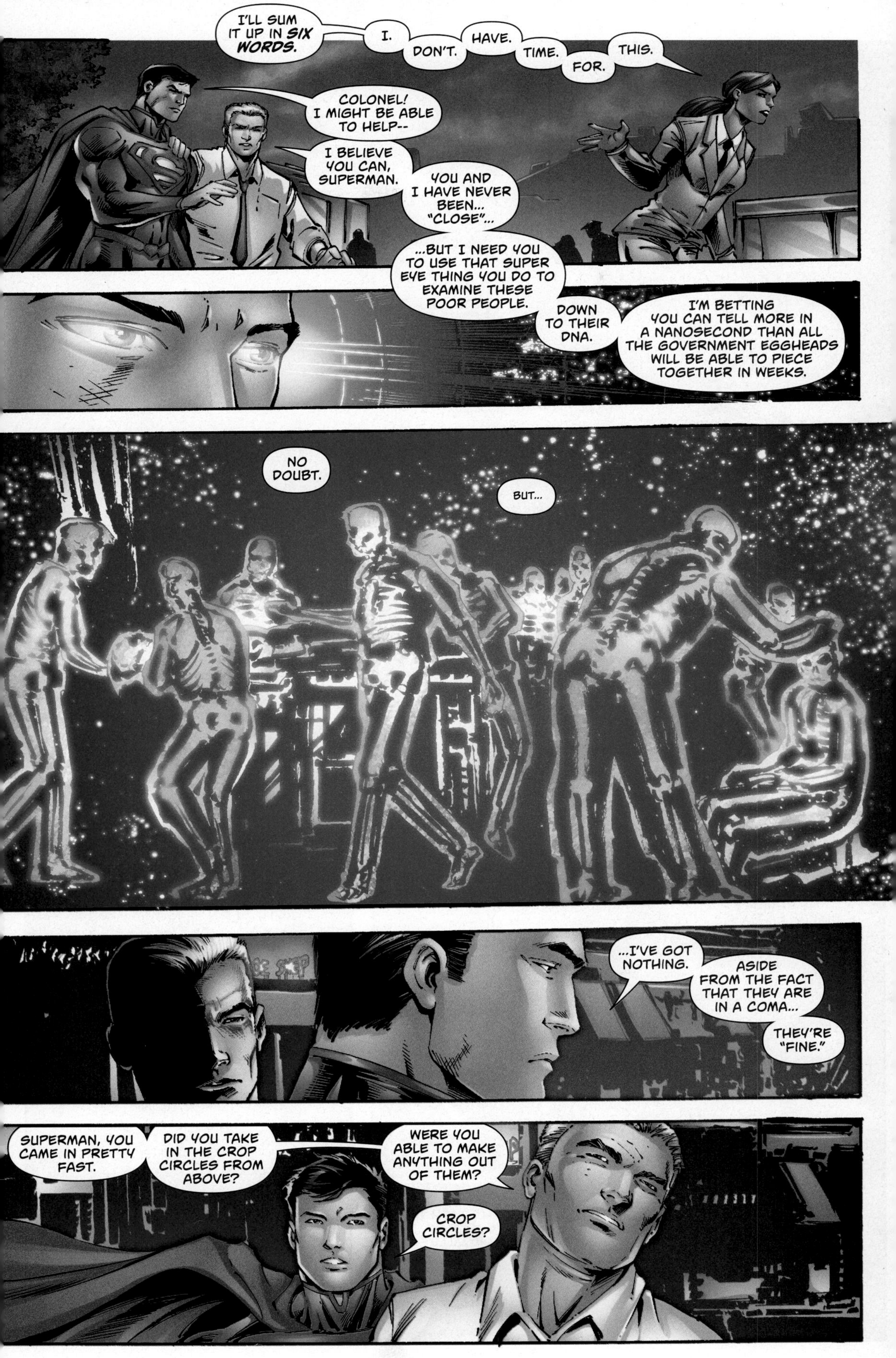
I'LL SUM IT UP IN SIX WORDS.
I.
DON'T.
HAVE.
TIME.
FOR.
THIS.
COLONEL! I MIGHT BE ABLE TO HELP--
I BELIEVE YOU CAN, SUPERMAN.
YOU AND I HAVE NEVER BEEN... "CLOSE"...
...BUT I NEED YOU TO USE THAT SUPER EYE THING YOU DO TO EXAMINE THESE POOR PEOPLE.
DOWN TO THEIR DNA.
I'M BETTING YOU CAN TELL MORE IN A NANOSECOND THAN ALL THE GOVERNMENT EGGHEADS WILL BE ABLE TO PIECE TOGETHER IN WEEKS.
NO DOUBT.
BUT...
...I'VE GOT NOTHING.
ASIDE FROM THE FACT THAT THEY ARE IN A COMA...
THEY'RE "FINE."
SUPERMAN, YOU CAME IN PRETTY FAST.
DID YOU TAKE IN THE CROP CIRCLES FROM ABOVE?
WERE YOU ABLE TO MAKE ANYTHING OUT OF THEM?
CROP CIRCLES?

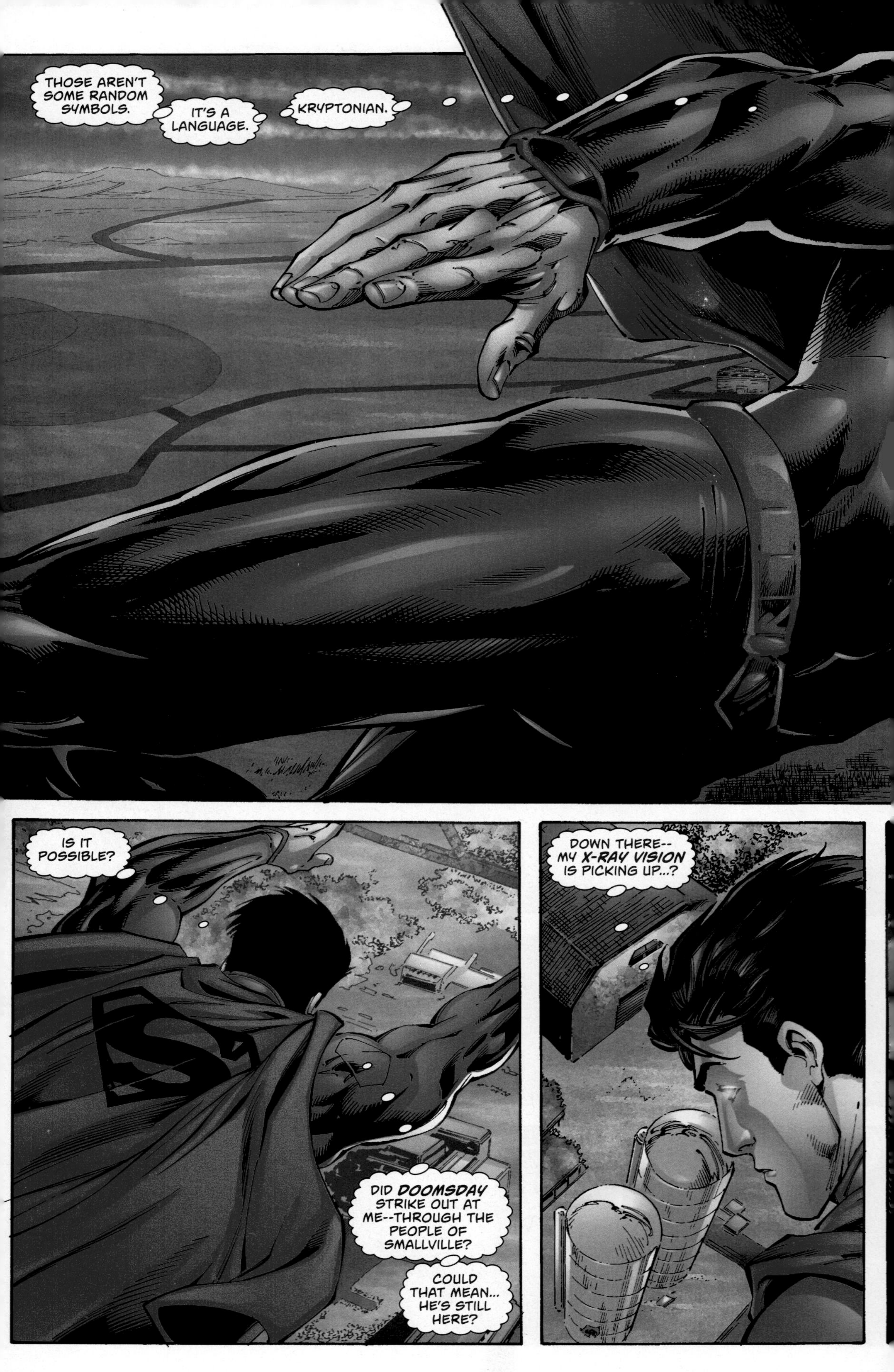
THOSE AREN'T SOME RANDOM SYMBOLS.
IT'S A LANGUAGE.
KRYPTONIAN.
IS IT POSSIBLE?
DID DOOMSDAY STRIKE OUT AT ME--THROUGH THE PEOPLE OF SMALLVILLE?
COULD THAT MEAN... HE'S STILL HERE?
DOWN THERE-- MY X-RAY VISION IS PICKING UP...?

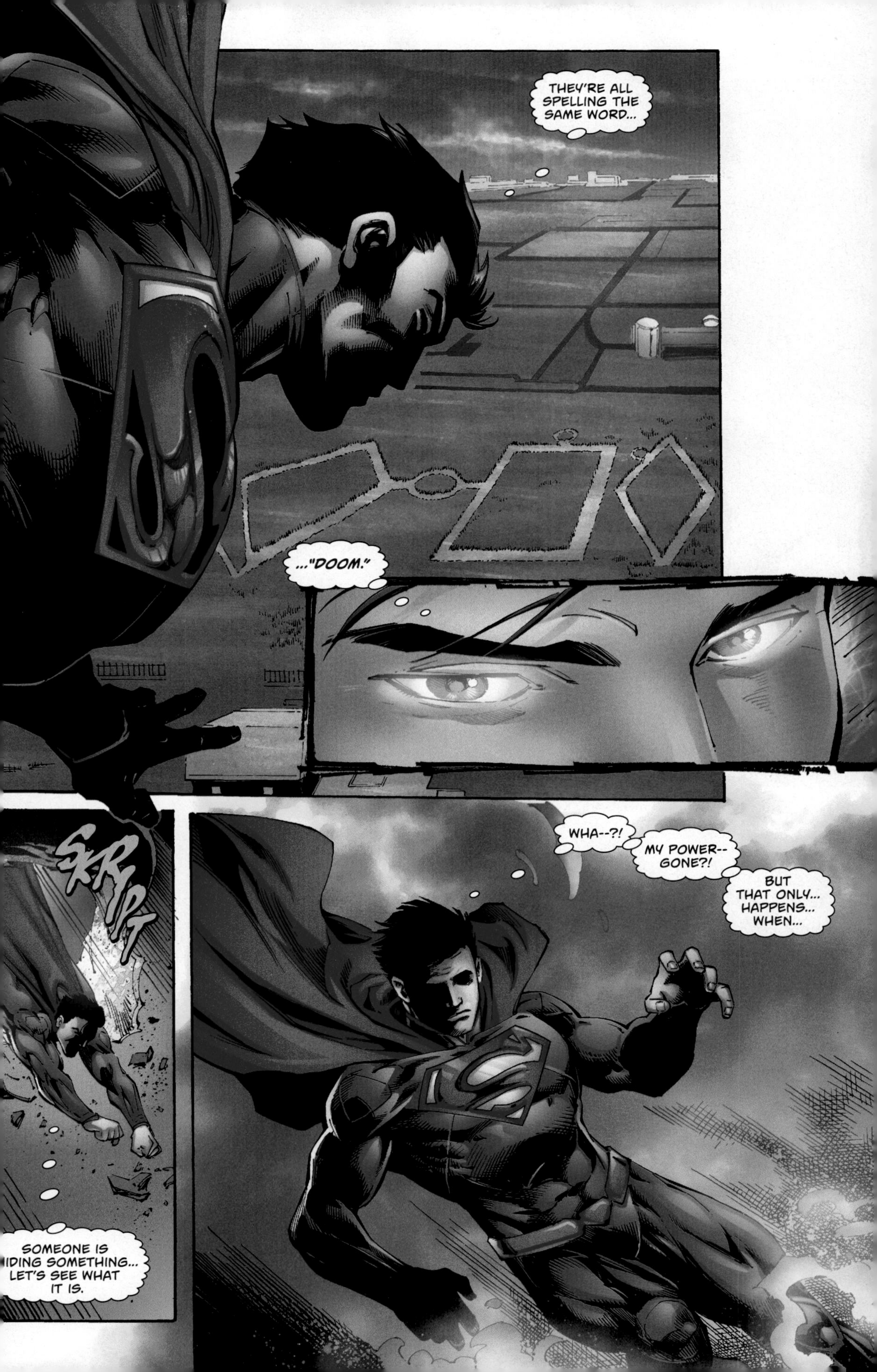
THEY'RE ALL SPELLING THE SAME WORD...
..."DOOM."
SKRRT
SOMEONE IS IDING SOMETHING... LET'S SEE WHAT IT IS.
WHA--?!
MY POWER-- GONE?!
BUT THAT ONLY... HAPPENS... WHEN...

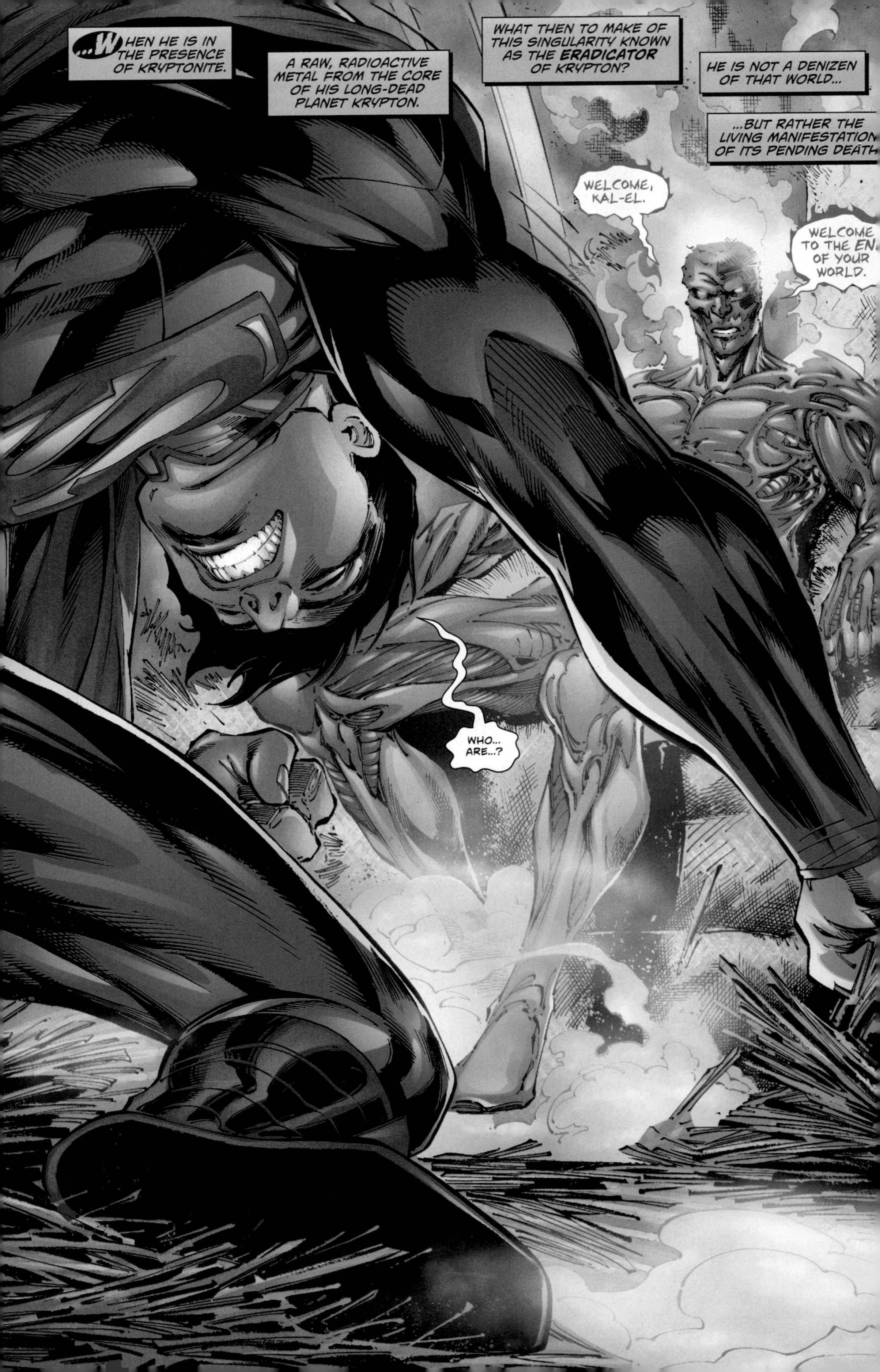
...WHEN HE IS IN THE PRESENCE OF KRYPTONITE.
A RAW, RADIOACTIVE METAL FROM THE CORE OF HIS LONG-DEAD PLANET KRYPTON.
WHAT THEN TO MAKE OF THIS SINGULARITY KNOWN AS THE ERADICATOR OF KRYPTON?
HE IS NOT A DENIZEN OF THAT WORLD...
...BUT RATHER THE LIVING MANIFESTATION OF ITS PENDING DEATH
WELCOME, KAL-EL.
WELCOME TO THE EN OF YOUR WORLD.
WHO... ARE...?

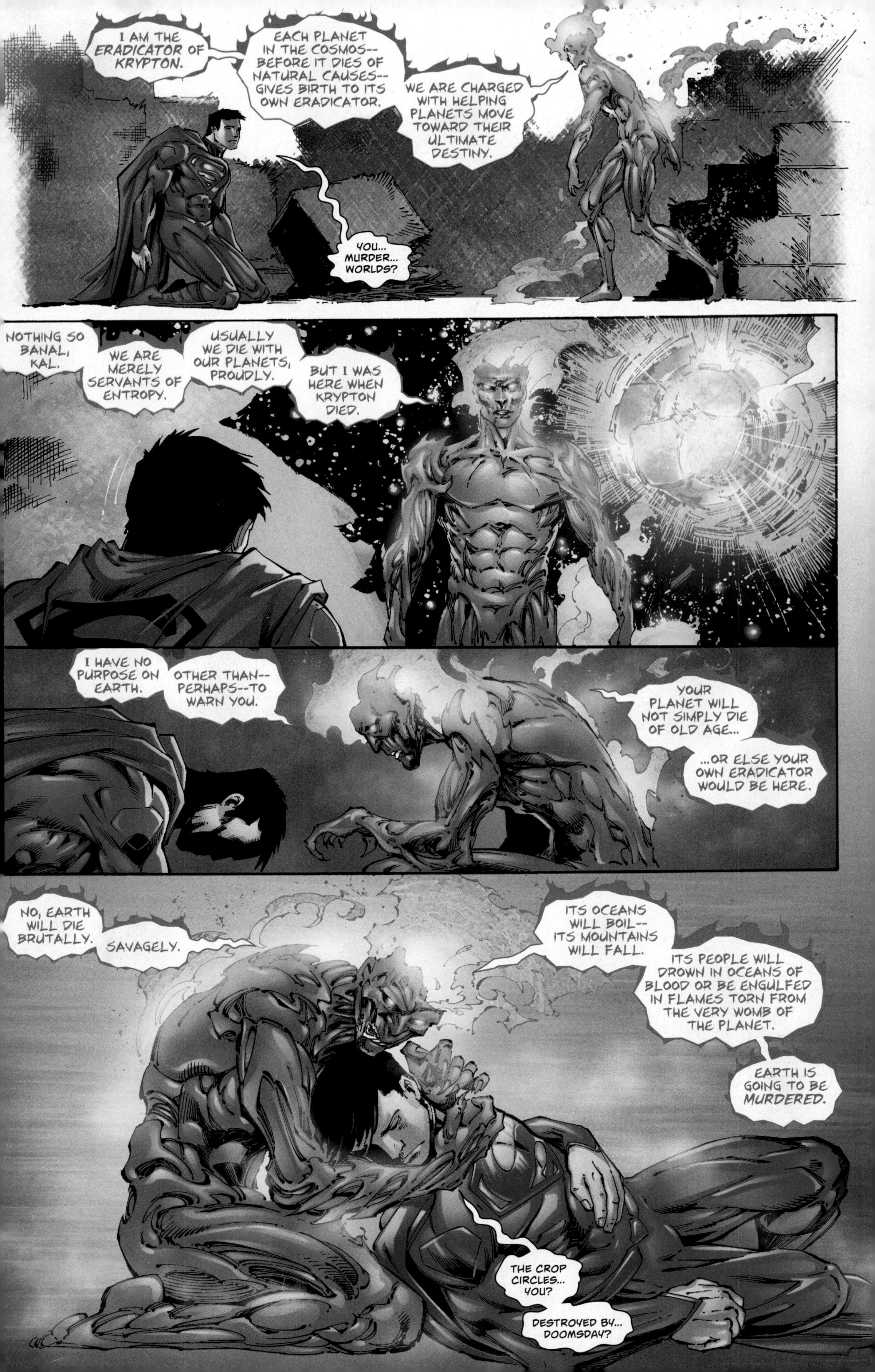

I AM THE ERADICATOR OF KRYPTON.
EACH PLANET IN THE COSMOS--BEFORE IT DIES OF NATURAL CAUSES--GIVES BIRTH TO ITS OWN ERADICATOR.
WE ARE CHARGED WITH HELPING PLANETS MOVE TOWARD THEIR ULTIMATE DESTINY.
YOU... MURDER... WORLDS?
NOTHING SO BANAL, KAL.
WE ARE MERELY SERVANTS OF ENTROPY.
USUALLY WE DIE WITH OUR PLANETS, PROUDLY.
BUT I WAS HERE WHEN KRYPTON DIED.
I HAVE NO PURPOSE ON EARTH.
OTHER THAN--PERHAPS--TO WARN YOU.
YOUR PLANET WILL NOT SIMPLY DIE OF OLD AGE...
...OR ELSE YOUR OWN ERADICATOR WOULD BE HERE.
NO, EARTH WILL DIE BRUTALLY.
SAVAGELY.
ITS OCEANS WILL BOIL--ITS MOUNTAINS WILL FALL.
ITS PEOPLE WILL DROWN IN OCEANS OF BLOOD OR BE ENGULFED IN FLAMES TORN FROM THE VERY WOMB OF THE PLANET.
EARTH IS GOING TO BE MURDERED.
THE CROP CIRCLES... YOU?
DESTROYED BY... DOOMSDAY?

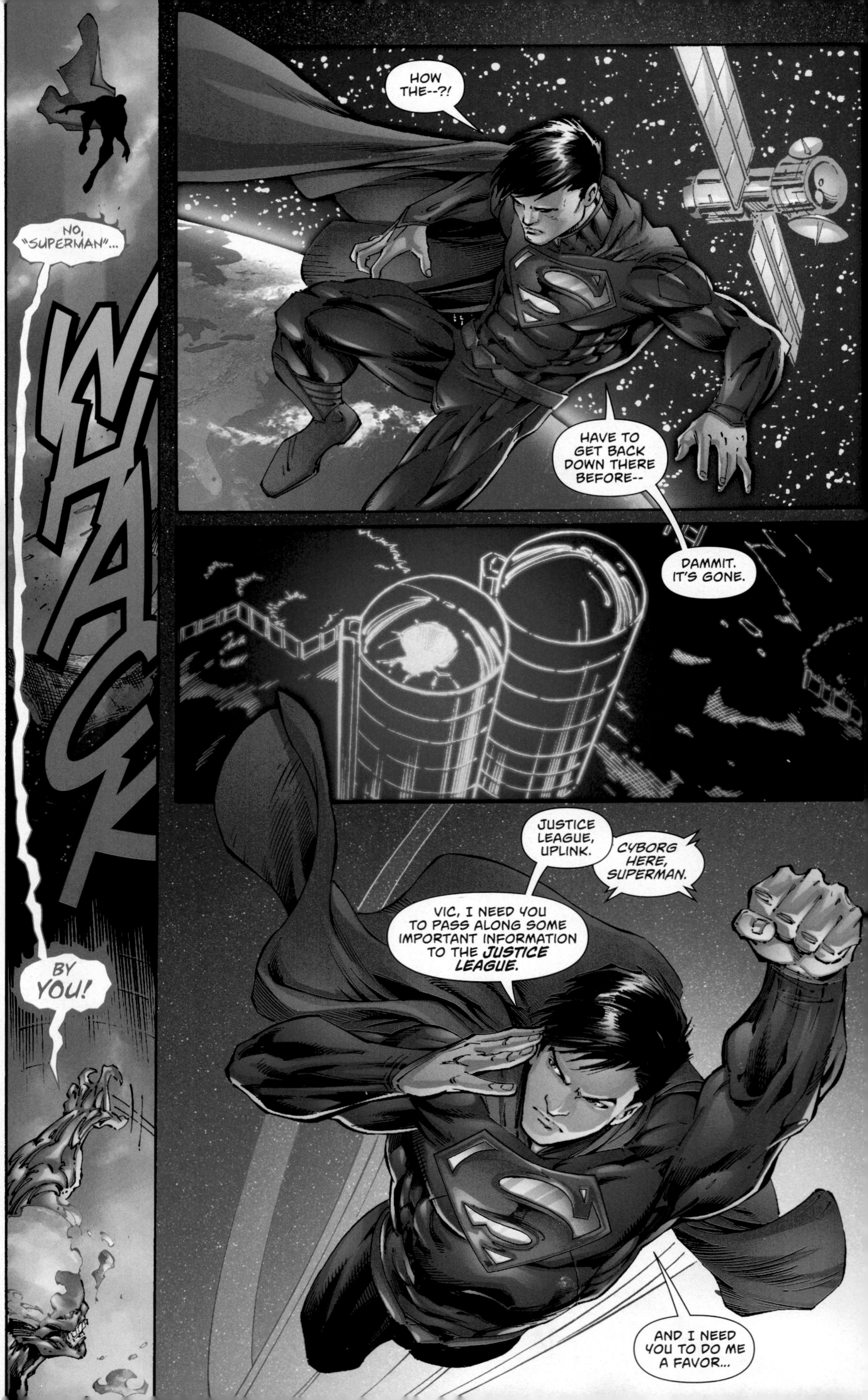
NO, "SUPERMAN"...
WHACK
BY YOU!
HOW THE--?!
HAVE TO GET BACK DOWN THERE BEFORE--
DAMMIT. IT'S GONE.
JUSTICE LEAGUE, UPLINK.
CYBORG HERE, SUPERMAN.
VIC, I NEED YOU TO PASS ALONG SOME IMPORTANT INFORMATION TO THE JUSTICE LEAGUE.
AND I NEED YOU TO DO ME A FAVOR...

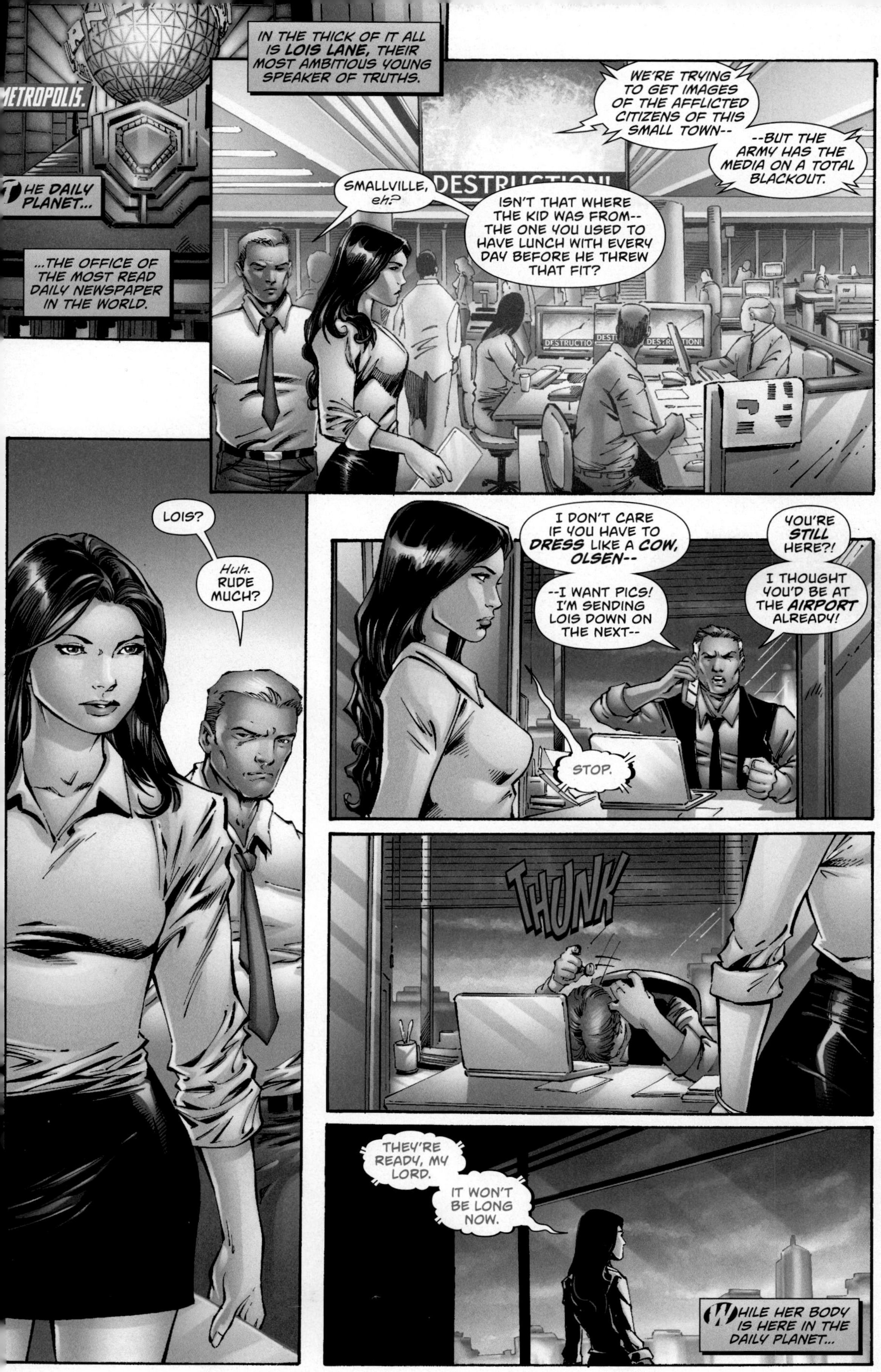

METROPOLIS.
THE DAILY PLANET...
...THE OFFICE OF THE MOST READ DAILY NEWSPAPER IN THE WORLD.
IN THE THICK OF IT ALL IS LOIS LANE, THEIR MOST AMBITIOUS YOUNG SPEAKER OF TRUTHS.
WE'RE TRYING TO GET IMAGES OF THE AFFLICTED CITIZENS OF THIS SMALL TOWN--
--BUT THE ARMY HAS THE MEDIA ON A TOTAL BLACKOUT.
DESTRUCTION!
SMALLVILLE, eh?
ISN'T THAT WHERE THE KID WAS FROM-- THE ONE YOU USED TO HAVE LUNCH WITH EVERY DAY BEFORE HE THREW THAT FIT?
LOIS?
Huh. RUDE MUCH?
I DON'T CARE IF YOU HAVE TO DRESS LIKE A COW, OLSEN--
--I WANT PICS! I'M SENDING LOIS DOWN ON THE NEXT--
YOU'RE STILL HERE?!
I THOUGHT YOU'D BE AT THE AIRPORT ALREADY!
STOP.
THUNK
THEY'RE READY, MY LORD.
IT WON'T BE LONG NOW.
WHILE HER BODY IS HERE IN THE DAILY PLANET...

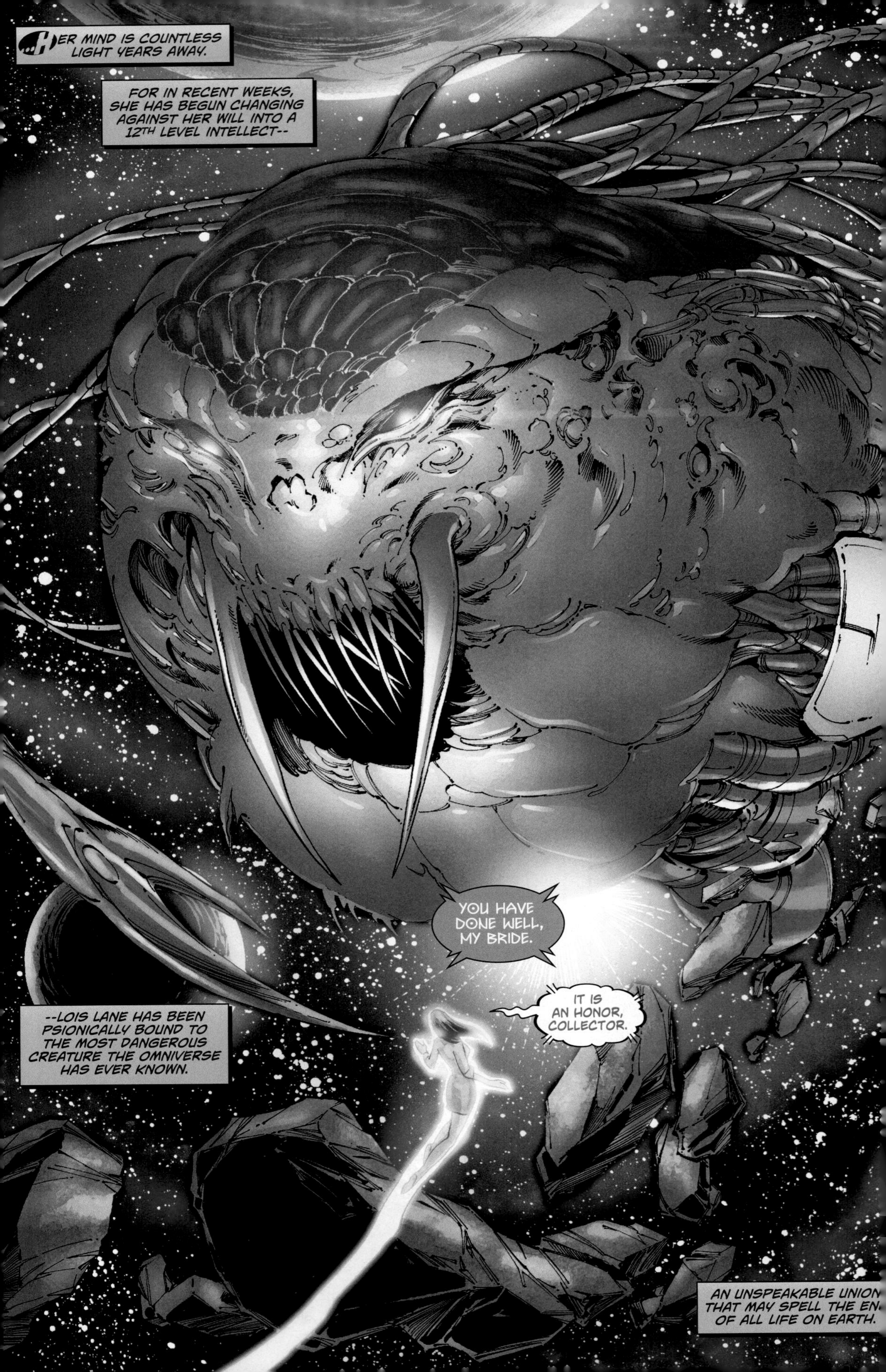
HER MIND IS COUNTLESS LIGHT YEARS AWAY.
FOR IN RECENT WEEKS, SHE HAS BEGUN CHANGING AGAINST HER WILL INTO A 12TH LEVEL INTELLECT--
YOU HAVE DONE WELL, MY BRIDE.
--LOIS LANE HAS BEEN PSIONICALLY BOUND TO THE MOST DANGEROUS CREATURE THE OMNIVERSE HAS EVER KNOWN.
IT IS AN HONOR, COLLECTOR.
AN UNSPEAKABLE UNION THAT MAY SPELL THE EN OF ALL LIFE ON EARTH.

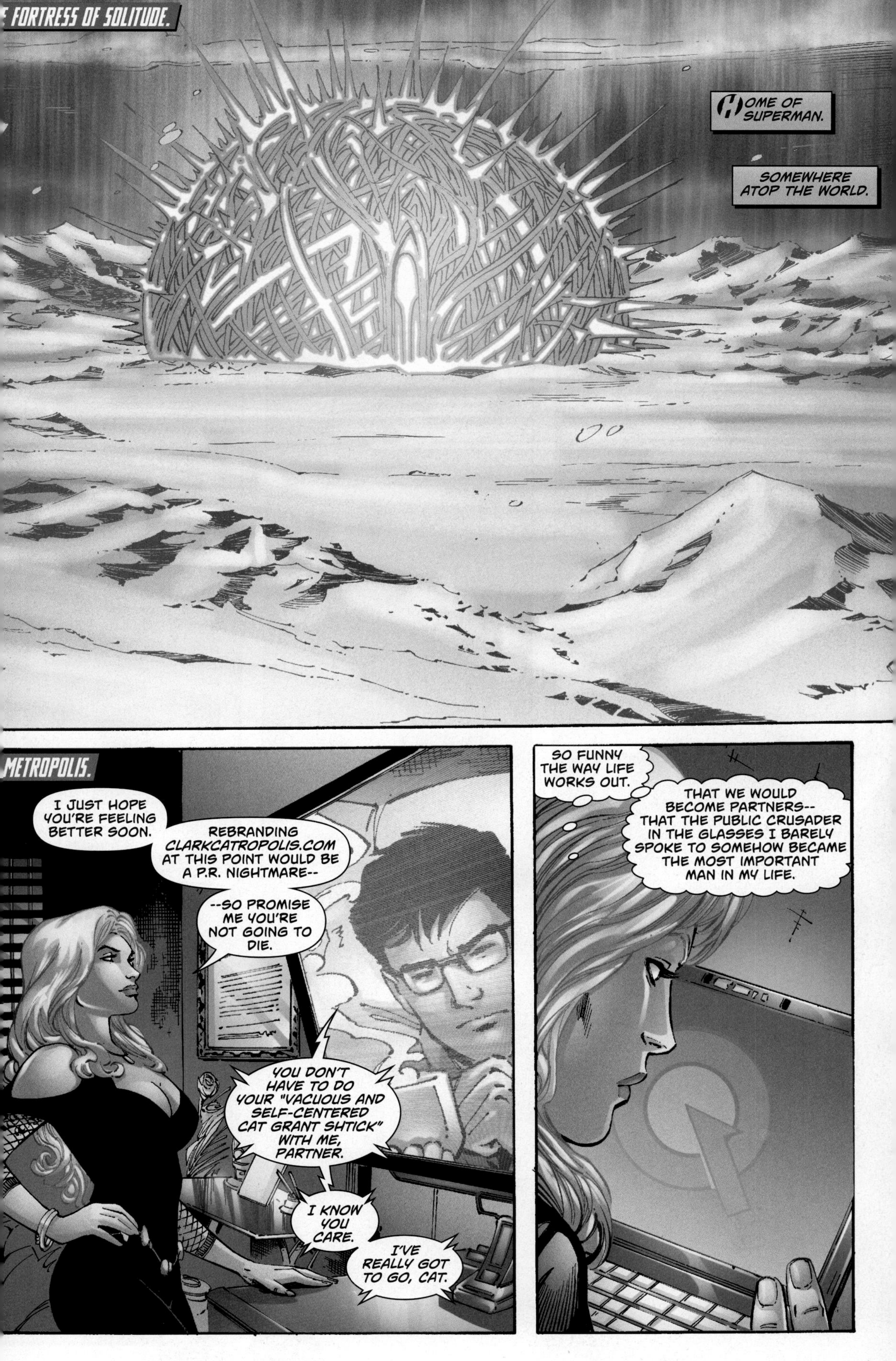
FORTRESS OF SOLITUDE.
HOME OF SUPERMAN.
SOMEWHERE ATOP THE WORLD.
METROPOLIS.
I JUST HOPE YOU'RE FEELING BETTER SOON.
REBRANDING CLARKCATROPOLIS.COM AT THIS POINT WOULD BE A P.R. NIGHTMARE--
--SO PROMISE ME YOU'RE NOT GOING TO DIE.
YOU DON'T HAVE TO DO YOUR "VACUOUS AND SELF-CENTERED CAT GRANT SHTICK" WITH ME, PARTNER.
I KNOW YOU CARE.
I'VE REALLY GOT TO GO, CAT.
SO FUNNY THE WAY LIFE WORKS OUT.
THAT WE WOULD BECOME PARTNERS-- THAT THE PUBLIC CRUSADER IN THE GLASSES I BARELY SPOKE TO SOMEHOW BECAME THE MOST IMPORTANT MAN IN MY LIFE.

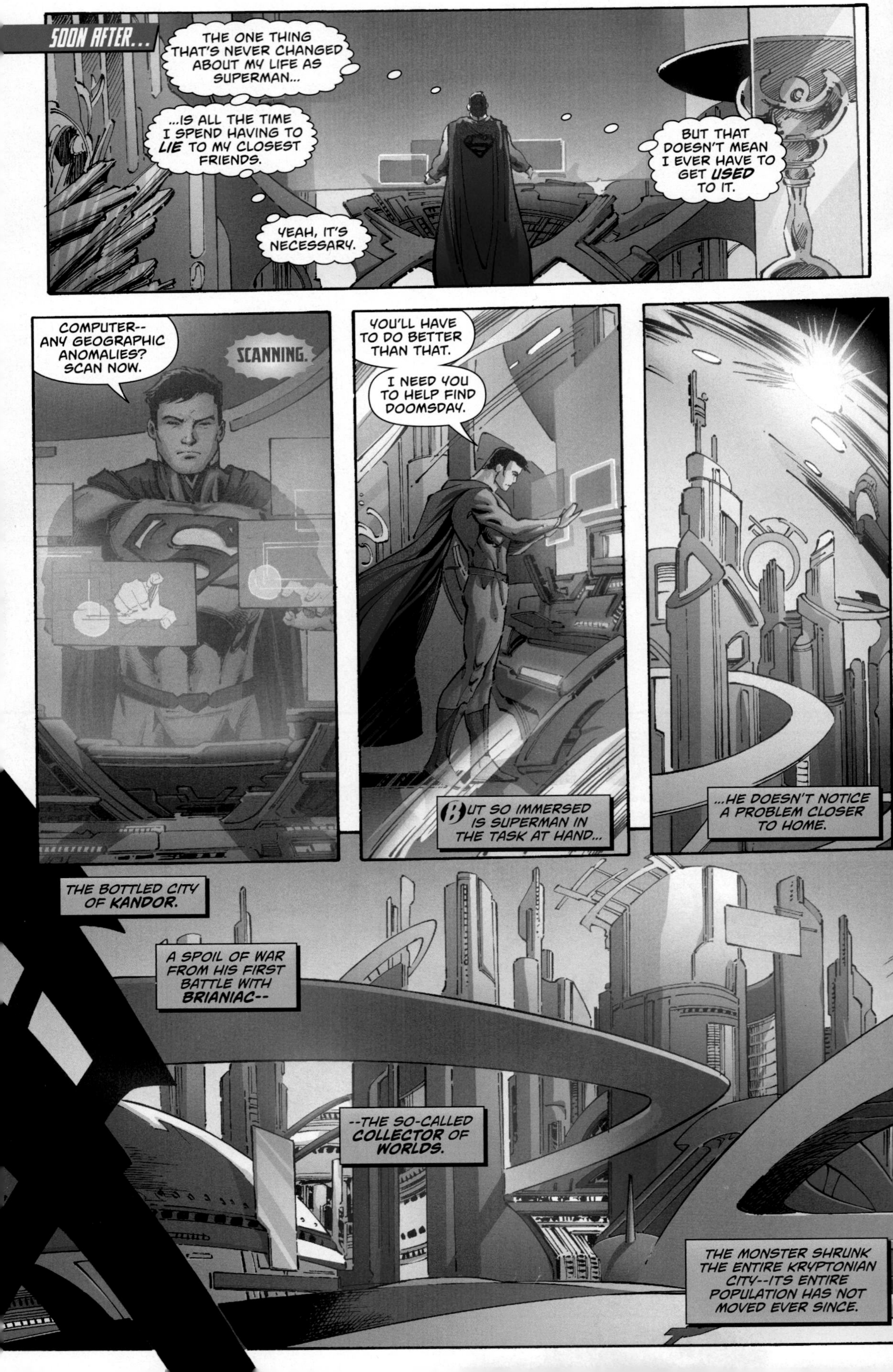
SOON AFTER...
THE ONE THING THAT'S NEVER CHANGED ABOUT MY LIFE AS SUPERMAN...
...IS ALL THE TIME I SPEND HAVING TO LIE TO MY CLOSEST FRIENDS.
YEAH, IT'S NECESSARY.
BUT THAT DOESN'T MEAN I EVER HAVE TO GET USED TO IT.
COMPUTER-- ANY GEOGRAPHIC ANOMALIES? SCAN NOW.
SCANNING.
YOU'LL HAVE TO DO BETTER THAN THAT.
I NEED YOU TO HELP FIND DOOMSDAY.
BUT SO IMMERSED IS SUPERMAN IN THE TASK AT HAND...
...HE DOESN'T NOTICE A PROBLEM CLOSER TO HOME.
THE BOTTLED CITY OF KANDOR.
A SPOIL OF WAR FROM HIS FIRST BATTLE WITH BRIANIAC--
--THE SO-CALLED COLLECTOR OF WORLDS.
THE MONSTER SHRUNK THE ENTIRE KRYPTONIAN CITY--ITS ENTIRE POPULATION HAS NOT MOVED EVER SINCE.

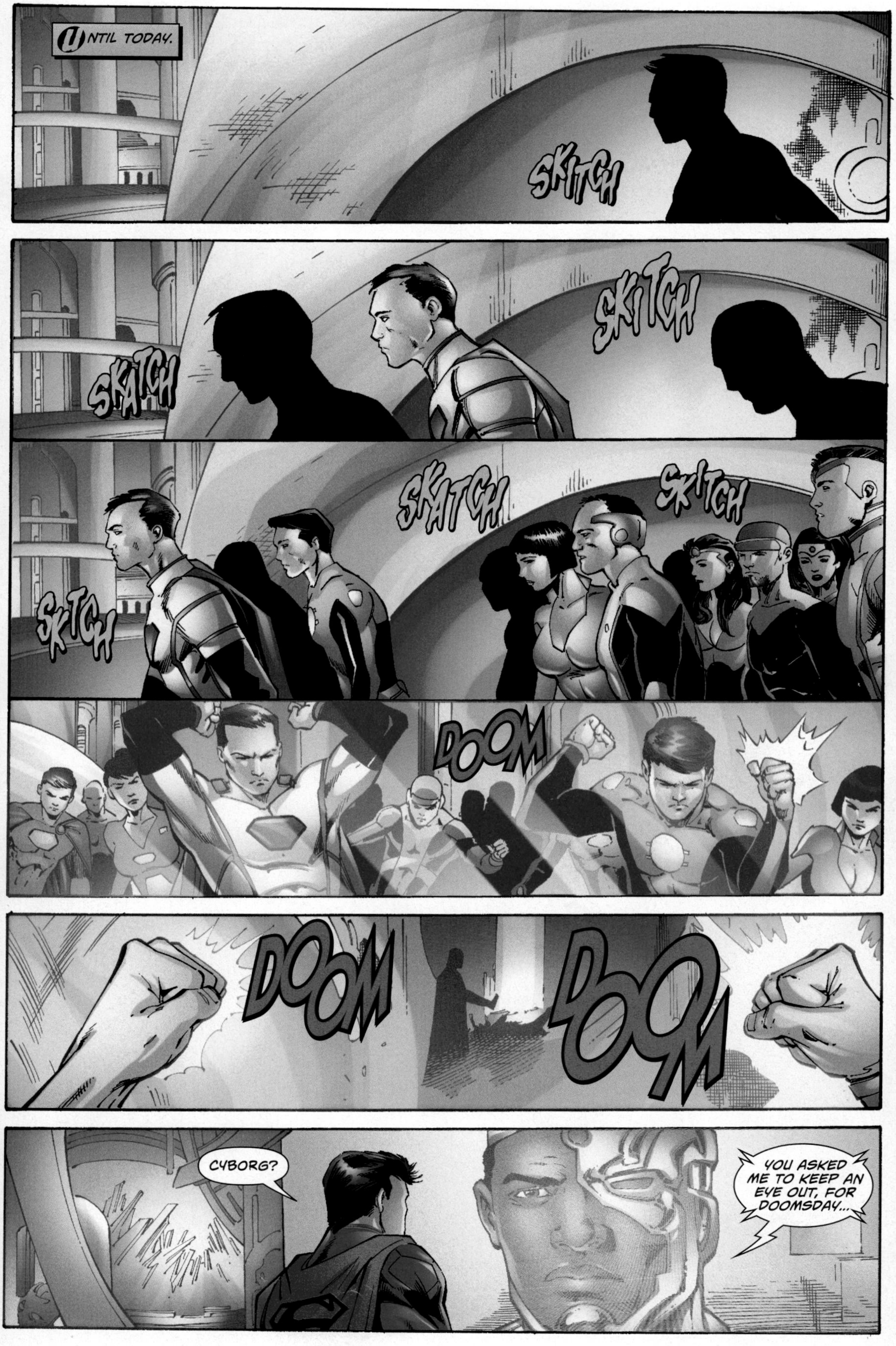
UNTIL TODAY.
SKITCH
SKATCH
SKITCH
SKTCH
SKATCH
SKITCH
DOOM
DOOM
DOOM
CYBORG?
YOU ASKED ME TO KEEP AN EYE OUT, FOR DOOMSDAY...

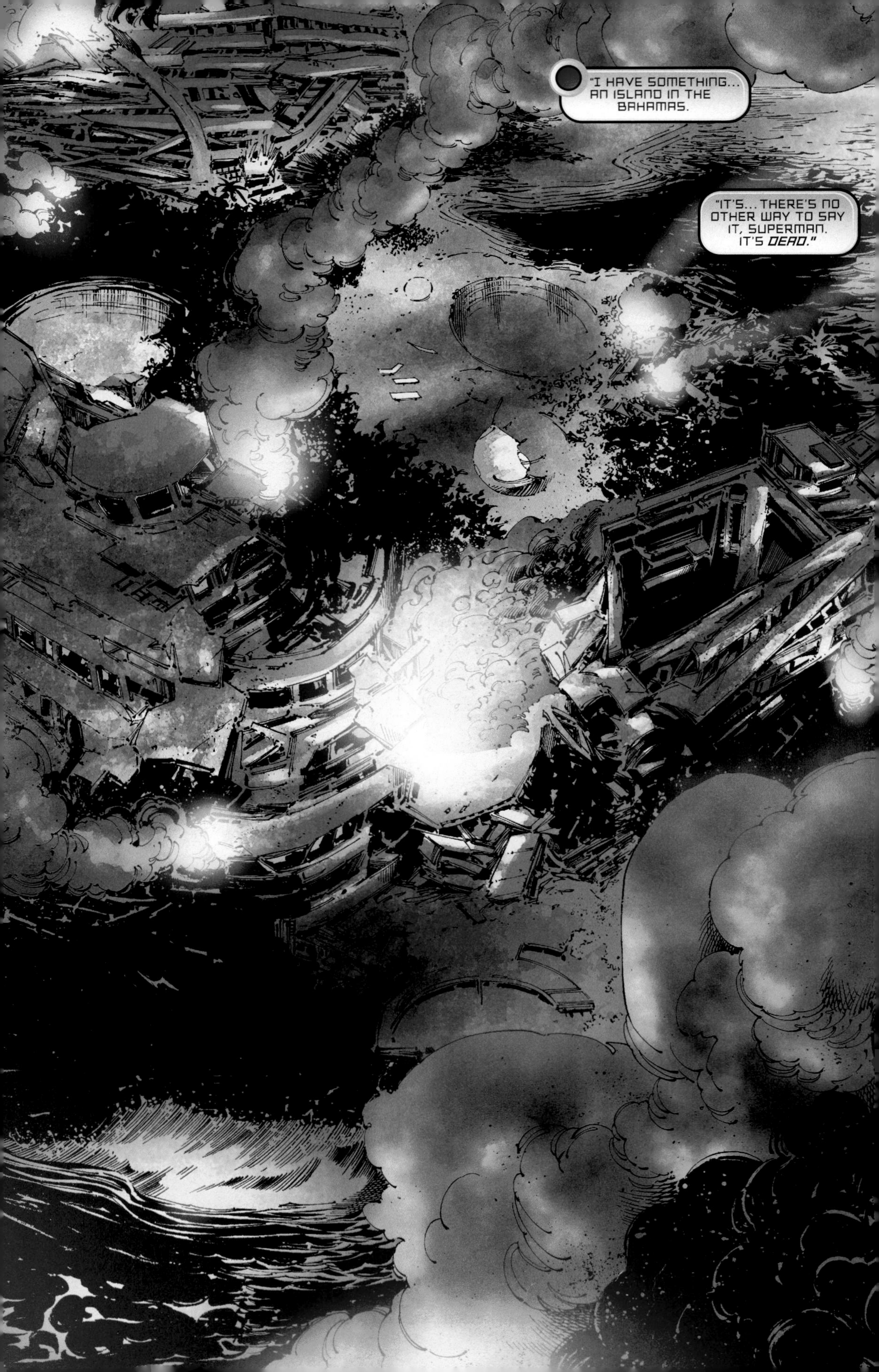
"I HAVE SOMETHING... AN ISLAND IN THE BAHAMAS.
"IT'S... THERE'S NO OTHER WAY TO SAY IT, SUPERMAN. IT'S *DEAD*."

INFECTED

SCOTT LOBDELL writer **ED BENES JACK HERBERT** pencillers **JAIME MENDOZA VICENTE CIFUENTES** inkers
PETE PANTAZIS JEROMY COX colorists cover art by **ED BENES, JONATHAN GLAPION** and **PETE PANTAZIS**

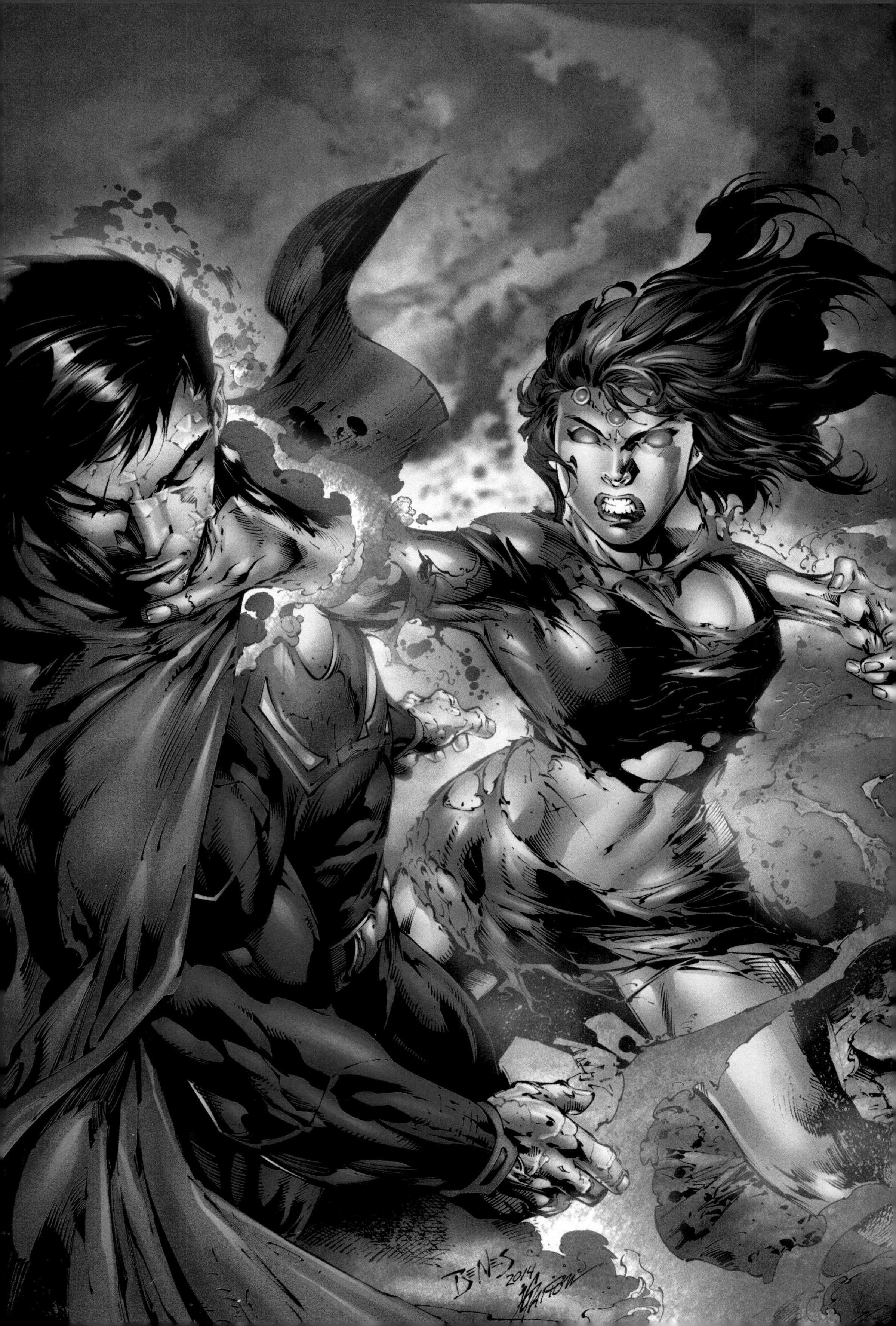

WORLD   U.S.   METROPOLIS   BUSINESS   OPINION   SPORTS   ARTS   STYLE   VIDEO

May 7, 20

Daily Planet

DAILY PLANET

SUPERMAN DOOMED!

BY LOIS LANE

It was DOOMSDAY around the world, both figuratively and literally.

A massive creature of unknown origin resembling one that SUPERMAN fought once before appeared first in the Bahamas, subsequently in Botswana and then Mumbai, India, causing untold destruction.

Doctor Silas Stone, of S.T.A.R. Labs, had been tracking the creature after its initial appearance in the Bahamas.

Photo by James Olse

Artist Rendition by Ken Lashley

"The creature was generating a corrosive force field that produced rap biological decay in anything that came within its radius."

Efforts by world governments to stop the creature were unsuccessful.

Members of the Justice League looked to halt the rampaging monster path of destruction by confronting it. The Man of Steel, in a display brute force never before witnessed, eventually defeated the monster tearing it apart.

This final battle took place in the midwestern town of Smallville, whe a day before its citizens fell inexplicably into a coma. Experts theorize t event was linked to the appearance of the behemoth. However, the destru tion of Doomsday has not revived them. And as Superman recovers fro this epic struggle, everyone is wondering what effect this battle has had the Last Son of Krypton himself.

Watch exclusive video footage of the destruction in the Bahamas.

"Doomsday" Origins
Recovery in the Northwestern
Indies
Newly appointed Senator Sam Lan
being considered at for "cleanup"
in the U.S.

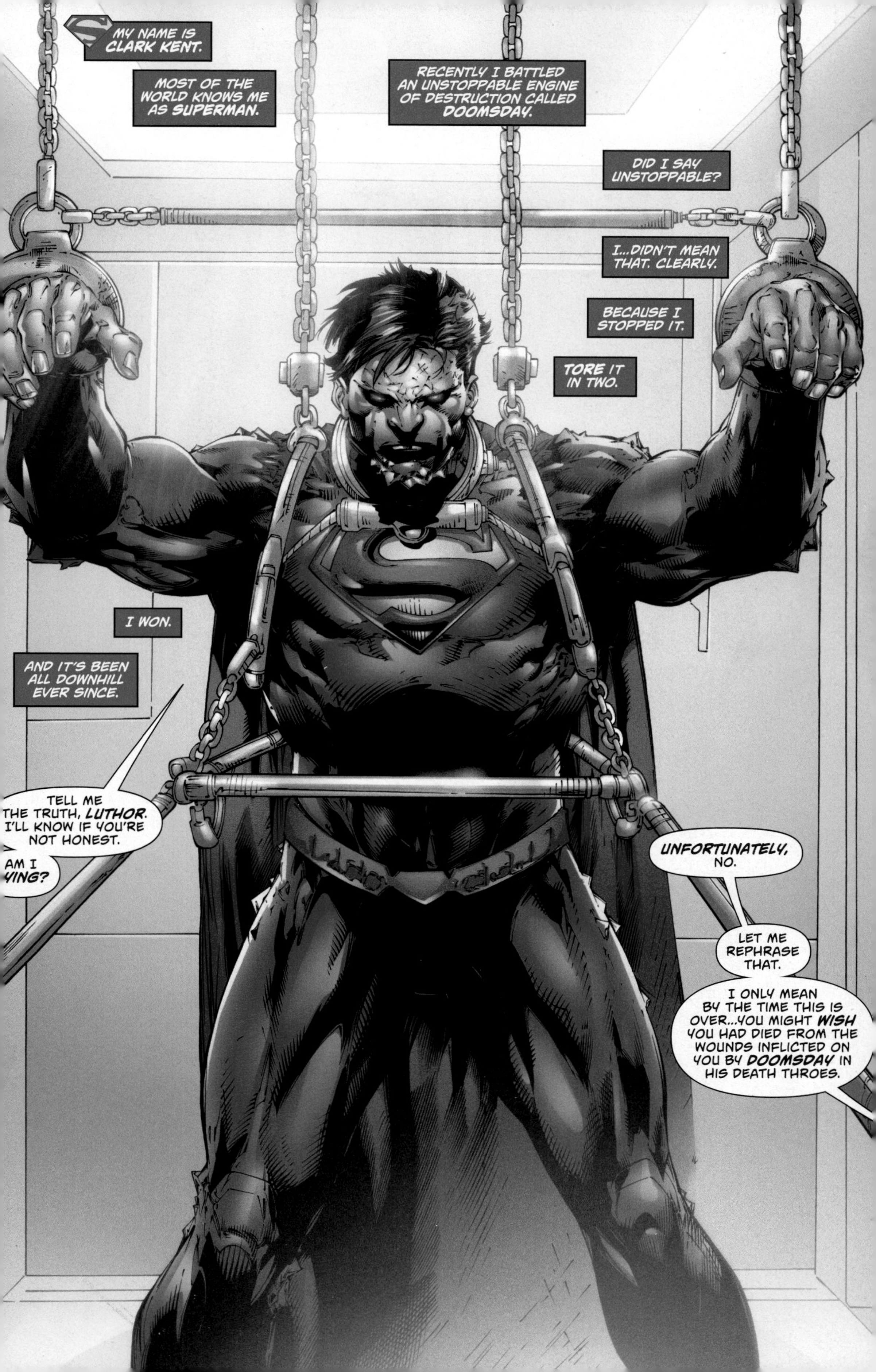
MY NAME IS CLARK KENT.
MOST OF THE WORLD KNOWS ME AS SUPERMAN.
RECENTLY I BATTLED AN UNSTOPPABLE ENGINE OF DESTRUCTION CALLED DOOMSDAY.
DID I SAY UNSTOPPABLE?
I...DIDN'T MEAN THAT. CLEARLY.
BECAUSE I STOPPED IT.
TORE IT IN TWO.
I WON.
AND IT'S BEEN ALL DOWNHILL EVER SINCE.
TELL ME THE TRUTH, LUTHOR. I'LL KNOW IF YOU'RE NOT HONEST.
AM I YING?
UNFORTUNATELY, NO.
LET ME REPHRASE THAT.
I ONLY MEAN BY THE TIME THIS IS OVER...YOU MIGHT WISH YOU HAD DIED FROM THE WOUNDS INFLICTED ON YOU BY DOOMSDAY IN HIS DEATH THROES.

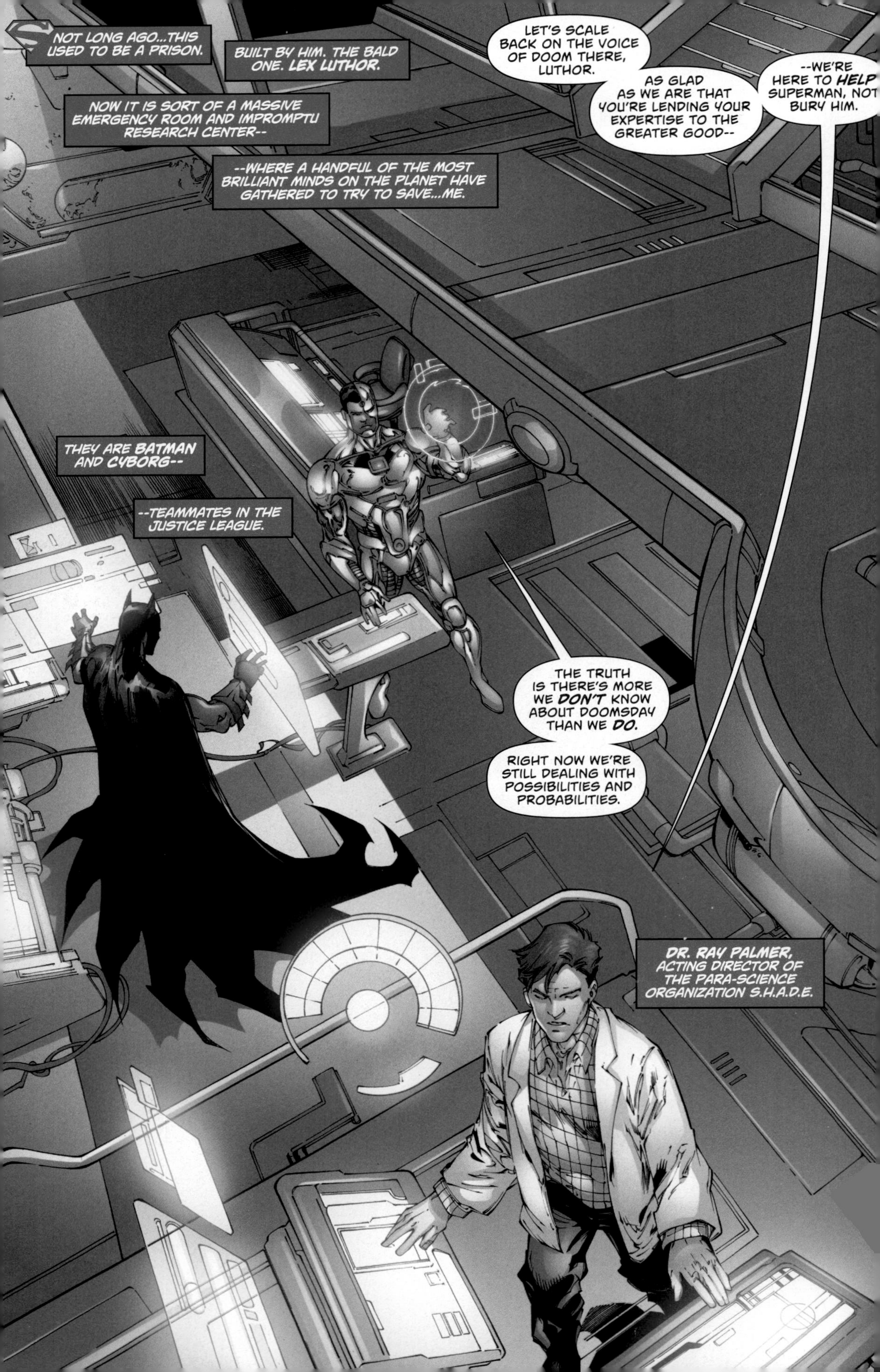
NOT LONG AGO...THIS USED TO BE A PRISON.
BUILT BY HIM. THE BALD ONE. LEX LUTHOR.
NOW IT IS SORT OF A MASSIVE EMERGENCY ROOM AND IMPROMPTU RESEARCH CENTER--
--WHERE A HANDFUL OF THE MOST BRILLIANT MINDS ON THE PLANET HAVE GATHERED TO TRY TO SAVE...ME.
LET'S SCALE BACK ON THE VOICE OF DOOM THERE, LUTHOR.
AS GLAD AS WE ARE THAT YOU'RE LENDING YOUR EXPERTISE TO THE GREATER GOOD--
--WE'RE HERE TO HELP SUPERMAN, NOT BURY HIM.
THEY ARE BATMAN AND CYBORG--
--TEAMMATES IN THE JUSTICE LEAGUE.
THE TRUTH IS THERE'S MORE WE DON'T KNOW ABOUT DOOMSDAY THAN WE DO.
RIGHT NOW WE'RE STILL DEALING WITH POSSIBILITIES AND PROBABILITIES.
DR. RAY PALMER, ACTING DIRECTOR OF THE PARA-SCIENCE ORGANIZATION S.H.A.D.E.

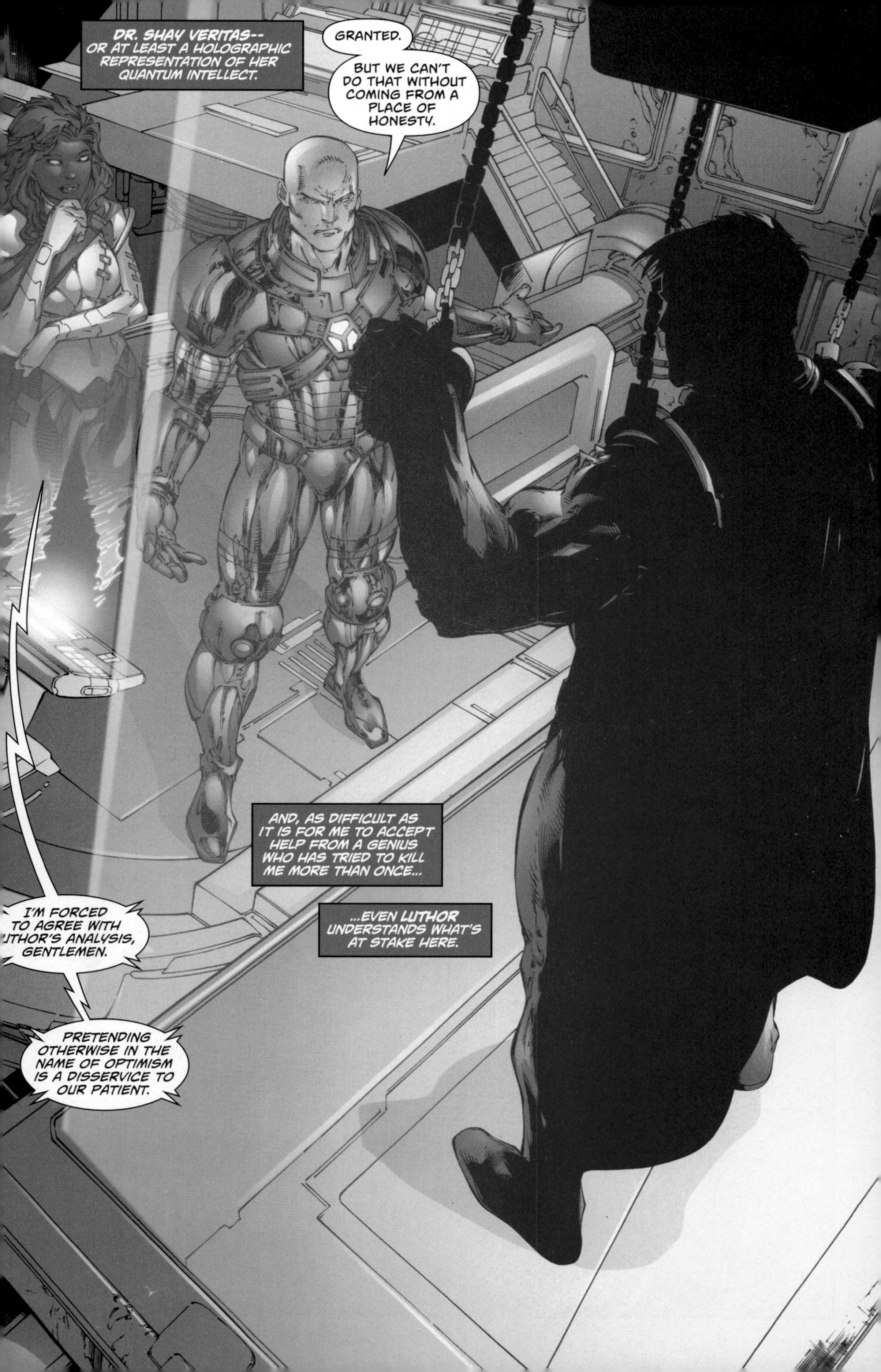
DR. SHAY VERITAS--
OR AT LEAST A HOLOGRAPHIC REPRESENTATION OF HER QUANTUM INTELLECT.
GRANTED.
BUT WE CAN'T DO THAT WITHOUT COMING FROM A PLACE OF HONESTY.
AND, AS DIFFICULT AS IT IS FOR ME TO ACCEPT HELP FROM A GENIUS WHO HAS TRIED TO KILL ME MORE THAN ONCE...
...EVEN LUTHOR UNDERSTANDS WHAT'S AT STAKE HERE.
I'M FORCED TO AGREE WITH LUTHOR'S ANALYSIS, GENTLEMEN.
PRETENDING OTHERWISE IN THE NAME OF OPTIMISM IS A DISSERVICE TO OUR PATIENT.

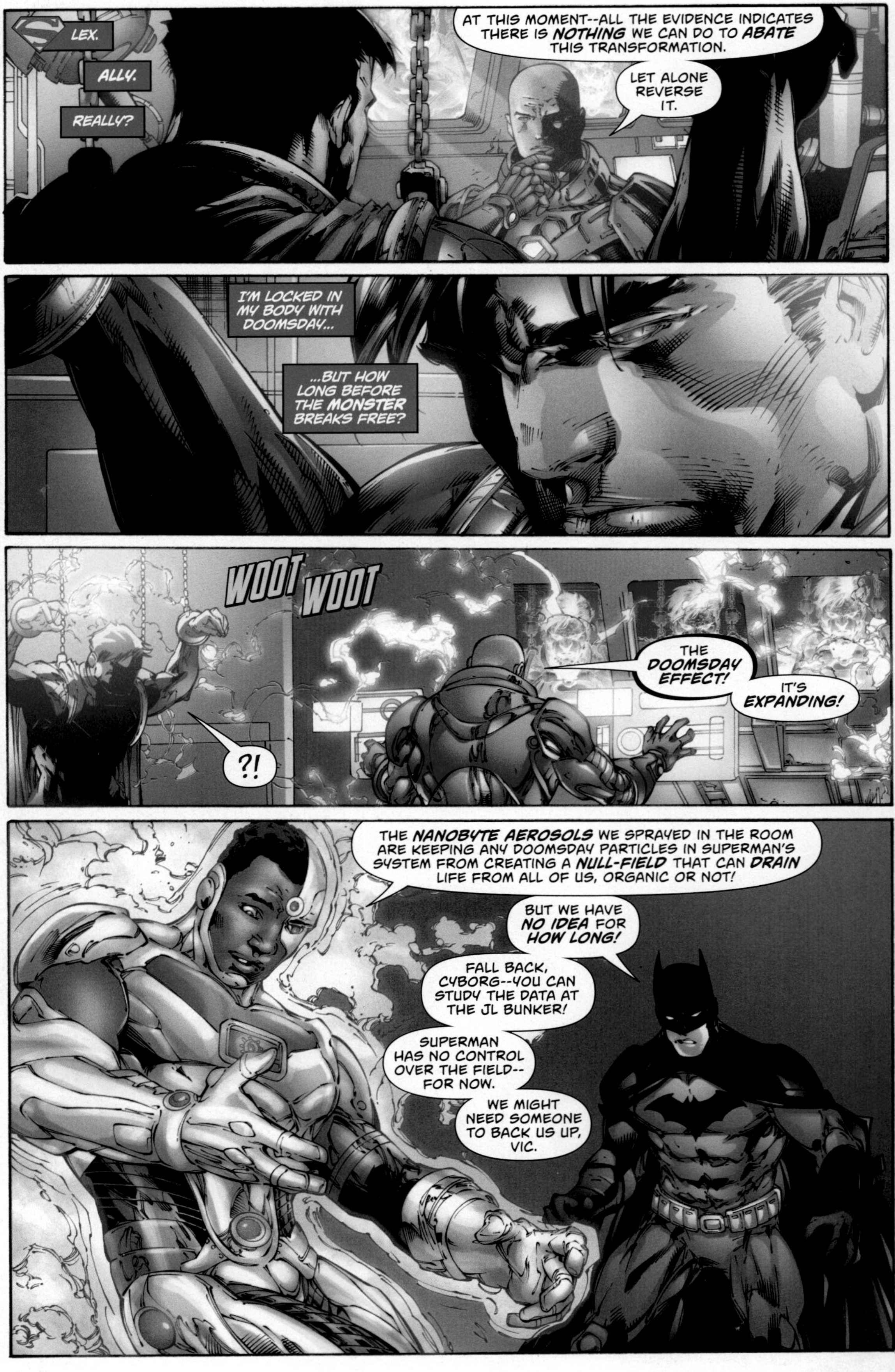
LEX.
ALLY.
REALLY?
AT THIS MOMENT--ALL THE EVIDENCE INDICATES THERE IS NOTHING WE CAN DO TO ABATE THIS TRANSFORMATION.
LET ALONE REVERSE IT.
I'M LOCKED IN MY BODY WITH DOOMSDAY...
...BUT HOW LONG BEFORE THE MONSTER BREAKS FREE?
WOOT WOOT
?!
THE DOOMSDAY EFFECT!
IT'S EXPANDING!
THE NANOBYTE AEROSOLS WE SPRAYED IN THE ROOM ARE KEEPING ANY DOOMSDAY PARTICLES IN SUPERMAN'S SYSTEM FROM CREATING A NULL-FIELD THAT CAN DRAIN LIFE FROM ALL OF US, ORGANIC OR NOT!
BUT WE HAVE NO IDEA FOR HOW LONG!
FALL BACK, CYBORG--YOU CAN STUDY THE DATA AT THE JL BUNKER!
SUPERMAN HAS NO CONTROL OVER THE FIELD-- FOR NOW.
WE MIGHT NEED SOMEONE TO BACK US UP, VIC.

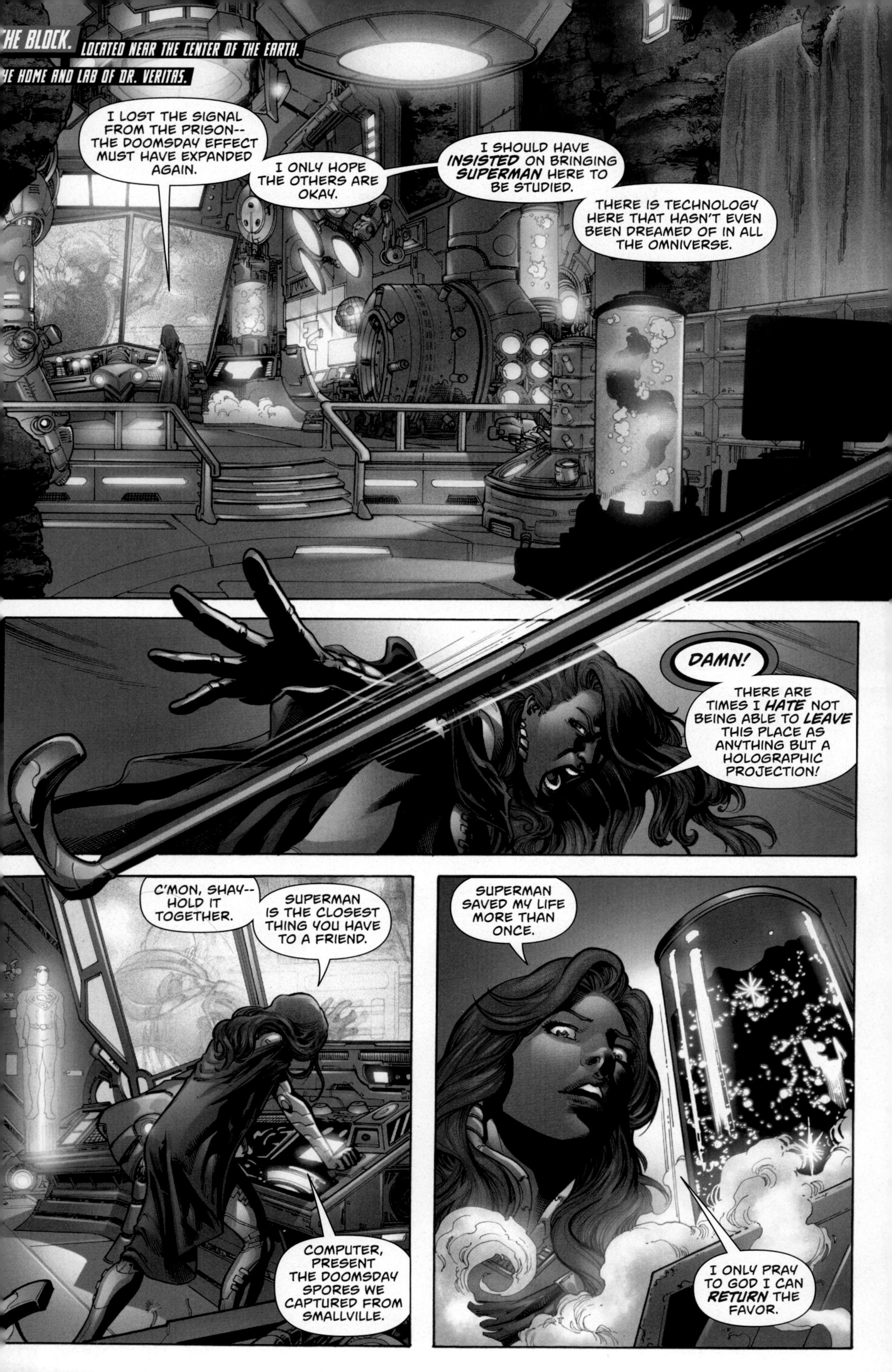
THE BLOCK. LOCATED NEAR THE CENTER OF THE EARTH.
THE HOME AND LAB OF DR. VERITAS.
I LOST THE SIGNAL FROM THE PRISON-- THE DOOMSDAY EFFECT MUST HAVE EXPANDED AGAIN.
I ONLY HOPE THE OTHERS ARE OKAY.
I SHOULD HAVE INSISTED ON BRINGING SUPERMAN HERE TO BE STUDIED.
THERE IS TECHNOLOGY HERE THAT HASN'T EVEN BEEN DREAMED OF IN ALL THE OMNIVERSE.
DAMN!
THERE ARE TIMES I HATE NOT BEING ABLE TO LEAVE THIS PLACE AS ANYTHING BUT A HOLOGRAPHIC PROJECTION!
C'MON, SHAY-- HOLD IT TOGETHER.
SUPERMAN IS THE CLOSEST THING YOU HAVE TO A FRIEND.
COMPUTER, PRESENT THE DOOMSDAY SPORES WE CAPTURED FROM SMALLVILLE.
SUPERMAN SAVED MY LIFE MORE THAN ONCE.
I ONLY PRAY TO GOD I CAN RETURN THE FAVOR.

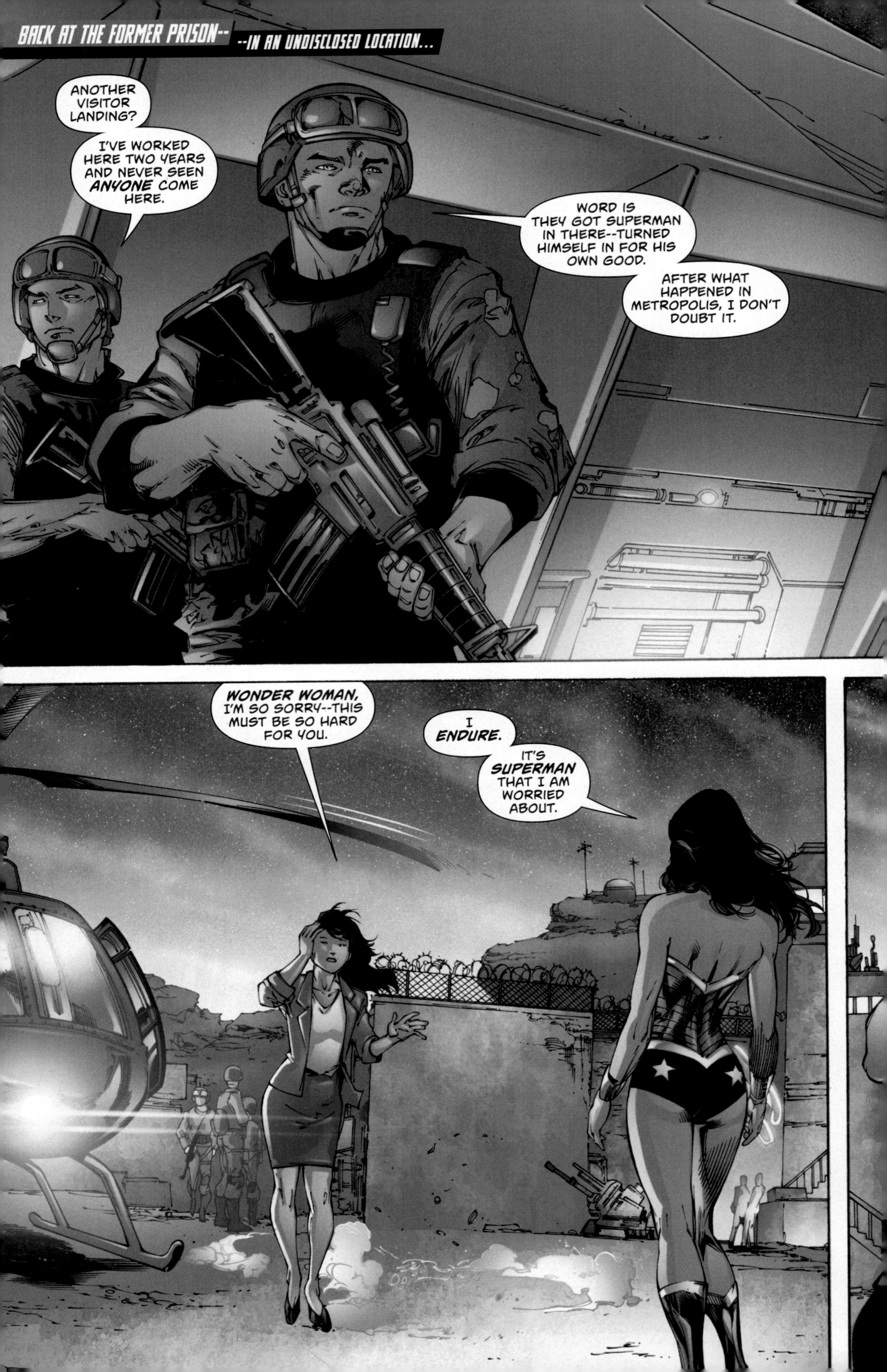
BACK AT THE FORMER PRISON--
--IN AN UNDISCLOSED LOCATION...
ANOTHER VISITOR LANDING?
I'VE WORKED HERE TWO YEARS AND NEVER SEEN ANYONE COME HERE.
WORD IS THEY GOT SUPERMAN IN THERE--TURNED HIMSELF IN FOR HIS OWN GOOD.
AFTER WHAT HAPPENED IN METROPOLIS, I DON'T DOUBT IT.
WONDER WOMAN, I'M SO SORRY--THIS MUST BE SO HARD FOR YOU.
I ENDURE.
IT'S SUPERMAN THAT I AM WORRIED ABOUT.

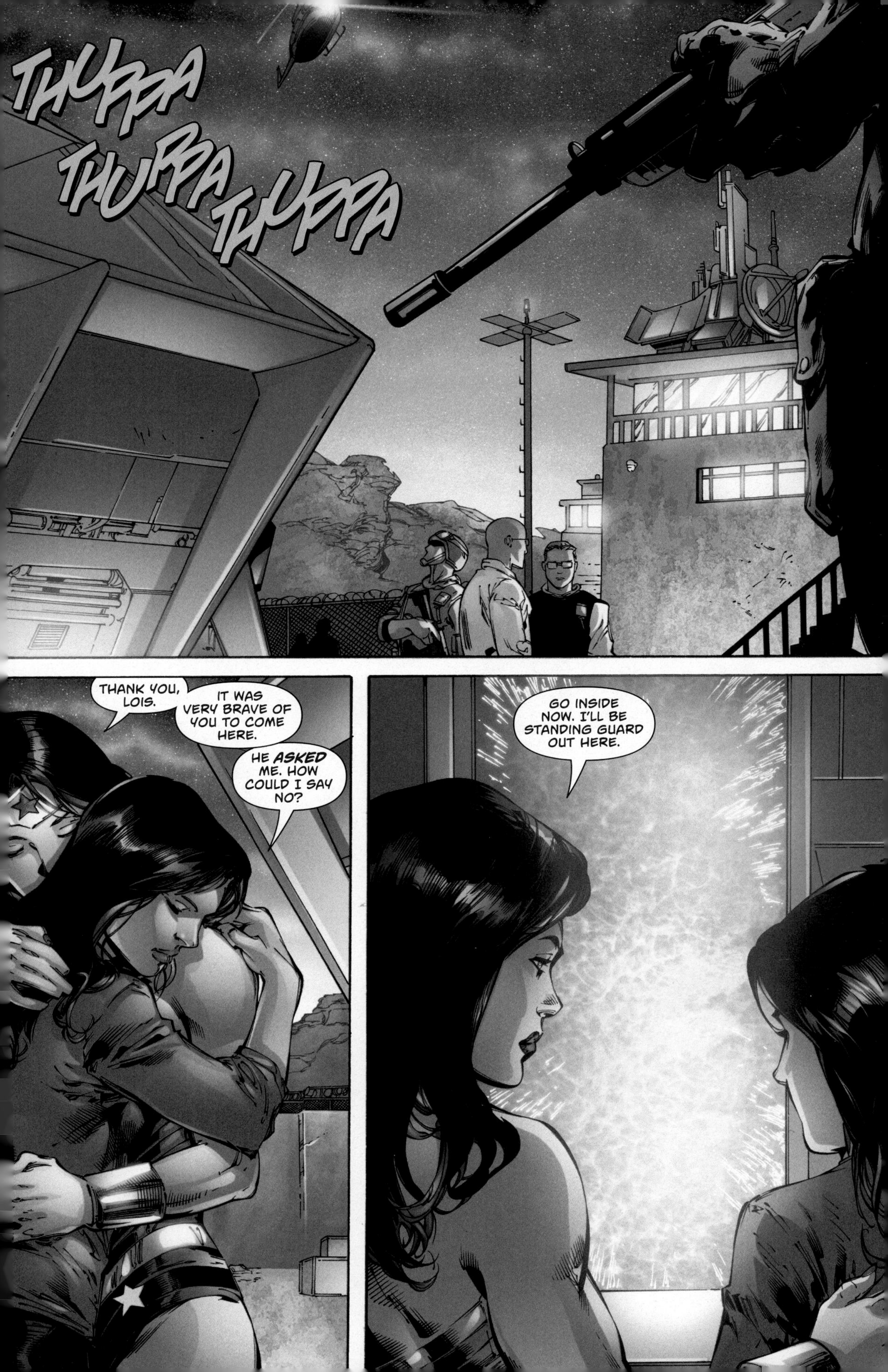
THUPPA
THUPPA
THUPPA
THANK YOU, LOIS.
IT WAS VERY BRAVE OF YOU TO COME HERE.
HE ASKED ME. HOW COULD I SAY NO?
GO INSIDE NOW. I'LL BE STANDING GUARD OUT HERE.

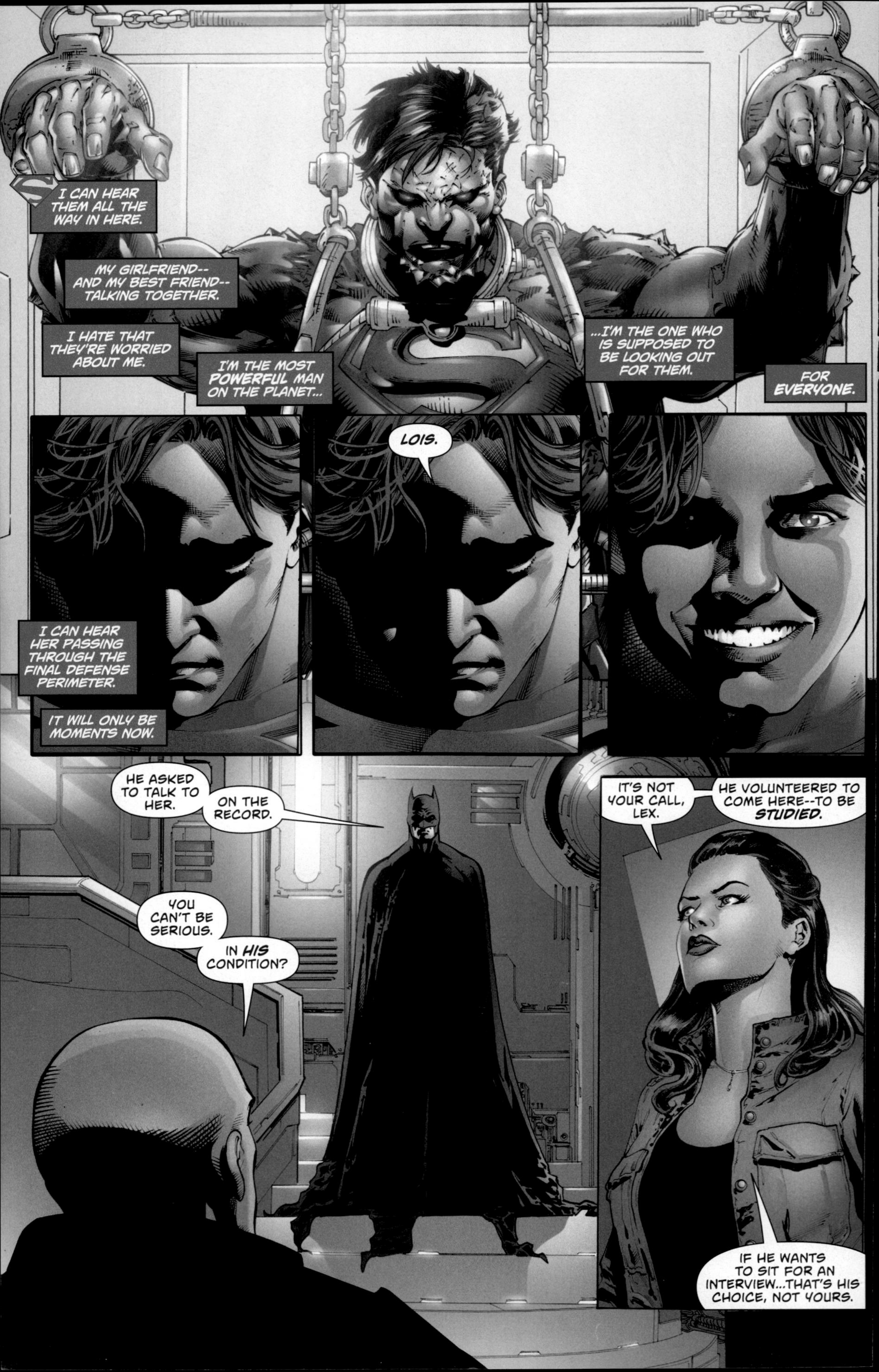
I CAN HEAR THEM ALL THE WAY IN HERE.
MY GIRLFRIEND-- AND MY BEST FRIEND-- TALKING TOGETHER.
I HATE THAT THEY'RE WORRIED ABOUT ME.
I'M THE MOST POWERFUL MAN ON THE PLANET...
...I'M THE ONE WHO IS SUPPOSED TO BE LOOKING OUT FOR THEM.
FOR EVERYONE.
I CAN HEAR HER PASSING THROUGH THE FINAL DEFENSE PERIMETER.
IT WILL ONLY BE MOMENTS NOW.
LOIS.
HE ASKED TO TALK TO HER.
ON THE RECORD.
YOU CAN'T BE SERIOUS.
IN HIS CONDITION?
IT'S NOT YOUR CALL, LEX.
HE VOLUNTEERED TO COME HERE--TO BE STUDIED.
IF HE WANTS TO SIT FOR AN INTERVIEW...THAT'S HIS CHOICE, NOT YOURS.

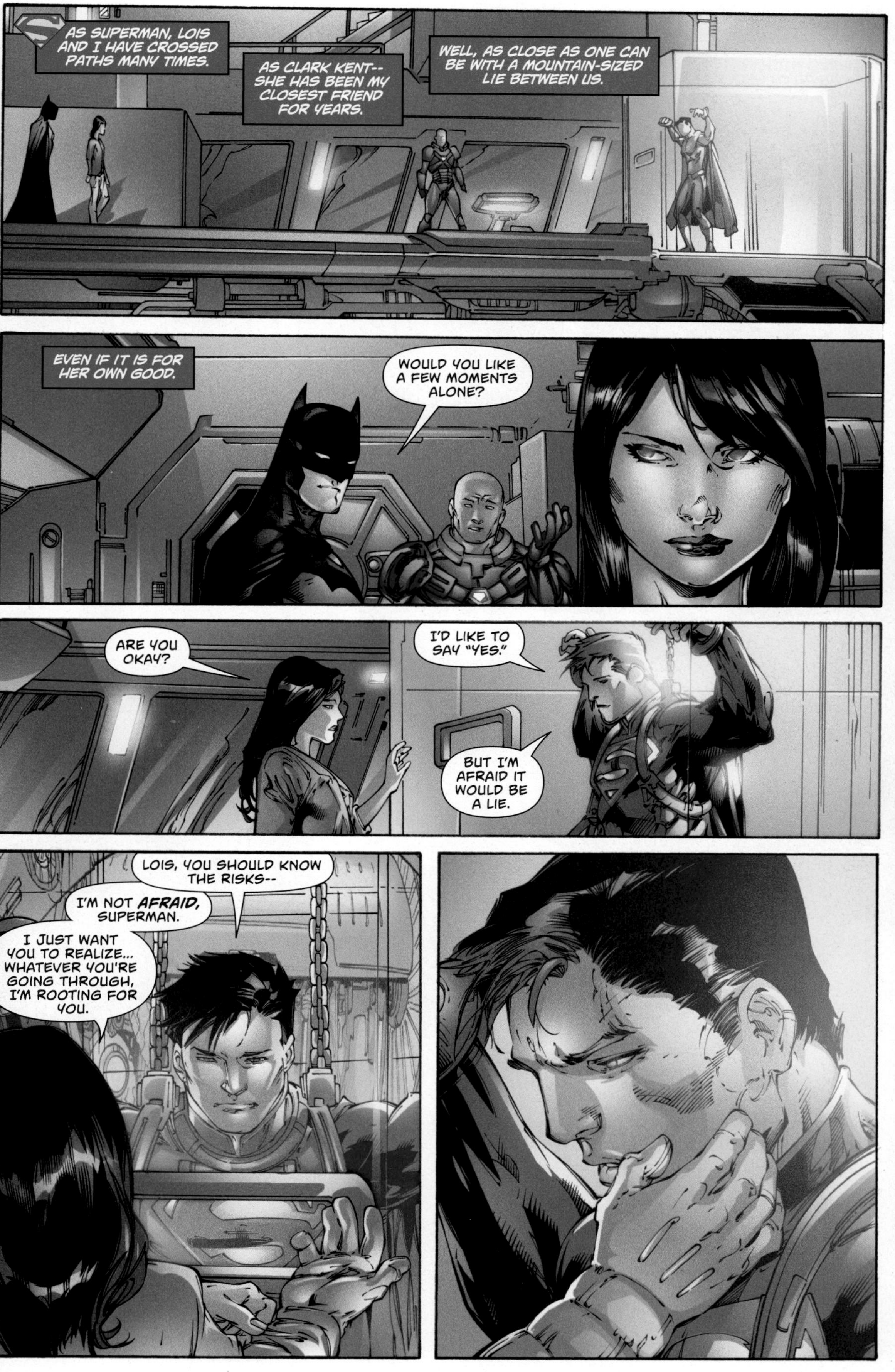
AS SUPERMAN, LOIS AND I HAVE CROSSED PATHS MANY TIMES.
AS CLARK KENT-- SHE HAS BEEN MY CLOSEST FRIEND FOR YEARS.
WELL, AS CLOSE AS ONE CAN BE WITH A MOUNTAIN-SIZED LIE BETWEEN US.
EVEN IF IT IS FOR HER OWN GOOD.
WOULD YOU LIKE A FEW MOMENTS ALONE?
ARE YOU OKAY?
I'D LIKE TO SAY "YES."
BUT I'M AFRAID IT WOULD BE A LIE.
LOIS, YOU SHOULD KNOW THE RISKS--
I'M NOT AFRAID, SUPERMAN.
I JUST WANT YOU TO REALIZE... WHATEVER YOU'RE GOING THROUGH, I'M ROOTING FOR YOU.

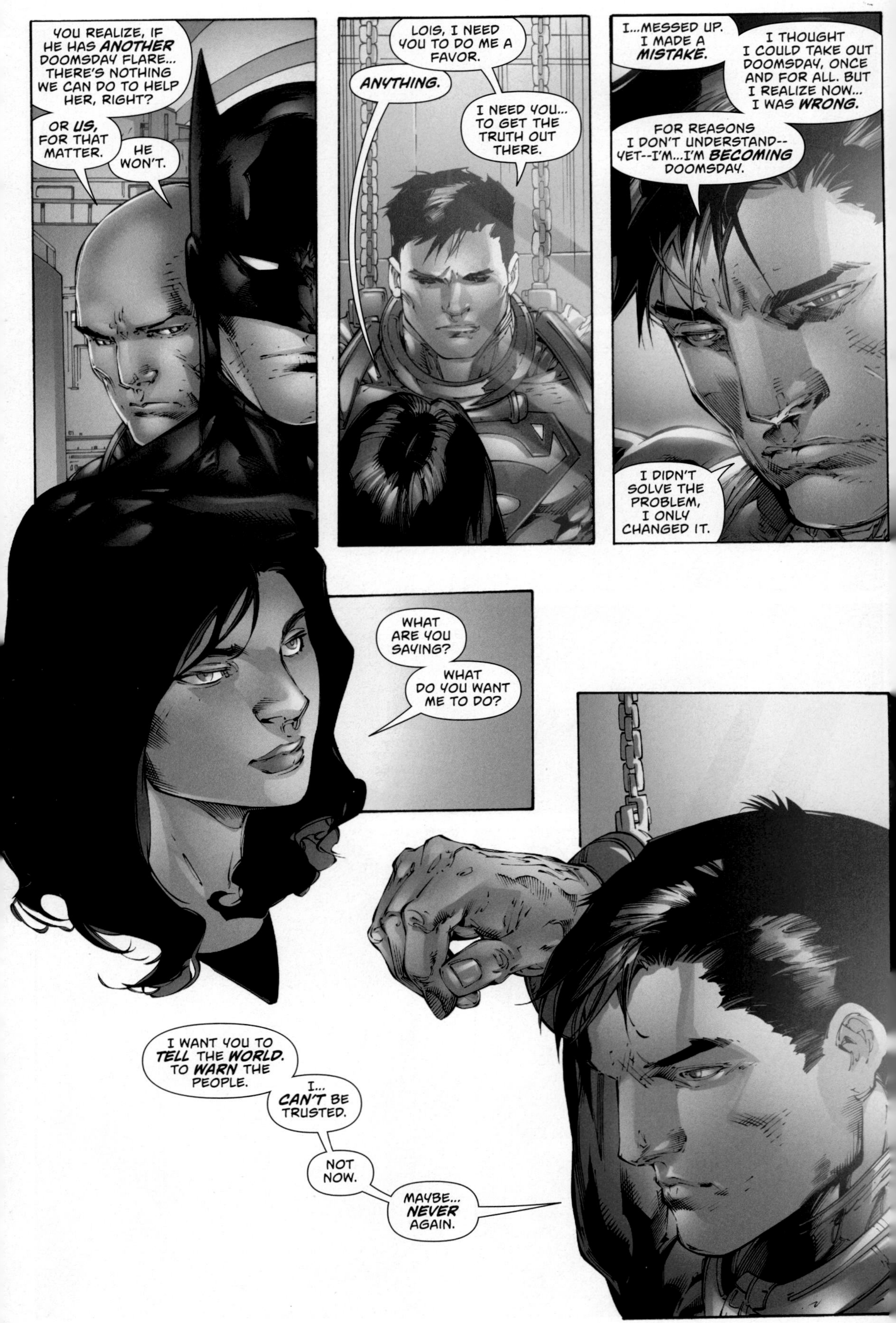
YOU REALIZE, IF HE HAS ANOTHER DOOMSDAY FLARE... THERE'S NOTHING WE CAN DO TO HELP HER, RIGHT?
OR US, FOR THAT MATTER.
HE WON'T.
LOIS, I NEED YOU TO DO ME A FAVOR.
ANYTHING.
I NEED YOU... TO GET THE TRUTH OUT THERE.
I...MESSED UP. I MADE A MISTAKE.
I THOUGHT I COULD TAKE OUT DOOMSDAY, ONCE AND FOR ALL. BUT I REALIZE NOW... I WAS WRONG.
FOR REASONS I DON'T UNDERSTAND--YET--I'M...I'M BECOMING DOOMSDAY.
I DIDN'T SOLVE THE PROBLEM, I ONLY CHANGED IT.
WHAT ARE YOU SAYING?
WHAT DO YOU WANT ME TO DO?
I WANT YOU TO TELL THE WORLD. TO WARN THE PEOPLE.
I... CAN'T BE TRUSTED.
NOT NOW.
MAYBE... NEVER AGAIN.

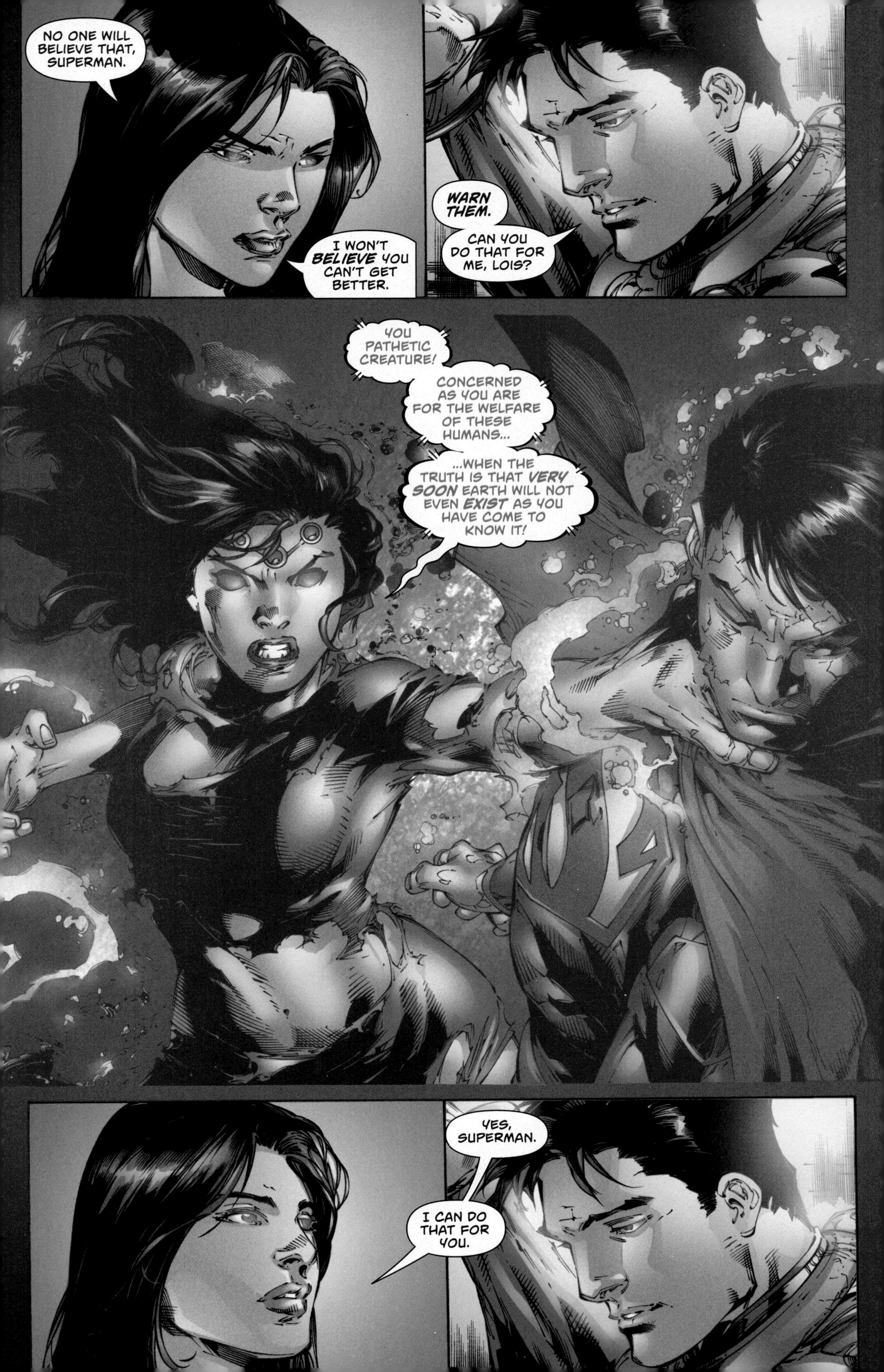
NO ONE WILL BELIEVE THAT, SUPERMAN.
I WON'T *BELIEVE* YOU CAN'T GET BETTER.
WARN THEM.
CAN YOU DO THAT FOR ME, LOIS?
YOU PATHETIC CREATURE!
CONCERNED AS YOU ARE FOR THE WELFARE OF THESE HUMANS...
...WHEN THE TRUTH IS THAT *VERY SOON* EARTH WILL NOT EVEN *EXIST* AS YOU HAVE COME TO KNOW IT!
YES, SUPERMAN.
I CAN DO THAT FOR YOU.

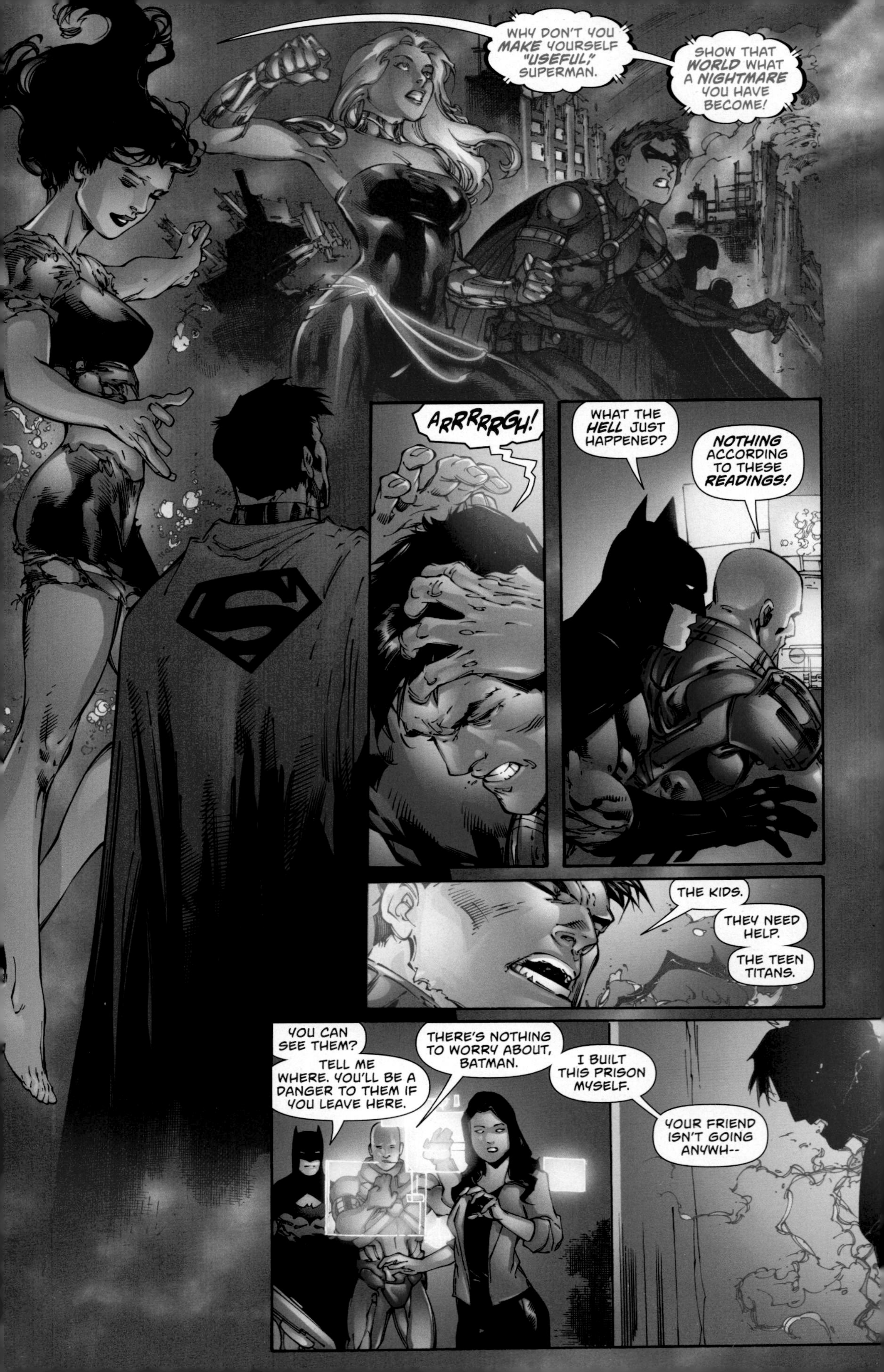
WHY DON'T YOU MAKE YOURSELF "USEFUL," SUPERMAN.
SHOW THAT WORLD WHAT A NIGHTMARE YOU HAVE BECOME!
ARRRRRGH!
WHAT THE HELL JUST HAPPENED?
NOTHING ACCORDING TO THESE READINGS!
THE KIDS.
THEY NEED HELP.
THE TEEN TITANS.
YOU CAN SEE THEM?
TELL ME WHERE. YOU'LL BE A DANGER TO THEM IF YOU LEAVE HERE.
THERE'S NOTHING TO WORRY ABOUT, BATMAN.
I BUILT THIS PRISON MYSELF.
YOUR FRIEND ISN'T GOING ANYWH--

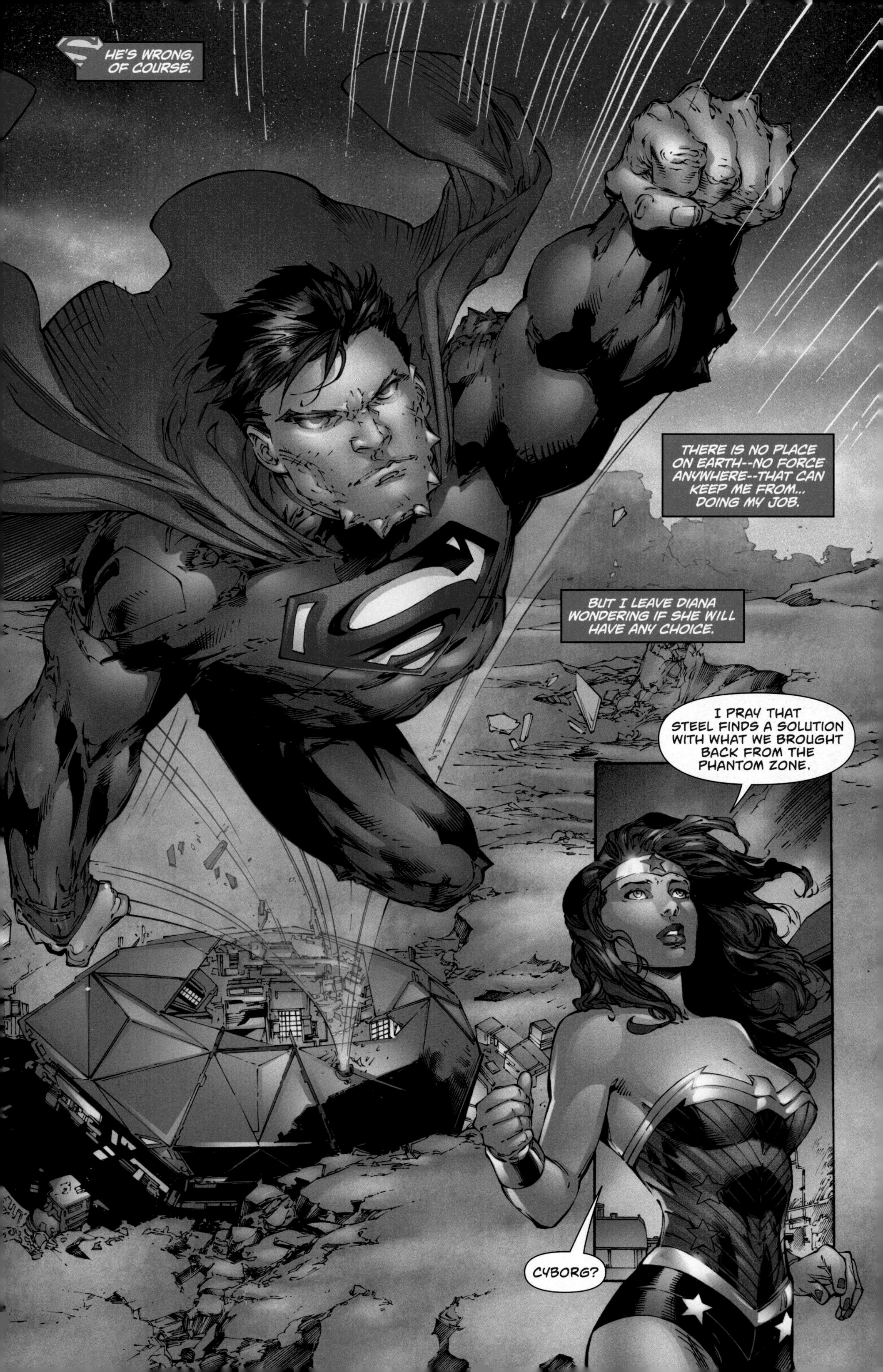
HE'S WRONG, OF COURSE.
THERE IS NO PLACE ON EARTH--NO FORCE ANYWHERE--THAT CAN KEEP ME FROM... DOING MY JOB.
BUT I LEAVE DIANA WONDERING IF SHE WILL HAVE ANY CHOICE.
I PRAY THAT STEEL FINDS A SOLUTION WITH WHAT WE BROUGHT BACK FROM THE PHANTOM ZONE.
CYBORG?

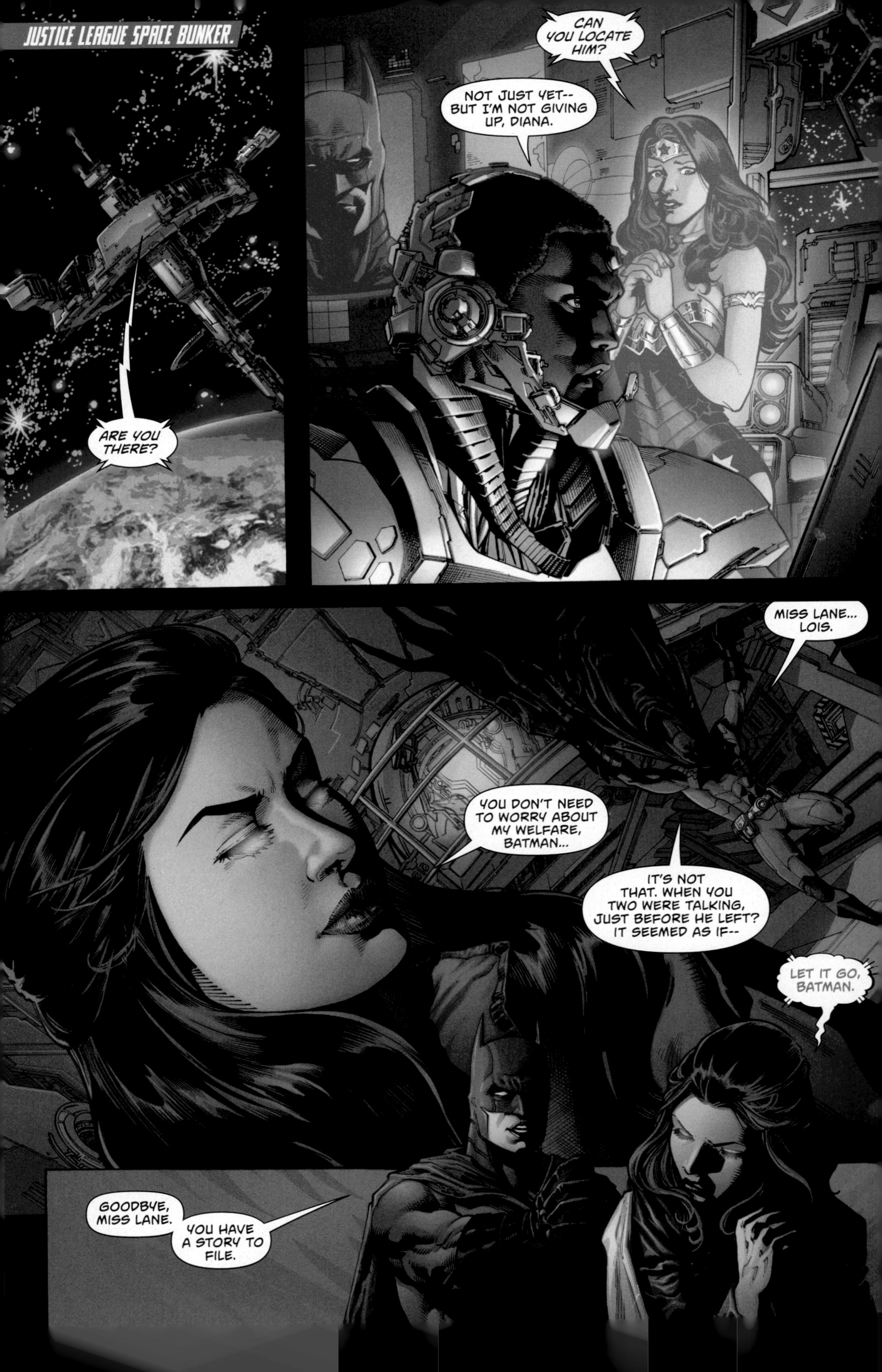
JUSTICE LEAGUE SPACE BUNKER.
ARE YOU THERE?
CAN YOU LOCATE HIM?
NOT JUST YET-- BUT I'M NOT GIVING UP, DIANA.
MISS LANE... LOIS.
YOU DON'T NEED TO WORRY ABOUT MY WELFARE, BATMAN...
IT'S NOT THAT. WHEN YOU TWO WERE TALKING, JUST BEFORE HE LEFT? IT SEEMED AS IF--
LET IT GO, BATMAN.
GOODBYE, MISS LANE.
YOU HAVE A STORY TO FILE.

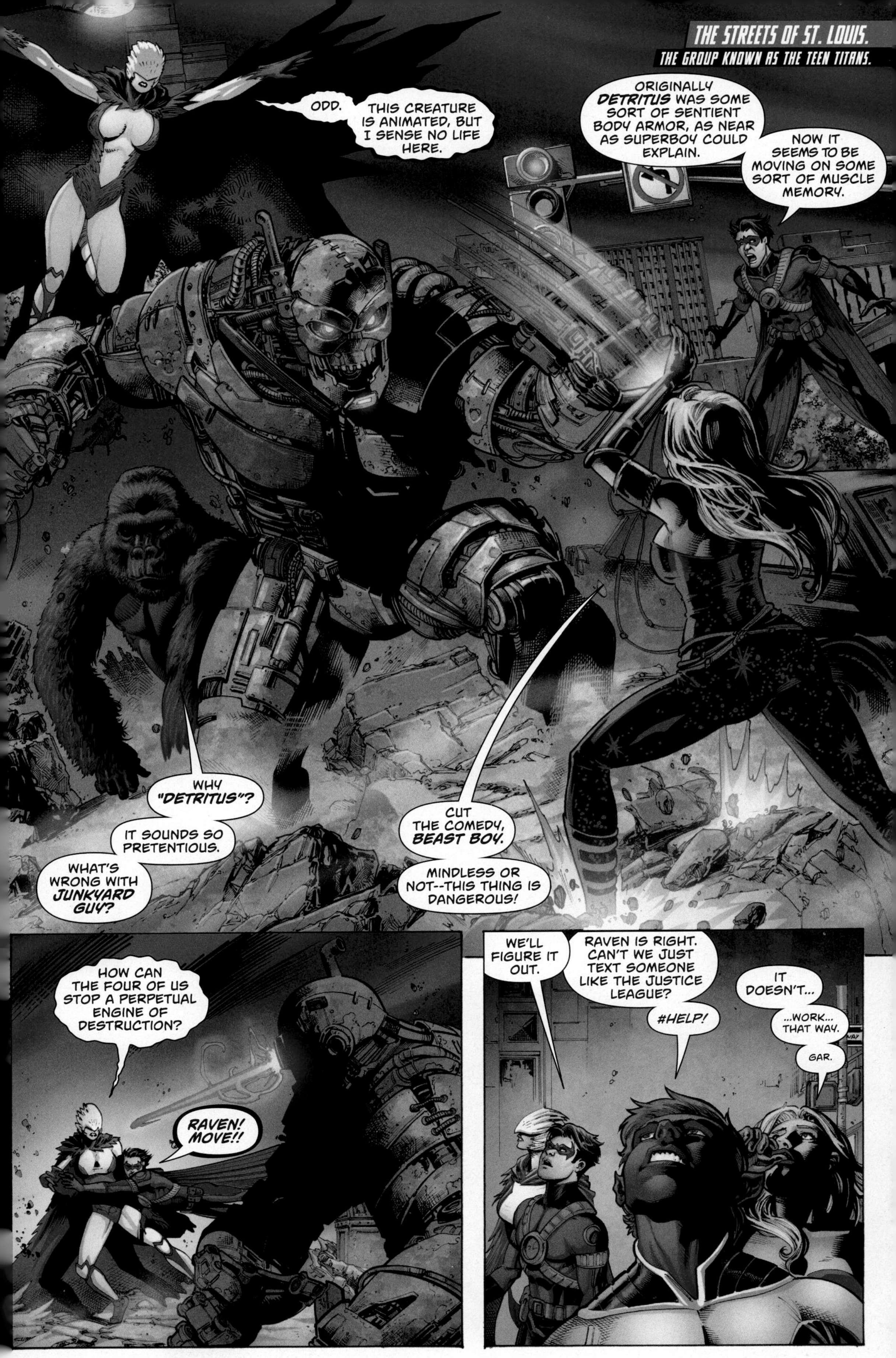
THE STREETS OF ST. LOUIS.
THE GROUP KNOWN AS THE TEEN TITANS.
ODD.
THIS CREATURE IS ANIMATED, BUT I SENSE NO LIFE HERE.
ORIGINALLY DETRITUS WAS SOME SORT OF SENTIENT BODY ARMOR, AS NEAR AS SUPERBOY COULD EXPLAIN.
NOW IT SEEMS TO BE MOVING ON SOME SORT OF MUSCLE MEMORY.
WHY "DETRITUS"?
IT SOUNDS SO PRETENTIOUS.
WHAT'S WRONG WITH JUNKYARD GUY?
CUT THE COMEDY, BEAST BOY.
MINDLESS OR NOT--THIS THING IS DANGEROUS!
HOW CAN THE FOUR OF US STOP A PERPETUAL ENGINE OF DESTRUCTION?
RAVEN! MOVE!!
WE'LL FIGURE IT OUT.
RAVEN IS RIGHT. CAN'T WE JUST TEXT SOMEONE LIKE THE JUSTICE LEAGUE?
#HELP!
IT DOESN'T...
...WORK... THAT WAY.
GAR.

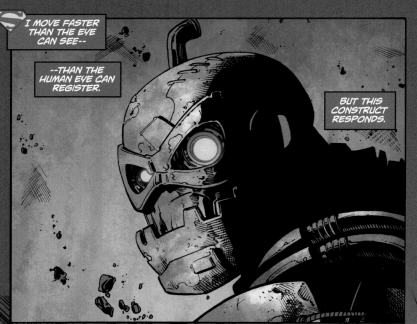

I MOVE FASTER THAN THE EYE CAN SEE--

--THAN THE HUMAN EYE CAN REGISTER.

BUT THIS CONSTRUCT RESPONDS.

CHARGING UP ITS DEFENSES.

BA-WA-BA-B

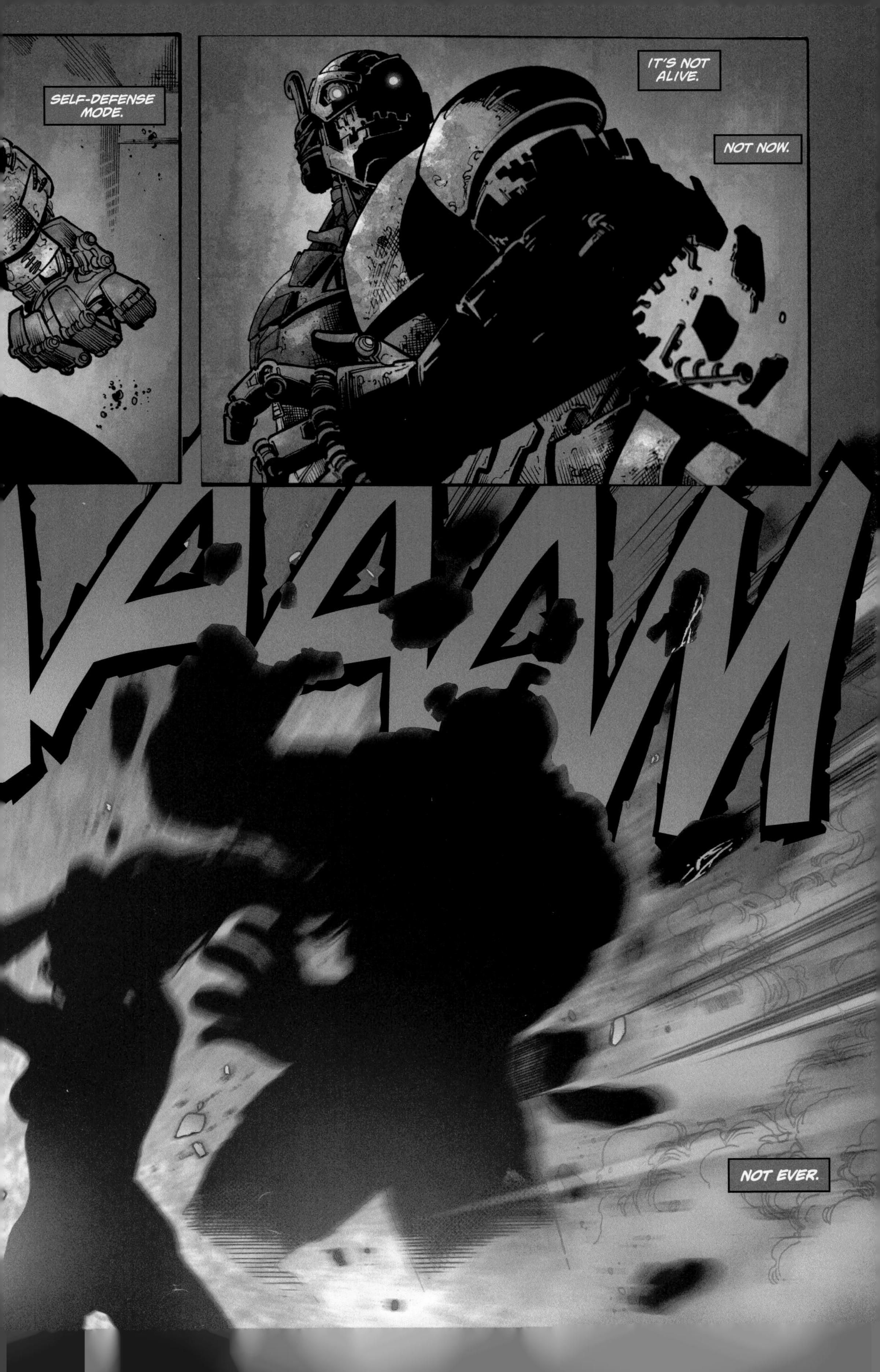
SELF-DEFENSE MODE.
IT'S NOT ALIVE.
NOT NOW.
KRAAM
NOT EVER.

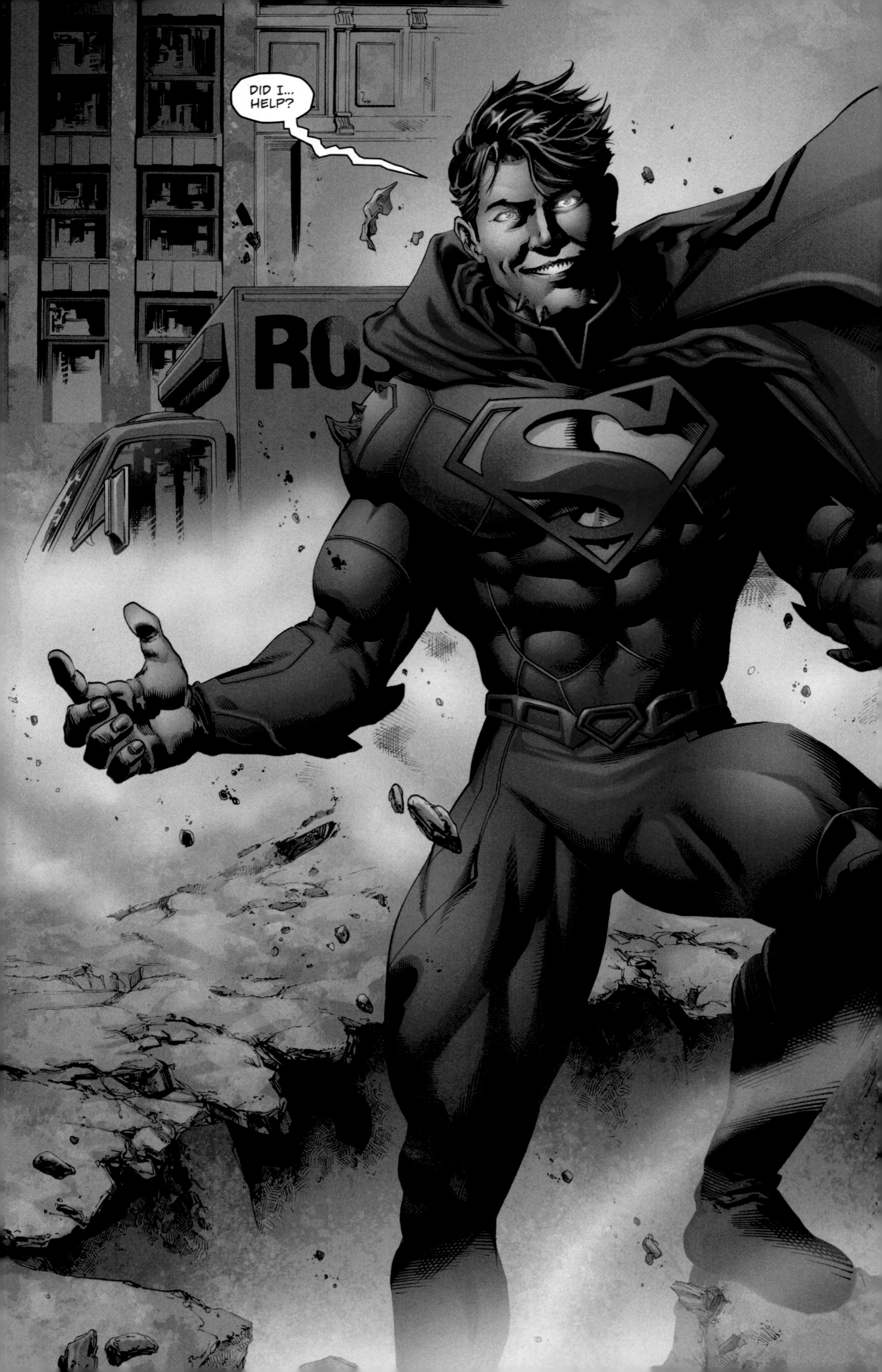
DID I...
HELP?
ROS

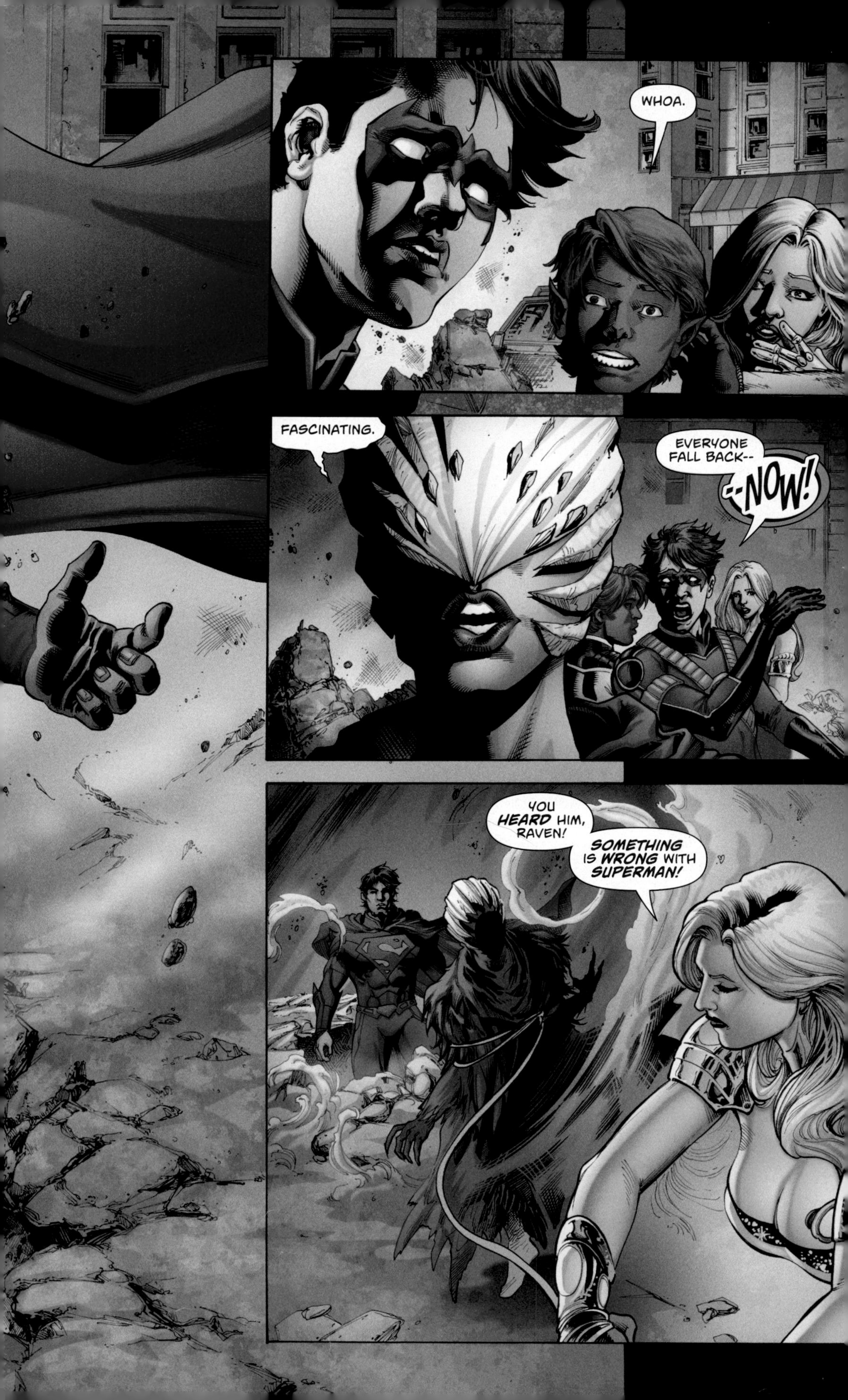
WHOA.
FASCINATING.
EVERYONE FALL BACK--
--NOW!
YOU HEARD HIM, RAVEN!
SOMETHING IS WRONG WITH SUPERMAN!

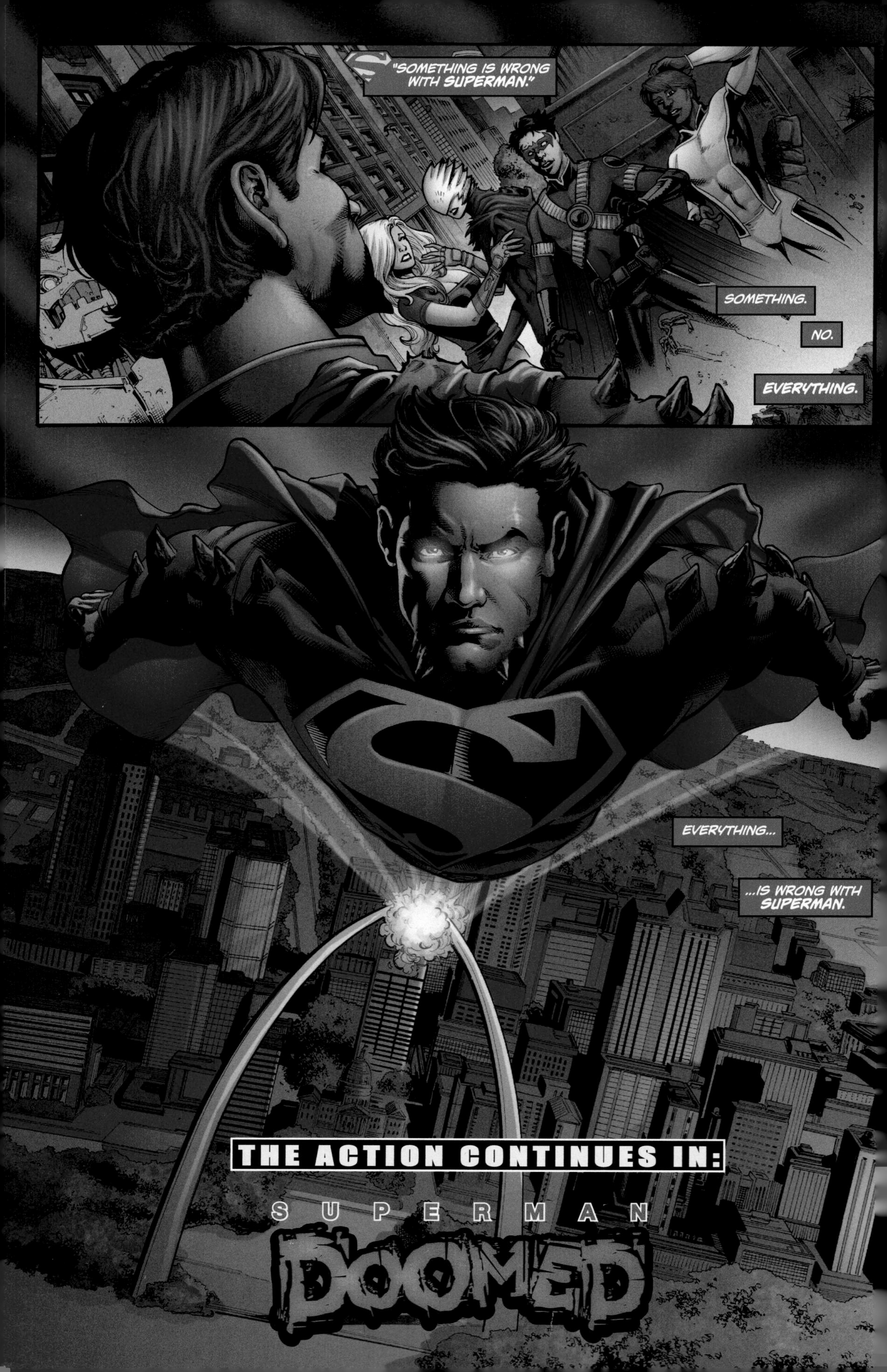
"SOMETHING IS WRONG WITH SUPERMAN."
SOMETHING.
NO.
EVERYTHING.
EVERYTHING...
...IS WRONG WITH SUPERMAN.
THE ACTION CONTINUES IN:
SUPERMAN
DOOMED

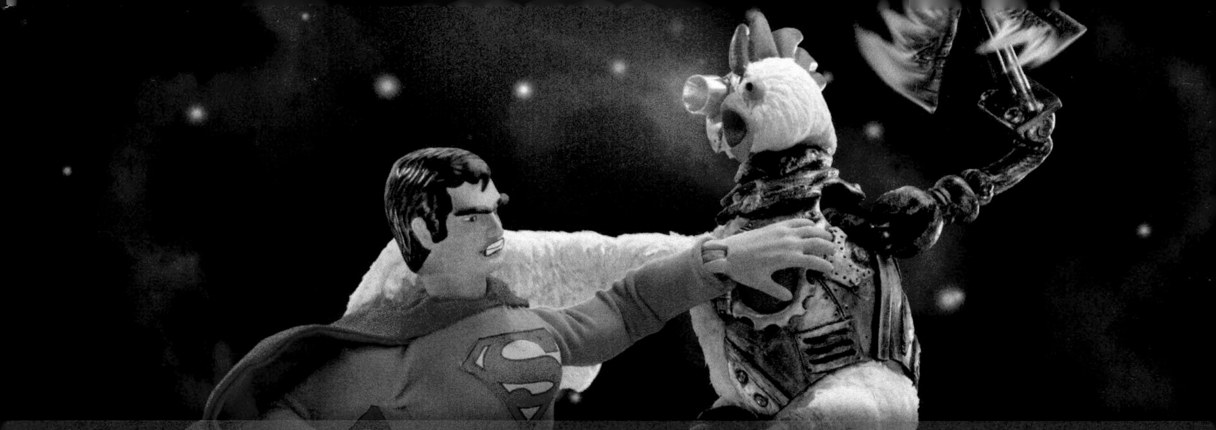

VARIANT COVER GALLERY

SUPERMAN #25
by Kenneth Rocafort

SUPERMAN #27
by Jon Katz, after Joe Shuster

SUPERMAN #28
by Jeff Wamester

SUPERMAN #29
by RC Stoodios

SUPERMAN #30
by Paul Coker

SUPERMAN #31
by Mike and Laura Allred

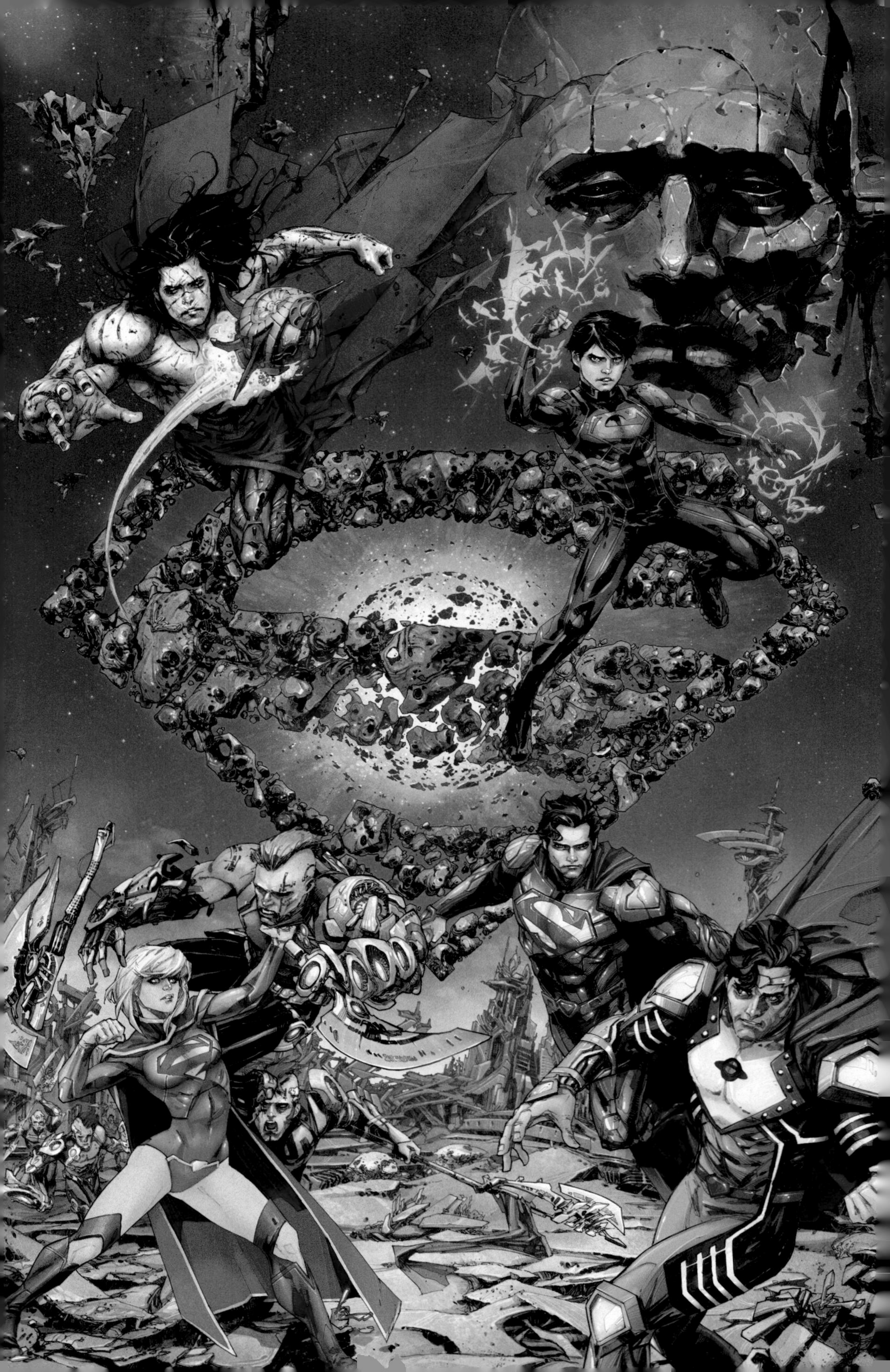

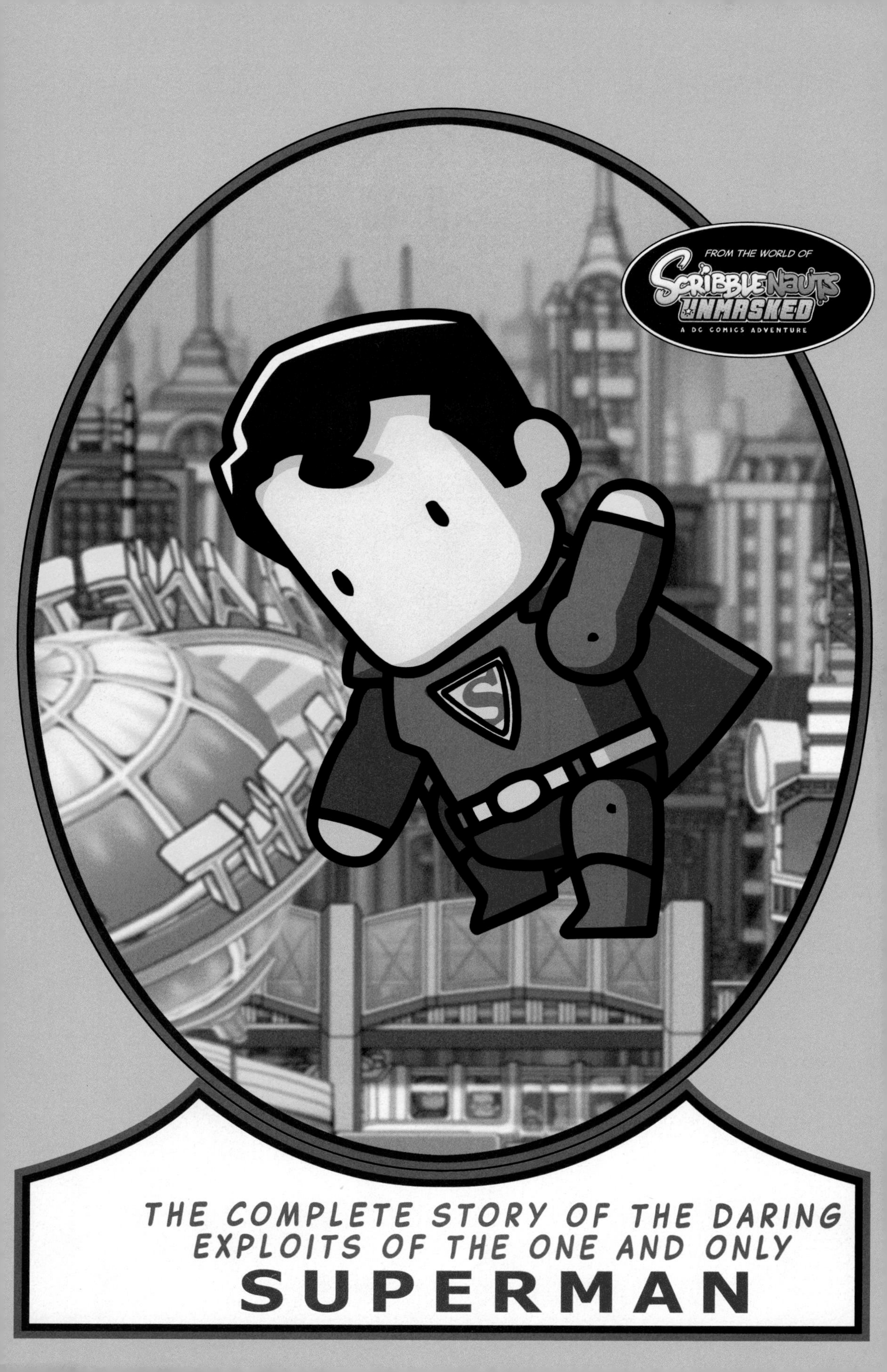
FROM THE WORLD OF
SCRIBBLENAUTS UNMASKED
A DC COMICS ADVENTURE

THE COMPLETE STORY OF THE DARING EXPLOITS OF THE ONE AND ONLY

SUPERMAN

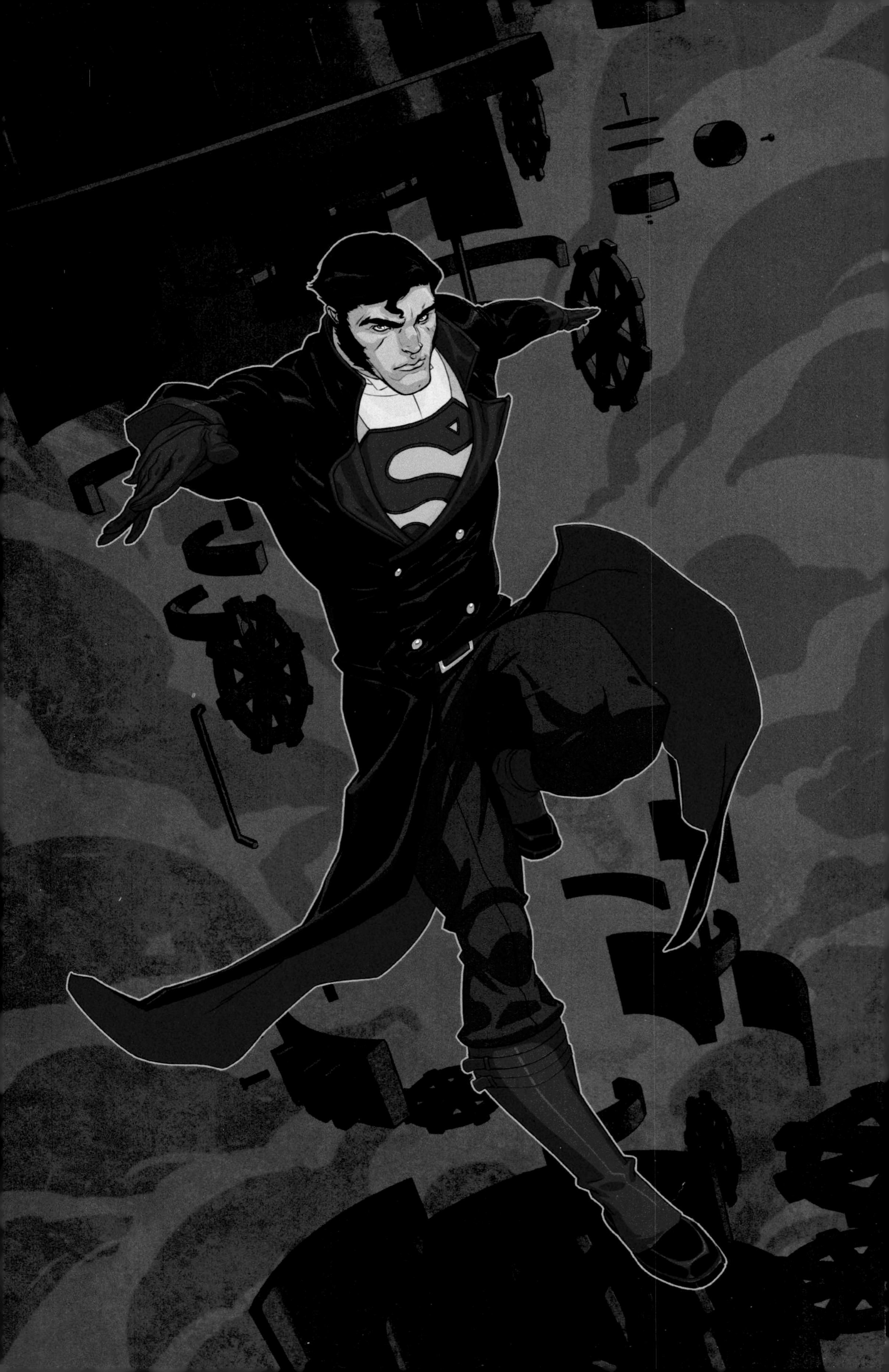

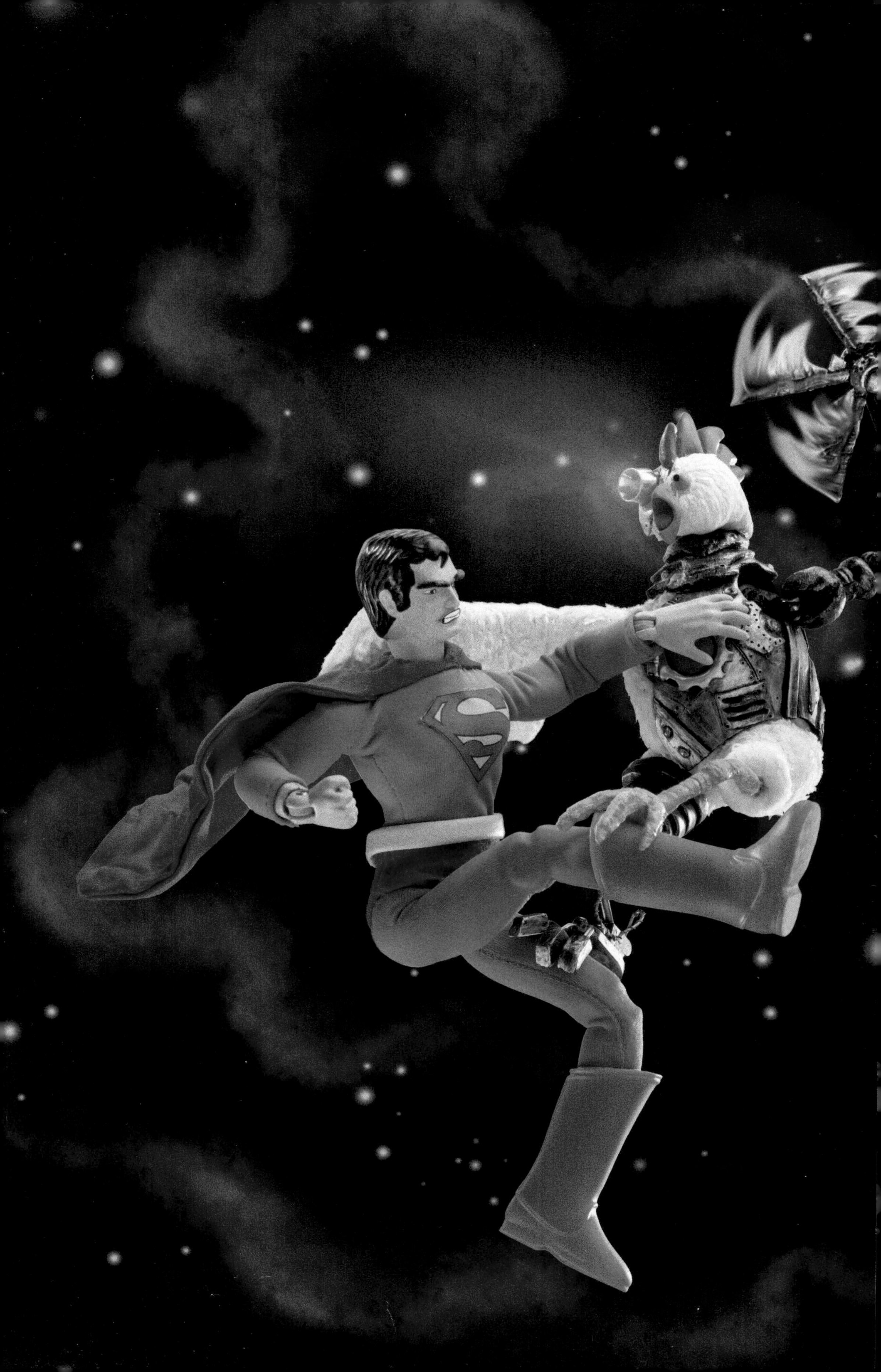

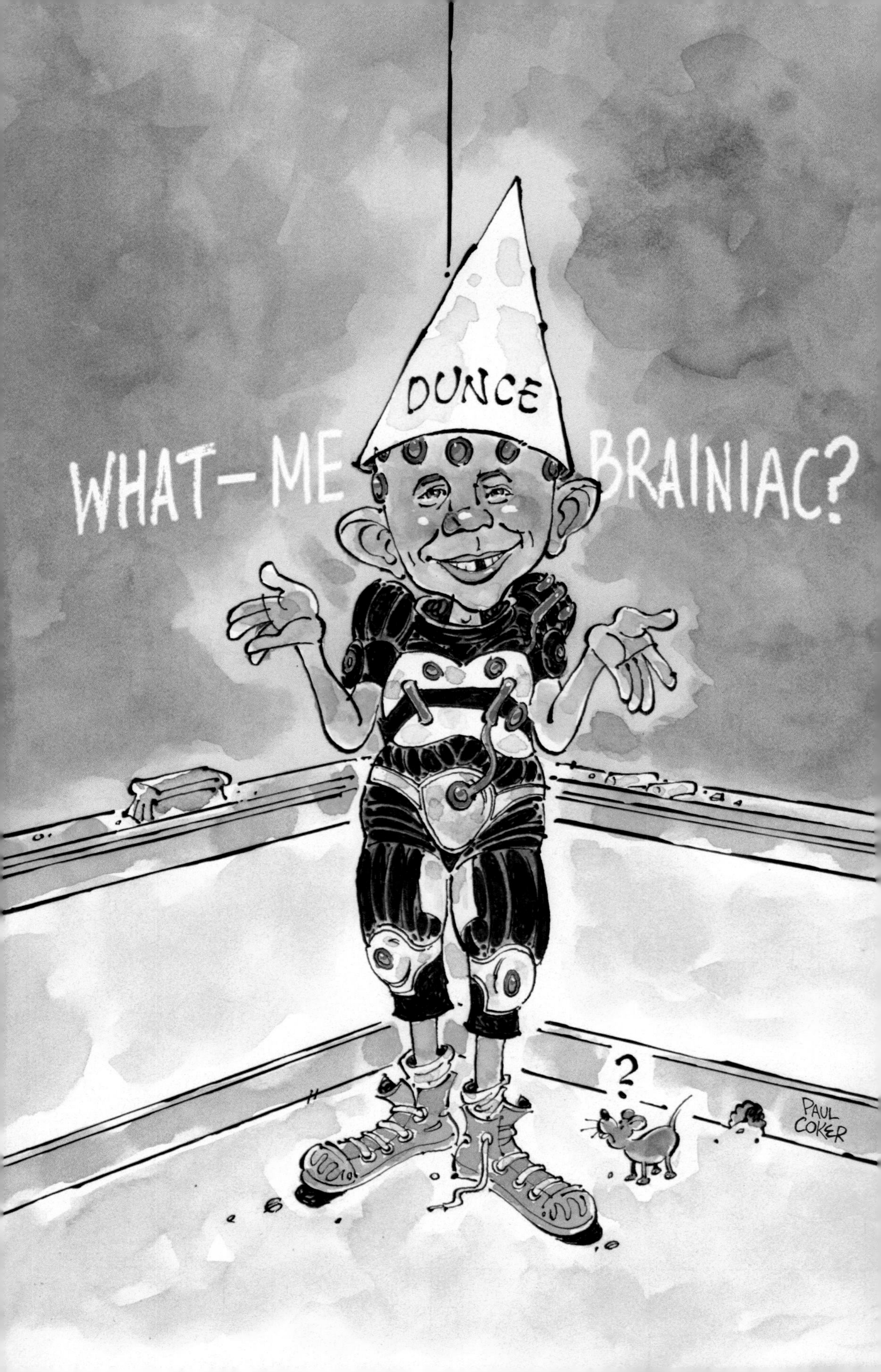
DUNCE
WHAT—ME BRAINIAC?
?
PAUL COKER

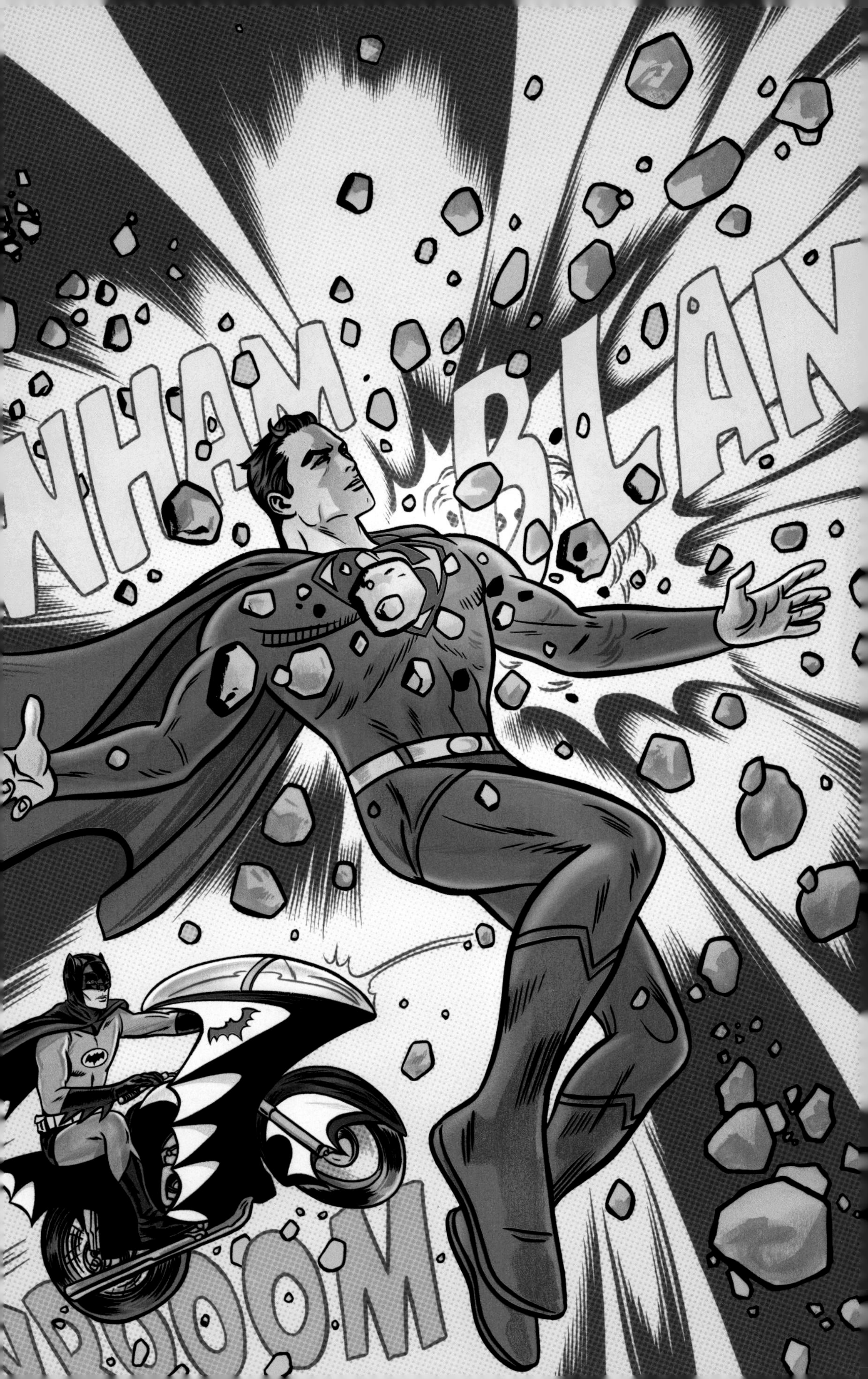
WHAM
BLA
ROOOOM

Sketches by Ken Lashley

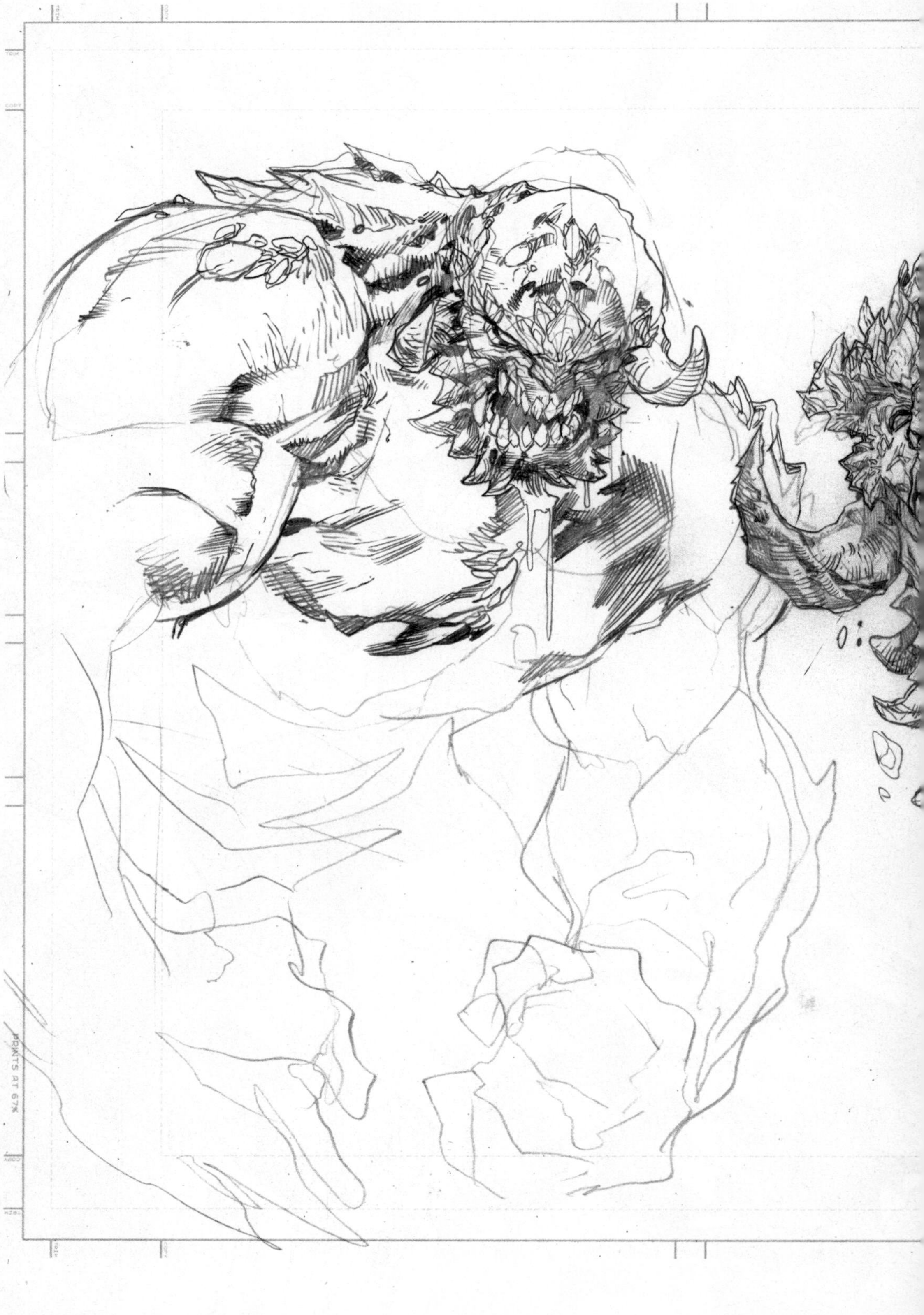

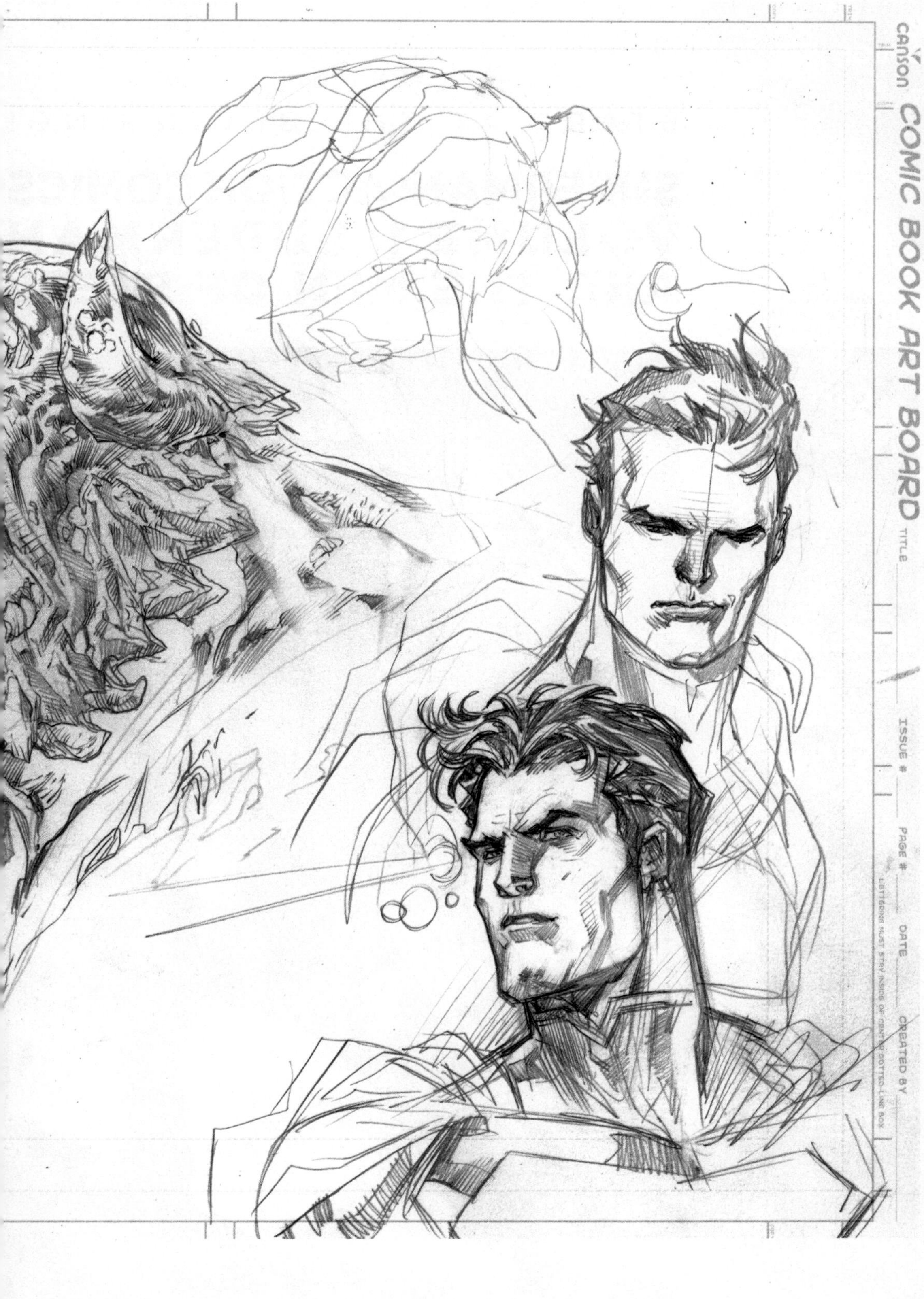
canson
COMIC BOOK ART BOARD
TITLE
ISSUE #
PAGE #
DATE
CREATED BY

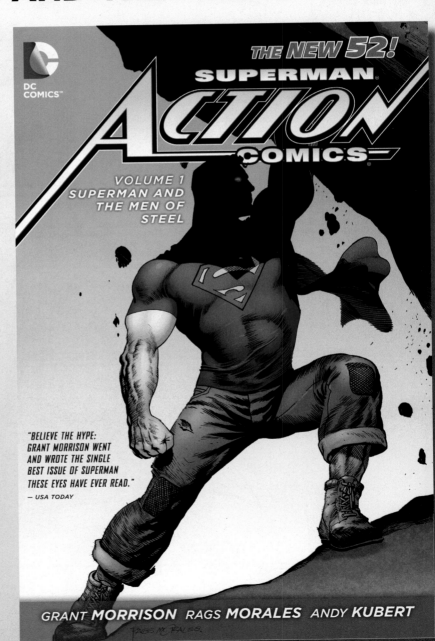

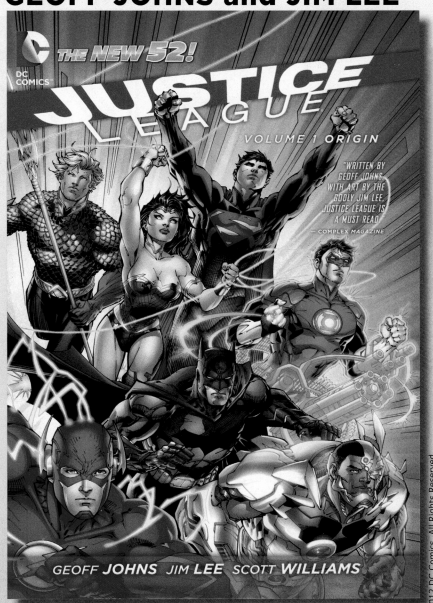

DC COMICS™

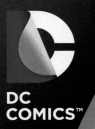

"ACTION COMICS has successfully carved
own territory and continued exploring Morriso
familiar themes about heroism and ideas."—I

"Casts the character in a new light, opens up fresh storyte
ing possibilities, and pushes it all forward with dynamic Ra
Morales art. I loved it."—THE ONION/AV CL

START AT THE BEGINNING!

SUPERMAN: ACTION COMICS VOLUME 1
SUPERMAN AND THE MEN OF STEEL

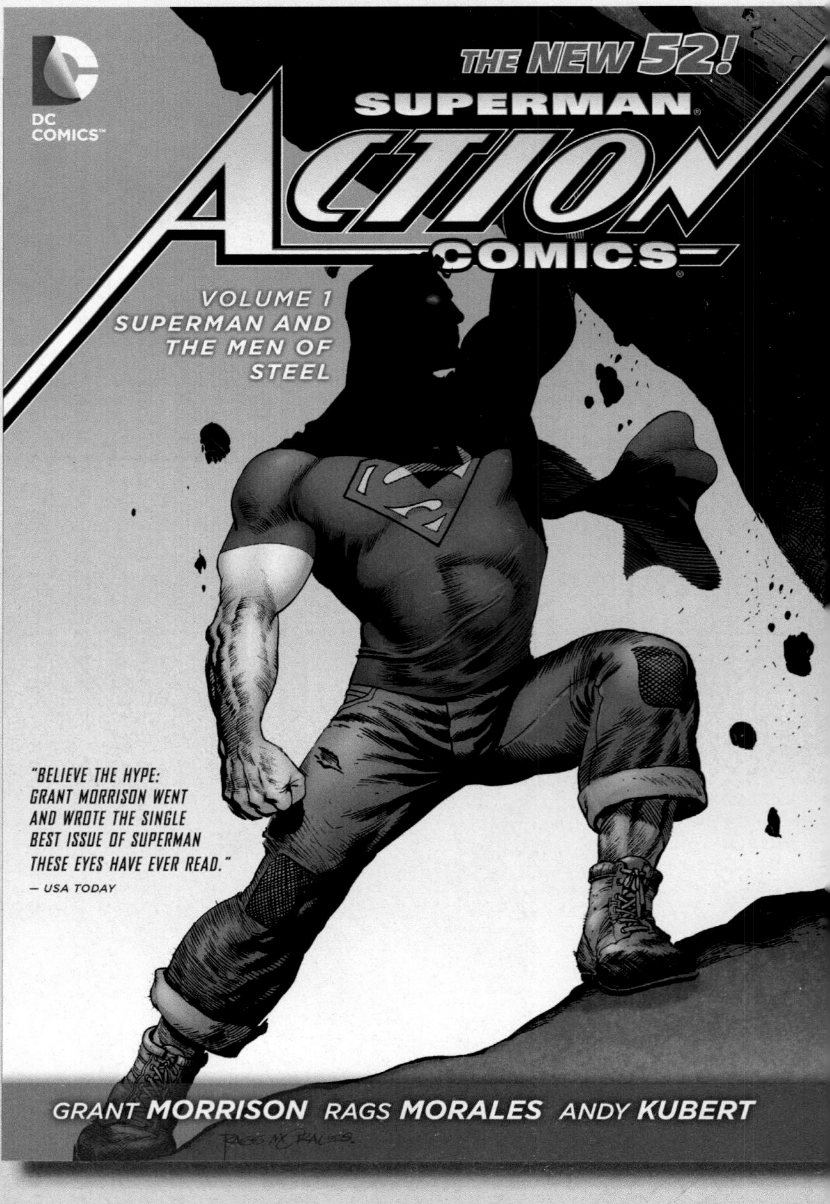
DC COMICS™
THE NEW 52!
SUPERMAN
ACTION COMICS
VOLUME 1
SUPERMAN AND
THE MEN OF
STEEL
"BELIEVE THE HYPE:
GRANT MORRISON WENT
AND WROTE THE SINGLE
BEST ISSUE OF SUPERMAN
THESE EYES HAVE EVER READ."
— USA TODAY
GRANT MORRISON RAGS MORALES ANDY KUBERT

SUPERMAN: ACTION COMICS VOL. 2: BULLETPROOF

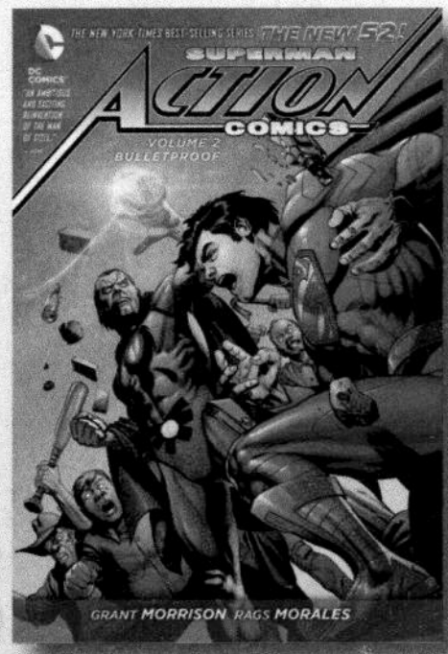
THE NEW 52!
SUPERMAN
ACTION
COMICS
VOLUME 2
BULLETPROOF
GRANT MORRISON RAGS MORALES

with GRANT MORRISON and RAGS MORALES

SUPERMAN: ACTION COMICS VOL. 3: AT THE END OF DAYS

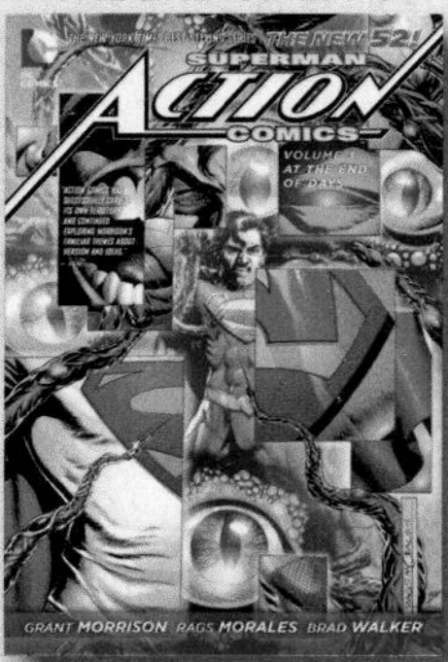
THE NEW 52!
SUPERMAN
ACTION
COMICS
GRANT MORRISON RAGS MORALES BRAD WALKER

with GRANT MORRISON and RAGS MORALES

SUPERBOY VOL. 1: INCUBATION

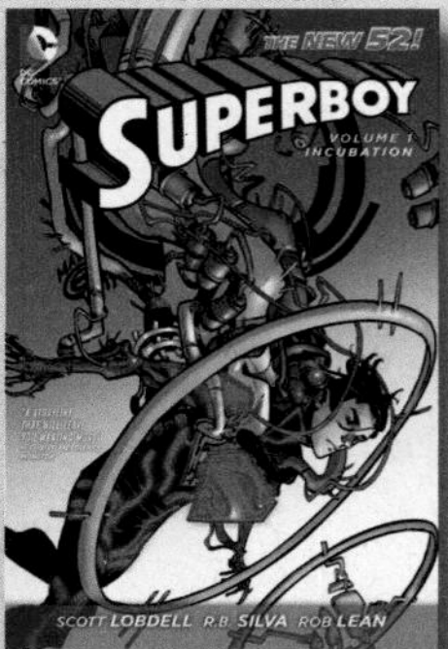
THE NEW 52!
SUPERBOY
VOLUME 1
INCUBATION
SCOTT LOBDELL R.B. SILVA ROB LEAN